National Security Intelligence

To Loch Lomond Bentley, RAF pilot
1913–1941
who paid the ultimate price in defense of the democracies

Jere W. Morehead
President, University of Georgia, who has encouraged and supported my
writing, teaching, and public service endeavors over the years

National Security Intelligence

Secret Operations in Defense of the Democracies

Third Edition

LOCH K. JOHNSON

polity

First published in 2024 by Polity Press

Polity Press
65 Bridge Street
Cambridge CB2 1UR, UK

Polity Press
111 River Street
Hoboken, NJ 07030, USA

ISBN-13: 978-1-5095-6033-2
ISBN-13: 978-1-5095-6034-9(pb)

A catalogue record for this book is available from the British Library.

Library of Congress Control Number: 2023921194

Typeset in 10/13pt Swift Light by
Cheshire Typesetting Ltd, Cuddington, Cheshire
Printed and bound in Great Britain by CPI Group (UK) Ltd, Croydon

The publisher has used its best endeavours to ensure that the URLs for external websites referred to in this book are correct and active at the time of going to press. However, the publisher has no responsibility for the websites and can make no guarantee that a site will remain live or that the content is or will remain appropriate.

Every effort has been made to trace all copyright holders, but if any have been overlooked the publisher will be pleased to include any necessary credits in any subsequent reprint or edition.

For further information on Polity, visit our website: politybooks.com

Contents

About the Author   vi
Illustrations   vii
Abbreviations   ix
Preface to the Third Edition: Roadmap to a Hidden World   xiv
Acknowledgments   xxiv

1 National Security Intelligence: The First Line of Defense   1

2 Intelligence Collection: Global Spying   40

3 Intelligence Analysis: Understanding World Affairs   73

4 Covert Action: Secret Attempts to Shape History   105

5 Counterintelligence: Guarding the Democracies   142

6 Safeguards against the Abuse of Secret Power   179

7 National Security Intelligence: Hidden Shield and Sword of the
  Democracies   218

Notes   240
Appendix   273
Suggested Readings   275
Index   285

About the Author

Loch K. Johnson is Regents Professor Emeritus of Public and International Affairs at the University of Georgia, as well as a Meigs Distinguished Teaching Professor. Born in Auckland, New Zealand, Professor Johnson received his PhD in political science from the University of California, Riverside. Throughout his career, he has written widely on the subject of national security; his most recent books include *Intelligence: The Secret World of Spies*, 6th edition, coedited with James W. Wirtz (OUP, 2023) and *The Third Option: Covert Action and American Foreign Policy* (OUP, 2022). He served as senior editor of the journal *Intelligence and National Security* for eighteen years, and has been a Distinguished Visiting Scholar at Yale University and at Oxford University.

Professor Johnson also served as special assistant to the chairman of the Senate Select Committee on Intelligence (the Church Committee); as the first staff director of the Subcommittee on Intelligence Oversight, U.S. House Permanent Select Committee on Intelligence; and as special assistant to Chairman Les Aspin of the Aspin–Brown Commission on the Roles and Missions of Intelligence. At the University of Georgia, he led the founding of the School of Public and International Affairs (SPIA) from 1997 to 2001.

Illustrations

FIGURES

1.1 Basic human motivations and the quest for national security
     intelligence: a stimulus–response model   12
1.2 The U.S. Intelligence Community (IC), 2024   23
1.3 The organization of the CIA   29
1.4 The CIA's Operations Directorate during the Cold War   30
2.1 The intelligence cycle   43
2.2 The relationship between a nation's sense of acceptable risk and
     its resources committed to intelligence collection and analysis   54
3.1 Frequency of NIEs by year, 1950–2005   87
4.1 The ebb and flow of U.S. covert actions, 1947–2024   120
4.2 A partial, heuristic "ladder of escalation" for covert actions   132
6.1 Auth on the lack of meaningful congressional oversight of
     intelligence prior to 1975   184
6.2 A cycle of intelligence shock and reaction by congressional
     overseers since 1975   206
6.3 A typology of roles assumed by intelligence overseers in the U.S.
     Congress   214

TABLES

3.1 Sample National Intelligence Council products, 1994   80
5.1 Key intelligence recommendations proposed by the Huston Plan,
     1970   145
6.1 Types of stimuli and key intelligence oversight responses by
     lawmakers since 1974   208
7.1 National security intelligence: A reform agenda for the United
     States   229

BOXES

3.1 Data on *PDB* reporting during the Nixon and Ford Administrations   75
3.2 Key Judgment excerpts from an NIE on climate change, 2021   83
3.3 Special Estimate (SNIE) excerpt on war in the Middle East, 1967   86
6.1 The *contra* section of the Iran–*contra* finding, 1981   182

PHOTOS

1.1	The Twin Towers	3
1.2	CIA Headquarters	27
1.3	Walter Bedell Smith	35
2.1	U.S. surveillance satellite	41
2.2	Oleg Penkovsky	64
2.3	Cuban missile crisis	66
3.1	Richard Moore	102
4.1	William E. Colby	108
4.2	President Salvador Allende Gossens	113
4.3	MQ-9 Reaper drone	124
5.1	Aldrich Hazen Ames	151
5.2	James Angleton	161
6.1	Admiral Stansfield Turner	180
6.2	Senator Frank Church	186
6.3	Lee H. Hamilton	215
7.1	General James R. Clapper	220
7.2	Avril D. Haines	221

Abbreviations

Every profession, including intelligence, has its abbreviations to ease communications among workers. A book on intelligence would be deficient without reference to this day-to-day language. An effort has been made to keep the acronyms in this book to a minimum, but occasionally they are included to provide a sense of how intelligence officers speak to one another within their organizations, as well as to avoid repeating long terms time and again. When these acronyms do arise, this glossary provides a ready guide for the reader.

AI	artificial intelligence
ATC	air traffic control
CA	covert action
CAS	Covert Action Staff
CASIS	Canadian Association of Security and Intelligence Studies
CE	counterespionage
CHAOS	cryptonym (codename) for an illegal CIA domestic spy operation against antiwar protesters in the 1960s and 1970s
CI	counterintelligence
CIA	Central Intelligence Agency (known by insiders as "the Agency")
CISA	Cybersecurity and Infrastructure Security Agency (Department of Homeland Security)
COCOM	combatant commander (Pentagon)
COed	"case officered" (a CIA foreign recruitment term)
COINTELPRO	FBI Counterintelligence Program
comint	communications intelligence
CNOs	Computer Network Operations
COS	Chief of Station (the top CIA officer in the field)
CTC	Counterterrorism Center (CIA)
DA	Directorate of Analysis
DBA	dominant battlefield awareness
DCI	Director of Central Intelligence

DCIA or D/CIA	Director of the Central Intelligence Agency
DDI	Deputy Director for Intelligence
DDNI	Deputy Director of National Intelligence
DDO	Deputy Director for Operations
DEA	Drug Enforcement Administration
DEC	DCI Environmental Center
DHS	Department of Homeland Security; also, Defense Humint Service (DoD)
DI	Directorate of Intelligence (CIA)
DIA	Defense Intelligence Agency
DNC	Democratic National Committee
DNI	Director of National Intelligence
DO	Directorate of Operations (CIA), also known at times earlier in the CIA's history as the Clandestine Services and the National Clandestine Services
DoD	Department of Defense
DoJ	Department of Justice
DS	Directorate of Support
DS&T	Directorate for Science and Technology (CIA)
DVE	domestic violent extremist
EIT	enhanced interrogation technique
elint	electronic intelligence
EPA	Environmental Protection Agency
FBI	Federal Bureau of Investigation
FISA	Foreign Intelligence Surveillance Act
FISC	Foreign Intelligence Surveillance Court
fisint	foreign instrumentation intelligence
geoint	geospatial-intelligence
GRU	Soviet Military Intelligence
HPSCI	House Permanent Select Committee on Intelligence
humint	human intelligence (espionage assets)
IC	Intelligence Community
ICBM	intercontinental ballistic missile
IG	Inspector General
imint	imagery intelligence (photography)
INR	Bureau of Intelligence and Research (Department of State)
ints	intelligence collection methods (as in "sigint")
IOB	Intelligence Oversight Board
IRBM	intermediate-range ballistic missile
IRTPA	Intelligence Reform and Terrorism Prevention Act (2004)
IS	Intelligence Studies

ISI	Inter-Services Intelligence (the Pakistani intelligence service); also, International Studies Association
ITT	International Telephone and Telegraph (an American corporation)
I & W	indicators and warning
KGB	Soviet Secret Police and Foreign Intelligence: Committee for State Security
KJ	Key Judgment (NIE executive summary)
KSM	Khalid Sheikh Mohammed, the Al Qaeda terrorist said to have been the mastermind behind the 9/11 attacks
LC	Library of Congress
MAD	mutual assured destruction
masint	measurement and signatures intelligence
MI5	British Security Service (counterintelligence)
MINARET	cryptonym for NSA warrantless telephone taps against Americans (pre-1975)
MIP	Military Intelligence Program
MRBM	medium-range ballistic missile
MSS	Ministry of State Security (Chinese equivalent of the CIA)
MVE	militia violent extremist
NBC weaponry	nuclear, biological, chemical armaments
NCA	National Command Authority
NCS	National Clandestine Service
NCMI	National Center for Medical Intelligence (DIA)
NCTC	National Counterterrorism Center
NED	National Endowment for Democracy
NEST	Nuclear Emergency Support Team (Energy Department)
NFIB	National Foreign Intelligence Board
NGA	National Geospatial-Intelligence Agency
NIB	National Intelligence Board
NIC	National Intelligence Council
NIE	National Intelligence Estimate
NIM	National Intelligence Manager (ODNI)
NIO	National Intelligence Officer
NIPF	National Intelligence Priorities Framework
NIP	National Intelligence Program
NOC	non-official cover
NPIC	National Photographic Interpretation Center
NRO	National Reconnaissance Office
NSA	National Security Agency
NSC	National Security Council

NSI	national security intelligence
OBE	overtaken by events (CIA analysis)
OC	official cover
ODNI	Office of the Director of National Intelligence
OLC	Office of Legal Counsel (Justice Department)
OPEC	Organization of Petroleum Exporting Countries
osint	open-source intelligence
OSS	Office of Strategic Services
PDB	*President's Daily Brief*
PDD	Presidential Decision Directive
PFIAB	President's Foreign Intelligence Advisory Board (as of 2008, PIAB)
phoint	photographic intelligence
PIAB	President's Intelligence Advisory Board
PM ops	paramilitary operations
PRC	People's Republic of China
PRISM	Codename for controversial NSA sigint program targeting, without a court warrant, suspected terrorists – including some Americans (post-9/11)
RFE	Radio Free Europe
RL	Radio Liberty
RMVE	racially (or ethnically) motivated violent extremist
SA Division	Special Activities Division
SAM	surface-to-air missile
SCIF	sensitive compartmented information facility
SDO	support to diplomatic operations
SecDef	Secretary of Defense
SFA	Space Force Agency
SHAMROCK	cryptonym for NSA program to read international cables from and to American citizens (pre-1975)
sigint	signals intelligence
SLBM	submarine-launched ballistic missile
SMO	support to military operations
SNIE	Special National Intelligence Estimate
SOE	Special Operations Executive (Great Britain)
SOG	Special Operations Group (CIA)
SSA	space situational awareness
SSCI	Senate Select Committee on Intelligence
STELLARWIND	generic cryptonym for controversial NSA warrantless wiretaps and metadata collection programs (post-9/11)
SVR	Foreign Intelligence Service of the Russian Federation (KGB successor)
techint	technical intelligence

telint   telemetry intelligence

TIARA   tactical intelligence and related activities

TOR   Terms of Reference (for NIE drafting)

215   Code number for NSA communications metadata program targeting U.S. citizens (post-9/11)

UAE   United Arab Emirates

UAV   unmanned aerial vehicle (drone)

UKUSA Agreement   a signals intelligence pact between the United Kingdom and the United States, signed in 1946 and later extended to include Canada (1948) as well as Australia and New Zealand (both in 1956) – the "Five Eyes"

USCYBERCOM   U.S. Cyber Command (an NSA co-agency)

USIA   United States Information Agency (Department of State)

U-2   CIA spy plane (with later Air Force Variations known as the A-12 and the SR-71)

VC   Viet Cong

WHO   World Health Organization

WMDs   weapons of mass destruction

YAF   Young Americans for Freedom (student group in the United States during the 1960s)

Preface to the Third Edition: Roadmap to a Hidden World

National security intelligence is a vast, complicated, and important topic, with both technical and humanistic dimensions – all made doubly hard to study and understand because of the thick veils of secrecy that surround every nation's spy apparatus. Fortunately, from the point of view of democratic openness as well as the canons of scholarly inquiry, several of these veils have been lifted in the past five decades. This partial unmasking occurred in the context of government inquiries into intelligence failures and wrongdoing, especially those in 1975 in the United States that looked into charges of illegal government spying by the American security agencies against law-abiding citizens. On the heels of these inquires came a more determined effort by academic researchers in the United States and other democracies to probe the dark side of their own governments. These developments gave birth to a new research discipline, known as "Intelligence Studies." In this volume, the endnotes and the Suggested Readings are a testament to the burgeoning and valuable studies on national security intelligence (NSI) that have accrued from thoughtful scholarly reflection on the activities of secret spy organizations.

This research on intelligence activities is being pursued by scholars in academe and think-tanks, as well as by professional historians within the spy agencies themselves. Examples from the latter include the first-rate scholarly work published by the Office of Historians located within America's most well-known espionage organization, the Central Intelligence Agency (CIA, often referred to by insiders as "the Agency"). Impressive, too, is the research written by scholars inside the intelligence agencies and academe that is published in a CIA in-house journal titled *Studies in Intelligence*. This journal is printed in both a classified and an unclassified format, the latter available for readers without a government security clearance. The other spy agencies also have talented historians who chronicle the work of their home organizations.

In search of a solid understanding of NSI activities, much remains to be accomplished by researchers, both inside and outside the secret agencies. Not surprisingly, national security imperatives prohibit full transparency in this sensitive domain of study, since (for example) the enemies of democracy would benefit from knowing the names of foreign agents recruited by the open societies as a defense against autocratic regimes abroad. Such agents would likely then be executed for treason. Similarly, if intelligence collection methods used by the democracies were revealed, the closed societies would be able to take evasive measures to thwart those methods. Yet, in a genuine democracy, the people must have at least a basic comprehension of all the activities of their government, even within the shadowy domain of intelligence operations. While honoring the boundaries of sensibly classified information meant only for use by a nation's intelligence professionals and top decision-makers, it is nonetheless incumbent on scholars, journalists, and public officials to help citizens understand the hidden dimensions of their governing institutions and why it is important that their secret agencies are supported and funded. Despite periodic failures, intelligence agencies in the democracies have time and again proven their value, even though secrecy is contrary to the basic norm of openness, and even though sometimes the secret agencies within open societies have trampled on fundamental tenets of liberty and privacy before being pulled back into their proper role.

The Cold War was, in large part, a struggle between espionage organizations in the democracies and in the world's authoritarian regimes, illustrating the centrality of maintaining secret agencies even within open societies.[1] Spy services have sometimes been the source of great embarrassment to the democracies, as with America's covert action disaster at the Bay of Pigs in Cuba (1961), along with the questionable assassination attempts against foreign leaders carried out by the CIA under ambiguous authority from both the Eisenhower and the Kennedy Administrations. Harmful to the reputation of America's democracy, too, were the domestic espionage scandals of the mid-1970s; the Iran–*contra* scandal a decade later; and, more recently, revelations about torture and other forms of prisoner abuse against suspect terrorists – desperate measures adopted by the CIA and U.S. military intelligence agencies in the global struggle against terrorism. Troubling, too, was the dragnet "metadata" collection of information about American citizens by the National Security Agency (NSA), the leading eavesdropping organization in the United States. Intelligence mistakes of analysis can have enormous consequences, too, as when the United Kingdom and the United States invaded Iraq in 2003 based in part on a faulty assessment that Saddam Hussein, the Iraqi dictator, was developing weapons of mass destruction (WMDs) that could soon strike London and Washington. Further, intelligence organizations and operations conducted by the larger nations can levy a costly burden on taxpayers, doubly hurtful to citizens in the current times of high inflation.

For all of these reasons, NSI deserves the attention of the public, closer study by the scholarly community, wider coverage by the reliable media, and improved accountability inside the governments of democratic societies.

The challenge is daunting. To some extent, a nation's intelligence organizations and its community of scholars are at loggerheads: the government prefers secrecy, while scholars hope for access to information – openness. Still, recent experience underscores that a nation can encourage intelligence scholarship and still maintain an effective secret service. Indeed, the more a public knows about intelligence, the more likely it is that its citizens will support the legitimate – indeed, vital – protective shield these agencies provide, as long as they operate within the boundaries of the law and acceptable moral limits.

In 2009, a survey of scholarship on intelligence in the United States concluded:

> The interdisciplinary field of intelligence studies is mushrooming, as scholars trained in history, international studies, and political science examine such subjects as the influence of U.S. and foreign intelligence on national decisions during the cold war, the Vietnam War, and Watergate; how spycraft shaped reform efforts in the Communist bloc; the relationship of intelligence gathering to the events of September 11, 2001; and abuses and bungles in the "campaign against terrorism." As the field grows, it is attracting students in droves.[2]

A more recent review of the intelligence studies literature found "pathbreaking" new research that had attracted scholars from multiple disciplines, along with a growing number of women researchers.[3]

Hundreds of universities and colleges in democratic societies around the world now offer formal courses on national security intelligence, all of which are in high demand. In the United States, this interest stems in part from the widely reported intelligence failures related to the 9/11 attacks and the flawed predictions about WMDs in Iraq that preceded America's entry into the Second Persian Gulf war in 2003. Two decades later, in 2021, the sudden collapse of the U.S.-supported regime in Afghanistan – under assault by resurgent Taliban rebels, the same faction that provided a safe haven in Afghanistan for the Al Qaeda terrorist group prior to its 9/11 attacks – was yet another intelligence failure. The result: a hasty, chaotic evacuation from that nation of U.S. troops and civilian personnel, along with thousands of Afghan citizens who had supported those Americans within their homeland. Further, a violent insurrection carried out by rightwing extremists against the U.S. Congress on January 6, 2021, as it carried out its constitutional duty to count the Electoral College voting results from the 2020 presidential election, was also never anticipated by the U.S. intelligence agencies, despite fragmentary threats that had appeared regularly in public forums and message boards on the Internet. Certainly, leading lawmakers on Capitol Hill were never warned about this danger. Students, not to mention government officials, want to know why intelligence failures occur and what can be done to prevent such shortcomings in the future.

Moreover, many young people in the democracies hope to join their governments as public servants in some capacity, whether as diplomats, lawmakers, staff aides, intelligence officers, or military personnel, to engage in activities that will help shelter the free nations against attacks from autocrats abroad and extremists at home. Others realize that governmental decision-making is based on information and, whether in the leafy groves of academe or within a metropolitan think-tank, they want to pursue a life of learning about the relationship between information and decisions. In addition, some – raised on exaggerated Hollywood depictions of intelligence operations – are drawn to the study of national security intelligence because it seems like an adventurous life. Despite their attraction to the derring-dos of James Bond, however, young intelligence officers soon discover that the writings of the sociologist Max Weber (an expert on bureaucracy) provide greater insight into the real world of espionage than the dramatic license exercised by spy novelist Ian Fleming and others responsible for cultivating overheated misperceptions of real-life intelligence activities.

In recent years, the most important development in the study of NSI has been the effort by scholars to move beyond memoirs written in retirement by former intelligence officers (which are of uneven quality, but sometimes include first-rate impressions). The objective has been to achieve a more rigorous application of research standards that address such questions as how nations gather and understand ("analyze") information on threats and opportunities that arise across the globe. Serious researchers also want to understand how and why spy agencies engage in aggressive covert action and counterintelligence operations. Important, as well, as least for democratic nations, has been the question of how to establish guardrails – legal and moral frameworks – against the abuse of power by a nation's secret agencies, whether operating at home or overseas. As this research evolves, studies on intelligence matters are increasingly based on empirical data, testable hypotheses, and theoretical frameworks – the underpinnings of reliable scholarly inquiry.[4]

In addition, scholars in intelligence studies have been engaged in the conduct of in-depth interviews with intelligence practitioners to learn more about the insider's point-of-view; and they have further benefited from an extensive number of intelligence documents released by governments in recent decades. In the United States, these papers include the Church Committee Report in 1975–6 (on domestic spying, covert action, and secret assassination plots); the Aspin–Brown Commission Report in 1996 (on counterintelligence and, more broadly, the state of U.S. intelligence after the Cold War); the Kean Commission Report in 2004 (on the 9/11 intelligence failures); the Silberman–Robb Commission in 2005 (on WMDs in Iraq); and, most recently, the Senate Homeland Security Committee Report and the House Select Committee Hearings on the intelligence failures related to the January 6, 2021, insurrection (2021–2).

In the United Kingdom, the list of valuable government reports includes the House of Commons Select Committee on Foreign Affairs Report and the Intelligence and Security Committee Report (both in 2003), as well as the

Butler Report and the Hutton Report (both in 2004). These inquiries examined flawed aspects of British intelligence reporting on WMDs in Iraq prior to the outbreak of war by Western powers against that nation in 2003. Useful, too, are the UKUSA Agreements (pronounced "Eu-Koo-SA") released to the public in 2010, which consist of documents from 1940–56 related to signals intelligence (sigint) cooperation between the United Kingdom and the United States (since 1946), along with Canada (1948), as well as Australia and New Zealand (both in 1956). Also released have been the findings of the Chilcot Committee (2010), with its final report on the 2003 war against Iraqi published in 2016. In Canada, the McDonald Commission Report on domestic intelligence abuse (1981) is another example of a valuable source for the discipline of intelligence studies.

When the leaders of a nation make a decision, the quality of information before them can be a significant determinant of success or failure. Researchers engaged in intelligence studies seek to know more about this information: where it comes from, its accuracy, how it is used (or misused), and what might be done to improve its reliability and timeliness. This field of study also attempts to learn more about covert action, which has led to much controversy in world affairs, as with the Bay of Pigs experience in 1961. That disastrous CIA paramilitary operation against Cuba stands in sharp contrast to the crucial role of the Agency's U-2 photographic intelligence that supported prudent and successful White House decision-making the following year in response to the nearly catastrophic Cuban missile crisis. More recently, America's use of Predator and Reaper unmanned aerial vehicles (UAVs or drones), armed with Hellfire and other types of missiles, is a new and highly lethal form of covert action, unleashed initially against Taliban and Al Qaeda *jihadists* across Afghanistan and the mountainous regions of northwest Pakistan in the aftermath of the 9/11 attacks. Tragically, these robotic aircraft have occasionally inflicted accidental deaths among noncombatants in the Middle East, Southwest Asia, and North Africa. Drone attacks have also been carried out by the Pentagon and the CIA against terrorist targets on the Horn of Africa, across the Maghreb, and in Syria and Iraq – wherever radical terrorist factions opposed to the democracies are encamped or operationally engaged in attacks against the open societies.

Intelligence researchers also study the question of treason: why it occurs and what counterintelligence methods can be employed to reduce its incidence. Further, they explore the question of how democracies can best maintain a balance between effective secret operations of intelligence agencies, on the one hand, and the privileges of a free society, on the other – the ongoing search by the democracies for a workable equilibrium between security and liberty.

*   *   *

In Chapter 1, this new edition begins with an overview of the three major intelligence missions: collection and analysis, covert action, and counterintelligence – each of which is replete with its own challenges and controversies. This opening chapter also looks at the multiple dimensions of the phrase "national security intelligence," or NSI, which includes a cluster of organizations, a product (secret reports to decision-makers), and a set of clandestine activities. Moreover, Chapter 1 introduces the eighteen major agencies that currently comprise America's "Intelligence Community" (IC). In addition, this chapter explains why accountability is vital to ensure these secret services adhere to the basic principles of democracy (which has not always been the case); it explores why the American intelligence agencies have been plagued by a lack of both institutional integration and a culture of working together toward providing the President and other policy officials with a holistic stream of accurate and timely reports about world affairs.

The next three chapters examine more closely each of the core missions, beginning in Chapter 2 with the topic of intelligence collection. The concept of an "intelligence cycle" is introduced as a useful theoretical framework for envisioning how the United States gathers information from around the world and transmits these findings to the White House and other high councils of government in the form of reliable analytic reports and oral briefings. As this chapter and the next disclose, the steps that intelligence takes while traveling from the field (say, a spy reporting from a remote location in the mountains of Tibet, or photographs taken by high-altitude surveillance satellites) to high decision-making councils are susceptible to many potential pitfalls.

Chapter 3 carries forward the story of how intelligence travels from the field into the hands of policy officials. This part of the story explores the challenge of intelligence analysis – the preparation of reports on global threats and opportunities that policymakers need to know about, based on the worldwide intelligence collection activities explored in Chapter 2. Together, the twin steps of collection and analysis comprise the first intelligence mission. Each of these stages of intelligence confronts a set of unique obstacles, though, and that is why collection and analysis warrant separate treatment in this book. Nevertheless, it should be remembered that intelligence gatherers and analysts are engaged as a team in an ongoing dialogue – a constant back and forth – about a nation's information needs as they work together to prepare reports for high-level councils of government.

Chapter 4 takes up the most controversial of the three intelligence missions: a resort to the use of covert actions that can be highly invasive, such as drone attacks by the CIA against terrorist cells around the world. This chapter sheds light on a vital normative question: by means of secret interventions abroad, should the United States and other democracies seek to channel the flow of history in a direction favorable to their own interests through the adoption of covert actions, despite the havoc such operations can wreak in a foreign country?

Chapter 5 peers into another one of the darkest chambers in America's Intelligence Community: counterintelligence and, its companion discipline, counterterrorism. This is the third core intelligence mission. These activities are designed to protect the United States and other democracies from the machinations of hostile foreign spy agencies and terrorist organizations. The failure of America to thwart the aerial terrorist attacks of 9/11, aimed at New York City and Washington, D.C. on September 11, 2001, is a painful reminder of how important – and difficult – the responsibility can be for shielding the democracies from peril.

In Chapter 6, the book turns to the subject of intelligence accountability, as examined from a U.S. constitutional perspective. James Madison and his colleagues who wrote the American Constitution in 1787 understood full well the dangers of concentrated power as grievously exercised against the colonies by King George III in the lead-up to their revolution against the British motherland. Just as power can be risky to freedom, secret power can elevate the challenge of preserving liberty in the open societies to even higher levels. Government surveillance technology has become increasingly sophisticated. Today, a nation's espionage agencies have an omni-surveillance capacity to know about all the communications of their citizens: whom we telephone, when, and for how long; about our political, social, and religious connections; our sexual orientations – everything we do, everything we are as human beings.

New espionage technologies – ubiquitous street cameras, facial recognition capabilities, cybertools that can delve deeper and deeper into our lives, "deep fakes" emerging throughout our social networks and media communications, advanced DNA tracking capabilities, vast data collection by Big Government and Big Business, artificial intelligence expanding the scope and methods of espionage and covert actions – all race forward at a fast clip, outpacing laws to govern these chilling developments, and raising serious questions about whether our new spy machines are becoming smarter than their human handlers against whom they might one day turn. In South Korea during the Covid-19 pandemic of 2019–22, government authorities gathered detailed intelligence on when people left for work and returned home, whether they wore masks in the subway, where they changed trains, which massage parlors and karaoke bars they frequented, their internet activities, their private health details. And this was in *South* Korea, a democracy; in North Korea, the epitome of a dictatorial counterintelligence state, one could multiple the degree of citizen surveillance by orders of magnitude.

If America's secret agencies were given full rein, there would be no way to resist an increasingly authoritarian government in the United States. As Senator Frank Church put it simply but movingly in 1975, during his Senate

Committee's inquiry into intelligence abuse in the United States, "There would be no place to hide."[5] Chapter 6 examines how, in a democratic nation, intelligence agencies can provide protection against foreign foes and domestic extremists without at the same time eroding the freedom and privacy of its own citizens. Open societies around the world continue to face, and always will, the same quest that motivated America's founders in 1787: a search for an acceptable balance between the imperatives of national security and – the very lifeblood of democracy – the right of liberty for every citizen.

Chapter 7 briefly reviews the central arguments made in the book, and assesses the state of intelligence in the United States since the election of the Donald J. Trump Administration in 2016. The Trump years, from 2017 to 2021, were a time of unprecedented conflict between the White House and America's spy agencies. In addition, this chapter offers a set of reform ideas designed to promote the twin objectives of improved performance by the intelligence agencies in the service of the democracies, along with strengthened safeguards to ensure fidelity of secret agencies to the rule of law within their own homelands.

*   *   *

Much has happened in the world since Polity published the first edition of this book in 2012 and even since the second edition in 2017. Among other topics, this third iteration addresses in greater depth the subject of cybersecurity. The misuse of cybertechnology has become a growing threat to free nations as a result of intensified cyberattacks carried out by the spy services of hostile autocratic foreign governments, terrorist cells, and old-fashioned criminals using advanced electronic "safe-cracking" tools. The intelligence services of China, Russia, North Korea, Iran, and others have flooded every form of media in the democracies with disinformation and misinformation, in the hope of weakening or even destroying democracy as a form of government in this tempestuous world.

Along with stealing government and industrial secrets from the democratic nations through electronic interventions, foreign dictators have attempted as well to shape the outcomes of free elections around the world using these high-tech methods. The autocrats have secretly supported candidates in the democratic societies who might be more in harmony with their own malignant objectives. In 2016, for instance, Russian intelligence operatives hacked into the computers of the Democratic National Committee (DNC), as well as voter-registration systems throughout the United States. According to senior U.S. intelligence officials, these influence operations directed by the Kremlin may well have played a significant role in tilting the presidential election outcome that year toward a victory for the Republican candidate, Trump. Russian President Vladimir V. Putin, a former KGB counterintelligence officer trained to view the United States as an arch-enemy attempting to humiliate and perhaps even destroy Russia, reportedly considered him a more friendly and malleable prospect for Moscow–Washington relations than his Democratic opponent, former Secretary of State Hillary Clinton.

This third edition also addresses several other new developments related to intelligence activities, such as the eroded relationship between the U.S. Intelligence Community and the presidency throughout the Trump years in the White House. Never before in the history of the United States had the nation's chief executive been so openly disdainful of the CIA, the Federal Bureau of Investigation (FBI), and their companion agencies. President Trump often referred to the IC as part of a "deep state" hidden within America's federal government – in his view, a dangerous, unelected bureaucracy advancing its own interests at the expense of the American people. A core reason why President Trump remained so hostile toward the intelligence agencies throughout his tenure was the commenting by some of America's spy chiefs – in public – that he owed his presidential victory to Russia's manipulation of the election outcome; some observers went so far as to allege collusion between Trump campaign officials and Russian intelligence officers. Such charges, though, have never been proven.

Another important topic since the previous edition is the horrific Covid-19 pandemic, which killed more than a million Americans and additional millions across the globe. The question addressed here is: did the IC anticipate the spread of this disease from China to the United States and other nations, providing leaders with advanced warning? In the future, is "global health intelligence" something the IC and other secret agencies in the democracies should include as a more central part of their burgeoning collection-and-analysis responsibilities?

To permit attention to these new intelligence challenges without turning this book into a tome, I have trimmed some material from earlier editions. My purpose has been to avoid converting this primer into an encyclopedic treatise on national security intelligence. The goal has been to provide a manageable introduction to intelligence studies without drowning the reader in minutia. Once the fundamentals of intelligence presented in this book are understood, the reader may then wish to consult the more specialized and detailed works offered in the Suggested Readings section at the end of this volume.

All non-fiction books ought to sail closely to the shores of factual evidence. This volume adheres to that fundamental precept. Important, too, though, are values within society – views on right and wrong, good and bad. This carries the writer and the reader into more subjective territory often referred to as normative analysis. This is permissible, I think, as long as the writer is clear about his or her value system. Thus, in this book, I occasionally address normative (value-oriented) topics; so let me be clear at the beginning about these perspectives. My studies of intelligence agencies since 1975 and my several years of service in the U.S. government (though not with any intelligence agency) have led me to a belief in the following important underlying values of democratic governance:

- that democracy, based on liberty and the rule of law, is far superior to any other form of government, and the comparison is not even close when contrasted with the brutally repressive regimes of authoritarian and totalitarian governments;
- that a central lesson of history is that power corrupts – a proposition dangerously magnified when power is secretly held; and,
- that intelligence agencies can provide valuable information to help protect the democracies against threats, internal and external, and thus they warrant concomitant funding and respect when operating within the law and propriety; but that, even in the open societies, they have also displayed a capacity to violate democratic norms and, therefore, must be subjected to well-crafted and carefully monitored safeguards against the abuse of secret power.

Facts and evidence, yes; but one will also find in these pages a normative undercurrent that reflects the values outlined above.

National security intelligence is an intriguing and meaningful pursuit. The subject ranges across many topics and academic disciplines. It holds a certain panache imparted by such topics as paramilitary operations, secret rendezvouses with foreign agents, space-based spying by glittering satellite, mole-hunting in dark passageways, lethal drone warfare, and the challenge of anticipating the next packet of tricks history intends to play in the affairs of mere mortals.

Welcome to the third edition, and to the mysterious and fascinating world of modern-day intelligence activities.

Loch K. Johnson
Salisbury, Connecticut

Acknowledgments

With pleasure, I acknowledge the wellsprings of my understanding of national security intelligence. These sources, include the hundreds of intelligence officers who have responded to my endless questions and requests for interviews since 1975. Among them, at the senior level, are former intelligence leaders Richard Helms, James R. Schlesinger, William E. Colby, George H.W. Bush, Adm. Stansfield Turner, William J. Casey, William H. Webster, Robert M. Gates, R. James Woolsey, John M. Deutch, and James R. Clapper.

In addition, providing wise counsel regarding the view of intelligence from Capitol Hill, have been lawmakers Les Aspin, Edward P. Boland, Frank Church, Wyche Fowler, Lee H. Hamilton, Angus King, Roman Mazzoli, Charles McC. Mathias, Jr., Keith Robinson, Richard S. Schweiker, and Walter F. Mondale (who also served as Vice President during the Carter Administration).

This book has benefited, too, from my opportunities to work as a staff aide in the Senate, the House of Representatives, and the White House. And I have learned so much from the research findings of my academic colleagues – the authors whose works are cited in the notes and bibliography that accompany this volume.

I would like to express my appreciation as well to Dr. Louise Knight, who originally approached me about writing a book like this for Polity in 2010. She is a wonderful editor and I am deeply grateful for her friendship and steady, unerring guidance. Helpful, too, at Polity was editorial assistant Inès Boxman, who provided valuable suggestions during the preparation of this third edition. And I owe a large debt of gratitude to Sarah Dancy, also at Polity, for her expert copyediting in both this edition and the previous one. She has a remarkable sensitivity for clear prose, and is a pleasure to work with as well.

Several colleagues served as readers-over-my-shoulder and provided thoughtful ideas. Among them, let me especially note my appreciation to Professor David M. Barrett of Villanova University. He is not only a premier scholar and teacher in the field of Intelligence Studies, but has also been a dear friend and professional colleague over the years. At the University of Georgia, I would further like to thank Dean of the School of Public and International Affairs (SPIA) Matthew R. Auer for his outstanding leadership and support of my research; President Jere W. Morehead, to whom this book is dedicated, for his remarkable stewardship of the University, his friendship, and his inspiring encouragement.

My greatest debt, as always, is to Leena S. Johnson, my discerning "in-house editor" and wife of many happy years; and to Kristin, our daughter, and grandchildren August and Loch – each a steady source of infectious enthusiasm and good judgment. Their encouragement made life infinitely more enjoyable for me during the challenges that come with writing a book.

1

National Security Intelligence:
The First Line of Defense

Only a few puffs of white cloud marred a perfect blue sky as American Airlines Flight 11 prepared to depart from Boston's Logan International Airport at 7:59 on Tuesday morning, September 11, 2001. Destination: Los Angeles. Passenger Mohamed Atta, short in stature and dour in countenance, had seated himself in 8D, business class. Four other men from the Middle East, equal to Atta in their unfriendly demeanor, sat near him in business and first class.

In the cockpit of the Boeing 767, Captain John Ogonowski and First Officer Thomas McGuinness went through the usual pre-flight checklist at the control panel. Everything was in order. The captain backed the plane out of its berth and taxied down the runway. He pulled back on a lever and headed for an altitude of 26,000 feet. Eighty-one passengers settled in for the scheduled five-hour flight and the crew's nine flight attendants bustled about in the kitchens, preparing for cabin service. At 8:14, fifteen minutes into the journey, a routine radio message from the Federal Aviation Administration's center for air traffic control (ATC) in Boston requested that Captain Ogonowski take his aircraft to a higher elevation, 35,000 feet. Contrary to standard procedure, the Captain failed to acknowledge these instructions. A commotion on the other side of the cockpit door had distracted him.

Just as the ATC message arrived in the cockpit of Flight 11, two of the men who had boarded the aircraft with Atta sprang from their seats in first class. With knives, they stabbed two flight attendants who were wheeling a beverage cart down the aisle. One of the attendants collapsed, mortally wounded; the other shrieked and clasped a hand over a cut on her arm. The assailants moved quickly to the cockpit door and forced their way inside.

In their wake, Atta raced from his seat and commandeered the controls of the airplane. Back in the passenger cabin, another of his companions knifed a male passenger in the throat and began to spray Mace throughout the business- and first-class sections. The poisoned air drove some passengers down the aisle, away from the front of the airplane; others huddled low in their seats. Speaking English with a heavy Middle East accent and wielding a knife in plain sight, the killer – muscular, intense, ready to strike again – warned that he had a bomb. One of his allies added in flawless English: "Nobody move. Everything will be okay. If you try to make any moves, you'll endanger yourself and the airplane. Just stay quiet." In the coach section, passengers remained unaware of the danger, believing that a medical emergency had arisen in first class.

Filled with Mace, the air in the front cabin was proving impossible to breathe. A flight attendant hid by the curtain that separated the coach and business sections and tried to reach the captain in the cockpit with an on-board telephone. When this failed, she called the American Airlines operations center in Fort Worth, Texas, and, with remarkable composure, explained in a low voice that a violent hijacking of Flight 11 was under way. Officials in Fort Worth also had no success with their repeated calls to the cockpit.

Twenty-five minutes had elapsed since take-off. The airplane was now flying erratically. It made a lurch southward, circled in a wide arc, and went into a sharp descent. Perhaps it was bound for the John F. Kennedy Airport in New York and a round of bargaining on the tarmac: a demand for a ransom, in exchange for the release of the aircraft and its hostages.

But the plane was flying so low. Far too low.

At 8:46, Flight 11 slammed into the ninety-sixth floor of the North Tower at the World Trade Center in lower Manhattan.

Instant inferno. Temperatures above the melting point for steel. Metal wrenching against metal. Immediate death for all those on board the airplane and an unknown number of office workers – the lucky ones who at least escaped the fiery end that would soon consume others in the building. Some people above the impassable impact site chose to leap from windows toward the streets, an eternity below, rather than perish in the searing flames.

Another aircraft – United Airlines Flight 175 – had also set off for Los Angeles from Logan Airport. Hijacked in coordination with Flight 11, it soon turned to the south as well, arced back toward the east, and plunged toward the skyscrapers of New York City, their windows glittering in the morning sunlight. The plane struck the South Tower of the World Trade Center at 9:03, about seventeen minutes after the North Tower impact.

Two other teams were part of the hijacking plot, later traced to Al Qaeda, a terrorist group sheltered by the Taliban regime in Afghanistan. Instead of New York City, however, they directed their confiscated airplanes toward the nation's capital city. At 9:27, American Airlines Flight 77, originally on its way to Los Angeles from Washington Dulles, smashed into the Pentagon like a huge missile, traveling at a speed of 530 miles per hour.

When terrorists took over the fourth plane, United 93, on its way to San Francisco, its passengers had already heard – in heart-wrenching cell phone calls with loved ones – about the fate of American 11 and United 175. At 9:57, several of the passengers decided as a group to rush the hijackers in a desperate attempt to prevent the plane from reaching its target – perhaps the Capitol or the White House. Their brave struggle lasted for several minutes, as the terrorist pilot at the controls attempted to throw them off balance by jerking the steering column from side to side and up and down. Undeterred by

Photo 1.1: The Twin Towers
A "bucket brigade" works to clear rubble and debris, hoping to find survivors of the deadly terrorist attack on the Twin Towers.

U.S. Navy photo by Photographers Mate 2nd Class Jim Watson.

these maneuvers, the passengers fought their way to the door of the cockpit. About to be overwhelmed, the terrorists chose to destroy the plane rather than surrender. The counterfeit pilot turned a lever hard to the right and rolled the aircraft over on its back. Within seconds, it fell from the sky and exploded in a fiery ball across a barren Pennsylvania field. In another twenty minutes of flying time it would have reached Washington.

In New York, the tragedy was not over. Under the extreme heat caused by the impact of large and fast-flying airplanes filled with volatile aviation fuel, the structural girders of the Twin Towers buckled and soon collapsed, sending office workers, tourists on the observation deck, and rescuing firefighters and police officers into a downward free fall to their deaths. Steel, glass, furniture, and bodies plummeted from the heavens. Massive grey and black plumes of dust and pulverized metal billowed throughout lower Manhattan as thousands of people in the streets below fled from the crumbling 125-story buildings. Blackness blotted out the sky, as if the sun had died that morning along with all the innocents in the Twin Towers and on the ill-fated airplanes.

When the dust settled, the extent of the tragedy eventually became all too clear: 2,996 people had perished in New York City, in Washington, and at a smoldering farmland near Shanksville, Pennsylvania. The United States had suffered its worst attack in history, surpassing the horrific Japanese bombing of Pearl Harbor in 1941.[1]

The importance of national security intelligence

Al Qaeda, operating out of Afghanistan, was responsible for the aerial terror-ism that had inflicted on America a painful – indeed, brutal – reminder of the importance of national security intelligence (NSI) in the fates, accidents, and destinies that make up the human condition. If only this nation's intelligence agencies could have provided the George W. Bush Administration with more thorough information about the intentions and capabilities of Al Qaeda, the United States might have been able to prevent the tragedy. If only the Central Intelligence Agency (CIA), America's most well-known espionage service, had been able to place an undercover agent high in the Al Qaeda organiza-tion, a "mole" who could have tipped off U.S. authorities about the planned hijackings. If only the Federal Bureau of Investigation (FBI), America's pre-mier domestic intelligence agency, had been more successful in tracking down two foreign terrorists known by the CIA to have flown to California from the Middle East in January of 2000 and would prove to be part of the Al Qaeda hijacking teams. The Bureau would have had better luck perhaps in apprehending these men if only the Agency had passed along its knowledge about their arrival in the United States more quickly to the Bureau's highest echelons, rather than – astonishingly – merely by way of more routine and time-consuming lower-level liaison channels. And if only FBI Headquarters in Washington had taken more seriously, and acted upon, reports from its own agents in Minnesota and Arizona that foreigners from the Middle East – who would also join the teams of Al Qaeda terrorists on 9/11 – were enrolled in flight training in those states and asking suspicious questions (reported by flight instructors to the Bureau) about how to maneuver U.S. aircraft in mid-air but with little interest in the take-off and landing phases of flight training.

There was a series of other "if only" possibilities, all lost. If only the National Security Agency (NSA), the largest of the U.S. spy organizations, had translated more quickly from Arabic into English intercepted telephone messages between leaders within Al Qaeda that hinted at an approaching attack on the United States from the skies. If only airport security offic-ers and American pilots had been warned about the immediacy of possible hijackings, considered a real likelihood by the CIA as early as 1995, and been provided with profiles and photographs of at least some of the 9/11 terrorists that the Agency had on file. If only the Clinton and Bush Administrations had taken more seriously the growing warnings from America's intelligence agencies about their discovery of more aggressive Al Qaeda planning to attack the American homeland – especially as red-flagged by the CIA in an August 6, 2001, *Presidential Daily Brief* entitled "Bin Laden Determined to Strike." These presidents could then have done much more to pump the brakes in response to IC warnings. Intelligence officers and political leaders alike made a staggering number of mistakes that otherwise might have halted this act of savagery against the innocent people who perished that terrible day in 2001.

In October 2023, Israel would suffer similar consequences as a result of its stunning intelligence failure to anticipate the initiation of war by Hamas terrorists, who, in a surprise attack by land, sea, and air, massacred hundreds of civilians in southern Israel – men, women, and children – and captured some two hundred more as hostages. Nor reportedly did U.S. intelligence have any forewarning of this elaborate Hamas invasion from the Gaza Strip. It was Israel's 9/11. It will take considerable future study to fully understand the "what ifs" of this calamity. How did two of the best intelligence services in the world so badly miss the warning signs of the impending attack? One thing seemed certain already: Israeli intelligence had failed to infiltrate the Hamas terrorist organization in Gaza with spies so as to track its scheming against Israel before an attack – a shocking failure of that nation's "human intelligence" or "humint."

In 2001, no one knew if the events of 9/11 were only the beginning of many assaults that would follow against the United States and other democracies, perhaps using chemical, biological, or even nuclear devices rather than airplanes as weapons. No further immediate attacks occurred, in part because of the enormous pressures directed against Al Qaeda around the world by America and its allies; nonetheless, tensions remained high in all the open societies about the chances of additional violence aimed against them by global terrorists. Indeed, before long, Al Qaeda and its loosely affiliated cells – whose leaders (Osama bin Laden chief among them) were thought to be hiding in the rugged mountain terrain of North Waziristan in Pakistan – did target other locations around the world, in London, Madrid, and Bali, for example. And Al Qaeda was further involved in assaults on American, British, and other international armed forces in Iraq and Afghanistan; in addition, it openly proclaimed its presence in Somalia, Yemen, and in parts of Pakistan, along with boasts of having infiltrated sleeper agents into all the major democracies. Al Qaeda terrorists were consistently aided and abetted by *jihadists* associated with the Taliban, the insurgent organization that provided Bin Laden and his associates with a safe haven in Afghanistan prior to and during the terrorist operations directed against the United States overseas and then at home from 1998 to 2001.

Nations in the West escalated the intensity of their intelligence activities against Al Qaeda and its affiliates (especially in the Middle East, Southwest

Asia, and Northwest Africa), in hopes of acquiring prior knowledge of possible future attacks in this reeling world, while at the same time crippling the ability of these groups by way of aggressive CIA paramilitary operations against them. Finally, in May 2011, after a decade of searching for Bin Laden, a U.S. Navy SEAL team – supported by intelligence gathered chiefly by the CIA and the NSA – raided a private compound in Abbottabad (a city north of the Pakistani capital, Islamabad) and killed the Al Qaeda leader.

Soon after Bin Laden's death, another global terrorist faction came to the forefront in the Middle East and North Africa. Known as ISIS, it proved to be an equally barbaric army of insurgents operating in Syria, Iraq, Libya, and other locations around the globe. This new organization demonstrated a sophisticated use of social media to recruit young men and women to its cause, far beyond what Al Qaeda had achieved. ISIS stands for Islamic State in Iraq and Syria; it is also known by some as the Islamic State, ISIL (Islamic State of Iraq and the Levant), or, in Arabic, *Daesh*. This terrorist group claimed credit for attacks not only in the Middle East and Libya, but also in Brussels and Paris, as well as inspiring a savage attack by local terrorists against tourists and French citizens in Nice. Adherents to ISIS's anti-Western agenda also engaged in mass shootings on its behalf in California (San Bernardino) and Florida (Orlando), along with a truck-ramming attack against random pedestrians in New York City. While Al Qaeda remains high on the U.S. and allied lists of major terrorist threats, it has been edged out of the top tier by the frequently demonstrated capacity of ISIS to spawn attacks against democracies.

The 9/11 event is presented as a beginning centerpiece for this volume because it was the single most important intelligence failure in the history of the United States. That dark experience presents many lessons about why intelligence agencies fail from time to time – a core question addressed throughout these pages. More contemporary illustrations examined in the book explore the involvement of Western intelligence agencies in support of Ukraine in its full-scale war against Russia, which began in 2022 (though with roots of discord reaching back over a decade); and in providing warnings about the outbreak of the Covid-19 pandemic. Further, in the case of the United States, the book examines the manner in which intelligence agencies and senior policymakers came into conflict with one another during the 2017–21 Trump presidency. While these high-level conflicts during the Trump years have already been widely reported, far less is known at this point about the success of Western intelligence in assisting the war effort in Ukraine, or in the tracking of the origin and dissemination of the Covid-19 virus. Western spy organizations, along with everyone else outside the few Chinese in the know, have yet to determine with assurance whether the pandemic stemmed from unsanitary "wet markets" in Hunan, China, or from an accident within a medical lab or a military facility in that city. Ukraine and

Covid-19 are both addressed in subsequent chapters, but definitive insights will have to await further research and the declassification of intelligence documents. Presently, intelligence about both topics is highly classified. Members of NATO are trying not to further inflame the Russian President, Vladimir V. Putin, by openly discussing their supportive role in the Ukraine war; and the Chinese have refused to be candid with the world about the unexplained origins in their country of the Covid-19 pandemic.

Other emerging threats are also explored in the chapters that follow. They include the ongoing danger of global terrorism; the new (or renewed is a better way to say it) conflicts between democracies and the superpower dictatorships of China and Russia – what some commentators view as a second Cold War unfolding in its early stages; and the challenge of domestic violent extremists (DVEs), like those who stormed the U.S. Capitol on January 6, 2021, as well as the most lethal variations of DVEs: racially or ethnically motivated violent extremists (RMVEs) and militia violent extremists (MVEs). Western intelligence organizations fear that these forms of indigenous extremism present an elevated threat to democracies, leading to possible mass-causality attacks perpetrated by alienated factions or individuals ("lone wolves") who may be anarchists, nihilists, or simply far-right populists opposed to progressive forms of government. Recent examples of this domestic terrorism in the United States include a DVE who threw a Molotov cocktail into a political office in Texas; a RMVE white supremist who killed two African Americans in Massachusetts; and an MVE who planned to take over a television station in Illinois to broadcast his anti-government message. In each of these examples, all of which occurred in 2021, the perpetrators were apprehended, convicted, and are now serving prison sentences. Ideally, intelligence would have discovered the plans for these attacks in advance, allowing authorities to prevent them – preferably by way of legally permitted surveillance operations, based on evidence-based warrants.

Mysteries and secrets

Intelligence practitioners speak of "mysteries," "secrets," and "puzzles." Mysteries are subjects that a nation would like to know about in the world – say, schemes hatching inside the hidden recesses of domestic terrorist organizations. Such matters, though, are difficult to fathom in light of the limited capacity of human beings to forecast the course of history. Who might be the next leader of Russia or China? Will Pakistan be able to survive the internal political unrest that constantly plagues that country? What brooding anarchist might aspire to bomb a government facility in the United Kingdom or North America, and when? These are highly complicated intelligence challenges. In contrast, secrets are more susceptible to human discovery and comprehension through the deployment of espionage agents and well-placed spy machines, combined with the skilled use of open-source materials that would include library, social media, and Internet research. A further category sometimes used by intelligence officials consists of puzzles. These are questions about world affairs that might be solved purely by way of open sources, without resorting to spying. Even secrets and puzzles though, let alone mysteries, can be difficult to unravel – for example, the number of nuclear submarines in the Chinese Navy; the identity of Russian agents who have infiltrated NATO's pool of staff experts; or the efficiencies of North Korean rocket fuel and the precise range of that hermit nation's long-range missiles and the potential kiloton yield-of-destruction they can carry.

With a reliable spy in the right place, with the skills of a talented library researcher, with surveillance satellites in the right orbits, or with reconnaissance aircraft able to penetrate enemy airspace, a nation might be able to uncover secrets and sort out puzzles. In the case of mysteries, though, leaders must rely largely on the thoughtful "best guesses" of intelligence analysts about the likely contours of an answer, based on hunches and as much empirical evidence as can be found through open sources and espionage. In a speech given on July 19, 2023, to an audience in Prague (reported by *Politico*), a candid leader of the British intelligence service MI6, Richard Moore, admitted his frustration in trying to fathom the status of an on-again, off-again renegade Russian paramilitary leader, Yevgeny Prigozhin, during the ongoing Ukrainian war. In June, Prigozhin had attempted a brief and half-baked coup against the Putin regime, even though the Russian President had been viewed as his friend and ally. The coup went nowhere and Prigozhin shut it down. As Moore recalled: "Prigozhin started off that day [in June] as a traitor at breakfast, he had been pardoned by supper, and then a few days later, he was invited for tea." Moore understandably concluded: "There are some things that even the chief of MI6 finds a little bit difficult to try and interpret in terms of who's in and who's out." In August, just two months after the aborted coup attempt, Prigozhin perished in a suspicious airplane crash north of Moscow.

Despite the difficulties, and to the extent they can afford it, prudent nations establish a robust intelligence capability to ferret out secrets and thoroughly research puzzles. They also attempt – insofar as human frailties allow – to plumb the depth of the world's mysteries.

Central themes

This is a book about a nation's efforts to uncover secrets and solve puzzles while at the same time pondering mysteries, as its leaders attempt to comprehend world affairs and make sound decisions in an often hostile global environment. These pages focus on the degree of intelligence successes and failures in forecasting world events, as well as the ever-present problem of guarding against the misuse of secret power by espionage agencies as they carry out their spying activities.

The inevitability of intelligence failures

Intelligence agencies in the West have helped protect democracies against a variety of dangers, from bellicose totalitarian regimes to terrorist organizations and extremists, whether at home or abroad. These agencies have sometimes fallen short in meeting their responsibility to provide a first line of defense against threats. The events of 9/11, followed by erroneous predictions in 2002 about the likely presence of weapons of mass destruction (WMDs) in Iraq, tragically underscored the chances for error by U.S. and other intelligence services in the democratic nations. Then came (among other examples) the faulty prognosis by America's intelligence agencies in 2021 about the viability of the U.S.-backed government in Afghanistan. Moreover, the intelligence agencies never anticipated how quickly the U.S.-trained Afghan military units would crater when America's troops withdrew from that country and the government fell as Taliban fighters stormed Kabul.

Nations and other organizations have periodically experienced significant intelligence failures, some of which have led to disaster. Hitler's espionage services predicted that Britain would be weak-kneed and unwilling to react with force against a Nazi invasion of Poland. Joseph Stalin assumed that he could depend on the Third Reich to honor a non-aggression pact signed with the Soviet Union early in World War II. President Franklin D. Roosevelt and his intelligence aides assumed that Japan would never be so reckless as to strike Pearl Harbor in 1941. As a result of human error and bureaucratic blunders, intelligence misjudgments have haunted leaders and their governments in regimes of every stripe, democracies and autocracies alike. Such failures are not just a rare exception to the rule. Self-delusion, mirror-imaging (that is, assuming other nations will behave in the same manner as one's own nation, despite cultural differences), bureaucratic rivalries that hinder intelligence-sharing, the lack of human agents or surveillance satellites in the right place at the right time, fear of delivering bad news to a national leader – the list of reasons for intelligence missteps goes on. How prescient the philosopher of war Karl von Clausewitz (1730–1831) was when he concluded that "many intelligence reports in war are contradictory, even more are false, and most are uncertain."[2] The same can be true in times of peace. This reality regarding the limits of intelligence is an uncomfortable truth woven like a dark thread through the pages of this volume.

While the reality of intelligence failures must be addressed in the hope of limiting their future occurrence, it should be remembered that espionage services in the democracies have recorded many successes as well. Throughout the Cold War, for instance, the United States and the United Kingdom had an accurate, detailed understanding of Soviet weaponry as it developed, including where these instruments of war were located. Further, if the weapons were being readied for warfare, the West would have had an early warning – thanks chiefly to human and technical intelligence-gathering capabilities (such as satellite surveillance). A surprise attack that caught the democracies off-guard, as America was at Pearl Harbor in 1941, would have been unlikely during the Cold War and after, thanks to the modern surveillance capabilities enjoyed by Western democracies (as well as their authoritarian adversaries). Such careful tracking of an adversary, especially a superpower like the Soviet Union – well versed in counterintelligence methods – was no mean feat during the Cold War. The successes made the large Western expenditure of funds on intelligence worth the cost.

In a more recent example of an intelligence success, Western spy services have been able to provide Ukraine – engaged in an existential struggle against a Russian invasion force in February of 2022 during the Biden Administration – with accurate information about Moscow's military plans and movements (including the precise location of Russia's generals), along with details on Moscow's disinformation operations against the Ukrainian government in Kyiv. A particularly valuable service provided by the West has been to disseminate early warnings to the Ukraine military about impending Russian attacks. The director of the CIA, William J. Burns, visited Ukraine three times between January 2022 and the end of 2023 for meetings with that nation's military and intelligence leaders. During the January visit, he informed Ukraine officials that the Russians planned to take over Kyiv's Antonov Airport the following month, a heads-up that allowed Ukraine time to prepare a defense against the use of this facility as a staging area for the Russians to attack the nation's capital. In subsequent trips, Burns provided additional warnings about specific Russian military objectives and tactics, including cyber consultations that helped block Moscow's efforts to hack the energy grid and other important databases in Ukraine. Further, among other instances of assistance, a shadowy intelligence group within the Energy Department (the Nuclear Emergency Support Team, or NEST) reportedly wired Ukraine with miniature sensors that can detect the presence of radiation from nuclear power-plant leaks or from a Russian nuclear weapon. NEST also has the capacity to confirm the identity of an attacker. This support, along with the supply of advanced weaponry from the West, significantly helped this smaller nation stand up to President Putin's plans to absorb Ukraine into the Russian empire.

Moreover, on a day-to-day basis, Western espionage agencies have provided their national leaders with helpful information about everything from worldwide political developments and economic trends to data on global environmental degradation, as well as the possible outbreak of pandemics. In this way, a nation's intelligence organizations can – and often do – contribute substantially to the goal of a knowledgeable, fact-based approach to policymaking.

The specter of intelligence scandal

Another truth, is that – regrettably – intelligence agencies (in the manner of all other human organizations, whether governmental or private sector) often fall prey to Lord Acton's well-known prophecy that "power tends to corrupt and absolute power corrupts absolutely."[3] From the point of view of democratic theory, he might have added: "especially secret power, hidden as it is from the guardians of liberty."[4] History reveals that, time and again, a nation's secret services have turned their disquieting capabilities for surveillance and manipulation against the very citizens they were meant to shield. Efforts within democratic regimes to maintain accountability over intelligence agencies ("oversight," in the awkward but widely used expression of American political scientists and government officials) has proven difficult and has often collapsed.

Neither of the themes that guide this book – the inability to predict future events with precision, and the acknowledgment that the misuse of secret government organizations can be a danger to open societies – should astound the reader. After all, intelligence agencies are made up of human beings, who must live their lives without the benefit of a crystal ball and do not possess the attributes of angels; consequently, one can expect failures and abuses. (The celebrated "Grand Strategy" course at Yale University begins with the reading of *Paradise Lost*, a drama by John Milton on the seeds of human corruption.) No mere mortal is omniscient; nor can any mortal lay claim to Kantian purity in the conduct of government affairs. Yet societies seem regularly taken aback by the occurrence of intelligence failures and scandals. Citizens and policymakers alike express amazement and dismay that their espionage services have been unable to provide a clairvoyant warning of impending danger; or that these agencies – even in the democracies – have illegally spied at home, not just against enemies abroad. In contrast to this naivety, the American founding father James Madison and his colleagues understood that nations were led not by angels, but by human beings of flesh and blood. As a result, government failures and the abuse of power were inevitable.

With the admirable common sense of a Midwesterner, President Harry S. Truman echoed Madison's cautionary words found in *Federalist Paper 51* about the importance of constitutional safeguards against government abuse. "You see," Truman reflected, "the way a government works, there's got to be a housecleaning every now and then."[5] Citizens in the democracies can throw up their hands in despair over the fact that intelligence errors and misdeeds

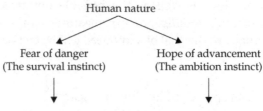

1 The search for information (The intelligence cycle)
2 Protection of information (Counterintelligence)
3 The search for an added advantage (Covert action)
4 Protection against the abuse of secret power (Accountability)

Figure 1.1: Basic human motivations and the quest for national security intelligence: a stimulus–response model.

are inescapable; or they can acknowledge the limits and the foibles of the human species and establish guardrails to lessen their effects. That is one of the core challenges laid down in this book.

Given the reality of persistent forecasting miscues and periodic corruption in government (which is especially hard to discern within the dark crevasses of an intelligence bureaucracy), why do democracies dedicate substantial resources to the establishment and support of spy agencies – seemingly a complete anathema to open societies? Are not the mistakes, as well as the risks to civil liberties, too great for democratic regimes to tolerate the presence of secretive organizations and their shadowy activities within the interstices of their otherwise largely transparent government institutions?

The answer is that all living species have a primordial desire to shield themselves from threats to their well-being, whether saber-toothed tigers in the Stone Age or aerial terrorism today. Thus, they establish – as well as they can – prudent defenses: everything from radar installations positioned in human societies to detect the approach of enemy bombers to, at a low level in the chain of life, motion-sensitive webs spun by spiders to warn of an intruder. As fundamental as the atom is to physics, so is the human instinct for survival to the creation of government institutions, including secret spy agencies. Moreover, reformers in open societies continue to hope that corruption within a democracy's intelligence services might be discovered early enough, and rooted out, before improper espionage activities manage to erode the bedrock democratic principles of liberty and privacy.

Beyond survival, humans are motivated by a sense of ambition (see Figure 1.1). Intelligence agencies can assist leaders in their efforts to know in advance not only about *threats* they may face, but about *opportunities* that may arise to advance the national interest. This book focuses on intelligence agencies within nation-states; but they are not the only organizations drawn to espionage. The basic drives of survival and ambition apply equally to nonstate organizations and factions around the world. They, too, often have their own intelligence apparatus, whether (for example) they are terrorist cells or global corporations.

Given the peril of modern WMDs – or even the simpler but still catastrophic use of such low-tech methods as hijacked aircraft assaults against skyscrapers or a large, speeding truck aimed at pedestrians (a terrorist method used in Nice in 2016 and in New York City the following year) – nations hope that their intelligence agencies, however imperfect, might provide at least some degree of warning. Nations are prepared to spend large sums of money from their treasury on the gathering of information about threats and opportunities, near and afar. Understanding that the world is complex and our knowledge is limited, the primary hope is to avoid devastating surprises like Pearl Harbor or the 9/11 attacks; or to gain an advantage over foreign competitors engaged in military, commercial, cultural, and political rivalries across the meridians.

The intelligence missions

Collection and analysis

In myriad ways, the activities of intelligence agencies are vital for understanding international affairs.[6] The most important intelligence mission is to collect reliable, timely information about the world, which is the traditional meaning of the word "spying," as well as to assess its meaning accurately – intelligence "analysis" (topics examined further in Chapters 2 and 3, respectively). Officers in the CIA and its companion spy agencies in the United States eschew use of the term "spying," They prefer the less tainted term "intelligence gathering." (The British novelist P.G. Wodehouse's main character in several popular novels, Jeeves – a clever valet of a rich and idle young Londoner by the name of Bertie Wooster – was once confronted by this query: "Spying, Jeeves?" asked Wooster. The valet's reply: "We prefer 'reconnaissance,' sir.") Collection, though, is in fact spying if done by clandestine means. Much of the CIA's work consists of other responsibilities, such as covert action, counterintelligence, internal management, and liaison activities – all quite different from old-fashioned (indeed, biblical) espionage operations. So those who are not involved in the handling of foreign agents blanch at being known as "spies" and, technically, they have a point, even though the core *raison d'être* of a nation's intelligence apparatus – as opposed, in the United States for example, to a reliance solely on open-source research in the Library of Congress – is to ferret out hidden information abroad that may be relevant to security concerns.

At the heart of decision-making in every nation is a scene where policy officials are seated around a table in a secure government conference room, as they decide which direction to take their society in its relations with other nations and international organizations. These deliberations are based on information from many sources: a vast flow of ideas and recommendations from personal aides, cabinet members, government agencies, intelligence liaison partners overseas, lobbyists, the media, academics, think-tank experts, and even, on occasion, friends and family. A well-known example of the latter was the urging by Nancy Reagan, President Ronald Reagan's wife, that he engage in the pursuit of *détente* with the Russians to overcome the negative poll ratings against him stemming from the Iran-*contra* intelligence scandal of the mid-1980s. Lobbyists – such as the oil, sugar, and automobile industries in corporate America, or peace activists in times of foreign wars – are also known to provide constant pressure on foreign policy officials in pursuit of their objectives.

Vital in this "river of information," to use a metaphor used by some U.S. officials, are data collected by a nation's secret services. Often this source of information sets the government's agenda and shapes final decisions, especially in a time of crisis. Given the centrality of secret agencies, one cannot fully comprehend the choices that a nation makes without an understanding of how they operate, and without knowing something about the scope and quality of the information they provide. Despite the many sources of data and guidance available to leaders, NSI resides at the heart of a nation's decision-making, largely because secret agents and spy machines can sometimes pry out information from foreign governments and terrorist organizations that are not available in the *Washington Post*, the *New York Times*, the *Financial Times*, or social media platforms and Internet sources. In some cases, the sought-after information can only be acquired by way of clandestine sources and methods.

Just as a nation's spy services have erred from time to time on questions of anticipated global events, so have its defenses against internal subversion – as witnessed in the United States by the surprise insurrection against the Congress by a riotous mob on January 6, 2021. Moreover, as a nation's secret agencies have abused their powers, so have its citizens had to suffer through domestic spy scandals. Conversely, as examples throughout this book will attest, the illumination provided by reliable intelligence has led to much better decision-making than if policy officials had been forced to act in the dark. Furthermore, safeguards established in the democracies during the 1970s and 1980s have often been successful in curbing abuses by a nation's espionage agencies before they occur, or at least have allowed the open societies to quickly address these missteps afterward, then further strengthen their procedures for intelligence accountability.

Covert action

While primarily devoted most of the time to the collection and analysis of information from around the globe, intelligence agencies may also engage in a second mission of covert action: the attempt to change the course of history secretly, through the use of propaganda, political interventions, economic sabotage, and paramilitary activities. (Paramilitary operations are secretive warlike activities, which might include assassination plots against the leaders of other nations and terrorist organizations; a more formal definition of covert action and a discussion of its various forms is presented in Chapter 4.) These "dirty tricks," as they are characterized by critics, can be attractive to leaders who seek quick and (they hope) quiet measures to gain an advantage over global competitors. Yet covert action has sometimes brought grief and disrepute to a nation for violating the canons of propriety and international law, erasing the important difference between the intelligence activities of the democracies and their authoritarian counterparts.

Counterintelligence

Every nation's intelligence apparatus has a third important mission, known as counterintelligence (the focus of Chapter 5), of which (broadly defined) counterterrorism is a part – although these two activities are managed by different units within the governments of the United States and the United Kingdom. Here the purpose is to guard a nation's secrets and institutions against secret penetration and deception operations carried out by hostile foreign governments and terrorist organizations – or, in extreme cases, their outright attack against democracies. Foreign adversaries will attempt to burrow into a rival (and sometimes even a friendly) government, mole-like, in search of secrets or to sow disinformation. The Soviets succeeded in penetrating the CIA and the FBI at high levels during the Cold War, as well as the British, German, and French intelligence services (among others), with harmful effects for these democracies. The democracies have done their best to return the favor, often succeeding.

Media reports citing intelligence officers in the democracies indicate that the secret services of Russia and China (among other autocratic regimes) have been spying against Western nations even more aggressively in recent years than they did during the Cold War (1945–91), chiefly in a quest for technical, military, and commercial secrets. Russia and China are also thought to have the capacity to disrupt the electricity grid in the United States (especially where military installations are located), raising the prospect of cyberwarfare against this crucial national infrastructure. In return, America and other democratic nations have the wherewithal to retaliate in kind. Every nation seeks to thwart the presence of foreign spies or terrorist "sleeper cells" in its midst. The end result is a game of cat and mouse played between malevolent intruders, on the one hand, and spy-catchers, on the other, within the inner sanctums of national capitals around the world.

The challenge of intelligence accountability

Further, for democratic regimes, the matter of intelligence accountability is critical to those who fear the possible rise of a Gestapo within their own society. In the United States, the *New York Times* discovered in 1974 that the CIA had resorted to spying against American citizens whose only transgression had been to protest the war in Vietnam – a right protected by the First Amendment of the American Constitution. In response to the disclosure of these intelligence abuses (which bore the CIA codename Operation CHAOS), Congress moved to reform America's espionage services and establish safeguards against a repeated misuse of their secret trust. This intelligence reform movement in the United States began in the 1970s with the Church Committee investigation (led by Senator Frank Church, a Democrat from Idaho), then spread around the world to other open societies. Intelligence accountability, explored in Chapter 6, continues to be a subject of scholarly research, as well as debate and practical experimentation inside the world's existing and would-be free nations.

This book's purpose

The objective in this book is to place the topic of national security intelligence under a microscope, particularly with an eye toward examining its flaws and how they might be addressed in order to strengthen democracy's shield against terrorists, Russian and Chinese cyberattacks, and other threats to the open societies. The topic of intelligence is often overlooked in college classes on International Affairs because it is especially difficult to conduct research into the hidden chambers of a government, even the more transparent ones. This initial chapter offers an introduction to NSI in the United States by presenting some basic definitions and organizational charts that are necessary to understand how secret agencies function.

Ideally, a book on NSI would examine the approaches taken in various democratic and nondemocratic societies – a comparative analysis of espionage practices around the globe. Some work of this nature has been undertaken.[7] This volume, though, will largely explore the American experience. One day, when more data become available about intelligence activities in a wide range of countries (both free and those that suffer under government repression), reliable comparative studies of espionage services will likely yield significant insights into the evolution and function of secret services in every part of the world. Until that time, as French Intelligence Studies scholar Sébastien Laurent has put it, "the Anglo-Saxon school of intelligence is the only show in town and currently enjoys an unrivaled global hegemony."[8]

In sum, this volume attempts to provide readers with a sense of the successes, as well as the failures and scandals, that attend the existence of secret agencies. This is an important mandate for Intelligence Studies (IS), one of the fastest growing subfields of International Relations. The IS discipline began in the early 1980s and has blossomed into a significant component of university and college courses on International Affairs throughout the English-speaking world and beyond. Drawing largely on American illustrations, this book demonstrates how each of the intelligence missions is plagued by periodic error and misdeed. It investigates what might be done to mitigate failure and abuse – that is, how a democracy can improve its odds for accurate indications and warnings (I&W) of danger at home and abroad, while promoting the rule of law even within a government's hidden corridors. Despite the inevitability of failure and scandal, steps can be taken to reduce their incidence. Intelligence agencies in the United States, the United Kingdom, and other democracies have also recorded many notable victories in the defense of global freedom, and these happier outcomes are examined as well in these pages.

NSI comprises a frustrating set of activities given the inherent weaknesses that attend the imperfections of humankind, including our inability to foresee the future, along with the penchant for some leaders to abuse power – especially when that power is conducted out of public sight. Nonetheless, on a trouble-ridden world stage characterized by uncertainty, ambiguity, fear, and peril, no nation can afford to be without the shield – the eyes and the ears – that intelligence agencies can provide. And sometimes vital, too, are the swords of covert action and counterintelligence they can unsheathe against the powerful enemies of the free societies that unfortunately have always existed in history.

A good starting place to develop an appreciation for the complexity of this topic is an exploration of the various meanings evoked by the phrase "national security intelligence."

The multiple dimensions of national security intelligence

Intelligence as secret information

Observers, and even intelligence specialists and practitioners, do not always agree on the precise meaning of national security intelligence. The English author Somerset Maugham, an intelligence officer in World War I, offered a brief definition in his short story entitled "His Excellency." In his experience, intelligence was basically "getting hold of little bits of information that are sometimes useful." Following one's nose and keeping one's eyes open; observing something here or there, confirming a suspicion for the umpteenth time. More formally, the major point of disagreement among specialists usually pivots around whether "intelligence" ought to be defined narrowly or broadly. Defined narrowly (as is most commonly the case), NSI focuses on the primary mission of a country's secret agencies, that is, the gathering (Maugham's perspective) and then the analysis of information that might help to improve policy decisions made by leaders who value data for the insights and decision advantage that facts and experienced interpretation can impart. Refined still further, the definition may focus strictly on the actual product of the collection-and-analysis process: a written report or an oral briefing that conveys a blend of secretly and openly derived information to a government official. The CIA has defined intelligence simply as the "knowledge and foreknowledge of the world around us – the prelude to Presidential decision and action."[9] From this perspective, NSI means information. Some choose to limit the meaning even further to only *secret information*: strictly the findings gathered by way of clandestine methods carried out by spies, satellites, reconnaissance aircraft, and electronic interceptions, then interpreted by expert analysts.

Intelligence as a set of missions

More broadly, NSI can refer as well to all three primary intelligence missions examined in this book: collection and analysis, covert action, and counterintelligence. One might imagine a government official in, say, Israel asking an intelligence director: "What mixture of secret operations might be most effective in first finding out more about, and then halting, Iran's development of a nuclear bomb?" Here the emphasis is on NSI as a combination of coordinated activities or secret options that a leader might consider to achieve a foreign policy goal. The sequence would be information acquisition and assessment, followed perhaps by aggressive methods of covert action or counterintelligence operations to subdue a threat. In this case, then, NSI refers to the array of basic *missions* pursued by secret government agencies.

Intelligence as a process

A third usage of the term may refer solely to the most preeminent among the trio of missions: collection and analysis. In this instance, the concept of NSI points to the means – that is, the *process* or *modus operandi* – by which information is gathered from the field. Perhaps the process would involve a document stolen by a British agent from a safe in Beijing, or a photograph snapped by a camera on a U.S. surveillance satellite orbiting above a North Korean vessel steaming through the South China Sea. The final phase is the transmission of this information to a government's decision-makers.

Intelligence as organization

Finally, NSI may refer to a physical place – perhaps a spy headquarters building in a nation's capital, or a tent staffed by intelligence officers in an encampment of soldiers bivouacked on a remote desert location. The people responsible for gathering and interpreting NSI belong to bureaucratic *organizations* – a nation's secret agencies. "Get intelligence on the line," an Army general might order, referring to a specific structural entity the commander needs to contact – such as a Special Forces reconnaissance unit on the front edge of a battlefield.

A holistic view of national security intelligence

In light of these various dimensions of NSI, thinking of the term purely as a final paper product or an oral briefing that combines secretly acquired and open-source information is too limiting – although certainly NSI is precisely that at its core. Still, intelligence is what intelligence does, and the secret agencies can spend much of their time engaged in covert action and counterintelligence, and not only in collection and analysis. Indeed, during times of overt warfare, and sometimes in between, aggressive overseas intelligence operations in the form of covert action have become preeminent – the tail that wags the intelligence dog.

During the 1980s, for instance, the Reagan Doctrine was on the cutting edge of the approach to American foreign policy adopted by President Ronald Reagan and his National Security Advisors. This "doctrine" (a description coined by the media, not the Administration) relied on the CIA to combat Soviet intervention in the developing world. The Administration embraced a bold escalation in the funding, magnitude, and frequency of covert actions directed against the Soviet Union. Of special concern were Soviet operations in poor countries around the globe. As in earlier stages of the Cold War, sometimes these fears were justified and sometimes they were imagined by nervous U.S. officials who genuinely feared that the Kremlin and its KGB had gotten a toehold everywhere – or officials (like the notorious Senator Joe McCarthy, Republican of Wisconsin in the 1950s) who used red-baiting as a useful political campaign tool. The most notable instances of secret interventions by the Reagan Administration occurred in the nations of Nicaragua, Afghanistan, and Poland. If one assumed during the 1980s that U.S. national security intelligence was all about the writing of top-secret reports on world affairs (or the actual documents themselves), one would have missed the profound significance of intelligence as a covert action mission considered vital by the Reagan Administration.

Similarly with counterintelligence. Every intelligence officer has an obligation to protect government secrets, and to support those offices within the
spy agencies that are officially responsible for this mole-catching mission.
Relegating counterintelligence to orphan status of minimal importance to a
country's security increases the odds of dangerous foreign penetration operations, which can lead to the riddling of an intelligence agency with traitors
who have succumbed to blandishments from foreign governments (typically,
secret cash payments) to spy against their own country. The end result of
counterintelligence failures is that the victimized nation loses its own stable
of agents abroad, who have been identified by the mole, captured, and often
executed by a foreign intelligence service. Moreover, a nation's intelligence
reports can be contaminated by the machinations of double agents, who
might be in a position to insert disinformation into these classified documents. In short, to focus only on intelligence collection and analysis and
covert action as the be-all and end-all of national security intelligence is to
lose sight of the indispensable counterintelligence responsibility to protect a
nation's secrets and otherwise shield the public against hostile agent penetrations and terrorist attacks.

Accountability is also often dismissed by some as a subject that is at best
tangential to NSI – indeed, some argue that the adoption of laws and regulations guiding secret operations simply interferes with effective espionage,
covert action, and counterintelligence, thereby endangering the very democracies the spy services were created to defend. In an open society, however,
intelligence officers and their directors – not to mention the squadrons of
lawyers who counsel them (some 140 in the CIA today, up from six in 1975
and two in 1947) – spend a fair amount of time dealing with intelligence
overseers: Inspectors General (IGs) stationed within government agencies,
executive oversight boards, legislative review committees, ad hoc special
panels of inquiry in Congress (or Parliament in the European capitals), and
select commissions appointed by democratic governments for special inquiries into intelligence failures and scandals. Again, assuming that intelligence
is what intelligence officers do, one would have to conclude that – at least
in democratic societies – NSI involves time spent by a country's spy chiefs
with intelligence supervisors. These chiefs are held accountable by all three
branches of government in the United States: the President and the IGs in the
bureaucracy beneath the White House, the lawmakers in Congress, and the
judges in the courts. All are expected to heed the warnings of James Madison
and Lord Acton about the high odds of power abuse.

NSI is decidedly not either covert action alone, or counterintelligence;
neither is it limited to meeting with congressional oversight panels. Yet it is
certainly more than gathering information about threats and opportunities
(collection); sitting with a cup of coffee and a computer, or a pencil, writing
up what all the incoming information means (analysis); and disseminating

classified reports to policy officials. Intelligence officials engage in *all* of these activities. Collection and analysis is usually of primary importance, but covert action will occasionally rush to the forefront of the intelligence agenda – as it did during the Reagan years and in the more recent struggles of the United States and its allies against global terrorism. Or as it did when an Aldrich Ames (a traitorous CIA officer) or a Kim Philby (a turncoat within MI6 in Britain) is discovered to be a mole within one's own government – in both of these cases, pawns of the Russian spy services – and intelligence managers suddenly rue their prior lack of adequate attention to the counterintelligence mission. Or when the acronyms of a nation's secret services – for example, CIA, FBI, MI6, or MI5 – are splashed across the newspaper headlines with allegations of failed analysis or scandalous conduct, and intelligence managers wish they had devoted more attention to oversight laws and procedures.

Some, quite possibly most, practitioners and scholars alike, will continue to prefer a narrow definition of NSI: the idea of intelligence as information – indeed, just secret information. Others, though, including the author of this book, embrace a more encompassing view, along the lines suggested by British intelligence scholars Peter Gill and Mark Phythian:

> Intelligence is the umbrella term referring to the range of activities – from planning and information collection to analysis and dissemination – conducted in secret, and aimed at maintaining or enhancing relative security by providing forewarning of threats or potential threats in a manner that allows for the timely implementation of a preventive policy or strategy, including, where deemed desirable, covert activities. The ultimate purpose of intelligence is to provide policymakers with a decision advantage as they cope with resolving problems that face their nation.[10]

Whatever definition one prefers, the critical point is that espionage agencies engage in several activities to support the interests of their home nation. In the spirit of capturing this diversity of responsibilities, this book suggests that *national security intelligence consists of a cluster of government agencies that conduct secret activities, including covert action, counterintelligence, and, foremost, the collection and analysis of information for the purpose of illuminating the deliberations of policy officials by way of timely, accurate knowledge of potential threats and opportunities.*

Since intelligence activities are carried out by people in hidden and tightly guarded government agencies and their units abroad, as a starting point a closer look at intelligence as an organization is in order. The key questions posed here including the following. What institutions are engaged in crafting the final products – reports and oral briefings to decision-makers – that reside at the heart of what is meant by national security intelligence, and what agencies and individuals engage in covert action and counterintelligence? Who within a nation's intelligence bureaucracy responds to government overseers? The organizational blueprint for the major spy organizations in the United States (see below) provides an illustration of what a nation's spy agencies actually do, and how they carry out their secret assignments (that is, their use of "tradecraft," in the jargon of professional intelligence officers).

Intelligence as a cluster of organizations: The American experience

A fundamental aspect of every nation's approach to spying is to recruit professional intelligence officers and support staff, stationing them in office buildings at home that are heavily fortified by fences, alarms, and armed guards, as well as in secret locations abroad. The U.S. espionage establishment has grown into a sprawling bureaucracy – among the largest ever devised by any society in history, surpassed in size only by the number of intelligence officers fielded by contemporary China. Moreover, since the 9/11 attacks, the funding for spy-related activities by the United States has risen dramatically. For example, the NSA budget doubled between 2001 and 2006, reportedly reaching some $8 billion a year.[11]

As displayed in Figure 1.2, the President and the National Security Council (NSC) stand at the pinnacle of America's behemoth security apparatus. Beneath this National Command Authority (NCA) reside the nation's eighteen major intelligence agencies, known as the Intelligence Community, or IC. This Community was been led from 1947 through 2004 by a Director of Central Intelligence (DCI) and, since 2005, by a new spymaster with the formal title of Director of National Intelligence (DNI), in charge of the Office of the DNI (ODNI). This Office is responsible for the management and coordination of the entire espionage establishment in the United States – providing (ideally) a core of gravity to curb the other IC agencies from flying off into distant orbits of their own choosing, rather than working together as a system. The goal was consolidation, as a remedy against intelligence fragmentation and concomitant confusion for policymakers. Some view the ODNI as an unnecessary added layer of bureaucracy in the Intelligence Community, while others argue that it engages in many useful leadership activities, such as reviewing CIA covert action proposals before they go to the White House for approval or rejection. The DNI is assisted by a set of deputies (DDNIs); a National Counterterrorism Center (NCTC), which absorbs about 40 percent of the ODNI staff and budget resources; and a panel, still housed at CIA Headquarters, of top-flight analysts who comprise the National Intelligence Council (NIC).

At times, the DNI and the D/CIA (Director of the Central Intelligence Agency, the title of the Agency's chief since 2005) can be rivals for authority in the IC, as discussed later in this book. When working together properly, however, the DNI provides overall direction and integration for the IC, and the D/CIA tends to operations – collection and analysis, covert action, and counterintelligence

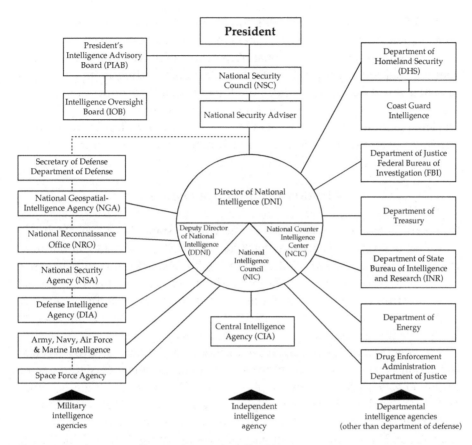

Figure 1.2: The U.S. Intelligence Community (IC),n 2024.
*From 1947 to 2005, a Director of Central Intelligence (DCI, based at the CIA) led the IC, rather than a DNI.

– at Langley, the Agency's well-guarded compound located near the township of McLean in Northern Virginia, across the Potomac River from Washington, DC. The D/CIA also usually leads briefings at the White House on daily intelligence reports, while the DNI focuses on the Community-wide coordination of intelligence activities. (For a listing of U.S. intelligence leaders in the modern era and their dates of service, see the Appendix.)

Some observers, including at the highest reaches of the IC, reject the notion that there are eighteen major U.S. intelligence agencies. As one former intelligence chief put it in a confidential email to the author: "There are 5 AGENCIES [original emphasis] and the rest are staff components supporting a larger department." An example of the latter is the Drug Enforcement Administration (DEA) within the Department of Justice. The "real IC" agencies he had in mind are the CIA, FBI, NSA, NGA, and DIA. These five are indeed behemoths within the Community, but reporting from the other agencies can be of high value, too, in various classified documents that make their way to the White House, Capitol Hill's Intelligence Oversight Committees, and other high-level intelligence consumers in America's government.

An examination of organizational frameworks within a government can be about as exciting as hot porridge for breakfast on a sizzling summer day; but knowing which agencies comprise the IC, and what their duties are, is a necessary first step toward understanding the world of America's spies. Hold on, for when it comes to a discussion of the organizations within an intelligence bureaucracy, the abbreviations are unfortunately numerous and unavoidable.

Military intelligence agencies

While the major secret agencies in the United States have evolved into a cluster of organizations known – in a classic misnomer – as a "Community," in reality these organizations display more the earmarks of rival tribes than a harmonious set of compatible institutions. Nine of the spy agencies are located within the framework of the Department of Defense (DoD), seven in civilian policy departments, and two – the CIA and the DNI – stand apart as independent organizations outside any policy department.

The military intelligence agencies include the National Security Agency, the nation's codebreaking, encrypting, and signals intelligence (sigint) organization, engaged primarily in telephone, as well as eavesdropping on email and other social media. Mobile telephone signals reach as high as 60,000 feet and are easily captured by NSA's orbital satellites, in conjunction with its large ground-based antennae in various location around the world. Within the NSA is the U.S. Cyber Command (USCYBERCOM), responsible for secret cyberactivity, both offensive and defense. One of the reasons the Eisenhower Administration ordered the CIA to engage in a coup against Iran in 1953 was to establish sigint facilities along the Soviet border; just one well-located sigint base alone produced vast quantities of data on Soviet long-range missile testing. Another approach involves the interception of electronic communications using spy planes circling the borders of a target nation – China, for example. Even when actual conversations cannot be intercepted, sometimes the fact of increased communications (known as "chatter") between Party A and Party B can alert NSA officials to activity that may warrant closer examination by the other intelligence disciplines, or (for short) the "ints."

The National Geospatial-Intelligence Agency (NGA) is dedicated chiefly to taking photographs overseas of enemy troop encampments, weaponry, and facilities (a method known as "imagery intelligence" or "imint" and, more recently, "geospatial intelligence" or "geoint"). For this purpose, the NGA employs intricate cameras mounted on satellites in space, as well as on lower-altitude unmanned aerial vehicles (UAVs or drones) and piloted reconnaissance aircraft. The National Reconnaissance Office (NRO) supervises the construction, launching, and management of America's s surveillance satellites. Much of this nation's intelligence is derived from its web of high-tech spy satellites, both sigint and geoint – some 3,400 of them in 2023 and largely impervious to most countermeasures.

In addition, on the military side of intelligence are the Defense Intelligence Agency (DIA), which analyzes a wide range of military-related subjects; and the four intelligence units of the Army, Navy, Air Force, and Marines, each focused on the collection and analysis of tactical intelligence from locations overseas – especially battlefields – where U.S. personnel serve in uniform. Within the DIA is a nontraditional and low-profile, but increasingly important, unit known as the National Center for Medical Intelligence, or NCMI. Here is the IC's first line of protection against the global emergence of pandemic pathogens, for we know that a range of coronaviruses will likely surface in the future. It has a significant advantage over the World Health Organization or the Centers for Disease Control, for it receives early reports from U.S. intelligence officers based in virtually every country in the world about possible health threats that could spread to the United States. Covid-19 in China, cholera in Liberia, Ebola in the Congo – wherever medical dangers may lurk, the CIA's clandestine corps takes a close look at indications of a potentially spreading disease, then forwards this warning to Langley as well as to the NCMI.

The newest of the IC organizations is yet another military organization known as the Space Force Agency. The SFA was established in 2020 and charged with addressing the question of how to keep outer space, which is becoming increasingly crowded with commercial and intelligence satellites, open and safe. Its area of responsibility begins at approximately 62 miles above earth. The SFA also focuses on methods to counter Chinese and Russian antisatellite weaponry. The organization's umbrella duty is to advance (to use its insider lingo) the "space situational awareness" (SSA) of the United States.

Together, these military agencies account for some 85 percent of the total annual U.S. spy budget of approximately $80 billion in recent years, and they employ about 85 percent of the nation's intelligence personnel.[12] The military intelligence services absorb such a great portion of the yearly funding for espionage because of the high costs of the "platforms" (machines) they use for intelligence-gathering – especially large, sophisticated, and expensive surveillance satellites, but also an expanding global fleet of drones.

Funding for intelligence in the United States comes from two separate budgets: the National Intelligence Program (NIP), which supports the large national spy agencies, such as the NGA, the NRO, and the NSA, all of which have chiefly military (though some civilian) spy missions; and the Military Intelligence Program (MIP), devoted mainly to tactical intelligence and related activities (TIARA). The boundary between the NIP and MIP, though, is "fluid, imprecise and subject to change," according to the Federation of American Scientists Project on Government Secrecy.[13] For instance, in 2006, the NGA received 70 percent of its funding from the NIP and 30 percent from the MIP; the following year, the respective figures were 90 percent and 10 percent. In 2010, to draw upon another one of the few years in which the U.S. government publicly disclosed these figures, the respective percentages were approximately 66 percent and 34 percent of the roughly $80 billion worth of intelligence expenditures.

In 2014, the NIP stood at $52.6 billion and the MIP at $19.2 billion, for a total of $71.8 billion. In 2016, the budget projections suggested a slight increase for the NIP, at $53.5 billion, and a decrease for the MIP, at $16.8 billion, or a total of $70.3 billion – a figure lower than the record-breaking spending in 2010, though an amount still vastly larger than America's aggregate spy budget before the 9/11 attacks (indeed, double the amount).

Civilian intelligence

Of the seven intelligence agencies embedded in civilian policy departments, four have been part of the Intelligence Community for decades and three are newcomers. Among the older agencies, the FBI is located in the Department of Justice (DOJ) and is assigned both a counterintelligence and a counterterrorism mission (in addition to its law enforcement duties); and the Office of Intelligence and Analysis is in the Department of Treasury, which includes among its duties the tracking of petrodollars and the elusive funding sources of terrorist organizations. The Bureau of Intelligence and Research (INR) is in the Department of State, the smallest of the older secret agencies but one of the most highly regarded for its well-crafted and often prescient reports; and the Office of Intelligence and Counterintelligence is in the Department of Energy and monitors the worldwide movement of nuclear materials (uranium, plutonium, heavy water, and nuclear reactor parts), while also maintaining security at the nation's weapons laboratories and nuclear weapons storage sites.

The three newcomer civilian agencies, all brought on board after the 9/11 attacks, include Coast Guard Intelligence; the Office of Intelligence and Analysis, in the Department of Homeland Security (DHS); and the Office of National Security Intelligence, located in the Drug Enforcement Administration (DEA). When admitted to the IC in 2001, Coast Guard Intelligence initially had its own direct line to the nation's DNI on the organizational ("wiring") diagrams for America's spy establishment; but when the second Bush Administration created the DHS in 2003, Coast Guard Intelligence became an offshoot of this new department, because of their common mission to protect the U.S. homeland and its coastline. Also within the DHS is the Cybersecurity and Infrastructure Security Agency (CISA), which partners with USCYBERCOM and the FBI to defend the United States against foreign cyberespionage and cyberwarfare. The DEA, America's lead agency in the global struggle against illegal drug dealers who peddle fentanyl, heroin, and other deadly narcotics in the streets and alleyways of the democracies, has been a part of the DoJ for decades, but became a member of the IC only in 2006.

The CIA

The last of the older agencies, and the eighth civilian intelligence organization, is the CIA – along with the ODNI, the only civilian agency in the IC and located outside a cabinet department. During the Cold War, the Agency enjoyed special prestige in the federal government as the only espionage entity formally established by the National Security Act of 1947. Equally important for its status and political clout in the nation's capital, the Agency served as the home office for the DCI – the titular leader of all the intelligence agencies. Critics say that, as a result of this stature, the Agency adopted a sense of entitlement and a reputation for being the most elitist of U.S. government agencies. (As noted earlier, since the end of 2004 the DCI office has been replaced by a Director of National Intelligence.)

Photo 1.2: CIA Headquarters
The Headquarters Building for the Central Intelligence Agency in Langley, Northern Virginia, near Washington, DC.
Source: Carol M. Highsmith Archive, Library of Congress, Prints and Photographs Division.

As the names imply, the Central Intelligence Agency and the Director of Central Intelligence were originally meant to serve as a focal point for the U.S. intelligence establishment, playing the role of coordinators for the IC's activities and the collators of its "all-source" (that is, all-agency) reports, in an otherwise highly fragmented array of spy organizations. R. James Woolsey, who held the position of DCI during the early years of the Clinton Administration, has described the job of America's intelligence chief in this manner: "You're kind of Chairman and CEO of the CIA, and you're kind of Chairman of the Board of the intelligence community."[14] He emphasized, though, that the DCI does not have the authority to give "rudder orders" to the heads of the various intelligence agencies (Woolsey served for a time as Undersecretary of the Navy). Rather, he continued, "it's more subtle" – a matter of personal relationships, conversations, and gentle persuasion: the glue of trust and rapport rarely discussed in textbooks, but the essence of successful government transactions in Washington and other national capitals in each region of the world. As an example of the internal structure of an intelligence agency, the CIA's organizational framework is displayed in Figure 1.3.

Today, the Agency consists of five "directorates," the newest of which is the Directorate for Digital Innovation, created in 2015. Admiral Stansfield Turner, who served as DCI during the Carter Administration (1977–81), has referred to the four directorates within the Agency during his tenure – Operations, Intelligence (now "Analysis"), Science and Technology, and Administration (now "Support") – as "separate baronies." His observation underscores the reality that the CIA has several distinct cultures within its walls that are not always in sync with one another, or with the leadership cadre – the Agency's panjandrums – on the seventh floor of the Headquarters Building at Langley. An illustration: the views of "nerdy" lab scientists in the Directorate of Science and Technology can be rather different from the "can-do" action officers overseas in the Directorate of Operations – "cowboys" who are skilled at blowing up bridges and mining harbors in enemy territory.[15] An additional structural feature of the CIA is its use of (currently) a dozen Mission Centers – special units designed to coordinate Agency operations in nontraditional, transitory domains. The most recent example is the creation at Langley of a Mission Center for Ukraine, which helps guide the IC's support for that besieged nation.

The DO/NCS

As Figure 1.4 illustrates, during the Cold War the Directorate of Operations (DO; earlier in its history known as the National Clandestine Service, or NCS) is led by a Deputy Director for Operations (DDO). The DO is the arm of the CIA that extends across the latitudes of the planet. Its officers operate for the most part out of Agency "stations" around the world, along with a few

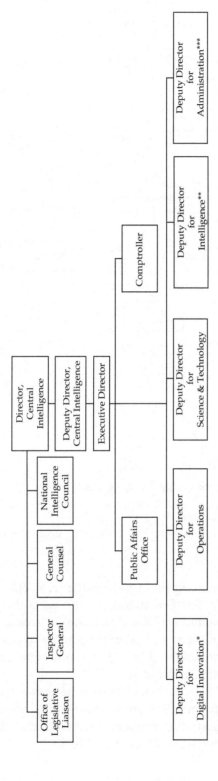

Figure 1.3: The organization of the CIA.

* A new Directorate created by the CIA in 2015.

** Now the Deputy Director for Analysis in charge of the Directorate of Analysis.

*** Now the Deputy Director for Support in charge of the Directorate of Support.

Source: Loch K. Johnson, *The Third Option: Covert Action and American Foreign Policy* (New York: Oxford University Press, 2022), p. 20. Used with permission.

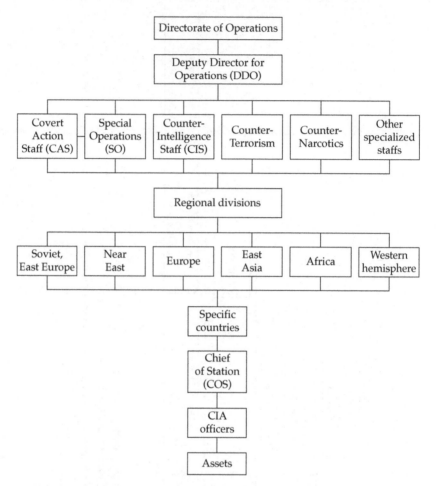

Figure 1.4: The CIA's Operations Directorate during the Cold War.

Note: The current structure of this highly secretive Directorate remains classified; but, substituting "Russia" for "Soviet," it is similar to what it was during the Cold War (1945–1991).

Source: Loch K. Johnson, *America's Secret Power: The CIA in a Democratic Society* (New York: Oxford University Press, 1989), p. 46.

smaller bases within some nations or on some battlefields. The stations have within their walls specially fortified rooms, known as SCIFs (pronounced "skifs" – sensitive compartmented information facilities), that are resistant to electronic eavesdropping attempts and permit Agency personnel to conduct top secret meetings overseas without fear of local counterintelligence officers or foreign intelligence services listening in.

The DO briefly readopted its National Clandestine Services name during the second Bush Administration; then when President Barack Obama came into office in 2008, this most controversial unit within the CIA reclaimed the previous DO tag. Its personnel abroad are referred to as "case officers," or, in a recent change of nomenclature, "operations officers." They are led by a chief of station, or COS, within each foreign country. The job of the case officer is to recruit locals, who are known as "assets" or, in Hollywood movies, "agents." An asset might be a speechwriter for a foreign ambassador, a chauffeur for a foreign cabinet member, or – if the CIA really strikes paydirt – a prime minister, president, chancellor, emperor, czar, emir, shah, sultan, king, or queen. Even a more lowly placed asset can be useful – a secretary at a munitions factory in India, for example, in a position to keep an eye open for new weapons planning ordered by the government. If successfully recruited, assets are directed by the CIA to engage in espionage activities against their own nations, as well as to support the Agency's counterintelligence and covert action activities within that country. In order to succeed, case or operations officers need to be gregarious individuals: charming, persuasive, and willing to take risks. For a foreigner to fall under their beguiling spell – or the attraction of the money the CIA may be offering – is to be "case officered" or "co-ed" in DO-speak.

The DA

At CIA Headquarters in Langley, analysts assigned to the Directorate of Analysis (DA) try to interpret and place into the context of world affairs the "raw" (unanalyzed) information gathered by operations officers and their assets, as well as by America's spy satellites and other machines. The CIA has the largest number of all-source analysts in the government. The job of these experts – the Agency's intellectuals – is to provide insight into what the gathered information means for Washington's decision-makers, especially how it may affect the security and international interests of the United States.

The DS&T and the DS

The Directorate of Science and Technology (DS&T) is the home of the CIA's "Dr. Q" scientists (a species of technically oriented intelligence officer made famous by James Bond movies) and assorted other "techno-weenies" who develop equipment to aid the espionage effort, from the crafting of wigs and other disguises to the engineering of tiny listening devices and exotic weaponry. The Directorate of Support (DS) is where the Agency's day-to-day managers reside. They meet payrolls, keep the hallways clean and hang artwork in the corridors at Langley, conduct polygraph ("lie-detector") tests on new recruits and periodically on employees, and maintain Headquarters security. Both the DS&T and the DS offer technical and security support to the Agency's operations abroad as well. During the Cold War, the Directorate of Administration (Support's earlier name) also engaged improperly in spying against anti-Vietnam War protesters, triggering the domestic spy scandal

in 1974 (Operation CHAOS), which resulted in major investigations into the
activities of the CIA and the other intelligence agencies.

Intelligence centers and task forces

To help overcome the fragmentation of America's Intelligence Community,
DCIs (and now D/CIAs), along with the nation's DNIs, have resorted to the
use of "centers," "task forces," and "mission managers" that focus on particular topics and are staffed by personnel from throughout the Intelligence
Community. For example, DCI John Deutch (1995–7) created an Environmental
Intelligence Center to examine how intelligence officers and private-sector
scientists could work together on the security and ecological implications of
global environmental conditions, using spy satellites to examine such matters
as the depletion of rain forests in Brazil, river water disputes in the Middle
East, and the extent of melting ice floes in the Arctic Circle.[16] The year 2023
was the hottest in the history of recorded temperatures. The Environmental
Intelligence Center sought to learn more about the effects of high temperatures on U.S. security and, more generally, on world affairs.

   Another DCI, William H. Webster (1987–91), established a special Iraqi Task
Force to focus on the intelligence support needed for the First Persian Gulf
War in 1990–1. More recently, DNI James R. Clapper (2010–17) has relied on
an Open Source Center (located at Langley where most of the IC's analysts
work, but reporting to the ODNI) to help integrate facts and figures available
in the public domain with secret information acquired from overseas.

Intelligence oversight boards

As shown in Figure 1.2 above, the IC also has two prominent oversight boards.
One is known as the President's Foreign Intelligence Advisory Board (PFIAB,
shortened after the 9/11 attacks to the President's Intelligence Advisory
Board, or PIAB, to emphasize that U.S. domestic spy agencies like the FBI
were equally vital in keeping the President informed about threats to the
nation). The other is called the Intelligence Oversight Board (IOB). Since its
creation in the 1950s, PFIAB/PIAB has had among its annual membership a
dozen or so presidential appointees (the numbers vary from administration
to administration) who are often prominent security, foreign policy, and
scientific experts. The latter have given the panel a special niche: helping the
President improve the science of espionage. Edward Land, the inventor of
the Polaroid camera, is an example of a much-valued PFIAB member during
the Eisenhower Administration. He significantly advanced the capabilities of
America's spy cameras attached to satellites in space. Some presidents, however, have used membership on the Advisory Board not so much as a means

for monitoring and improving U.S. intelligence, but rather as a prestigious White House sinecure for political allies who contributed money to their election campaign – a corruption of the panel's original intent.

The IOB, now folded into the PIAB as a subcommittee, is small, with only three or four members at any given time. On rare occasions it has conducted a serious inquiry into charges of intelligence improprieties (such as a controversial NSA domestic intelligence collection program in 2013, discussed in Chapter 6). It, too, has become largely an honorific assignment, though – more cosmetic than effective as a vigilant protector against the abuse of secret power.

Not displayed in Figure 1.2, but nonetheless an integral part of the IC, are the House and Senate Intelligence Committees, known formally as the Senate Select Committee on Intelligence (SSCI, with the unfortunate pronunciation "sis-see") and the House Permanent Select Committee on Intelligence (HPSCI, pronounced "hip-see"). They were established by Congress in 1976 and 1977, respectively. The DCIs have complained periodically that there should have been just one joint committee rather than two separate committees; but it was prudent to establish two oversight panels, just as it is wise to fly in a plane with two engines, rather than just one. Sometimes SSCI has operated effectively, while HPSCI has been relatively dormant, and vice versa. Their central role in maintaining accountability over the IC is explored in Chapter 6.

An "iron pentagon"

Added to this official complex of organizations are a plethora of smaller intelligence units in the federal government, as well as many private institutions that are hired by the U.S. intelligence agencies to help them with their missions – the "outsourcing" of intelligence. A *Washington Post* investigation in 2010 – and the only published report with this level of detail – discovered the existence of 1,271 government organizations involved in intelligence work of one type or another, and an additional 1,931 private intelligence-oriented companies.[17] The most notorious example of the latter in recent years was the Blackwater firm (renamed Xe Services in 2009, then Academi in 2011), based in North Carolina. This group of security experts and paramilitary officers provided protection to American intelligence officials and diplomats in Iraq and Afghanistan during the U.S. interventions in those countries, among other locations. Blackwater reportedly even entered into the CIA's plans for executing terrorist leaders over far-flung areas of the earth's surface – an idea that was scrubbed when Blackwater officers developed a reputation for overzealous operations overseas. They had gone rogue or, in MI6 slang (drawn from Urdu), "nut-cut." For example, in 2007, Blackwater guards armed with machine guns and grenade launchers killed seventeen unarmed Iraqi civilians at Nisour Square in Baghdad, including children.

In his famous farewell address, President Dwight D. Eisenhower warned the American people about a "military–industrial complex" – an expression of his concern that defense contractors might gain "unwarranted influence" over lawmakers, providing them with campaign contributions in exchange for appropriations to build an endless supply of new weaponry (with the concomitant corporate profits these weapons would accrue). Political scientists speak of this alliance as an "iron triangle" composed of interest groups, bureaucrats, and politicians. In Eisenhower's description, the points of the triangle were the weapons manufacturers (Lockheed, for instance), admirals and generals in the Pentagon, and key lawmakers on the Armed Services and Appropriations Committees. The alliance yielded lucrative profits for the manufacturers; new planes, ships, and tanks for the military brass; and defense jobs back home, for which lawmakers could claim credit and advance their re-election prospects. Presidents would come and go, but the iron triangle persisted – and often defied presidential leadership.

In more recent years, added to this venerable triangle are two more geometric points in the security establishment: outsource groups (like Academi) and the nation's weapons laboratories (where weapons systems are developed). This "iron pentagon," to coin a phrase, represents an even more potent and sophisticated security coalition than the triangle that Eisenhower found disconcerting in 1959. Accompanying the old lobbying efforts on behalf of new weaponry is an added corporate interest: intelligence dollars appropriated by Congress in large sums for spy platforms, such as the costly satellites used by the NGA, the NRO, and the NSA. Yet another corporate interest: the mass production of drones for the wars in Iraq, Afghanistan, Ukraine, and elsewhere. In addition, Academi and its proliferating counterparts – all with well-funded lobbying strategies – are attracted by congressional appropriations for security, counterintelligence, and covert action support.

A flawed plan for U.S. intelligence

Like the intelligence organizations of other nations, the American espionage system has been built without any grand design. Rather, these agencies have evolved in response to a series of pressures: national emergencies; new technological developments (better eavesdropping capabilities, for example, have led to a greater emphasis on – and a larger staff and building for – NSA's sigint operations); the priorities of intelligence leaders (Allen Dulles in the 1950s concentrated on his favorite method of spying, human intelligence – the traditional use of agents recruited locally to engage in espionage on behalf of the United States – as well as covert actions); and the lobbying skills of bureaucrats (the master: J. Edgar Hoover of the FBI, who from 1924 until his death in 1972 shaped "the Bureau" into one of the most highly regarded

Photo 1.3: DCI Smith
Walter Bedell Smith in 1945 during WWII. He would serve as the U.S. Ambassador to the Soviet Union from 1946 to 1948 and then as the Director of the CIA from 1950 to 1953.
Source: Dutch National Archives.

– some would say feared, racist, and unsupervised – organizations in the government of the United States).

When Vice President Harry S. Truman became the nation's leader after Franklin D. Roosevelt's death, he was stunned by all the intelligence reports pouring into his office. They required him, in his own words, to "look through a bunch of papers two feet high." Instead, he wanted to receive information that was "coordinated so that the President could arrive at the facts."[18] Frustrated, the new President turned to the idea of establishing a strong, statutory espionage organization: a *Central* Intelligence Agency. It soon became evident to President Truman, however, that the creation of a truly focused spy system would come at too steep a price, in light of an even more urgent goal he desired: the consolidation of the nation's military services.

The creation of a new Department of Defense would provide an umbrella to bring the services closer together. The President wished to avoid complicating this core objective by carrying out at the same time a quest for intelligence consolidation, which was bound to roil the military brass. They viewed a powerful new CIA as a threat to their own confederal and parochial approach to intelligence. As a top Agency official recalled, "The one thing that Army, Navy, State, and the FBI agreed on was that they did not want a strong central agency controlling their collection programs."[19] So Truman and his aides entered into a compromise with the armed services in the hope that this would produce the desired goal of military unification. They tried to improve intelligence coordination to some extent, but without letting that sensitive subject anger the Pentagon and erase its support for the higher goal of military unity. The result was a series of retreats from centralized intelligence, as exhibited in the diluted language regarding the CIA and its leader, the DCI, in the National Security Act of 1947. This law provided for only a weak DCI. In this sense the Agency was, from the beginning, as scholar Amy B. Zegart has remarked, "flawed by design."[20] In the observation of historian Michael Warner: "For the duration of the Cold War, the White House kept nudging successive Intelligence Directors to provide more leadership for the intelligence community." He concluded, however, that a towering obstacle persisted: "Cabinet-level officials . . . saw no reason to cede power to a DCI."[21]

Redesigning the leadership of American intelligence: The ODNI

In the waning days of 2004, when the memory of the surprise 9/11 attacks was still green, Congress – intensely lobbied by the grieving families of many who perished on that day in 2001 – finally addressed the need for intelligence reform. The key provision of the much amended 600-page law, titled the Intelligence Reform and Terrorism Prevention Act (IRTPA, pronounced "ert-pa"), was the creation of an Office of the Director of National Intelligence, or ODNI.

This new leadership position, though, was still nowhere near dominant enough to draw all the IC agencies together into one cooperative harness. Some compared it to being a caretaker of a cemetery: a DNI presides over a lot of people, but the office can't get them to move – or even listen. The DNI would have to go on sharing authority with the Secretary of Defense (SecDef) over military intelligence – the same situation faced by the DCI before Congress enacted the IRTPA legislation.

Frustrated by the meager authority of the ODNI, the first appointee to run the Office, Ambassador John D. Negroponte, soon fled back to the Department of State after serving for less than two years as DNI. His successor, former NSA director Admiral Mike McConnell, after serving two months as DNI, could offer only a euphemistic description of a job that he had clearly found unwieldy. It was, in his words, a "challenging management condition."[22] In particular, he complained about his inability to dismiss incompetent people. "You cannot hire or fire," he told a reporter.[23] In 2009, McConnell resigned and was replaced by another former admiral, Dennis C. Blair, who would take up quarters in a new (and sumptuous) headquarters building for the ODNI, located at Liberty Crossing in Northern Virginia.

Before long, Admiral Blair found himself embroiled in a squabble over who should appoint the top intelligence officer in each U.S. intelligence station overseas: the D/CIA, who would name the COS (as was current practice), or the DNI, who would name a "DNI Rep." The outcome provides an illustration of how enfeebled the ODNI is. Blair claimed the right, as the nation's top intelligence leader, to make these appointments, even though they had traditionally been selected by the head of the CIA (who, prior to 2005, was dual-hatted as DCI). As the new DNI, Blair issued a memorandum announcing that, henceforth, he would select each of the top U.S. intelligence officials overseas, whether a COS recommended by the D/CIA or a DNI Rep.

The following day, in response to this claim, the D/CIA at the time, former member of the House of Representatives Leon E. Panetta (D, California), countered with a memorandum of his own that ordered Agency employees around the world to disregard the DNI's message. Panetta – prodded by the Director of the National Clandestine Service (the name then for the DDO), who does the actual selection of station chiefs – reasoned that the CIA had traditionally named the nation's COSs abroad for good reason: it was the Agency that had almost all the intelligence billets in each of the stations overseas, so its officers could recruit local spies – humint – for the United States. These delicate relationships could be torn asunder if suddenly these CIA assets had to deal with case officers who were not even led in the field by the Agency; therefore, Panetta argued, it made sense to have Langley's officers remain in charge of U.S. intelligence leadership responsibilities in foreign nations. For instance, in the United Kingdom, Blair could make a case for naming the NSA senior representative as the "DNI Rep" in the United Kingdom, given the greater importance there of the sigint relationship (over humint). (The British sigint agency, the Government Communications Headquarters, or GCHQ, is vastly larger than its MI6 humint counterpart.) Here was the crux of the argument advanced by Admiral Blair.

Both arguments had some merit. On Panetta's side, it is true that U.S. intelligence officers in most stations are there to recruit indigenous assets, the job primarily of the CIA. Yet, in some countries where signals intelligence is a forte – the United Kingdom and Australia, for example – America's intelligence officers serve chiefly as liaison personnel for sigint cooperation. In these instances, it made some sense for the COS to be assigned not from the CIA but from the NSA, America's sigint organization. Blair wanted to be able to make these determinations on a case-by-case basis, rather than simply have the CIA in charge everywhere around the globe. Moreover, if the ODNI had been created in December 2004 to serve as America's intelligence chief, shouldn't Blair be calling the shots? He obviously thought so, but the White

House eventually sided with Panetta in this dispute. President Barack Obama and his Vice President, Joseph R. Biden, Jr., may have bent naturally toward Panetta, a fellow Democratic and former member of Congress. Perhaps, too, they were concerned about a rumor circulating in Washington that Blair's gambit was an attempt by the military to further weaken the CIA, and that the DNI would soon name large numbers of senior military intelligence officers to COS positions around the world.

Blair, the D/CIA's superior at least on organizational charts, was reportedly furious about what he perceived to be Panetta's insubordination. A *New York Times* reporter with an intelligence beat viewed the brouhaha as "further evidence that the intelligence overhaul five years ago [IRPTA] did little to end the longstanding rivalries of the Intelligence 'Community' or clearly delineate the chain of command within American the spy bureaucracy."[24] The Admiral resigned in 2010 – yet another "short-timer" at the ODNI. President Obama replaced him with a seasoned intelligence official, former Air Force general James R. Clapper, who had headed up both the DIA and NGA earlier in his long intelligence career. In confirmation hearings, he vowed to establish better working relations with Panetta – and he did, through patience, steady telephone dialogue, and frequent cordial meetings together, sometimes joined by President Obama.

A dream still on hold

General Clapper, well aware of the weaknesses in the ODNI, nonetheless expressed a determination during his Senate confirmation hearings to bring greater cohesion to the Intelligence Community. To enhance IC integration, he established a team of fifteen or so (the numbers varied from time to time) National Intelligence Managers, or NIMs, with specific portfolios related to world regions or specific issues (such as WMD counterproliferation). The NIM for the Western Hemisphere, for example, was expected to pull together "all-source intelligence" from throughout the IC in preparing reports on America's neighbors to the north and south for the President as well as other top government consumers of intelligence. DNI Clapper also focused on improving the "intelligence fusion centers" scattered around the United States in selected state capitals – a post-9/11 blending of federal, state, and local law enforcement and intelligence capabilities designed to counteract, at the grassroots level, germinating domestic terrorism and other national security threats. Thanks to his half-century of experience in intelligence work, along with his widespread friendships among senior intelligence professionals, General Clapper had considerable success during his 2010–17 tenure in managing the IC. His successors have found it difficult to match these fortuitous advantages and (as discussed later in the volume) the ODNI has largely become an ambiguously defined and hesitant institutional flagship for the IC.

In trying to make espionage agencies more effective as a shield for the democracies – that is, less prone to failure and scandal – organizational reform at the DNI level of intelligence management is just part of the challenge. The intricate core mission of collection-and-analysis also cries out for improvements, as examined in the next two chapters.

2

Intelligence Collection:
Global Spying

Early one morning in October 1994, Secretary of Defense William J. Perry – a tall, thoughtful man with a PhD in mathematics – greeted the Chairman of the Joint Chiefs of Staff, General John Shalikashvili, in the SecDef's spacious office at the Pentagon. Under his arm, the General carried a portfolio of satellite photographs of Iraq. He spread the images across a conference table. Using a pointer, Shalikashvili directed Perry's attention to a disturbing set of pictures. Improbable as it might have seemed, coming just three-and-a-half years after a U.S.-led coalition had knocked Saddam Hussein's army to its knees, elements of the Republican Guard (Saddam's elite troops), supported by mechanized infantry, armor, and tank units, were moving at a rapid clip southward toward Basra, a mere thirty miles from the Kuwaiti border. The force was aimed like an arrow at the Al Jahra heights overlooking Kuwait City, in an apparent repeat of the same maneuver that led to the Iraqi conquest of Kuwait in 1990 and the entry of the United States and a coalition of allies into the first Persian Gulf War. At its current rate of speed, the Republican guard would stream across the Kuwaiti border within a couple of days.

Perry quickly ordered a U.S. armored brigade stationed in Kuwait to the Iraqi border. With a mounting sense of uneasiness, the SecDef and the top Pentagon brass waited as young captains and lieutenants brought new batches of satellite imagery into Perry's office over the next twenty-four hours. Upwards of 10,000 Iraqi troops had amassed in an area near Basra. Steadily the number rose to 50,000, some camped within twelve miles of the border. The American brigade had arrived, but consisted of only 2,000 lightly armed Marines.

While the United States also had 200 warplanes in the area on standby alert, the Iraqi armored force dwarfed the American presence. President Bill Clinton ordered 450 more warplanes to Kuwait, along with the 24th Mechanized Infantry Division and a Marine contingent from Camp Pendleton in California. The aircraft carrier *George Washington* steamed at maximum speed toward the Red Sea from the Indian Ocean. None of these forces, though, would arrive in time to block an invasion of Kuwait. Perry and Shalikashvili faced the prospect of a rout that would quickly wipe out the small American brigade assembled at the border.

Photo 2.1: U.S. Surveillance Satellite
Illustration of a DSCS-3 satellite, currently in orbit as part of the Defense Satellite
Communications System, which provides military communications for the United States.
Source: U.S. Airforce.

Perry and Shalikashvili waited nervously for the next set of satellite photographs. When the pictures arrived, the two men both breathed an audible sigh of relief. The Iraqi troops had suddenly halted and some elements were already turning back toward Baghdad. The good news was that imagery intelligence (geoint) may have prevented the outbreak of another war in the Persian Gulf. Using these timely photographs to pinpoint the location of Iraqi troops, Perry had been able to put in place an American brigade as a barrier against Iraqi aggression. "Had the intelligence arrived three or four days later, it would have been too late," he told the Aspin–Brown Commission as it looked into the possibilities of U.S. intelligence reform in 1995.

The episode revealed, however, troubling intelligence weaknesses as well. Even though vital information had arrived in time for the Secretary of Defense to put up some semblance of resistance at the Kuwaiti border, the thousands of troops in the Republican Guard could have overwhelmed the single Marine brigade. The best Perry could hope for was that the Marines might intimidate Saddam and make him think twice about another invasion. Fortunately, the bluff worked. Retrospective studies of the satellite imagery taken of Iraq before the crisis disclosed palpable clues that, for weeks, Saddam had been gathering a force near Baghdad for another invasion of Kuwait. The photos revealed trickles of Iraqi troops and armor moving toward Basra that would soon turn into a threatening flood of armed aggression. Intelligence analysts in the CIA's National Photographic Interpretation Center (NPIC, now a part of NGA) had missed these signs, as had everyone else at the Agency.

The problem had not been a lack of information: high-ranking government officials have daily access to enough imagery and other intelligence data to smother every desk in the Pentagon – including some 700 photographs every day from U.S. surveillance satellites. Findings in more recent years include, for example, Chinese construction of hundreds of new long-range missile silos across its countryside. Photos don't always speak for themselves, however, and at the time of the October 1994 crisis nobody had scrutinized them carefully enough, day-by-day, to notice the accretion of troop buildups that signaled the possibility of a gathering invasion force. "Had we analyzed the data better from technical intelligence collection, in this case: satellite photography," said Perry, looking back at the crisis, "we could have had a seven-to-ten-day earlier alert. Better humint might have given this alert, too."[1]

The message from the SecDef was clear: the U.S. Intelligence Community still had much room for improvement when it came to support for military operations (SMO), along with a host of other collection-and-analysis responsibilities. This chapter examines key strengths and weaknesses of this preeminent mission for the secret agencies of every nation – what a DCI once referred to as "the absolute essence of the intelligence profession."[2]

The intelligence cycle

The phrase "collection and analysis" is used here as shorthand to describe a complex process for the gathering, analysis, and dissemination of information to decision-makers. A convenient way of envisioning this flow is the theoretical construct known as the "intelligence cycle" (see Figure 2.1). This schema is a heuristic device meant to make more understandable the complex reality of how intelligence actually works on a day-to-day basis. Despite its oversimplification of a complicated, interactive process with many stops and starts, accompanied by ongoing dialogue between collectors and analysts, the "cycle" does lay out well the major phases in the life of an intelligence report as it travels from the field to the office of a government decision-maker.[3] The first three phases are known as planning and direction, collection, and processing. Since these steps are all closely related to the collection of intelligence from around the world by spy agencies, they are the focus of this chapter. Chapter 3 that follows will then examine the final three phases, each of which relates to intelligence analysis and production.

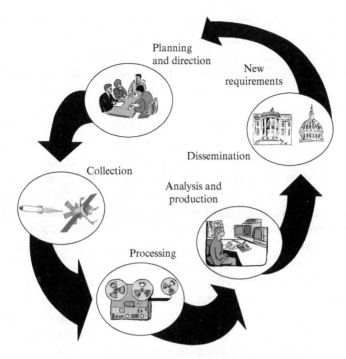

Figure 2.1: The intelligence cycle.

Source: Adapted from *Fact Book on Intelligence*, Office of Public Affairs, Central Intelligence Agency (October 1993), p. 14.

Planning and direction

The beginning of the intelligence cycle is critical. Unless a potential target is clearly highlighted when officials gather to establish intelligence priorities ("requirements" or "tasks"), it is unlikely to receive much attention by those who collect information – or, in the first place, even attract the funding necessary to carry out the collection. The world is a large and fractious place, with about 195 nations (estimates vary slightly) and a plethora of groups, factions, gangs, cartels, and terrorist cells, some of which have adversarial relationships with the democratic societies. A former DCI, R. James Woolsey (1993–5), observed after the Cold War that the United States had finally slain the Soviet dragon during that superpower standoff, but "we live now in a jungle filled with a bewildering variety of poisonous snakes."[4]

At some point, the degree of danger posed by foreign adversaries or domestic subversives becomes self-evident, as with the 9/11 attacks by Al Qaeda or the insurrection against the U.S. Congress on January 6, 2021. Intelligence officers and government officials, though, are like other mortals: rarely able to predict exactly when and where danger will strike. As former Secretary of State Dean Rusk once put it: "Providence has not provided human beings with the capacity to pierce the fog of the future."[5]

"Intelligence is an imperfect science," a senior U.S. intelligence officer has observed. "It's what you know, and it can change in a blink of an eye."[6] The outbreak of a genocidal war in Rwanda in 1993 provides an illustration. Les Aspin recalled: "When I became Secretary of Defense [in 1993, at the beginning of the Clinton Administration], I served several months without ever giving Rwanda a thought. Then, for several weeks, that's *all* I thought about. After that, it fell abruptly off the screen and I never again gave much thought to Rwanda."[7] The central African nation had become the "flavor of the month" for policymakers and intelligence officers as they scrambled to find information about the civil war that had erupted there. Surprise events like this one are known as intelligence "pop ups" or "ad hocs." Intelligence expert Mark Lowenthal notes how these international surprises can sometimes dominate the intelligence cycle and divert attention from established formal targets of perceived danger or opportunity. He refers to this sudden displacement of anticipated events (such as the ongoing Russian aggression in Ukraine that rekindled in 2022) and the demands they make on the time of policymakers and intelligence officers as "the tyranny of the ad hocs."[8]

The Iranian revolution in 1979 offers a further example of the difficulties intelligence analysts face in anticipating future events. A top CIA analyst on Iran has recalled that, on the eve of the revolution:

> We knew the Shah [the "king," in Farsi] was widely unpopular, and we knew there would be mass demonstrations, even riots. But how many shop-keepers would resort to violence, and how long would Army officers remain loyal to the Shah? Perhaps the Army would shoot down 10,000 rioters, maybe 20,000. If the ranks of the insurgents swelled further, though, how far would the Army be willing to go before it decided that the Shah was a losing proposition? All this we duly reported; but no one could predict with confidence the number of dissidents who would actually take up arms, or the "tipping point" for Army loyalty.[9]

An additional instance of a threat shrouded in ambiguity was the Soviet Backfire bomber during the Cold War. Analysts in the CIA concluded the bomber was a medium-range aircraft, which its specifications seemed to indicate. Yet DIA analysts pointed out that if the Soviets operated the bomber in a certain manner, sending its pilots on a one-way, no-refueling, kamikaze-style mission, then clearly its range would be much longer. From the DIA's point of view, under these conditions the Backfire bomber was a weapon of strategic significance that could reach the United States, not one solely for tactical operations on the Soviet perimeter.

Sometimes differences in analytic conclusions appear driven by political considerations. For example, when North Korea failed to put a satellite into orbit in 2009, some DIA analysts concluded that the country's technical capabilities were far less significant than Cassandras on the hawkish side of military planning had warned. Other analysts, though, attempted to "hype the threat" of North Korean missiles in order to "scare people" – so observed Philip E. Coyle III, a former director of weapons testing at the Pentagon. Their goal, according to Coyle, was the promotion of the Pentagon's costly and controversial antimissile program.[10]

In the United States, the job of evaluating the nature of threats and determining concomitant intelligence priorities is known as a "threat assessment."[11] Experts and policymakers convene to evaluate the dangers that confront the nation, starting at the beginning of every incoming administration in the January that follows the presidential election year, with periodic meetings thereafter and occasional emergency gatherings to re-evaluate fast-breaking intelligence targeting priorities. Recently, these dangers have been divided into two groups of concerns: first, superpower competition – military, economic, diplomatic, and espionage – with Russia and China since the end of the Cold War; and, second, transnational dangers that range from pandemics to climate change.

National security officials in the U.S. government establish a ladder of priorities, starting with the most dangerous threats at the top. This set of dangers is labeled Tier 0 in the schema of some administrations – the highest risk level reserved for an existing war where U.S. troops or America's foreign policy interests are vitally involved. A recent illustration has been the war in Ukraine, where the West has provided intelligence along with such weaponry as portable drones and anti-aircraft systems. The drones are equipped with various cameras and sensors, which beam photographs and data back to a command center. The objective of this assistance has been to restore Ukraine's borders as existed prior to a Russian "shadow" invasion of Eastern Ukraine in 2014. The level just below on the ladder of escalation is Tier 1A, reserved for the ever-present threat posed by nuclear-armed Russian and Chinese military forces, along with cyberattacks against the United States from these two superpowers (and their partners). Especially sobering, however remote the possibility, is the possibility of attacks ordered in Moscow and Beijing – or any other nation, such as North Korea – using WMDs (nuclear, biological, chemical: NBC weaponry) against the United States.

China is generally considered by U.S. intelligence analysts as the most worrisome competitor on the planet for the democracies, followed closely by Russia, although they pose different challenges. China holds the threat of an economic chokehold on the world, while the Russians are engaged in loose rhetoric about the possibility of using tactical nuclear weapons in Ukraine, which could well lead to a nuclear war between NATO nations and Russia – a global conflagration, with radioactive clouds floating around the surface of the planet. Both China and Russia are burnishing their military arsenals and, another characteristic they have in common, both are engaged in massive surveillance and disinformation operations against the United States and its democratic allies. Among all the world's nations, China now has the largest conglomerate of spy agencies. Little wonder the CIA has undertaken a major recruitment program among American citizens to hire China experts.

Questions of international commerce are considered important, too, for those involved in threat assessments. The economic dimension of U.S.–Chinese international competition, along with the efforts to tame Russian aggression in Ukraine through Western trade sanctions, elevates "economic" (or "financial") intelligence to the high 1A level. During the Cold War, roughly 40 percent of the CIA's collection-and-analysis resources were focused on matters related to the global flow of goods and services – say, clandestinely acquired intelligence regarding the likely negotiation positions of Japanese trade officials scheduled to meet with State Department personnel about a mutual reduction in tariffs on the sales of automobiles in one another's countries.

Also on this high perch, at least for some individuals involved in shaping the U.S. threat assessment, is the danger of homeland ("domestic") unrest, similar to the insurgency inflamed by the rhetoric of President Donald Trump against lawmakers on January 6, 2021. Based on Trump's inspiration, his supporters attacked the Congress during its constitutionally mandated counting of Electoral College votes. The Biden Administration and others remain concerned about the possibility of another assault – perhaps this time better armed and organized by insurrectionists – against the federal government by former President Trump's "army." The Trump insurgents evidently believed his claim that the 2020 presidential election was stolen from him – rigged by the Biden campaign and its backers. They also apparently believe that the FBI, the CIA, and other "deep state" intelligence agencies have been "weaponized" to battle against Trump's bid for another term in the White House in the 2024 presidential election. These "Trumpites," a faction that includes the most conservative Republican members of Congress, vow to take on the "corrupt" U.S. intelligence agencies through official investigations by committees run by the GOP in the House of Representatives and, if necessary, through armed resistance.

In 2023, rumors were rife around the country that, if they were to happen again, insurrections would be much better prepared to propel forward a Trump victory in the 2024 election, even if it required widespread violence and – some of his most extreme advocates argued – civil war between coastal elites in the United States and the rural common men and women within Trump's MAGA ("Make America Great Again") movement. Even more likely, counterterrorist experts reasoned, was an enraged lone wolf attack against a government building in Washington – or a state capital – by a single Trump supporter (or by a small group of MAGA members, not unlike Timothy McVeigh's attack against Oklahoma City's Murrah Building in 1995).

Moving downward in recent priorities, Tier 1B might include a listing of global terrorist organizations, plus concern about the proliferation of WMDs beyond the current nations that already possess unconventional weaponry. Of special concern is the global spread of nuclear warheads and the raw materials used to make these instruments of mass annihilation. At this level as well would likely be the machinations of North Korea (a nuclear power with long-range missiles able to carry nuclear warheads toward targets across the oceans), Iran (strongly anti-American and a potential nuclear power), and the unpredictable Syrian regime.

The evaluation of global dangers would continue down the ladder toward lesser – but still genuine – concerns at Tiers 2,3, and 4, depending on the perceived level of a threat posed by a country or by an unsettling change in world affairs: say, Tier 2 for U.S. border security against narcotics and illegal immigrants and 3 for a monetary crisis in Mexico that might affect U.S. investments in that country, and vice versa. At Tier 4 are the least dangerous topics, though still worthy of attention by the intelligence agencies. This level will receive the least robust funding for intelligence collection. An example might include studying more about the likely election outcomes in Latin America or possible leadership succession in India and Hungary.

A new claimant for America's intelligence-collection resources is the threat of global environmental degradation. During the Clinton Administration, Vice President Al Gore periodically fretted aloud in NSC meetings about the vanishing ice floes and the imperiled lives of polar bears. That particular concern failed to capture the interest of hardcore global strategists in the Cabinet Room of the White House, but the environmental dangers posed by climate change related to possible river overflows and the flooding of military bases in the United States and overseas was another matter. The training of U.S. forces and the testing of war-fighting equipment at these bases was serious business for the non-tree-huggers and polar bear skeptics at Council meetings. At subsequent NSC gatherings during the Clinton years, though, the fact that melting ice floes would have an effect on hiding places for America's nuclear submarines drove home the importance of climate-change intelligence more convincingly for the military-oriented threat-assessment participants than the plight of vanishing Brazilian forests or hapless polar bears stranded on ice floes drifting in the Artic Sea.

The broadening of thinking about intelligence priorities to include environmental matters was a product of the end of the Cold War, which provided the opportunity to think more expansively about security threats to the United States. NSC participants understood above all that a Soviet intercontinental ballistic missile strike would come with speed and result in the immediate extinction of the United States and the U.S.S.R. Both would be consumed in nuclear witch fires, turning them into piles of smoldering radioactive rubble. In contrast, environmental threats move more slowly: degradation of the ozone layer, deforestation, erosion of the coral reefs, melting of the world's ice floes, rising sea levels, vanishing clear air to breath and clean water to drink, the destruction of crops, and the spread of human and animal diseases incubated in the hot-house temperatures beginning to blanket the planet. For most U.S. intelligence planners, however, keeping an eye on Russia and China continued to be a far more immediate concern than melting sheets of ice in the oceans.

Decision-makers at all levels of government, and in every country, tend to focus on the immediate horizon, not on what the distant future may hold. Repairing potholes and bridges in New Orleans in 2004 gained immediate attention among local politicians, as opposed to spending the large sums of money necessary to prepare dikes for the unlikely arrival of a Level 5 hurricane – which is exactly what would sweep across the city the following year, causing billions of dollars worth of damage to one of America's favorite cities. Or concentrating on Iraq as a mortal danger to the United States between 1990 and 2000, rather than pouring money into establishing security measures – tightened airport security, sky marshals in commercial airplanes, closer surveillance of Al Qaeda members – toward preventing the act of aerial terrorism that would stun the United States in 2001. Both the Clinton and Bush II Administrations chose to ignore this possible danger, even though they had been forewarned by the CIA's Counterterrorism Center as early as 1995.[12]

The absence of an immediate Soviet threat in 1991 – the Soviet Union no longer existed – gave some breathing room, though, to officials in Washington during their NSC threat-assessment powwows. Into this space came new tasking considerations, such as a focus on environmental threats to democracies. Another policymaking dimension was at work in the case of environmental intelligence: a key personality – Vice President Gore was by this time attending NSC meetings. While still in the Senate, he had already questioned the CIA in 1990 about its potential capacities to use spy satellites as a means for exploring environmental trends on the earth below, based on the fact that these machines had been watching the planet's surface from space for more than thirty years. As a CIA science officer has observed, "We have photographed the evolution of the planet."[13] Once Gore became Vice President in 1993, he had the status to raise at NSC meetings, which normally dealt with such esoteric topics of missile velocities and throw-weights, the matter of doomed polar bears. Audible groans from Pentagon brass would sometimes greet Gore's forays into environmental security issues. Working his way through this skepticism, he nonetheless convinced President Clinton to declassify more than 800,000 spy-satellite photographs related to the research concerns of U.S. environmental scientists, distributing them to university research labs and to scientists in the private sector.

Although the DOD continued to rake in most of the budgetary poker chips reserved for intelligence-tasking purposes, some of the threat-assessment ante now went toward protecting the United States – and Mother Earth – from the slow-motion ruination that climate change was inflicting. With Gore's backing, DCI John Deutch (1995–7) created a DCI Environmental Center (DEC) at the Agency and, for the first time in U.S. intelligence tasking, a serious interest in "environmental security" entered into NSC and IC planning and spending. High among the DEC's priorities was the statistical modeling of environmental futures, creating alarm systems that could alert NSC members to impending ecological events potentially harmful to the United States and – an argument often used by Gore – its military forces spread around the globe.

As the world was becoming more aware of climate-related threats, which were growing exponentially, the State Department found itself increasingly involved in diplomatic negotiations related to ecological concerns, such as the Kyoto Conference on Greenhouse Emissions in 1997. International conferences require intelligence backup and the CIA soon had a fresh set of intelligence consumers: that portion of the nation's diplomatic corps focused on the global environment. Beyond the State Department, the DEC discovered other opportunities to demonstrate the value added of "green intelligence" to new clients. One of the first examples of a new CIA intelligence consumer was the International Affairs Division of the Environmental Protection Agency (EPA) in 1996.[14]

The DEC also entered into a compact with top environmental scientists in the nation's universities, think-tanks, and industry, through a project known as MEDEA (pronounced "ma-day-a"), named after the sorceress of Colchis in Greek mythology who assisted Jason of the Argonauts steal the Golden Fleece.[15] The *quid* for the *pro quo* was for the scientists to help the CIA think through the national security implications of environmental degradation, in return for access by nongovernment scientists to geoint that had mapped the evolution of the planet's surface since the advent of modern space-based surveillance technology in the United States. While the IC dedicated only 1 percent of its satellite-collection capabilities for this ecological tasking, that still contributed valuably to environmental security – once a shunned orphan at NSC meetings.

Some wished to push the intelligence boundaries farther in this new pursuit of environmental intelligence, tasking CIA officers abroad and their humint assets to keep an eye out for a wide spectrum of useful "green" data. Yet former DCI and later Secretary of Defense Robert M. Gates (1993–5) complained to members of the Aspin–Brown Commission in 1995 that "the intelligence agencies are not looking for more work." As he put it: "They're overwhelmed already."[16] One could understand this perspective, especially given this planet's wars; rebellions; pandemics; famines; the rise and fall of empires; millions of refugees and migrants on the move, whether by land or sea; environmental calamities, from wild fires and floods to rising global temperatures and vanishing rain forests; agricultural failures; industrial squalor; the proliferation of autocracies; human trafficking; global drug cartels; arms of all kinds sold on the black market. The list goes on in this fractious, wounded world. Gates further told a reporter at the time that "the CIA is probably more heavily tasked today by policymakers that at any time in the past."[17] Aspin–Brown Commission staff conversations with intelligence officers at Langley elicited unambiguous ridicule about environmental tasking for operations officers at the CIA – the men and women overseas on the cutting edge of U.S. espionage and covert action activities. It struck operatives as a "rather squishy" mandate; and another DO officer inquired with a smirk: "What are we supposed to do, creep around Patagonia counting the number of blind rabbits?"[18] This was a reference to scientific findings that retinal damage in local rabbits was one measure of the harm being done by a hole in the ozone layer above Argentina. Said another DO skeptic: "I'm concerned about questions of military and political instability. If the DEC wants to know if the Dnieper River is polluted, they can go find out for themselves."[19]

During the Bush II Administration, MEDEA lost much of its steam. In 2008, though, it went through a revival with support from the Obama Administration. The CIA established a Center for Climate Change and National Security in 2009. Subsequently, the Trump presidency closed the doors altogether on MEDEA. Yet despite the IC's constant wrangling with this Administration (examined further in Chapter 7), its analysts managed to write the nation's first National Intelligence Estimate (NIE) on global climate change (discussed in Chapter 3)

Another important new candidate for increased intelligence resources is the growing concern about global pandemics, stimulated by the fact that millions of people worldwide died from the Covid-19 disease that emanated from China in 2019 and rapidly traveled from continent to continent over the next three years. Worldwide, the Covid-19 virus led to the deaths of nearly 7 million people, according to the World Health Organization (WHO). Moreover, various estimates by economists suggest that the financial losses resulting from the disease rose to as high as $14 trillion in the United States alone by the end of 2023. Better surveillance regarding the expansion of this disease outbreak would have given nations more lead time to produce preventive vaccinations. Prior to the sudden emergence of Covid-19, international organizations – let alone individual countries around the world – failed even to maintain lists of high-security labs where particularly dangerous organisms are kept for study.[20] At least, though, the National Center for Medical Intelligence (NCMI) provided the Trump Administration with a heads-up that the Covid-19 outbreak in China had the potential to reach pandemic proportions. The NCMI had a strong advantage over the WHO: namely, access to DIA and CIA secret humint reporting from China and other countries, with intelligence assets noticing strains on hospital ERs in various countries, along with signs of the virus in Syrian refugee camps and multiple other sources that pointed toward the Covid threat. Although NCMI was able to insert this data into the *President's Daily Brief (PDB)* repeatedly in 2019 and 2020, policy advisors in the White House were reportedly reluctant to bring this bad news to the attention of President Trump.

The Pentagon remains the most voracious consumer of intelligence. This is especially true when military operations involving the United States are under way, which the Congressional Research Service in the Library of Congress estimates has been the case every year but nineteen since the nation was founded in 1789. The combatant commanders (COCOMs) – the four-star officers who lead U.S. troops, sailors, and air personnel around the world – are always hungry, understandably, for information that will help to protect their forces and, in wartime, to advance America's battlefield objectives. As emphasized in Chapter 1, this devotion to SMO – support to military operations – tends to dominate the intelligence budget and targeting priorities.

Despite this large investment of funds dedicated to military matters, mistakes are made. In 2002, America's secret agencies were initially far off the mark in their prediction that the Saddam Hussein regime was developing a robust WMD program that threatened the United States. For instance, this analysis relied heavily on what turned out to be an unreliable Iraqi defector, a German intelligence asset codenamed "Curveball" (discussed later in the chapter). Once the U.S. invasion against Iraq began the following year, however, the IC performed well. U.S. forces benefited from full battlefield transparency, knowing the location of practically every Iraqi tank, plane, boat, and even combat patrol. This dominant battlefield awareness (DBA, in Pentagonese) was remarkable in the annals of warfare. The same had been true during America's earlier invasion of Iraq in 1990–1. In both instances, the outcome was victory – one that came quickly in the first war, though much more slowly in the second. Best of all, in both instances the United States suffered relatively few casualties compared with other major wars. America's military firepower was the most vital ingredient in these successes, but DBA played a significant role as well. For adversaries, fighting the United States in the post-Cold War era became equivalent to wearing a blindfold while confronting a superpower with seemingly omniscient vision – at least at the tactical level of battlefield operations. This tilt of the Intelligence Community toward SMO has had its critics. They would prefer to see more funding for what might be called support to diplomatic operations, or SDO – gathering intelligence from around the world that might help to advance U.S. interests through diplomacy: a focus on peacemaking through negotiations that might head off war-fighting in the first place.

In addition to producing a threat assessment during the planning and direction phase of the intelligence cycle, important, too, are calculations about global opportunities. Intelligence is expected to provide a "heads up" regarding both dangers and chances to advance America's global aspirations.

Whether related to threats or to opportunities, bias and guesswork enter into the picture, along with the limitations that accompany the inherent opaqueness of the future. On which tier should policymakers place China's anti-U.S. propaganda? Iranian weapons developments? Warfare in Sudan? Rising global temperatures? Tracking potential pandemics? Inside the White House Cabinet Room, or in comparable forums of other democracies, the arguments fly around the room regarding the proper hierarchy of concerns. This is not an academic exercise. The outcome determines the priorities for multibillion-dollar spending on intelligence collection and analysis. The result of these top-secret debates is to pinpoint locations on the world map where spies will be infiltrated, telephones and computers tapped, surveillance satellites set into orbit, reconnaissance aircraft dispatched on overflight missions, and potentially deadly covert actions directed.

All too frequently in this process, intelligence officers are left in the dark about the "wish lists" in the minds of frenetically overscheduled policy officials, who assume the secret agencies will somehow divine their needs. An obvious solution: more regular discussions between the two groups – spies and the nation's leaders, the producers and the consumers of intelligence – to ensure that the secret agencies fully understand the top priorities of the nation's decision-makers. Yet try telling that to a high-level and besieged – indeed, snowed-under – policymaker. Nor are these "tasking" debates purely objective. Politics matters. Perhaps among those involved in the NSC deliberations are MAGA adherents with their pro-Russian, anti-NATO point of view, as was the case during the Trump Administration; or national security experts who are pro-Ukraine and pro-NATO, as during the Biden Administration.

Participants may also bring their favorite hobbyhorse to the proceedings: Gore on polar bears, say, or a MAGA proponent on the need for a modernized arsenal of U.S. nuclear weaponry. Or someone (or some faction within the NSC) convinced that fentanyl is the greatest danger confronting the United States, joining heroin and other narcotics illegally smuggled across U.S. borders to kill more Americans by way of overdoses than car crashes, H.I.V., or gun violence – some 10,000 deaths each year. Thus, so the argument would go, the DEA should receive a substantial share of the nation's intelligence budget, in order to trace and intercept these drugs more effectively as they transit to the United States from the labs of Mexican cartels, from China, and even from Canada. Intelligence leaders find themselves trying to deal not just with facts about threats and opportunities – horrific in themselves when it comes to the global threat of deadly narcotics – but with various subjective policy preferences and ideological inclinations among NSC members as well.

Then there is the reality of hierarchy within the NSC. Not all members are equal. At the top are the President and Vice President, followed by the Secretaries of Defense and State. Their priorities carry special weight, as when (with virtually no debate) President Jimmy Carter ordered funding for a small-scale (and still classified) covert action he had decided would be useful – even though the former Georgia governor had been strongly opposed to this approach to foreign policy during his successful 1976 presidential campaign.

It should be noted, too, that different nations – even among the democracies – are apt to have differing threat perceptions. Al Qaeda, ISIS, and other *jihadi* terrorist organizations, the global proliferation of WMDs, state-sponsored cyberattacks against American targets, and almost anything to do with China and Russia have recently been top-ranking intelligence concerns for the United States and the United Kingdom. In many African nations, however, AIDS and poverty are often considered the gravest threats to national security, or the dangers of Ebola and other deadly diseases. In Brazil, crime is high on the list; in New Zealand, a high priority in past years has been the encroachment of Japanese fishing vessels into the Tasman Sea, robbing Kiwi seafarers of their fishing rights in their own off-shore waters – although, more recently, the most pressing New Zealand intelligence concerns have centered on white supremacist mass shootings and other terrorist attacks, like the one directed by a lone-wolf killer in 2019 against the membership of two mosques in the South Island city of Christchurch. For Norway, a persistent key threat concerns fishing rights in the Barents Sea, as well as Russia's dumping of radioactive and other waste north of the Kola Peninsula. These variations in intelligence priorities can make it challenging for the secret services in the democracies to work together in sharing their information resources in a common response to threats.

Another key question looms behind discussions of intelligence threats and opportunities. How much information is enough? The answer depends on the chances a nation's leaders are willing to take about the future – how much "information insurance" they desire. The relationship between intelligence and risk is depicted in Figure 2.2. The fewer the risks a nation is willing to accept, the more intelligence it seeks. At the same time, though, the more intelligence a nation gathers, the more both the costs and the likelihood of information overload rise. With too much intelligence pouring in, a nation finds itself inundated with data and, ironically – in this data swamp – less able to analyze what it all means. Relevant, too, is the extent of a nation's global interests. Asked if the United States collected too much information, DCI William E. Colby (1973–6) replied: "Not for a big nation. If I were Israel, I'd spend my time on the neighboring Arab armies and I wouldn't give a damn about what happened in China. We are a big power and we've got to worry about all of the world."[21] In 2003, during the tenure of DCI George Tenet, a National Intelligence Priorities Framework (NIPF) was created as a management tool for evaluating how well the IC was meeting its goals of stating "requirements" (key targets), along with fulfilling all the other steps in the intelligence cycle that follow the planning phase.

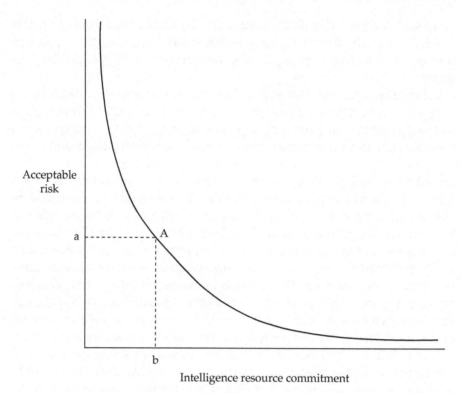

Intelligence resource commitment

Figure 2.2: The relationship between a nation's sense of acceptable risk and its resources committed to intelligence collection and analysis.

Source: Adapted from Loch K. Johnson, *Bombs, Bugs, Drugs, and Thugs: Intelligence and America's Quest for Security* (New York: New York University Press, 2000), p. 136.

Intelligence collection and the "ints"

The second phase in the intelligence cycle is collection: going after the information that policymakers have requested during the first phase of threat-assessment meetings (plus items that the Intelligence Community presumes, on its own accord, that leaders will want to know at some point). The objective may be as prosaic as gathering little bits of information that might be useful to a nation's leaders; poking around to uncover whatever one might find out about an adversary; spotting something here, something there, such as confirming the specifications of an enemy's latest missile for the twentieth time or checking on that nation's grain production yields over the past year. Here is a realistic example of a MI6 asset-placement during the Cold war, as sketched out in Mick Herron's spy novel, *Standing by the Wall*: "An accounts officer at the second-largest machine-parts factory in the GDR [the German Democratic Republic – East Germany], the output of which cast interesting light on agricultural requirements in the Eastern bloc."

Throughout the Cold War, the highest intelligence collection priority – and one ably performed by the intelligence services of the democratic nations – was to learn about the capabilities and locations of Soviet armaments, especially nuclear weaponry. This was sometimes a dangerous endeavor, as underscored by the more than forty U.S. spy planes shot down by the Soviet Union and its allies during this era. Intelligence-gathering in the Cold War – though important – was arguably less pressing than it is today, since at least the world understood then that the bipolar tensions between the superpowers defined international affairs. Now, as Joseph S. Nye, Jr. and William A. Owens have noted: "With the organizing framework of the Cold War gone, the implications are harder to categorize, and all nations want to know more about what is happening and why, to help them decide how much it matters and what they should do about it."[22] Napoleon made it clear in his era what he expected from his intelligence officers. His orders were to map out "accurately defiles and fords of every description . . . interrogate the priest and the postmaster . . . establish rapidly a good understanding with the inhabitants . . . intercept public and private letters." The great general further insisted on knowing "the length, width and nature of the roads" in enemy territory, along with the "depth and width" of rivers, "the number of houses and inhabitants of towns and villages . . . the heights of hills and mountains."[23]

A recent analysis of worldwide ship and airplane movements suggests how difficult it is for the intelligence services in the Western democracies just to keep track of global transportation flows – a matter of some significance because ships might carry materials (uranium, for instance) in violation of international sanctions levied against some countries, or, worse still, WMDs bound for rogue nations or terrorist factions. Each year, "worldwide maritime activity includes more than 30,000 ocean-going ships of 10,000 gross tons or greater," noted a DNI report in 2009, and there are "over 43,000 fixed airfields worldwide with over 300,000 active aircraft."[24] These figures, which have significantly risen since that tabulation, alone add up to a dizzying collection challenge. Moreover, on the counterterrorism front, during the first half of 2010 alone, the NCTC received 8,000–10,000 pieces of information related to global terrorist organizations, along with some 10,000 names of likely terrorists and more than forty specific threats and plots.[25]

In trying to understand this more complicated world that we now live in following the end of the Cold War in 1991, intelligence can provide valuable "cat's eyes in the dark," to use the British intelligence expression. Even wealthy nations, though, are unable to blanket the globe with expensive surveillance "platforms" designed for "remote sensing" – reconnaissance aircraft, satellites, and ground-based listening posts. The world is simply too vast and budgets are always finite. Still, satellite and airplane photography plays a central role in a nation's defenses. Imagery eased the hair-trigger anxieties of the superpowers during the Cold War – a major contribution of modern intelligence. Through the use of spy platforms, both ideological encampments – the United States and the Soviet Union – could watch one another's armies, aircraft, and ships at sea; as a result, the unlikely success of a Pearl Harbor-like surprise attack allowed tensions – and fingers on nuclear triggers – to relax a bit on both sides of the Iron Curtain that ringed the Soviet Empire. As DCI William E. Colby observed, fear and ignorance were replaced by facts for decision-makers.[26]

Before the United States had the capacity to count and trace Soviet weaponry with accuracy, Washington worried that Moscow was far ahead in armaments – the "bomber gap" and the "missile gap" that haunted America policymakers in the 1940s and 1950s, respectively. As a result of U-2 flights over the Soviet Union and, later, satellite surveillance over that vast territory with eleven time zones, the United States discovered there were indeed bomber and missile gaps; but, contrary to conventional wisdom, they favored the United States. The Americans had outpaced the Soviets in weapons production.

George J. Tenet, who served Presidents Clinton and George W. Bush as DCI (1997–2004), referred early in his tenure to what he viewed as the basics of intelligence: stealing secrets and analyzing the capabilities and intentions of America's adversaries.[27] Every intelligence agency has its own set of methods for acquiring secrets. In the United States, this "tradecraft" is referred to colloquially by the abbreviation "ints," short for "intelligence disciplines or collection methods." Imagery or photographic intelligence becomes "imint," or "geoint" in new terminology. Without the untrained eye of a professional photo-interpreter, the white-and-black lines in these sophisticated photographs can look more like a depiction of the static that plagued early television than landing strips and hangars on Russian military airfields.

Signals intelligence, "sigint," is an umbrella designation for a range of operations that collect against electronic targets, such as telephones overseas and other forms of communications ("comint," or communications intelligence), plus a variety of other types of electronic intelligence ("elint"), including data emitted by weapons during test flights ("telint," for telemetry) and emissions from enemy weapons and radar systems ("fisint," for foreign instrumentation signals). Nations with the resources to field such operations (the well-to-do nations) have sigint facilities stationed around the globe to spy on adversaries – and sometimes even friends. The Covid-19 pandemic boosted attention to global health surveillance by way of "medical sigint" – the interception of telephone conversations between health professionals (along with other intelligence sources for monitoring the spread of diseases, such as monitoring activities in the emergency room departments of foreign hospitals).

A recent illustration of how sigint facilities are spreading around the world: the *Wall Street Journal* reported in the summer of 2023 that the U.S. Intelligence Community had just discovered China was operating a sigint station aimed at the American homeland from a base in Cuba, just ninety miles off the Florida coastline. The Chinese were reported to have paid Cuba several billion dollars for this opportunity to spy on the United States – a payment that was a significant boon to the sagging economy of that island nation. The Republican Party blamed the Democrats for this development, until the Biden Administration responded publicly that it was aware of this base and that it had been established by the Chinese during the Trump years in the White House. Subsequent newspaper reports reminded the public that the Russians had also chosen Cuba during the Cold War for its largest sigint post abroad, spying on the United States in this manner for decades. For Washington officials, the revelation of foreign espionage activity against the United States was not a cause for war; every nation is involved in some aspect of these secret activities. Indeed, Americans operate the largest sigint network in the world. During the Cold War, for instance, the United States benefited from NSA listening bases located in China on its border with the Soviet Union; and, today, China is encircled by listening posts staffed by the intelligence services of various allied democracies, including NSA reconnaissance aircraft, ships at sea, or land-based antennae in the region. What was intolerable in the 1960s was not Moscow's sigint sites in Cuba, but the Kremlin's placement on the island of missiles with nuclear warheads in 1962 capable of striking the United States in minutes, leading to the most dangerous superpower crisis of the Cold War.

Last but not least among the "ints" is human intelligence, "humint." The value of this side of espionage was displayed again in the uncovering by U.S. assets in Cuba of the Chinese sigint base established there in 2023, among many other examples. The CIA asset Oleg Penkovsky inside the Soviet Union provided extremely valuable intelligence to the United States on Soviet missile-base designs. His secret drawings of these sites provided to the CIA alerted Washington authorities in 1962 to the presence of Soviet missiles in Cuba and led to U-2 imint that confirmed the threat. Here was humint and technical (machine) intelligence (or "techint") working together synergistically. Humint can be especially helpful when assets are able to report on the details of foreign weapons systems while they are still on a production line; or when they are able to gain access to inner sanctums where terrorists are planning their next attack. In another illustration, helpful as well is asset information about the likely bargaining positions of foreign diplomats in approaching trade negotiations.

The life of a humint asset has many complications and dangers, though, as he or she watches from the shadows, the alleys, and the byways in a foreign nation. The British novelist Rudyard Kipling wrote in *Kim*, the eponymous title of a book about an MI6 asset in India, that a humint asset "must go alone – alone and at the peril of his head. Then, if he spits, or sits down, or sneezes other than as the people do whom he watches, he may be slain." Death by a bullet to the back of his skull was the fate that greeted Penkovsky when he was uncovered by KGB counterintelligence officers in the aftermath of the Cuban missile crisis. Little wonder that, in remarks at the Aspin Security Forum in Colorado in 2023, D/CIA William J. Burns referred to some intelligence activities overseas as "hard jobs in hard places."

Within each of the ints, intelligence professionals fashion ingenious techniques for purloining secrets from adversaries – say, the contents of a laptop computer owned by a Russian government engineer in charge of weapons designing. The methods can range from sophisticated devices that track foreign military maneuvers by way of telescopic lenses on satellites orbiting deep in space, to multiple listening devises across the surface of the planet or hidden deep within the planet's oceans and seas. Even animals can play a role in intelligence gathering, as with the implanting of miniature microphones inside the breasts of pigeons trained to roost on the window ledges of foreign embassies. Gutted rats – soaked in pepper sauce to deter feral cats – have also been used by the CIA for alley-way "dead drops," that is, places to hide messages, cash, and film for foreign assets; and seals and dolphins have been trained for underwater missions by U.S. Navy Intelligence.

Another prominent intelligence discipline is "osint," or open-source intelligence. This type of information is gleaned from non-secretive sources, such as libraries or foreign media outlets. Is there information in the public domain about whether the desert sands near Tehran are firm enough to support U.S. helicopters, or must an intelligence asset be deployed to find out the answer? This was an important matter in 1979, when the Carter Administration planned a rescue of U.S. diplomats held in the American embassy in Iran. The DCI at the time, Admiral Stansfield Turner, had to send a special intelligence unit into Iran – a dangerous undertaking – to answer this question. The sand proved firm enough, but the mission eventually had to be aborted when U.S. military helicopters collided in the desert before they were able to fly into Tehran for the rescue attempt. Today, the DNI's Center for Open-Source Intelligence studies what information remains missing in the early osint drafts of intelligence reports that will have to be acquired through clandestine means, because the answers are nowhere to be found in library books, newspapers, magazines, or the Internet.

Since the end of the Cold War, roughly 90 percent – some say as much as 95 percent – of all intelligence reports are made up of osint material, such as information from blogs on the Internet that can offer revealing glimpses into the secretive Iranian society. Based on this statistic, some critics have suggested that policymakers in the United States should simply obtain their information about world events from the Library of Congress (LC) and close down the secret agencies, saving the nation upwards of $80 billion a year. The LC, however, does not have agents around the world to gather the secret – and sometimes the most important – "nuggets" of information that go into intelligence reporting. Nor does it have the long experience of the CIA and its companion agencies in analyzing foreign countries, putting together national security reports, and disseminating them in a timely manner to senior decision-makers around the bureaucracies in Washington – including the presentation of oral briefings to the President and other top officials (an art form in itself).

The newest and most technical int – measurement and signatures intelligence, or "masint" – can be valuable, too. Run chiefly by the DIA, here the methodology involves testing for the presence of various materials or substances, perhaps telltale vapors emitted by the cooling towers of foreign nuclear plants that might contain radioactive particles. These particles could indicate the presence of a "hot" reactor engaged in uranium enrichment. Other chemical and biological indicators have been secretly planted by CIA agents from time to time that might reveal the presence of illicit materials, as with waste fumes in a factory that point to the production of nerve gas. Between 1994 and 2008, for example, the intelligence unit in the U.S. Energy Department reportedly spent some $430 million on nuclear detection equipment at international border crossings, especially along Russia's frontiers.[28]

One of the most celebrated technical collection programs carried out by the CIA was an effort in 1974 to raise a disabled Soviet submarine from the bottom of the Pacific Ocean, an operation known as Project Jennifer. Officials in the Agency realized from satellite geoint that the Soviet vessel, at the time skimming along on the ocean's surface, had experienced a fire on board, causing it to sink rapidly beneath the waves. Under orders from DCI Colby, the Agency called upon Howard Hughes for assistance in retrieving the submarine. The eccentric billionaire was in the business (among other lucrative pursuits) of mining the ocean floors for valuable ore, such as magnesium. He owned a ship, the *Glomar Explorer*, capable of lowering wire cables deep enough into the Pacific to hoist the ore from the depths. Perhaps the *Glomar* could capture the submarine in its cable netting and pull the vessel to the surface. Hughes agreed to help, in return for a tidy $350 million, and the challenging recovery mission was under way. The dramatic attempt to raise the sub was only partially successful; half the prize fell back to the ocean floor, as the submarine was accidentally sliced in half by the *Glomar*'s slipping wire jaws. Still, the Agency viewed the capture of even half a Soviet submarine, which carried nuclear missiles and advanced communications equipment, as quite a coup.

Unfortunately, the Project Jennifer operation leaked to the media and a return trip to snare the rest of the ship was impossible once the Soviet Navy had been alerted to the position of its missing sub in the ocean. The actual contents of the captured half of the submarine remain classified, but insiders claim the project was worth the costly price tag. Critics, though, questioned why the Agency decided to pay a king's ransom for access to an obsolete Soviet submarine.[29] When the operation leaked to the media in 1975, Senator

Frank Church said: "If we are prepared to pay Howard Hughes $350 million for an obsolete Russian submarine, it's little wonder we are broke." His Senate colleague Barry Goldwater (R, Arizona) had a different view: "Frankly, if they hadn't gone out and raised that sub, I'd be mad."[30]

Humint versus techint

Intelligence professionals make a distinction between humint and techint collection – the latter an acronym for "technical intelligence" that lumps together all the machine-based means of gathering information. The vast majority of funds spent on collection go into techint. This category includes geoint and sigint satellites; large, land-based NSA listening antennae; and reconnaissance aircraft, such as the U-2 and A-12 spy planes in the United States, and their successor the SR-71, as well as the popular Predator, a drone fielded over Afghanistan, Iraq, and other nations in the Middle East and Southwest Asia following the 9/11 attacks. The Predator and its cousins, such as the larger Reaper and small (some even insect-sized) UAVs, are attractive to intelligence planners because of their mobility and their capacity to spy without endangering the life of a pilot. When the larger UAVs are equipped with missiles, they are able not only to spy but also to obliterate enemy targets that appear in their camera lens – a form of paramilitary covert action. Awed by the technological capabilities of spy machines, nations that can afford it spend sizable amounts of resources on their construction and deployment, prodded by the intelligence component of the "iron pentagon" lobby within their societies. One recent satellite program cost $9.5 billion, according to reliable newspaper reporting, and that amount was just for one of the simpler types of satellites used only in daylight hours and clear weather.[31]

This fascination with intelligence hardware continued into the age of terrorism and more recently into the renewed time of conflict between the United States and its chief global competitors, China and Russia, even though these platforms are less apt to be useful against the ghost-like targets that terrorists often are or against the well-hidden activities of rival superpowers. Cameras on satellites or aircraft are unable to peer inside the canvas tents, roofed mud huts, mountain caves, or deep underground caverns in the Middle East, Southwest Asia, and Iraq, where ISIS members meet to plan their deadly operations, or into the bunkers dug far beneath the surface of the earth as a hiding place for the North Korean construction and storage of atomic bombs. As an intelligence expert notes, often one "needs to know what's inside the building, not what the building looks like."[32] Recently released documents from the era of the Carter Administration included this revealing observation from NSC staffer Paul Henze about the limits of technical intelligence collection: "While we now enjoy nearly real-time photography from satellites ... we are not much closer than we were thirty years ago to knowing what goes on in the minds of the top men in Moscow or Madrid, Peking [now Beijing], Algeria or Brasilia, what Arab leaders say to each other when they get together or how French elections are going to come out." Similarly, a group of U.S. intelligence officers has emphasized that "technical collection lends itself to monitoring large-scale, widespread targets."[33] This approach is less effective against discreet and carefully concealed WMDs or terrorist cells.

Still, at times, techint can be a strong arm of counterterrorism – especially sigint telephone interceptions as an ISIS member (for example) speaks to a commander. Valuable, as well, are spy cameras strapped to the wings of low-altitude drones that can quickly deliver back to the United States high-resolution images of secret activities in distant lands. For example, in Afghanistan and Pakistan in the wake of 9/11, Taliban and Al Qaeda leaders were forced into hiding for fear of being spotted by U.S. geoint machines, whether surveillance satellites or reconnaissance aircraft (piloted or of the drone variety). As Richard Barrett noted at the time: "This lack of face-to-face contact with their subordinates and the enemy is sapping their authority. Taliban leaders have also had to limit their telephone communications for fear of giving away their locations, and have had to find less reliable and efficient ways to discuss strategy and pass orders to the field."[34] None of these U.S. intelligence capabilities, though, prevented the Taliban military from finally taking over Afghanistan in 2021.

In contrast to techint spending, the United States devotes just a single-digit percentage of its annual intelligence budget to foreign humint. Human spies are much less expensive than their machine counterparts. Moreover, within five years after the end of the Cold War, the CIA had experienced a 25 percent decline in case officers around the world, with fewer than 800 in the field. The FBI reportedly had more "special agents" (the Bureau's term for its operational officers) in New York City than the CIA had case officers across the globe.[35] On occasion, sigint satellites capture revealing information about adversaries – say, telephone conversations between international drug lords. Further, the photography yielded by geoint satellites is of obvious importance on such matters as the whereabouts of Chinese naval vessels, trucks transporting ISIS soldiers into Iraq, the unloading of missile parts carried in the hulls of Chinese freighters steaming toward Karachi ports (despite official denials in Beijing and Islamabad), Hamas rocket emplacements in Gaza, or the construction of sophisticated nuclear reactors in Iran. In the case of terrorism, though, a human agent well situated inside ISIS or Al Qaeda could be worth several billion-dollar satellites.

A category of humint tradecraft is the use of intelligence officers operating under deep or "nonofficial" cover, known by insiders as "NOCs." Cover involves assuming a false identity in order to have a reasonable excuse for being in a foreign country and roaming around in search of useful information to send back to headquarters. In contrast to CIA officers stationed overseas and working in official U.S. government facilities with official cover (OC), a NOC exists outside in the local society – say, as an archaeologist, investment banker, vagabond artist, yachtsman, or oil-rig operator. Acting as a NOC can be a difficult assignment. The intelligence officer must maintain his or her cover during the day, then undergo a metamorphosis at night into a spy in search of local recruits.

One of the most controversial forms of cover for U.S. intelligence officers has been for a NOC to pretend to be a journalist. If the "journalist" is caught engaging in espionage or recruiting foreign assets, he or she will not only be arrested and jailed (and, in some places in the world, killed on the spot) but will have brought believable suspicion, too, on the corps of genuine foreign media reporters inside that nation. Beginning in the late 1970s and continuing through the 1980s, the CIA promulgated a series of internal regulations that prevent its officers from claiming to be accredited American journalists or otherwise involve that profession in espionage or other spy activities (such as helping to recruit a local asset). This has led some intelligence leaders to complain periodically that the CIA is running out of ways to conceal its operations officers abroad. Yet, on the other side of the equation is the fact that, in a democracy, spies should not be confused with legitimate journalists; after all, a free press is an essential ingredient of an open society. When spies mask themselves as journalists, they corrupt the important relationship that exists between an open society and a media that is free of government ties.

A NOC frequently operates in remote locations where, as a senior CIA operative has put it, "diarrhea is the default setting."[36] Skulking around in the darkness, rain, and cold may be one's habitual working environment. No feather beds. Given the privations and risks involved in the life of NOC, the financial reward will have to be higher than the usual salary for intelligence officers if good recruits are to be attracted to this important challenge. According to several authoritative reports, intelligence officers under OC enjoy the comfort and safety of working under the auspices of the State Department overseas, as part of the embassy "country team" led by the ambassador.[37]

Convincing middle- or upper-class Agency recruits to adopt a life of crepuscular furtiveness, rather than the comfort of working inside a facility overseas with fellow Americans who enjoy official cover, can be a difficult sell – despite the nimbus of dangerous glamour and the daydreams of recruiting mysterious Romanian countesses in ancient castles. The NOC role can be hazardous in another respect; an intelligence officer in this role operates without the emollient of U.S. government immunity. If caught while engaged in espionage activities, he or she is likely to be arrested and imprisoned by local authorities and released to the United States only when – and if – an exchange of prisoners can be arranged.

For all these reasons, the Agency has shied away from the use of NOCs, although other nations have adopted this approach with great effectiveness

– such as the Soviet Union in New York City during the Cold War, as well as Russia and China today. Both of these nations also have a strong reliance on journalistic cover for their NOCs. An OC officer is unlikely to meet a member of ISIS at an embassy cocktail party overseas, but a NOC operating in, say, northeast Pakistan might have a chance of recruiting a local "cut-out" (an intermediary asset) who can in turn attempt a recruitment pitch to a Qaeda or Taliban operative. Official government socials, though, will remain a useful "hunting ground" for meeting potential recruits from major target countries, like Russia, as was the case during the Cold War.

The recruitment of human assets abroad is viewed by many CIA officers as the life-blood of intelligence. Yet, whether relying on NOC or OC tradecraft, humint is no panacea. During the Korean War, for example, almost all of America's South Korean assets recruited to infiltrate the north were either killed or captured. The same was true with its South Vietnamese assets sent into North Vietnam during that war from 1964 to 1973. Moreover, within closed societies like China and Iran, local spies are difficult to recruit; and even if successfully recruited, they are often untrustworthy. Neither boy scouts nor nuns, they have been known to fabricate reports, sell information to the highest bidder, and scheme as false defectors or double-agents (methods discussed further in Chapter 5). During the Cold War, all of America's assets in Cuba and East Germany proved to have been doubled back against the United States.[38]

A recent example of humint treachery is the German intelligence asset in 2002, by the name of Rafid Ahmed Alwan al-Janabi and prophetically codenamed "Curveball." A former Iraqi scientist who defected to Germany, he persuaded the German intelligence service (the Bundesnachrichtendienst, or BND) that biological WMDs existed in Iraq at the onset of war against that nation conducted by the United States and its allies in 2003. Curveball wrongly identified (for example) Iraqi trailers in a satellite photograph as storage locations for biological weapons when, in reality, the trailers were mobile laboratories used in the production of hydrogen and helium for weather balloons. The CIA took the bait through its intelligence liaison relationship with the Germans. Only after the war began in Iraq did Curveball's bona fides fall into doubt among German and CIA intelligence officials; he was, it turned out, a consummate liar, trying to soak the BND for money.[39]

It takes a considerable amount of time to train a clandestine officer before he or she is ready to recruit foreign assets – upwards of seven years. Fluency in the local language is a huge plus. Moreover, a case officer must learn the delicate art of handling an asset, a "very close relationship" that requires motivating the foreign local to engage in espionage, continue to produce valuable information, and maintain a double life in risky circumstances.[40]

Despite these drawbacks, humint can provide extraordinarily helpful information, as famously illustrated by the clandestine reporting to the CIA

Photo 2.2: Oleg Penkosvky
America's most celebrated humint asset, the Russian Oleg Penkosvky, with a guard in a Moscow court where he was found guilty of treason in 1963. He was soon executed by the KGB.
Source: Associated Press.

by Penkovsky during the Cold War. He was not recruited by a U.S. case officer overseas; he was a "walk-in" who volunteered to spy for the British and the Americans. To establish his bona fides, Penkovsky tossed classified Soviet intelligence documents over the wall of the U.S. and U.K. embassies in Moscow. The American officials feared, however, that he was a "dangle" meant to trick the United States. So his overture was initially rebuffed. He then tried the British Embassy in Moscow, and MI6 quickly determined that he was a legitimate "volunteer." Subsequently, based on reassurances from MI6, the Americans accepted his services, too. In 1962, from 30,000 feet over Cuba, the CIA's fleet of U-2 reconnaissance aircraft spotted the six-pointed Star of David design that, according to Penkovsky's reporting to the CIA, was the configuration of a Soviet missile base. To say the least, it bears emphasizing that this was eye-opening geoint – worth more, at least in this instance, than a billion-dollar satellite (see the case study below of the missile crisis).

Based on occasional humint successes like Penkovsky, the United States and most other countries persevere in their quest for reliable espionage assets overseas. Following the 9/11 tragedy, coupled with the errors made by the IC with respect to wrongly alleged WMDs Iraq in 2002, the Kean and the Silberman–Robb Commissions criticized America's lack of assets in important parts of the world. President George W. Bush authorized a 50 percent increase in the recruitment of CIA operations officers, leading in 2004 to the largest incoming class in the Agency's history.[41]

In an appraisal of humint, former DCI Colby observed: "It's one of those things you can't afford to say no to, because sometimes it can be valuable." He added: "You can go through years with nothing much happening, so then you cut off the relationship. Since nothing had happened there for ten years, we were in the process of closing the [CIA's] stations in El Salvador and Portugal – just before these countries blew up!" Colby's conclusion ended with a reference to covert action (the focus of Chapter 4 in this volume): "I think you'll always have some humint, and it'll pay off. And remember that the human agent is also available to somehow engage in the manipulation of a foreign government."[42] Former Secretary of State Dean Rusk, who served in both the Kennedy and the Johnson Administrations, has observed: "I regret our relying so heavily on technical intelligence, which produces limited information, at the expense of the old-fashioned spy on the ground who steals information, infiltrates groups, and eavesdrops on conversations."[43]

Former DCI Robert M. Gates agrees that humint has been valuable, despite the alarming number of double agents that the United States has had to deal with during and since the end of World War II. While acknowledging the contribution made by techint towards America's understanding of Soviet strategic weapons, Gates recalls that "a great deal of what we learned about the technical characteristics of Soviet conventional weapons we learned through humint."[44] Two of the most important duties of an intelligence service is to report on both the military capabilities and the intentions of foreign adversaries. Gates adds that when it came to probing into the Kremlin's intentions during the Cold War, not just its capabilities, humint also provided important insights. Humint can address the matter of human intentions in ways that are impossible for machines – although with artificial intelligence (AI) on the rise, who knows what techint may be able to achieve in coming years? Unlike a machine, however, a well-placed human asset might be in a position to pose a question to a foreign leader, such as: "What will you do if the United States does X?" As former CIA officer John Millis has written: "Humint can shake the intelligence apple from the tree, where other intelligence collection techniques must wait for the apple to fall."[45]

The Cuban missile crisis of 1962

Pilots of the high-altitude U-2 spy planes, built in record time through close coordination between the CIA, the U.S. Air Force, and Lockheed Corporation

Photo 2.3: Cuban Missile Crisis
U-2 photography from October 15, 1962, of a Russian nuclear missile base on the island of Cuba.
Source: National Security Archive.

in the 1950s, had come to know the contours of Cuba well during the late 1950s and early 1960s. In an operation referred to inside the Agency as Project NIMBUS, overflights across the island from west to east and back again had become standard operating procedure in the spring of 1962.[46] Since the CIA's disastrous paramilitary attempt to overthrow Fidel Castro by way of the Bay of Pigs paramilitary invasion the year before, regime change in Cuba continued to be a high priority for the Kennedy Administration, and the nearby island remained under close surveillance.

Just as sabotage and assassination plots against Castro remained a part of Washington's secret agenda, so did America's clandestine surveillance of the island, since Cuba had become Moscow's favorite Marxist-Leninist showcase in the developing world – the only socialist revolution that had succeeded in Latin America. As rumors grew among the CIA's assets on the ground in Cuba about intensified Soviet activity on the island in late 1961 and early 1962, the frequency of the U-2 reconnaissance missions increased. By May 1962, a year after the Bay of Pigs, the number of monthly flights had doubled and would rise further as the year unfolded and the rumors continued. Most of the flights originated from Laughlin Air Force Base in Texas and Edwards Air Force Base in California. Designed to fly as high as 73,000 feet and equipped with high-resolution cameras, the U-2 was a major breakthrough in aerial reconnaissance, although the plane was thin-winged and fragile, difficult to steer, and vulnerable to wind turbulence.[47]

Reports from CIA humint sources in Cuba suggested the arrival of a sizable number of Soviet troops on the island. More troubling still, these assets had spotted large cylindrical objects on the ground, and new Soviet encampments were being constructed in the palm forests of western Cuba. Senator Kenneth Keating (R, New York) had commented publicly about stories he had heard from some of his Cuban American constituents in New York, to the effect that the Soviets were importing missiles to the island. The CIA grilled its Cuban assets about these stories. The vast majority of the spies, though, were unreliable, offering conflicting and often fabricated reports – any "intelligence" to keep themselves on the Agency payroll.

Yet a few of the more trusted assets also claimed to have seen odd activities across Cuba, including the unloading of large objects from Soviet freighters in the port of Havana. In response to this humint, the Agency stepped up its U-2 reconnaissance flights. Bad weather intervened, though, and prohibited aerial photography throughout most of August 1962. Even more important than the unpredictable weather was the political opposition in the Department of State to further U-2 surveillance of the island.[48] Secretary of State Dean Rusk and others thought the flights were too risky; a conventional surface-to-air missile (SAM) in Cuba might be able to shoot down one of the reconnaissance aircraft and escalate the pressure in the United States from the Republican Party to invade this communist outpost in the Caribbean. Caution prevailed in the Kennedy Administration. Not until October 14 – after a full month of U-2 grounding ordered by President Kennedy in deference to Dean Rusk and the State Department – did the spy aircraft take flight again over the island, recording hundreds of photographs of the terrain below each day.

These fresh images were transmitted quickly to specialists in the CIA's National Photographic Interpretation Center. The black-and-white lines on the photos, difficult for the untrained eye to interpret, provided unmistakable clues to expert eyes: the Soviets were indeed constructing missile bases in Cuba. Shockingly, the photos ("imagery") revealed the presence of WMDs – indeed, missiles tipped with nuclear warheads. Earlier, Agency analysts had forecast that the Soviet Union would never be so rash as to introduce such weaponry into a country so close to the United States. John A. McCone, the DCI at the time, a successful California businessman turned spy chief, had predicted that, on the contrary, Moscow might attempt this provocative move. According to McCone's reasoning, President Nikita Khrushchev of the Soviet Union might try to redress the lop-sided intercontinental ballistic missile (ICBM) advantage enjoyed by the United States in 1962 – an estimated

17:1 edge – by placing shorter-range nuclear missiles close to the American homeland. Further, Khrushchev was no doubt inclined to do what he could by way of protecting a Marxist ally and protégé from a possible full-scale invasion of Cuba by U.S. military and CIA paramilitary forces, as possibly foreshadowed by the Agency's small-scale Bay of Pigs operation.[49]

Ominously, the U-2 photographs taken on October 14 over Cuba displayed a Star of David pattern on the ground near San Cristobal, just like the one Penkosky had warned about. The reality was both clear and disturbing: the Soviets had taken the fateful step of introducing missiles into their Central American satellite – and not just any rockets. These were medium- and intermediate-range ballistic missiles (MRBMs and IRBMs) bearing nuclear warheads capable of reaching – and annihilating – cities anywhere in the United States east of the Mississippi River. Half of America population centers could be converted into radioactive dust in less than a half-hour.

The next day, October 15, the CIA informed the White House about the presence of this advanced Soviet weaponry just off the American coast. Now the frequency of U-2 reconnaissance missions over Cuba shot upwards to several each day in a frantic search for additional missile sites. Low-level photography taken by Navy and Air Force aircraft complemented the U-2 imint and, together, they revealed still more missile trailers, erectors, vehicles, and tent areas in the Star of David design.

The reconnaissance missions yielded thousands of feet of film, some of which President Kennedy later presented to the public in a press conference as evidence in support of his allegations against the Soviet Union. Reports on the ground in Cuba from assets remained unreliable for the most part, but here was hard imagery of Soviet nuclear mischief – irrefutable empirical evidence in the form of photographs. The film pinpointed forty-two Soviet missiles in all, as well as the presence of Ilyushin-28 (IL-28) medium-range bombers, MIG-21 fighter aircraft, anti-aircraft missile batteries, and short-range battlefield rockets.

The U-2 photographs were a blessing to the President; it was a "moment of splendor," recalled a senior CIA analyst.[50] President Kennedy was elated to learn, based on the imagery, that the missiles would not be operational (that is, ready for firing) for some time – perhaps as long as a fortnight. Kennedy could now resist pressures from the Pentagon for a quick invasion; intelligence from the CIA had given him some breathing room to consider other options.

Had the United States, fearful the Cuban rockets were ready for firing, sent in a land force in the early days of this crisis, the Pentagon and the White House would have discovered that – however vital it had been – the intelligence from the U-2 flights and asset reporting suffered from potentially fatal gaps. After the end of the Cold War, conferences on the Cuban missile crisis held with U.S. and Soviet participants disclosed that, unbeknownst to the

CIA and the White House at the time, the Soviets had more than 200 tactical nuclear warheads on the island as well as the missiles, along with atomic bombs inside the cargo hatches of the IL-bombers and five times more troops than estimated by U.S. intelligence (some 40,000 instead of 8,000). Moreover, early in the crisis, the Kremlin had given local Soviet commanders discretionary authority to use the tactical weapons and release the bombers for flight to the United States if an American army invaded the island.[51] Reflecting back on those tense days, former Secretary of Defense Robert S. McNamara expressed his belief that an invasion would have triggered a nuclear war in Cuba, which would have led to a strategic response between the two superpowers – in other words, a thermo-nuclear third world war that would have destroyed much of the United States and the Soviet Union.[52] The Cuban missile crisis was an excellent example of how important intelligence can be to presidential decision-making in times of emergency; but it also stands as an illustration of how even saturated surveillance coverage of a relatively small target – an island in the Caribbean – can miss vital information.

Strengthening intelligence collection

"Many elements make up a decision," Secretary of State Rusk once told an interviewer. "First, though, one must grapple with the facts. What is the situation?"[53] In determining the situation overseas, no single int is sufficient. Success depends on all of the collection disciplines working together, just as an engine performs best when all of its cylinders are firing. Employing a different metaphor, intelligence officers sometimes refer to this synergism as the "Black & Decker" approach: using every tool in the toolbox while searching for as much information as possible. Former DCI Woolsey offered the example of North Korea. "That nation is so closely guarded that humint becomes indispensable to know what is going on," he said. "This humint then tips off sigint possibilities, which in turn may suggest where best to gather imint. These capabilities, ideally, dovetail with one another."[54]

At the end of the Cold War in 1991, efforts were made in Washington, DC to trim the defense and intelligence budgets. Some advanced the argument that intelligence capabilities associated with the various ints could be surged – that is, quickly moved – from one global location to another, depending on where the latest crisis emerged. Others, though, maintained that intelligence had to have a steady worldwide presence; only in this way could potential crises be anticipated. This surge-versus-presence debate led most participants to conclude that, yes, saving money was important and some technical collections systems could be moved from one hot spot to another; however, expert analysts at CIA Headquarters in Langley, with specific knowledge about a single country or region, were considered far less fungible. One can't be an expert on everything; one must specialize. Similarly, operations officers overseas who might have expertise in Latin American affairs, and were able to speak Spanish or Portuguese, could not perform effectively right away in Kabul or Islamabad. Thus, a consensus emerged that whereas the Intelligence Community would have to maintain global presence when it came to int collection and analysis, it could more easily surge some techint capabilities, including the use of drones, listening devices, reconnaissance aircraft, and satellites.

Both survey data and case studies of collection operations indicate that humint can be particularly important when targeting terrorists, narcotics dealers, human traffickers, and weapons proliferators.[55] Much can be done, however, to improve both techint and humint. Techint collection must constantly overcome advances in deception and denial activities carried out by adversaries, such as the camouflaging of their weapons facilities and the encryption of telephone calls.[56] Humint, though, is most in need of reform; even observers sympathetic to this approach have serious reservations about its effectiveness. The United States has a "moribund Clandestine Service," concluded one experienced field officer, evoking the earlier name of the DO; and the House Permanent Select Committee on Intelligence warned that humint is headed "over a cliff" as a result of poor management.[57] An agenda for humint reform in the United States would embrace at least these initiatives:

- an increase in the number of case (operational) officers in key parts of the world, especially NOCs;
- the development of additional cover arrangements overseas (such as international business enterprises), to reverse what DCI Colby once referred to as the "melting ice floe of cover"[58] – that is, the increasing unwillingness of the State Department, U.S. newspapers and magazines, universities, and religious groups to provide shelter and false identification for America's intelligence officers abroad, for fear of jeopardizing the safety of their own genuine employees;
- the improvement of foreign language training;[59]
- the recruitment of more citizens with ethnic backgrounds relevant to the strategic "hot-spots" of the world, such as the Middle East and Southwest Asia;[60]
- an improved sharing of humint findings across the Intelligence Community;[61] and,
- strengthened intelligence liaison relations, both humint and techint, among all democratic regimes determined to defeat terrorists, drug dealers, and other international criminals – although with a closer vetting by the United States of shared sources to avoid future "Curveball" deceptions by unscrupulous assets.[62]

The processing of intelligence

In the third phase of the intelligence cycle, the collected intelligence must be decoded if encrypted; interpreted if a satellite photograph; translated if in a foreign language; and generally put into a form that a president, prime minister, senior bureaucrat, or lawmaker can readily comprehend. This is known as processing: the conversion of raw intelligence, such as satellite geoint or email intercepts in Urdu, into a readable format.

Intelligence pours into the capitals of the larger nations like a fire hose held to the mouth, to use a simile often expressed by former NSA director, Admiral Noel Gayler. Each day, well over 4 million telephone, fax, and email intercepts flood the nation's sigint agency – often in difficult codes that must be deciphered or exotic languages that must be translated. Hundreds of satellite photographs arrive at the NGA every day. This volume is unlikely to dissipate. Every minute, for instance, 1,000 people around the world sign up for a new cell phone. A further problem is that nations are always short on foreign language translators, photo interpreters, and codebreaking mathematicians. In response to a query about the major challenges facing U.S. intelligence, it is no wonder that Vice Admiral J.M. "Mike" McConnell remarked when he was NSA director: "I have three major problems: processing, processing, and processing."[63] Almost every intelligence expert agrees that the collection of information worldwide has far outraced the ability of intelligence services to process the data.

The day before the 9/11 attacks, the NSA intercepted a telephone message in Farsi from a suspected Al Qaeda operative. Translated on September 12 – too late to be of any use – the message unnervingly proclaimed: "Tomorrow is zero hour."[64] Whether a more rapid translation might have led to a tightening of U.S. airport security procedures on the morning of September 11, thereby thwarting the attacks, is anyone's guess; but it may have. Today, the vast majority of information gathered by spy agencies is never examined; it gathers dust in warehouses. An estimated 90 percent of what the IC collects is never examined by human eyes; and as many as 99 percent of the telephone intercepts gathered by the NSA are never analyzed.[65] A leading expert on the NSA and sigint has noted that this agency collects from intercepted Internet traffic alone "the equivalent of the entire textual collection of the Library of Congress 2,990 times every day. Of this intake, according to NSA only 0.025 percent of the intercepted Internet material is selected for review by the agency's analysts." Even that amount is equivalent to "119 times the size of the entire collection of the Library of Congress."[66]

To improve processing, "watch lists" are used to scan for key topics like "bombs," "*Daesh*," "ISIS," "Ukraine," or "nuclear weapons"; and in the future, AI technology holds out promise for sorting through these intelligence haystacks more quickly and efficiently. Here is a supreme challenge for the government's IT specialists: improving the nation's capacity to sift rapidly through incoming intelligence data, separating the signals from the noise, the wheat from the chaff.

In the United States, additional IT challenges present themselves. The computers in the eighteen intelligence agencies still need to be fully integrated so that collectors and analysts can communicate better with one another from agency to agency in search of "all-source" integration of gathered intelligence. Presently, the connections remain spotty. This data integration must also be carried down to the state and large-city levels of government, where intelligence "fusion centers" are being developed for counterterrorism purposes. These local officials stand on the front lines of counterterrorism and threats from homegrown extremists; they urgently seek intelligence assistance from the federal IC. Further, as these attempts at improved organizational integration are pursued, steps must be taken to ensure that the channels of information-sharing are protected by firewalls that guard against cybertheft and manipulation by hostile intelligence services and domestic radicals. These are tall orders for IT specialists, many of whom prefer to rake in big money with jobs in Silicon Valley rather than work for their country on government wages.

The next phase of the intelligence cycle turns to "analysis," a vital topic explored in the following chapter.

3

Intelligence Analysis:
Understanding World Affairs

Analysis lies at the heart of the intelligence cycle: the task of bringing insight to the information that has been collected and processed. The intelligence analyst must be like Sherlock Holmes in "The Blue Carbuncle": someone whose "business is to know what other people don't know." Standing alone without further interpretation by intelligence experts, the data that flows to the Intelligence Community from human assets and spy machines is "like a big stew" (as former CIA official Peter Ernest has described it). The task of the analyst is to search for the pattern woven by the multiple threads in the intelligence that has been collected; or, using a different metaphor, to discern the picture out of the various pieces of the jigsaw puzzle. Gathering facts, attempting to make sense of them in a timely fashion, then getting them out to those who make decisions – that's the NSI's core responsibility.

The method of intelligence analysis is straightforward enough: namely, hiring smart people to pore over all the information from open and clandestine sources before presenting the findings to key decision-makers in written reports and oral briefings. The *Washington Post* reported in 2010 that the IC produces some 50,000 intelligence reports each year.[1] If these reports and briefings are unable to provide reliable insights into the meaning of the information gathered from around the world, then each of the preceding steps in the intelligence cycle – which annually cost billions of dollars to carry out – is for naught.

Here's the bad news: intelligence analysts will always be taken by surprise from time to time, a fate guaranteed by the dilemmas of incomplete information, the uncertain light of the future, and the frailties of the human condition. As Intelligence Studies scholar Richard K. Betts underscores:

> Intelligence failures are not only inevitable, they are natural. Some are even benign (if a success would not have changed policy). Scholars cannot legitimately view intelligence mistakes as bizarre, because they are no more common and no less excusable than academic errors. They are less forgivable only because they are more consequential. Error in scholarship is resolved dialectically, as deceptive data are exposed and regnant theories are challenged, refined, and replaced by new research. If decision makers had but world enough and time, they would rely on this process to solve their intelligence problems. But the press of events

precludes the luxury of letting theories sort themselves out over a period of years, as in academia. My survey of the intractability of the inadequacy of intelligence, and its inseparability from mistakes in decision, suggests one final conclusion that is perhaps most outrageously fatalist of all: *tolerance for disaster.*[2]

In a similar vein, Secretary of State Dean Rusk often advised DCIs during the Cold War that intelligence reports ought to start off with the honest caveat: "Damned if we know, but if you want our best guess, here it is." The limits of national security intelligence have been summed up succinctly by a former American intelligence officer, who offers this reality check: "Because intelligence collection is a human endeavor, failure is inevitable."[3]

Not all the news is bad, though. Western nations have taken long strides toward improving their intelligence capabilities against the enemies of democracy. The enormous amount of money spent on intelligence each year by the United States and its allies has allowed their officials to deploy the largest and – at least in terms of spy machines – the most sophisticated espionage apparatus ever devised by humankind. This brings in a torrent of information, much of which improves the safety of the open societies. China, though, is rapidly gaining ground in the race for global intelligence coverage, across the ints.

Still, while the Western intelligence services usually perform with a high rate of success in closely watching the military, diplomatic, and economic maneuvers of the autocratic regimes, occasionally things go wrong. As a character in spy novelist Mick Herron's *Standing by the Wall* puts it: "That was the trouble with the spy game: there were too many imponderables." Perhaps nothing underscores this reality better than the surprise attacks of 9/11; the IC thought Al Qaeda was a *foreign* threat, not a group that could strike the American homeland. This wake-up call was followed by the added intelligence misjudgment about the likely existence of WMDs in Iraq. As it turned out, they simply weren't there. Intelligence reports come in many forms. They can be short, such as: a situation report ("sit rep") on a specific area of unrest in the world; a CIA report filed back to Headquarters from the field (known as an "Aadwolf"); and "baseball card"-sized biographical sketches of foreign leaders for policymakers to easily carry with them on diplomatic missions overseas. And they can be long, for example: a dissertation on an important topic, such as likely leadership succession possibilities in Russia after Putin. Sometimes this reporting proves highly accurate; sometimes it is wrong. Most of the reports are in between. The most prestigious intelligence product in the United States is the *President's Daily Brief* (PDB). Another prestigious report is the National Intelligence Estimate (NIE), which is usually about twenty pages long but can be much lengthier for especially tangled topics.

The *President's Daily Brief*

From among the hundreds of classified reports prepared each year by the Intelligence Community, the *PDB* is the most heralded among America's national security decision-makers. Former DCI George Tenet referred to it as "our most important product," and Thomas Kean, Chair of the 9/11 Commission in 2003–4, dubbed it the "Holy Grail of the nation's secrets."[4]

The *PDB* is distributed by CIA couriers each morning to the President and a few top cabinet officials and aides. The number of recipients has varied from administration to administration, rising to as many as fourteen in the Clinton Administration and as few as five in the Reagan Administration, six in the second Bush Administration, and eight in the Obama Administration. The document often sets the agenda for early morning discussions in high councils – a "catalyst for further action," in the words of a NSC staff aide.[5]

When the DNI Office was created in 2004, the *PDB* shifted officially from being a CIA to a DNI report. In reality, though, it continued to be assembled by the Agency (where most of its contributors reside and where it is produced), and is usually also briefed by the D/CIA rather than the DNI. The latter is simply too busy dealing with the challenges of IC-wide institutional issues to spend the necessary hours – as many as four or five a day – preparing for the Oval briefing. The format of the *PDB* has varied over the years, though it has always had three core objectives: readability, logical reasoning, and factual fidelity based on the IC's wide network of sources and methods. The document is normally fifteen to twenty pages long and printed in impressive four-color graphics that vividly display, for example, global economic trends in color-coded lines on graphs. For decision-makers who prefer a computer presentation to a paper document, the *PDB* is also available (since the Obama Administration) in a secure electronic format. See Box 3.1 for a summary of some *PDB* reporting to Presidents Richard M. Nixon and Gerald R. Ford.

Box 3.1: Data on *PDB* reporting during the Nixon and Ford Administrations

The declassified *PDB*s from the Nixon and Ford Administrations include about 2,500 documents and 28,000 pages. These documents were the primary vehicle for summarizing the day-to-day sensitive intelligence and analysis, as well as late-breaking reports, for the White House on current and future national security issues. President Richard Nixon, as a once practicing attorney, preferred to review the *PDB*s on longer legal-size paper, and this format was carried into the Ford Administration. At the beginning of the Nixon Administration from 21 January to 28 April 1969, the CIA delivered morning and afternoon *PDB*s to accommodate National Security Advisor Henry Kissinger, who requested the most current intelligence as fast-breaking events were unfolding. These afternoon *PDB*s for Kissinger were referred to as "Late Notes." By the close of 1969, the *PDB* had become quite lengthy – generally ten pages or more – and its format included a table of contents to manage the increasing breadth of intelligence issues.

President Gerald Ford requested more detailed reporting and analysis, and these *PDB*s were often close to twenty pages with lengthy Annexes. Publishing the *PDB* every day except Sunday was a twenty-four-hour process, and the *PDB* staff managed the final product from identifying topics for articles in the product until "it went to bed" to be published in the early hours the following morning. Specific criteria for the *PDB* articles generally reflected what the Agency inferred about the interests of the President, as well as what the writers and reviewers – the Director of the *PDB* Staff, the Deputy Director for Intelligence or DDI [now called the Deputy Director of Analysis] and the Director of CIA – believed should be brought to the attention of the President on any given day.

Nixon received his first *PDB* as President on January 21, 1969, and Ford on August 9, 1974. From January 21 to April 28, 1969, the CIA delivered afternoon *PDB*s to NSA Kissinger, who requested these "Late Notes." According to former DCI Richard Helms, "I was never sure how often Nixon ever glanced at the *PDB*." By the time Nixon was President, staff [at the CIA] worked in three eight-hour shifts, with the end of the night shift occurring at 7 a.m. after the *PDB* was delivered. With Kissinger as Nixon's gatekeeper, each CIA director – Helms, James R. Schlesinger, and William E. Colby – was distanced from President Nixon, with the NSC taking the lead in providing the daily intelligence briefing to the President. Under the direction of Kissinger, the lengthened, detailed *PDB* delivered beginning on January 21, 1969, had three sections: "Major Problems," "Other Important Developments," and a final section, an "Annex," which captured longer analytic products on specific topics. Often times, the content of the Annexes were products drawn from reporting prepared by the Directorate of Intelligence, accompanied by assessments from the wider Intelligence Community, such as National Intelligence Estimates.

Source: Summarized from Celia Mansfield, CIA Historical Programs Coordinator, *Strategic Warning in the Early Détente Era: The President's Daily Briefs delivered to Nixon and Ford*, Center for the Study of Intelligence, CIA (2015).

The *PDB* – "the book," as it is known inside the CIA – is designed to grab the attention of harassed policymakers and provide them with "current intelligence" about events that have just transpired around the globe during the previous twenty-four hours, commenting perhaps on the health of an aging foreign leader or the deployment of a new Chinese weapon system. The rationale for producing and disseminating such briefs would have been well understood by British Prime Minister Benjamin Disraeli (1874–80), who is reputed to have observed that "the most successful man in life is the man who has the best information." This aphorism would be true, of course, for the most successful woman as well.

Both the spiral-bound, glossy paper hard copy and the secure laptop version are attractive and easy to read. Substantively, the *PDB* focuses on topics known to be high on a president's policy agenda, rather than the daily smorgasbord offered readers by regular newspapers. The document attempts, further, to integrate information gathered secretly from around the world through the eyes and ears of humint and techint sources fielded by the intelligence agencies. Here is the concept of "all-source fusion" at work, which permits "one-stop shopping" for information on global events – exactly what in earlier days President Truman lamented he never had. The *PDB* comes with another important service unavailable to ordinary newspaper subscribers: instant follow-up oral briefings designed to answer specific questions posed by its VIP readership – six or sixty minutes of additional information offered in a supplementary oral briefing, depending on the interest and patience of the policymaker. This creates a rare opportunity for a president or other top official to talk back to their "newspaper" and actually receive some immediate responses.[6]

During a typical year of the Clinton Administration, for instance, forty-two follow-up oral briefings took place in the offices of *PDB* recipients; and the CIA sent an additional 426 memoranda to those readers who requested more detailed written answers to their queries. About 75 percent of these follow-ups occurred by the next working day.[7] Thus, the *PDB* is more than a document: it is a *process*, allowing intelligence officers to interact with decision-makers and provide useful supportive information and insights. As an NSC staffer noted during the Carter Administration, this interaction keeps "the CIA boys hopping, but, most importantly, it lets them know what is of interest at any given time to the President."[8]

Presidents and some other subscribers in the small "witting circle" of *PDB* recipients have sometimes complained about the quality of the document. George W. Bush, for instance, received the *PDB* and oral briefings during his first presidential campaign in 2000, along with other leading candidates, a service provided by the CIA since 1952 to presidential contenders.[9] This son of a former D/CIA and president said he found them unhelpful, and remarked: "Well, I assume I will start seeing the good stuff when I become President" – without realizing that the IC was already giving him its best material.[10] Yet when George Tenet served as the senior intelligence director on the NSC staff in the mid-1990s, he observed that the *PDB* was, "for the most part, a high-quality product. There are days when it's not earth-shattering; there are days when it's really interesting."[11]

The Aspin–Brown Commission's examination of whether the Chinese were selling M-11 missiles to Pakistan between 1989 and 1995 provides an example of the value added by the *PDB*. At the time, reporting in public newspapers was filled with ambiguities about the alleged weapons sales.[12] The spy agencies, however, possessed geoint and sigint that moved the case from one of speculation to a level of strong evidence that the Chinese were indeed providing Pakistan with missile components, though lying about it in public and in diplomatic channels with the United States. The sighting of "cylindrical objects" at the Sargodha Missile Complex in Pakistan and "unidentified, suspicious cargo" being unloaded in the Karachi harbor provided useful humint clues. When coupled with telephone intercepts between Pakistani and Chinese officials alluding to "cylindrical objects" being unloaded from Chinese ships in Karachi harbor, and – the clincher – geoint from U.S. satellites of missile launchers at Sargodha, the President had more information about the weapons controversy in the *PDB* than he could have found anywhere in the open-source literature. With respect to the vital geoint data, in the Chinese proverb, "Better to see once than to hear a hundred times."

The National Intelligence Estimate

While the *PDB* is an example of *current intelligence*, a National Intelligence Estimate (NIE) concentrates on longer-range reporting, based on *research intelligence*. An NIE offers an appraisal of a foreign country or international situation, reflecting the coordinated judgment of the entire IC. "Estimates," as NIEs are sometimes called (or "assessments" in Britain), are the outcome of an intricate gathering and evaluation of intelligence drawn from all IC sources, relying on each of the ints.[13] They are not limited to the task of predicting specific events (which the *PDB* often attempts); indeed, their primary responsibility is to assist the President and other senior personnel by providing background research on foreign leaders, unfolding situations abroad, and the military, economic, and diplomatic activities of other nations. Many NIEs set down on paper (or in a computer format), and often rank, a range of possible outcomes related to developments inside a foreign nation or terrorist faction; or they will address the likely long-range pathway of a situation simmering somewhere in the world that could threaten the United States or present an opportunity for the advancement of America's global interests. An Agency official has offered this definition of an Estimate: "A statement of what is going to happen in any country, in any area, in any given situation, and as far as possible into the future."[14]

A range of NIE topics

An NIE is sometimes initiated by a formal request from a senior policymaker for an appraisal and prognosis of events and conditions in some part of the world. In an overwhelming majority of cases, however, the IC itself generates NIE proposals – 75 percent of them in one recent year.

In this manner, the IC attempts to "push" intelligence toward the consumer, rather than wait (perhaps endlessly) for it to be "pulled" from the intelligence agencies by incontinently busy and distracted officeholders (the intelligence consumers), whose in-boxes are silted with assignments that demand immediate attention. A further potential complication in having one's intelligence reports read and taken seriously: as John Steinbeck put it in *The Winter of Our Discontent*, "no one wants advice – only corroboration." As for potential subjects for an Estimate, the possibilities cover a wide front, as shown by these examples from the Carter Administration (a list that illustrates how some problems never go away):

- the balance of strategic nuclear forces between the United States and the Soviet Union [or, today, Russia and China];
- the conventional military balance in Europe;
- the prospects for a closer alliance between the Soviet Union and China [or now Russia and China];
- the outlook for cohesiveness within the Atlantic Alliance [think today of NATO and how unpredictable its unified support for Ukraine in its war with Russia may be as events unfold in 2024 – whether these are election results in NATO nations or outcomes on the battlefield]; and
- the significance of the developing world's international debt problems.[15]

Preparing Estimates

In the preparation of a NIE, a panel of intelligence experts (known since 1980 as the National Intelligence Council, or NIC – officially a part of the ODNI, but physically located at CIA Headquarters in Langley) initially examines the merits of each proposal in consultation with analysts throughout the Community, as well as with senior policy officials. If the decision is to move ahead in the drafting of a NIE, the NIC determines which segments of the IC can best contribute to the document and then provides these agencies with an outline of objectives, asking them to respond with their facts and insights by a certain deadline. This outline is known as the Terms of Reference, or TOR. As one NIC document explains: "The TOR defines the key estimative questions, determines drafting responsibilities, and sets the drafting and publication schedule."[16] For examples of a range of NIC products publicly reported in 1994, see Table 3.1.

Table 3.1: Sample National Intelligence Council products, 1994

National Intelligence Estimate (NIE)	NIEs address subjects of highest concern to senior US policymakers. They are approved by the DCI and the National Foreign Intelligence Board (NFIB). Twenty to forty pages in length.
Fast-track NIEs	Accelerated NIE.
NIE President's Summary	Shorter version of NIE distributed only to the President, members of the cabinet, and other top U.S. policymakers. Three to four pages in length.
NIE Update Memorandum	Follow-up to a NIE presenting new information or analysis. Coordinated within the Intelligence Community but does not require DCI or NFIB approval. Three to four pages in length.
Intelligence Community Assessment	Addresses important subjects but ones not requiring presidential attention; coordinated but not submitted to NFIB for approval.
National Intelligence Council Memorandum	Short memorandum coordinated by Intelligence Community but does not require CIC or NFIB approval. Three to four pages in length.
Warning Memorandum	A memorandum of a possible crisis situation. Prepared for senior US policymakers, receives DCI and NFIB approval. Two to three pages in length.
Warning Committee Report	A report coordinated within Intelligence Community but does not require DCI or NFIB approval. Published monthly or bimonthly. Three to four pages in length.
Regional Forecast Memorandum	A memorandum coordinated within Intelligence Community but does not require DCI or NFIB approval. Published monthly or bimonthly. Three to four pages in length.
Monthly Global Warning Report	Reports on critical hotspots throughout the world, does not require coordination or approval. Three to four pages in length.

Note: The NFIB (formerly the U.S. Intelligence Board or USIB) is an overarching interagency intelligence review panel. [Today, the list of NIC products has grown in number, but the items above still remain the essential reports. In place of "DCI," the approval chiefs would now include both the DNI and the D/CIA.]

Source: *A Guide to the National Intelligence Council*, CIA (1994), p. 42, with an introduction by then NIC Chairman Joseph S. Nye Jr. (who would later serve as Dean of the Kennedy School at Harvard University).

In response to the TOR, data and ideas pour back to the NIC from around the IC and are shaped into a draft NIE by one or more of the senior analysts who comprise the NIC, in continual dialogue with experts further down the chain of analysts. Since 1973, the most senior analysts on the NIC have been known as National Intelligence Officers, or NIOs. These men and women are expected to have "the best in professional training, the highest intellectual integrity, and a very large amount of worldly wisdom."[17] The ten to sixteen or so NIOs (the number varies from time to time) are considered *la crème de la crème* of intelligence analysts, drawn from throughout the Community as well as from academe, think-tanks, the military, and occasionally from congressional staff. A recent set of NIOs consisted of four career intelligence officers, five analysts from universities and think-tanks, three from the military, and one from the legislative staff on Capitol Hill. Further, the NIC consults regularly with some fifty experts across the country who hold security clearances but are not within the official IC framework.

For the dozen NIOs in the Clinton Administration (1993–2001), here is a listing of their "portfolios": Africa; Near East and South Asia; East Asia; Russia and Eurasia; Economics and Global Issues; Science and Technology; Europe; Special Activities (a euphemism for covert action); General Purpose Forces; Strategic and Nuclear Programs; Latin America; and Warning. The NIOs work closely with the DNI's National Intelligence Managers to bring about the kind of synergy in the IC that leads, recall, to the ultimate goal of all-source fusion: a blend of all the findings from the ints throughout the IC into comprehensive intelligence reports for decision-makers.

The best-known IC efforts to consult with outsiders for a critique of a NIE came in 1976, by way of a "Team A, Team B" review of an Estimate on Soviet military intentions and capabilities.[18] NSC staff selected the two teams. The CIA's own Soviet experts comprised Team A, and academics comprised Team B, led by Harvard University Russian historian Richard E. Pipes, known for his strongly hawkish views on the Soviet Union. Pipes and the members of his panel were convinced the Agency had gone soft. Its liberal "civilian" outlook, reinforced by "naive" arms-control experts in the scholarly community, had led (so Team B argued) to a NIE that downplayed the Soviet plan for world conquest. In the Team B view, the Soviets were subtly seeking – and could well achieve – a first-strike, war-winning strategy against the United States rather than pursue the dreamy policy of peaceful coexistence supposedly hoped for by liberals. Team B accused the CIA of miscalculating Soviet expenditures on weapons systems, thereby underestimating the formidable strength of the Red Army and its WMDs. Team A, in turn, charged the Pipes panel with exaggerating the Soviet peril. The upshot of this attempt at "competitive analysis" using outsider reviewers was that the CIA trimmed back on some of its more sanguine views about Moscow's intentions, adopting Soviet military production figures that were slightly more in line with the Team B projections.

During the drafting of a NIE, the NIO in charge will send the first draft back to each of the intelligence agencies working on the study and so begins the process of interagency editing, as specialists from throughout the IC hammer the final document into shape. An analyst recalls this editing process in painful terms: "It was like defending a Ph.D. dissertation, time after time after time."[19] The NIC makes the penultimate judgment on the appropriateness of the data and conclusions presented in each Estimate, then sends the document along to the National Intelligence Board for further review. The NIB is made up of senior representatives of the IC and is chaired by the DNI, who is also in charge of the NIC and has the last say on an Estimate before it is distributed to senior policymakers.

In the past, a few intelligence directors have occasionally so disliked an Estimate produced by the intelligence bureaucracy that they have written one themselves on the topic in lieu of sending forward the NIC version. This practice is rare, however, and carries with it the danger of an Estimate becoming too personalized or even politicized.[20] Sometimes, though, intelligence chiefs can be correct and the bureaucracy wrong, as when DCI John McCone rejected the conclusion of an Estimate that predicted the Soviets would be unlikely to place missiles in Cuba in the early 1960s. The best approach, however, is to rely on well-trained and experienced analysts; then, if the DNI, the D/CIA (or some other high official in the IC) disagrees with their evaluation, he or she can forward a dissent to policymakers as an addendum to the official NIO version or in a separate classified letter.

The bulk of the NIE drafting resides in the hands of junior analysts within the IC – specialists who study the daily cable traffic from the country (or other topic) in question. At a higher level, the NIOs are expected to keep in touch with the various intelligence agencies that have contributed to the Estimate. Obviously, the tenor of the language in a NIE is all-important, especially the confidence levels evinced in the document (whether high, medium, or low – or some finer gradation between these general categories). The NIOs must be careful not to claim more than the evidence can support, especially in the NIE's executive summary (called "Key Judgments," or KJs) found at the beginning of the document. (For an example, see Box 3.2 on "Climate Change," written and classified in 2021.) This may be the only portion of an Estimate read by a harried (or sometimes perhaps lazy) policy official, and it needs to convey the caveats that can serve as an antidote to overly assertive and simplistic conclusions.

The question of dissent

Especially tricky has been the question of how to represent dissenting views in an Estimate. The individual intelligence agencies sometimes have quite different perspectives on a world situation. Military intelligence organizations

Box 3.2: Key Judgment excerpts from a NIE on climate change, 2021

In 2021, the Intelligence Community published its first NIE focused on climate change. The Estimate offered three KJs:

Key Judgment 1: Geopolitical tensions are likely to grow as countries increasingly argue about how to accelerate the reductions in net greenhouse gas emissions that will be needed to meet the Paris Agreement goals. Debate will center on who bears more responsibility to act and to pay – and how quickly – and countries will compete to control resources and dominate new technologies needed for the clean energy transition. Most countries will face difficult economic choices and probably will count on technological breakthroughs to rapidly reduce their net emissions later. China and India will play critical roles in determining the trajectory of temperature rise.

Key Judgment 2: The increasing physical effects of climate change are likely to exacerbate cross-border geopolitical flashpoints as states take steps to secure their interests. The reduction in sea ice already is amplifying strategic competition in the Arctic over access to its natural resources. Elsewhere, as temperatures rise and more extreme effects manifest, there is a growing risk of conflict over water and migration, particularly after 2030, and an increasing chance that countries will unilaterally test and deploy large-scale solar geoengineering – creating a new area of disputes.

Key Judgment 3: Scientific forecasts indicate that intensifying physical effects of climate change out to 2040 and beyond will be most acutely felt in developing countries, which we assess are also the least able to adapt to such changes. These physical effects will increase the potential for instability and possibly internal conflict in these countries, in some cases creating additional demands on US diplomatic, economic, humanitarian, and military resources. Despite geographic and financial resource advantages, the United States and partners face costly challenges that will become more difficult to manage without concerted effort to reduce emissions and cap warming.

Key Takeaway: We assess that climate change will increasingly exacerbate risks to US national security interests as the physical impacts increase and geopolitical tensions mount about how to respond to the challenge. Global momentum is growing for more ambitious greenhouse gas emissions reductions, but current policies and pledges are insufficient to meet the Paris Agreement goals. Countries are arguing about who should act sooner and

> competing to control the growing clean energy transition. Intensifying physi-
> cal effects will exacerbate geopolitical flashpoints, particularly after 2030,
> and key countries and regions will face increasing risks of instability and
> need for humanitarian assistance.
>
> *Source: Climate Change and International Responses Increasing Challenges to US National
> Security Through 2040*, National Intelligence Estimate, National Intelligence Council, Document
> 10030-A (October 2021) Washington, DC.

are notorious for their "worst-case" approach to estimating – a result, critics
contend, of pressures on analysts applied by the Department of Defense and
the military–industrial complex to justify larger military budgets by frightening the American people and their representatives in Congress with testimony
about dire threats from abroad. Conversely, military intelligence officials
often consider the CIA and INR as too "civilian" and unable to understand the
true nature of foreign military dangers.

The clash of differing views among intelligence agencies can be healthy, if
driven by an objective weighing of facts rather than policy bias and ideology.
Debate among analysts can provide policymakers with a range of views,
instead of just the lowest common denominator. Sometimes NIEs are diluted
to a tapioca consistency that robs policy officials of the nuances they need
to understand. One NIC Vice Chair remembers that Estimates were "all too
likely to produce a hedged and weasel-worded result."[21] Further, agency dissents have been relegated to obscure footnotes on occasion, if included at all.
The best NIC managers have been careful to ensure that dissents are stated
at some length in the text of the NIE, not hidden in a footnote – if only to
avoid the resentment of dissenting agencies that have had their findings and
judgments shunted aside. Some dissenting agencies insist that their contrary
opinions be highlighted boldly in the text, often in a boxed format obvious to
every reader, and placed as well in the KJ section of the document. This is a
useful practice that encourages debate.

The internal liaison challenge

An additional responsibility of intelligence managers is to ensure that NIOs
and other designated intelligence analysts maintain good liaison relationships with consumers. "The difficulty lies not only in predicting the future,
in a world of many variables, incomplete data, and intentional deception,"
writes one intelligence officer, "but in convincing policy makers that the
prediction is valid."[22] President Lyndon B. Johnson once explained, using a
country analogy, why some policymakers are reluctant to hear from intelligence officers. "When I was growing up in Texas," he recalled at a private
dinner party in Washington, DC, "we had a cow named Bessie. I'd get her in

the stanchion, seat myself and squeeze out a pail of fresh milk. One day, I'd worked hard and gotten a full pail of milk, but I wasn't paying attention and old Bessie swung her s –-smeared tail through that bucket of milk. Now, you know, that's what these intelligence guys do. You work hard and get a good program or policy going, and they swing a s – -smeared tail through it."[23]

Experience has shown that unless a policymaker knows and feels personally comfortable with an NIO or other intelligence briefer, he or she is less likely to pay attention to an Estimate. Rapport between consumer and producer also provides analysts with a better understanding of the information needs of the policy departments, lowering the chances that an intelligence report will be irrelevant to current policy concerns and become merely a "self-licking ice cream cone."[24] Too close a relationship, though, can undermine the vital quality of objectivity in the intelligence process – the danger of politicization.

The timing and frequency of NIEs

An NIE can be written quickly, in two to four weeks – or in less than a day in emergencies; in two to six months during normal times; or as long as three years on a slow track. Historically, it has taken on average about 200 days to produce an Estimate – that is, seven months or so. Those studies readied on a fast-track basis during a crisis have their own name: a special NIE or SNIE (pronounced "snee"). During the Suez Canal crisis of 1956, for example, the IC crafted a SNIE on Soviet intentions within a few hours and, in May 1967, in a one-day SNIE turnaround on the eve of an Arab–Israeli War (see Box 3.3). Analysts hope, though, to have at least three months to produce a thorough Estimate.

From 1947 to 2005, the IC produced 1,307 NIEs, averaging twenty-three a year.[25] The numbers have fluctuated over the years (see Figure 3.1), a reflection of the DCI's priorities and an administration's interest in receiving Estimates.[26] Added into the mix are changing world circumstances that may or may not require the preparation of new NIEs. In times of war, for example, policymakers are likely to be focused on current intelligence that reports on immediate battlefield exigencies, with NIEs pushed to the back burner.

NIE hits and misses

The dean of early CIA analysts, Sherman Kent, commented on the goal of in-depth analysis. "The guts of the matter," he said, "is the synthesizing of the pieces and setting them forth in some meaningful pattern which everyone hopes is a close approximation of the truth."[27] Still, the end result remains something of a best guess, resulting from discussions among the top analysts in the IC. As Kent once put it, "estimating is what you do when you do not know." One enters "into the world of speculating."[28] However shrewd the

---

Box 3.3: Special Estimate (SNIE) excerpt on war in the Middle East, 1967

Military capabilities of Israel and the Arab States

Summary

Israel could almost certainly attain air supremacy over the Sinai Peninsula in less than 24 hours after taking the initiative or in two or three days if the UAR struck first. It would lose a third to half of its air force. Armored striking forces could breach the UAR's double defense line in the Sinai in three to four days and drive the Egyptians west of the Suez Canal in seven to nine days. Israel could contain any attacks by Syria or Jordan during this period.

General assessment

1. The Israel Defense Forces (IDG) are at a numerical disadvantage to the combined strength of its Arab neighbors in terms of aircraft, armor, artillery, naval vessels, and manpower. Nonetheless, the IDG maintain qualitative superiority over the Arab armed forces in almost all aspects of combat operations.

TOP SECRET
[declassified April 2004]

Note: UAR stands for the United Arab Republic, a sovereign state in the Middle east from 1958 to 1961 in the present territories of Egypt and Syria.
Source: David S. Robarge, "CIA Analysis of the 1967 Arab-Israeli War: Getting It Right," *Studies in Intelligence* 49/1 (2005): 1–7; repr. in Loch K. Johnson and James J. Wirtz, eds., *Intelligence: The Secret World of Spies*, 6th edn. (New York: Oxford University Press, 2023), pp. 113–18.

---

forecasts, they still remain hunches. It is better than blind luck – as with the throwing of animal entrails in the sand to predict the future, in the manner of Julius Caesar in ancient days – because the judgments are based on expert research and knowledge. Nonetheless, they are a far cry from certainty.

At times, NIEs have been as accurate as an expensive Swiss watch; on other occasions, they have been wide of the mark. Examples of successful predictions (among many others) include: the likely conduct of the Soviet Union in world affairs during the Cold War (Moscow would try to expand its influence and territory, but would avoid the risk of general war);[29] the launching of the Soviet Sputnik in 1957; the Sino-Soviet split of 1962; the Chinese A-bomb test in 1964; the development of new Soviet weapon systems throughout the Cold War;[30] developments in the Vietnam War (1964–75); the Arab–Israeli War of 1967; the India–Pakistan War of 1971; the Turkish invasion of Cyprus in

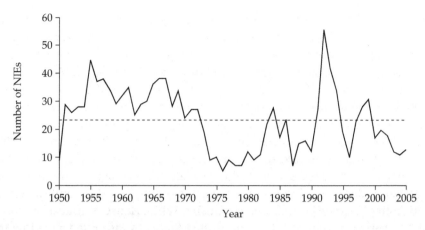

Figure 3.1: Frequency of NIEs by year, 1950–2005.

Note: The broken line in the figure represents the mean number of NIEs produced annually during this sample period. The high point in the production of Estimates came (perhaps not surprisingly) from 1991–93, when for the first time a former CIA analyst – Robert M. Gates – had become DCI.

Source: Central Intelligence Agency, 2006.

1974; the Chinese invasion of Vietnam in 1978; the mass exodus from Cuba in 1978; the Soviet invasion of Afghanistan in 1979; the sharp deterioration of the Soviet economy just before the end of the Cold War (1984–9); the investment strategies of the Organization of Petroleum Exporting Countries (OPEC) consistently over the years; the rise and fall of political leaders around the world, including the breakup of Yugoslavia in the 1990s; the threat of "aerial terrorism" in 1995, presaging the 9/11 attacks (but, unfortunately, without sufficient details to intercept the airplane hijackers before they carried out their plan); forecasting the difficulties of a post-invasion Iraqi society in 2002; and assisting the Ukrainians anticipate the when and where of Russian military operations against their nation in 2022–3.

Most of the IC's major mistakes during the Cold War were about what the Kremlin intended, not what weapons systems the communist empire possessed. The ability to track the numbers and capabilities of Soviet weaponry was vital during the superpower confrontation, and remains so today with Russia (and China). Moreover, weapons-reduction negotiations with the Russians and others contiunue to depend on the ability of the intelligence agencies to detect any significant violation of arms accords – a process known as verification. "Trust but verify" was a famous and wise arms control slogan adhered to by the Reagan Administration during the 1980s.

Examples on the debit side of analysis include: the failure to predict the outbreak of the Korean War in 1950, or the initial placement of Soviet offensive missiles in Cuba in 1962; the reporting – especially by U.S. Air Force Intelligence – of a (nonexistent) bomber and missile gap between the Soviet Union and the United States in the 1950s and early 1960s; underestimating during the Vietnam War the supplies coming to the Viet Cong through Cambodia; underestimating the pace of the Soviet strategic weapons program throughout the Cold War; faulty forecasts about the Soviet invasions of Hungary in 1956 and again in Czechoslovakia in 1968, the Arab–Israeli War in 1973, and the fall of the Shah of Iran in 1979; and a lack of precise predictions about the collapse of the Soviet empire in 1989–91 – although the CIA tracked its economic decline and rising political turmoil more closely than critics concede.[31] Mistakes regarding supposed WMDs in Iraq in 2002 arose as a result of limited humint in the country, poor vetting of the few humint sources that were available (Curveball, for instance), overreaction to an earlier underestimating of Iraq's weapons prowess in 1990, and too close political ties between the DCI and the Bush II White House.[32] Attacks by "lone wolf" terrorists have also taken the United States by surprise from time to time, as in San Bernardino, California (2015) and Orlando, Florida (2016), along with more recent mass shootings in various locations in the United States by domestic extremists armed with AK-style rifles.

More recently, the IC was taken by surprise with the sudden cratering of the government in Kabul as U.S. forces departed from Afghanistan in 2021. The Afghan Army disintegrated overnight in the face of Taliban invaders, despite the years and billions of dollars spent by the United States and its allies in training and arming these soldiers to defend their homeland. On top of that came the loss of life of 2,461 Americans in uniform stationed in that country. Even the Covid-19 pandemic proved impossible for intelligence analysts to fully understand. Did it germinate from "wet" shopping markets in China, where the sale of bats and other exotic foods takes place in unsanitary conditions? Or was the disease a product of a Chinese biological laboratory accident? Despite considerable effort to answer this question, no one knows for sure one way or the other – at least outside of officials in Beijing.

In a nutshell, NIEs have been uneven in their capacity to provide officials with accurate forecasts about history's probable trajectory, especially when it comes to details. Long-range prognosticating is a skill that diminishes the farther one attempts to peer into the future. "The CIA Directorate of Science and Technology has not yet developed a crystal ball," Frank Church cautioned; he added: "Though the CIA did give an exact warning of the date when Turkey would invade Cyprus [in 1974], such precision will be rare. Simply too many unpredictable factors enter into most situations. The intrinsic element of caprice in the affairs of men and nations is the hair shirt of the intelligence estimator."[33] When it comes to predictions, recall too Professor Betts's conclusion at the beginning of this chapter that "some incidence of failure [is] inevitable." The bottom line: in a reeling world with multiple "iron curtains" concealing the disquieting activities of authoritarian regimes, information is usually scarce or ambiguous, and the situation in question may be fluid and changing. Former intelligence officer Arthur S. Hulnick advises that "policy makers may have to accept the fact that all intelligence estimators can really hope to do is to give them guidelines or scenarios to support policy discussion, and not the predictions they so badly want and expect from intelligence."[34]

This realistic sense of limitations is unhappy news for presidents and cabinet secretaries who seek clear-cut answers, not hunches and hypotheses; but such is the reality of national security intelligence. It bears repeating, though, that having intelligence agencies closely examining world affairs is better than operating blindly. As a CIA analyst writes: "There is no substitute for the depth, imaginativeness, and 'feel' that experienced, first-rate analysts and estimators can bring to the often semi-unknowable questions handed them."[35] Even if NIEs are less than perfect instruments for forecasting future events, they have the virtue of gathering together in one place a dependable set of facts about a situation abroad. This frees up decision-makers to focus attention on sorting out the disagreements they might have over which policy options to choose. Former NSA Director William Odom states this case: "The estimate process has the healthy effect of making analysts communicate and share evidence. If the NIEs performed no other service, they would still be entirely worth the effort."[36] Almost fifty years ago, Kent noted, too, that "the intelligence estimate will have made its contribution in the way it promoted a more thorough and enlightened debate."[37]

The Iraqi NIE controversy

Caught up in the swiftly moving events that followed hard upon the 9/11 attacks in 2001, DCI George Tenet never got around to ordering the preparation of an NIE on Al Qaeda or on suspected Iraqi WMDs. Neither did the White House. Reportedly, advisors to President George W. Bush feared that a full-blown Estimate on the WMD question would reveal "disagreements over details in almost every aspect of the Administration's case against Iraq."[38]

The lack of an NIE on Iraqi WMDs at the very time the United States was engaged in an important internal debate over whether to launch a war against Saddam Hussein's regime was unfortunate. Rumors about WMDs in Iraq were rife and inflamed by references to "mushroom clouds" appearing on American soil, expressed to the American public by President Bush and National Security Advisor Condoleezza Rice (among others in the Administration).[39] Tenet has admitted his error: "An NIE on Iraq should have been initiated earlier, but at the time I didn't think one was necessary. I was wrong."[40]

Senators Richard Durban (D, Illinois) and Carl Levin (D, Michigan), both members of the Senate Select Committee on Intelligence, believed at the time that a NIE would be important in the debate over a possible war against Iraq. They insisted on a formal written assessment and persuaded SSCI Chairman Bob Graham (D, Florida) to send a letter on September 10, 2002, to Tenet requesting that an Estimate on Iraq be prepared as soon as possible.[41]

Tenet replied that he would be unable to produce the kind of comprehensive NIE on Iraq that Graham sought, because of other pressing intelligence duties – this despite the fact that the United States was on the precipice of a major war! Nevertheless, he promised to furnish, as soon as possible, a less elaborate Estimate on the subject of WMDs in Iraq.[42] The DCI ordered a "crash project" to meet SSCI's request. The ninety-page NIE went to the Senate about three weeks after the request – too hastily prepared, in the view of critics. One reporter called it "the worst body of work in [the CIA's] long history."[43] The document arrived at SSCI's quarters in the Hart Office Building in early October and Tenet went to brief the committee's members on its main points. In retrospect, Senator Graham feels the DCI seemed to skate over dissenting views that downplayed the Iraqi WMD threat.[44]

Senators Graham, Durbin, and Levin next sought to have the NIE declassified for public consumption, except for portions that might disclose sensitive intelligence sources and methods. They made the request on October 2, 2002, and two days later Tenet delivered an unclassified, twenty-five-page version of the longer document. The problem, from Graham's point of view, was that the new version "did not accurately represent the classified NIE we had received just days earlier."[45] Missing was the sense imparted in some passages of the longer, still-classified document that Saddam, if left alone, posed no immediate danger to the United States or his neighbors. In Graham's opinion, Tenet had diluted the original document to keep in step with the opinion of the White House that Saddam was a serious menace to the United States.[46] Republican Senator Chuck Hagel (Nebraska) concluded that the condensed NIE was "doctored" to suit the political needs of the White House.[47]

The Key Judgments section of the original NIE was not released until July 16, 2003 (the invasion of Iraq began four months earlier, on March 19, 2003). Only on June 1, 2004 – almost a year into the war in Iraq – did Tenet provide a more complete, but still redacted, version of the KJ section. In a report released in July 2004, SSCI concluded that the NIE's KJs were, for the most part, "either overstated, or were not supported by the underlying intelligence reporting."[48] Then only much later, in 2007, in a memoir published as the war in Iraq lingered on, did Tenet acknowledge that "we should have said, in effect, that the intelligence was not sufficient to prove beyond a reasonable doubt that Saddam had WMD." The DCI said that he now believed "more accurate and nuanced findings would have made for a more vigorous debate – and would have served the country better."[49]

Current versus research intelligence

A vital question for any nation is how many resources should be devoted to the production of current intelligence, at the expense of preparing more deeply considered products of research intelligence like the NIE. In capitals around the world, most policy officials prefer to receive current rather than research intelligence. Indeed, policymakers in the United States have rated NIEs eighth in value among the intelligence products they received, according to former CIA senior analyst Mark M. Lowenthal, who has noted further that the Intelligence Community has more recently "put its greatest emphasis on shorter, more current products," a response to "a fairly consistent decline in policymaker interest in intelligence community products as they get longer and more removed from more current issues."[50]

The upshot is that about 80–90 percent of the analytic resources of the U.S. Intelligence Community is now dedicated to clarifying for policymakers what happened today and yesterday, and what is likely to happen tomorrow – the essence of "current intelligence."[51] According to Lowenthal, the IC has "gotten out of the knowledge-building business. Now it is: current, current, current."[52] A former CIA deputy director for intelligence points out, however, that "a bunch of research intelligence is done, not necessarily estimative – just everything we know about subject X. Then someone says, 'It's about time we do a formal Estimate.'"[53]

A yardstick for intelligence reports

Whatever the type (current or research-oriented), all intelligence reports should attempt to honor the basic canons of professional analysis. Among the major hallmarks of an outstanding intelligence report, the first requirement is to get the facts right. In this sense, intelligence analysis resembles university research, with its emphasis on fact-driven conclusions – only government analysts have access to all the secret int data that can enrich the reality of what they are writing about. On the downside, analysts face the pressures of time constraints: policymakers want information *now*, not tomorrow or in a few months. Another difference is that intelligence analysts are expected to stay away from policy prescriptions. That's the job of policymakers. The analyst's job is to provide policymakers with the best Truth – objective assessment – he or she can muster. In contrast, many university researchers propose policy recommendations based on their findings.

Accuracy

In 1999, the American comedian Jay Leno quipped that "CIA" must stand for "Can't Identify Anything." He directed this remark toward the wrong U.S. intelligence service. In fact, a rookie intelligence officer in the NGA accidentally forwarded to a NATO bomber pilot in Europe out-of-date coordinates for an arms depot in Serbia (a country NATO was at war against at the time). That building, unfortunately, had been recently sold to China as a space for its embassy in Belgrade. Several Chinese were killed in this accidental bombing and many people in China and elsewhere continue to believe the bombing was done on purpose. Obviously, the intelligence agencies must provide accurate information, although within limits of course; no realistic policymaker expects IC clairvoyance about future world events. What can be expected, though, is that the analyst has carefully gathered and laid out all the facts – not pulled the incorrect data out of a drawer.

Timeliness

Important, too, is the quality of timeliness. History runs on nimble feet, and if intelligence reports lag too far behind events, they are likely to be of little use to a decision-maker. The result may be the dreaded (for an analyst) acronym "OBE" scrawled across a report: "Overtaken by events."

Relevance

Policymakers have no interest in receiving an intelligence report on local elections in Greenland when their in-box is filled with decisions that have to be made about such events as the ongoing war between Russia and Ukraine, or atrocities in a Sudanese civil war. Sometimes intelligence analysts wish to write about their own interests or specialty, perhaps derived from their PhD dissertation topic – for example, "Rural Politics in Outer Mongolia." If analysts are out of tune, however, with the consumers they serve when it comes to a topical focus, they may as well go on a fishing trip; consumers will have no time for their esoteric analysis. Again, the egotistic "self-licking ice cream cone" phenomenon.

The best intelligence reports are tailored to address the most pressing problems awaiting action within a decision-maker's in-box. This reality underscores the value of close – yet nonpolitical – ties between intelligence producers and consumers, brought about by forward liaison teams and periodic meetings between the two groups. In 1996, the International Affairs Division of the EPA experimented with having a CIA forward-liaison staffer attend its daily management meetings. This CIA officer was able to learn close-hand what problems the EPA was addressing. As a result, she could then return the next day with helpful data and reports from the DCI's Center for Environmental Intelligence. The EPA and the CIA quickly established a good working relationship, which gave the EPA valuable information about global environmental matters drawn from the IC's extensive satellite and other forms of image surveillance of the Earth's surface. Here is an example of a model consumer–producer relationship.

Readability

Considerable effort goes into making intelligence reports inviting to read: the four-color quality of the *PDB*, for instance, fully equipped with charts, graphs, and photographs – all on high-quality paper. It is not enough to write a solid intelligence assessment about some event or condition in the world; the report must be *marketed* as well, to catch the attention of bustling policy officials. The language must be straightforward, too, even if the subject is economics and the temptation to use econometrics and abstract jargon is great. Policymakers have a low tolerance for the obscure, and few have doctorates in economics.

Brevity

Like many overworked government leaders, the great Secretary of State George Catlett Marshall placed a premium on succinct reporting. When George F. Kennan became the first director of the Policy Planning Staff in the State Department, he asked Marshall what his instructions were. "Avoid trivia," the General replied. British Prime Minister Winston S. Churchill felt the same way. In a compliment to one of his favorite policy advisors, Churchill referred to him as Lord Heart-of-the-Matter during cabinet meetings. Praise descends upon those analysts – report writers and oral briefers – who cut to the chase. As legendary CIA analyst Douglas J. MacEachin liked to tell CIA recruits: "A snappy march through the evidence, followed by a delineation of the analytic logic for any conclusions makes for a short, punchy paper." Or, as Shakespeare put it snappily: "Brevity is the soul of wit."

Imagination

The best analysts attempt to think imaginatively about how an adversary might try to harm the United States and other democracies, peering ahead as best they can to comprehend challenges that have not yet fully developed but which could become major dangers at some point in the future. Would a terrorist organization resort to aerial terrorism aimed at the skyscrapers of New York City? Here was a question insufficiently weighed up by analysts – and policymakers – before the 9/11 attacks that would ultimately provide a tragic and irrevocable answer. Analysts must think creatively in addressing possible global developments. What are the most vulnerable targets inside the United States today for traditional military adversaries, terrorists, and foreign intelligence services? What are the likely strategic objectives of China in the South China Sea, or Russia on its border with Eastern Europe beyond Ukraine? What are the odds that a missile might strike the United States without anyone in Washington knowing who fired it – a troubling "attribution" problem? How likely is it that a pandemic might again sweep from China or Africa and around the world? To what extent is environmental degradation dangerous to U.S. national security interests?

Jointness

The United States presently has eighteen major intelligence agencies, plus a range of ints, for a reason: the world is large and several approaches to intelligence-gathering are necessary to ferret out the information Washington leaders hope to have. Yet a fragmented flow of information to decision councils from eighteen different "hoses" around the IC would be overwhelming and confusing. Instead, contemporary presidents and other leaders (just like Truman in 1947) want all-source fusion – the thoughtful blending of all the int findings into comprehensive intelligence reporting. This requires the sharing and integration of intelligence findings, which the Kean Commission inquiry found to be the weakest link in America's IC in the run-up to the 9/11 tragedy.

Objectivity

Intelligence reports must be free of political considerations and attempts to please decision-makers – a cardinal requirement. The Nazi Foreign Minister Joachim von Ribbentrop issued orders to his ministry stating that anyone who reported intelligence that contradicted the views of Der Führer should think again, hinting that a person found guilty of this offense would face an unpleasant outcome.[54] With these sorts of edicts traveling out from Berlin to the various bureaucratic entities of the Third Reich, the end result was predictable: Hitler and his retinue descended deeper and deeper into self-delusion, cut off from accurate information about the progress of the war against Britain, Russia, the United States, and other allied powers.

A strong sense of professional ethics keeps most intelligence officers in the democracies on the straight and narrow path of honest reporting. Occasionally, though, some individuals have set aside this sense of ethics, as when DCI Allen Dulles failed to stand up to inflated DoD estimates on Soviet bomber production rates; or when DCI Richard Helms deleted a paragraph from an Estimate on Soviet missilery, under pressure from the Nixon Administration to paint a more frightening portrait of America's Cold War enemy.[55] This "politicization" of intelligence is much more likely to come from the consumer side of the intelligence equation, as the less scrupulous of democracy's policymakers cherry-pick intelligence reports and otherwise bend and twist the findings to suit their own political agendas. The most effective guard against the politicization trap is to engage in unalloyed honesty with policymakers about a report's evidence, premises, and inferences.

Specificity

Finally, and among the most difficult objectives of all, the best intelligence reports carry a sufficient degree of specificity to provide policymakers with an ability to take action. Intelligence officers are often able to monitor an increase in the flow of messages between members of an adversarial group or nation – perhaps, the telephone conversations of ISIS lieutenants. This kind of "traffic analysis" that reveals an increase in enemy communications – more "chatter" – can be valuable, triggering a greater concentration of ints toward the target. Yet even more useful would be a quick deciphering of the encoded messages and translation of them into English, which might point to an enemy's precise attack plans. In short, vague airport "orange alerts" about possible terrorist attacks provide little help; what is necessary are a terrorist organization's detailed attack plans – *actionable intelligence, timely delivered*. The analyst must be explicit and honest, though, about the limits of data in a report, clearly conveying a sense of his or her level of confidence about the findings.

This list of intelligence reporting attributes adds up to a lofty set of standards, on top of which comes the necessity of reliable access to top policymakers. Given a lack of rapport at the level of intelligence dissemination, the intelligence will likely go unread or fall on deaf ears. (As Intelligence Studies scholar Gregory F. Treverton has said to the author, here is a key question – especially in this age of ubiquitous disinformation: "Is anyone listening?") That is why the relationship between top intelligence managers – the DNI and the various IC agency directors – and senior policy officials is so important. DCI James Woolsey was rarely able to sit down with President Clinton and talk about intelligence findings; William Casey, despite his many deficiencies as DCI, enjoyed open access to President Reagan and, as a result, could return to Langley with full knowledge of the main foreign policy problems confronting the Administration. The current (as I write) D/CIA, William J. Burns, also enjoys access to President Joe Biden. Access, access, access – an indispensable ingredient for the achievement of initial intelligence "tasking" (that is, recall, the official listing of desired targets for intelligence collection worldwide) and, at the other end of the "intelligence cycle," for the dissemination of key analytic findings.

Often the Intelligence Community will fall short of these demanding standards, because of inadequate collection (during the war in Vietnam, for example, the CIA was never able to penetrate the North Vietnamese government with an effective spy[56]); the slow translation of foreign language and coded materials; flawed analyses; the political misuse of reports by policymakers; or a lack of timely access to the President and other top officials. Despite such challenges, the secret agencies must aim for the highest possible quality in intelligence reporting; policymakers must constantly resist the temptation to twist these reports for political purposes; and both the producers and consumers of intelligence must develop bonds of trust and rapport – but not a political alliance – in their common quest for better information to guide decision-making.[57]

As for NIEs, they often make a contribution in the mix of products for policymakers, but improvements are necessary. Estimates have to be more nuanced, with dissents – sometimes known by analysts as "footnote wars" – boldly presented ("flagged"), including both within the body of the text and in the Key Judgments or "executive summary" portion of the report. Their production levels ought to rise as well (in one year under DCI George H.W. Bush, the Intelligence Community produced only five NIEs); they need to be shorter (usually thirty pages or less, rather than one hundred pages as is sometimes the case); and they should be completed in six months at the most – and much faster in emergencies. Moving the ODNI to Langley would also make sense from the point-of-view of the NIE production process (and also the *PDB*). After all, the vast majority of the government's top strategic analysts are located in the CIA's Directorate of Analysis (DA) and the NIC, not in the ODNI at Liberty Crossing, miles away from Langley. The production facilities for the *PDB*, NIEs, and other intelligence reports are also at Langley.

Co-location

Some reformers have long believed that the preparation of intelligence reports could be improved by having a closer relationship between operatives and analysts at the CIA. The operatives in the DO enjoy "ground truth" about countries overseas, since that is where they serve on the ground, using official or nonofficial cover. This gives them a certain inside knowledge, from café life and back-alley meetings to the nuances of local slang. The analysts are experts about foreign countries, too, and periodically travel abroad, but for shorter periods of time. Their primary knowledge comes from study within their home agencies; they typically have a PhD that reflects their advanced book-learning and research on international affairs and comparative politics. Though quite different in their career paths and daily experiences, both groups can bring something to the table when a specific nation or region is the focus of U.S. attention. Yet operatives and analysts traditionally have offices in separate corridors at the CIA, behind doors with combination locks that bar any outsiders from entering. This can have unfortunate consequences.

For example, in the planning that went into the Bay of Pigs covert action in 1961, the DO operatives were enthusiastic and confident about the prospects of a relatively easy overthrow of Fidel Castro; the people of Cuba would supposedly rise up against the dictator once the Agency had landed its paramilitary force on the island beaches. In another part of the CIA, however, DI analysts with expertise on Cuba understood that an uprising was highly unlikely; as they spelled out in a SNIE in December 1960, the people of Cuba revered their leader (Fidel Castro) and would resist a CIA invasion force door-to-door in Havana and across the island. The DO could have benefited significantly from rubbing shoulders with their colleagues in the DI (as the DA was then called). Perhaps that interaction would have brought a stronger dose of realism to the DO's planning. Nor was President Kennedy made aware of the DI's views on the unlikely success of this scheme. The head of the Bay of Pigs planning, Richard Bissell, was enthusiastic about the paramilitary operation and the possibility of a promotion that a successful overthrow of

Castro might bring to him personally in the CIA leadership hierarchy. He had some hallway knowledge of the skeptical SNIE, but never detailed enough to bring it to the President's attention.[58]

Aware of this physical and cultural distance between the DO and the DI, John Deutch took steps as DCI in 1995 to improve the cooperation between the two groups at Langley, by physically moving together elements of both Directorates. In 2009, D/CIA Leon Panetta announced there would be "more co-location of analysts and operators at home and abroad" in the coming years, adding that greater fusion of these separate Agency units "has been key to victories in counterterrorism and counterproliferation."[59] In 2010, he announced the formation of a CIA Counterproliferation Center to combat the global spread of WMDs. In the Center, which would report to Panetta and further upward to the DNI's National Counterproliferation Center, operatives and analysts would work together cheek-by-jowl in the spirit of co-location.[60] Panetta's successor John Brennan, who assumed office in 2013, pushed the CIA even further in this direction, with a major integration of operatives and researchers through the Agency's Headquarters Building.

Intelligence dissemination

Once prepared by analysts, intelligence reports are distributed to those who make decisions (and their top aides). This may seem easy enough, but even this phase of the intelligence cycle is rife with possibilities for error. For one thing, as often alluded to earlier in this volume, policy officials are often too busy to read documents provided to them by the IC. "I rarely have more than five minutes each day to read intelligence reports," an Assistant Secretary of Defense (a former Rhodes scholar and Harvard University professor) told the Aspin–Brown Commission in 1995.[61] Other barriers to listening by the intelligence consumer audience, which can lead to the disregard or warping of the value-added that decision-makers could gain from careful attention to the facts and thoughtful assessments provided by IC reporting, include arrogance, shortsightedness, laziness, and the corrosive effects of power. That a nation may spend a king's ransom on the collection and analysis of national security intelligence, only to have the findings ignored by distracted decision-makers, is a troublesome paradox. No wonder Intelligence Studies scholar Betts concludes that "the typical problem at the highest levels of government is less often the misuse of intelligence than the non-use."[62] Misuse occurs as well, though – all too often, as when leaders select the portions of a report they like and dismiss the rest (known as intelligence cherry-picking).

In 2003, Secretary of State Colin Powell of the Bush II Administration addressed the UN Security Council in a successful attempt to convince that organization's membership that a U.S. invasion of Iraq was justified. Without sufficient probing into the authenticity of intelligence reports from the CIA and its companion agencies, the Secretary declared that Baghdad did indeed possess unconventional weaponry – a "fact," he added, that was based on "solid intelligence." The intelligence was not solid and proved wrong. From the vantage point of retirement years later, Powell wished ruefully in his memoirs that he had posed tougher questions to the leaders of the IC about their hunches related to WMDs in Iraq; he regretted that neither he nor his aides had stood up during their intelligence briefings that proceeded the Iraqi invasion and said: "We really don't know that! We can't trust that! You can't say that!" Instead, the Bush II Administration slipped further and further into a make-believe world that led to an expensive and unnecessary war.

Always of concern is the proper personal relationship between analysts and decision-makers. If a NIO becomes too cozy with those in power, the danger of politicization rises as the analyst may be tempted to bend intelligence in support of policy objectives – what is known as "intelligence to please." Yet if the NIO is too detached and unaware of the policy issues faced by a decision-maker, an intelligence report risks being completely ignored. It is worth emphasizing again: the skillful analyst will carefully navigate between this Scylla and Charybdis, developing rapport with policymakers to understand better their in-box pressures, while keeping a distance from the politics of an administration.

An important debate on this topic revolves around whether DNIs, D/CIAs, and other intelligence managers and analysts should enter into discussions with decision-makers about policy recommendations. Or should they, rather, maintain a strict "no-cross zone" between the presentation of facts – a universally acknowledged intelligence duty – and commenting on ideal policy directions? Richard Helms, DCI from 1966 to 1973, argued for neutrality; so did the pioneering CIA analyst Sherman Kent, who believed that a high wall should exist between intelligence and policy officers. As Helms put it:

> My view was that the DCI should be the man who called things the way he saw them, the purpose of this being to give the President one man in his Administration who was not trying to formulate a policy, carry out a policy, or defend a policy. In other words, this was the man who attempted to keep the game honest. When you sit around the table and the Secretary of State is propounding this and defending this, and the Secretary of Defense is defending this and propounding that, the President has the right to hear somebody who says: "Now listen, this isn't my understanding of the facts" or "That isn't the way it worked."[63]

Other intelligence officials, though, such as DCIs John A. McCone (1961–5) and William J. Casey (1981–7), have taken an active – often aggressive – role in debates over policy options.[64] McCone even strongly recommended a military invasion of Cuba in 1962 during the missile crisis; and Casey is known to have torn up a NIE on Mexico and written his own version – one that portrayed

Mexico as highly susceptible to communist influence and a growing danger to the United States. Whatever one's philosophy on this subject of intelligence activism versus neutrality, it might be difficult at times in practical terms to stay apart from the policy fray as an intelligence officer. A senior analyst has noted: "When it's 8:30 at night and the Undersecretary of State says, 'What do you think I should do?', you can't say at that point: 'That's not my job, Mr. Secretary.' You just can't do that."[65] One solution followed by DCI Woolsey was to stay out of policy debates until after the formal NSC meeting was over and the Cabinet Room in the White House cleared; then, if asked, he offered President Bill Clinton his personal views at that time.

At any rate, the most important obligation of an analyst or an intelligence manager is to resist political pressures from those in high office to twist intelligence in a manner that suits an administration's policy preferences, at the expense of the true, factual meaning of an intelligence report. Here is the soul-destroying sin of politicized intelligence – the gravest hazard to the successful completion of the intelligence cycle.

With respect to the Iraqi WMD controversy in 2002, the DCI at the time, George Tenet, had an obligation to spell out for President George W. Bush the weaknesses in the intelligence reporting. Shortcomings in the Iraqi WMD data were improperly dealt with in Great Britain as well. The Prime Minister's communications director gave the British people the impression that Iraq had WMDs that could strike the British Isles, even though MI6's intelligence reporting on this subject noted only that Iraq probably had tactical (not strategic) WMDs that might well be used against a British and American invasion force on the battlefield in Iraq. Neither the Prime Minister nor the Director of MI6 ever corrected the distorted record presented by the UK's political leaders, which helped turn British public opinion more toward a pro-invasion stance out of fear that Saddam Hussein harbored nuclear, and perhaps even chemical and biological, weapons that could rain down on London and other targets close to home.[66]

The ongoing quest for better collection and analysis

Despite the well-intended efforts of many intelligence officers and policy-makers to make the intelligence cycle function smoothly, serious questions remain about the usefulness of the information provided by the IC to high councils of government. Even with the staggering amount of money spent each year on gathering and analyzing NSI, many consumers find its products lacking. "We never used the CIA stuff," recalled a former U.S. ambassador and assistant secretary of state. "It was irrelevant."[67] A survey of intelligence consumers conducted by the Senate Select Committee on Intelligence during the 1980s revealed widespread disdain toward the value of the IC's analytic work. Most widely reported was the sweeping indictment of the CIA expressed by Senator Daniel Patrick Moynihan (D, New York), for – in his view – the Agency's failure to predict the fall of the Soviet Union.[68]

Moreover, in the months prior to the 9/11 attacks against the United States, the CIA and the FBI blundered repeatedly in their counterterrorism activities, from failing to investigate suspicious behavior by foreigners in the United States seeking flight training for large commercial airliners to mix-ups in tracking known terrorists who entered the nation in early 2001 and would soon join other 9/11 hijackers.[69] The intelligence mistakes then multiplied in 2002 with the poor collection of information and faulty analysis related to suspected WMDs in Iraq. Examples include German intelligence and CIA gullibility over the trustworthiness of Curveball, as well as toward the pro-war lobbying in Washington of a self-serving Iraqi exile group; confusion over whether Saddam Hussein had purchased large amounts of yellow-cake uranium from Niger; facile (and false) conclusions reached about how Iraqi fire trucks spotted in the Iraqi desert indicated the presence of a biological weapons capability; how UAVs that the U.S. Air Force firmly believed were conventional surveillance aircraft were seen by others in the IC as carriers for unconventional weaponry; speculation on the likely progress of an Iraqi WMD program based on extrapolation (and overestimation) to compensate for known underestimating errors in 1990; taking at face value Saddam's blustering that he had WMDs, rather than considering the possibility (which turned out to be true) that his rhetoric was a hollow attempt at a deterrence posture designed to frighten Iraq's archenemies in Tehran and keep them at arm's length. The list goes on.[70]

Yet, despite mistakes, the IC has also consistently provided valuable data and insights to policymakers about world affairs. The Aspin–Brown Commission summarized some of the successes that occurred following the end of the Cold War:[71]

- discovering North Korea's nuclear weapons program;
- blocking the sale of radioactive materials to renegade nations;
- uncovering the black-market sales of illegal WMDs;
- supporting battlefield operations in the Middle East;
- backstopping many international negotiations with reliable information;
- helping to break up drug cartels, among them the Cali organization in Colombia;
- thwarting various terrorist activities, including the capture of Carlos the Jackal, as well as the ringleader of the 1993 World Trade Center bombing and the leader of the Shining Path terrorist group in Peru;
- providing information that supported diplomatic peacekeeping initiatives around the world;
- disclosing, and thus foiling, assassination plots perpetrated by other countries overseas;

- revealing unfair global trade practices, thereby improving the chances of success for U.S. business enterprises in the developing world;
- pointing to countries that have violated trade sanctions, as well as alerting officials to approaching financial crises in foreign nations; and,
- collecting information about human rights abuses around the world, as well as warning about ecological problems and humanitarian crises.

This is only a partial list from the years 1992–5. Since then, America's spy agencies have recorded many additional successes, including the capture or killing of a large number of Al Qaeda's leaders in Pakistan (Bin Laden among them) and ISIS members in Syria, Iraq, and Libya; the tracking and countering of other ISIS- and Qaeda-affiliated terrorist cells in such places as Syria, Somalia, and Yemen; support for the wars in Iraq and Afghanistan; surveillance assistance in the responses to a variety of natural disasters, not only abroad but (with special clearances from Congress and the White House) at home as well; early warnings to President Trump in the *PDB* about the impending threat of the Covid-19 virus emanating from China; and helping the Ukraine military resist Russian aggression.

The United States and other democracies, along with their adversaries, will continue to seek improvements in their knowledge of world events. On the collection side, this will mean spending more money on technical platforms and human agents to bring about greater transparency to the planet. On the analysis side, it will mean continuing to search for the brightest and most thoughtful citizens a government can find to work as analysts: smart, dedicated, patriotic individuals who can help decision-makers make better sense of history as it unfolds – especially those threats that could be harmful to the future of global democracy.

The importance of allied intelligence liaison relations

Vital for success will be cooperation among the intelligence services of the democracies through what is known as "foreign intelligence liaison" or "burden-sharing." The world is too vast for any one democracy alone to monitor for threats and opportunities; they need cooperation from one another. As President Biden told DNI Avril D. Haines in 2023: "You have to get out there and start sharing because we've got to help them see what you're seeing."[72] Understanding this reality, five democratic nations have famously combined some of their espionage activities into a cooperative intelligence alliance for mutual protect, known as the "Five Eyes" and consisting of Australia, Canada, New Zealand, the United Kingdom, and the United States. Members of the Five Eyes share a common language, a devotion to democratic principles, cultural affinities, and a long period of trustful relationships. A recent example of their cooperation with one another was a joint advisory released in

Photo 3.1: Richard Moore
Richard Moore, chief of the UK's MI6, meets with Charles, Prince of Wales (the future King Charles III) at MI6 Headquarters in London, October 21, 2021.
Source: Office of the Chief of the Secret Intelligence Service.

2023 regarding the likely expansion of Chinese intelligence operations, from spying against the democracies to potentially actively disrupting Western communications and other vital infrastructure systems.

While this pact could be enlarged to include nations such as Germany and Japan, both of which have strong intelligence services, the prospect remains controversial. This is true not only because there are language and cultural barriers at play, but also stemming from the fact these two nations were mortal enemies to the democracies not that long ago in World War II. Of course, German and Japanese societies have changed dramatically since 1945 and are now valued members of the global democracy club, but memories linger and movement in the direction of expanding the Five Eyes membership has been slow. Further, once that door is opened, what about the other democracies? How large can an intelligence alliance become without losing its efficiency and ability to keep its secret activities secure?

Intelligence liaison arrangements can be dicey, as the Curveball example underscored in the lead-up to the 2003 war in Iraq; the spying for Russia by the rising Norwegian government official Arne Tretholt from the mid-1970s to 1985; and the MI6 Kim Philby defection to the Soviet Union in the 1960s after he insinuated himself closely with the CIA while serving in Washington,

DC. More recently, a member of the German Federal Intelligence Service (the BND) responsible for cybersecurity was found guilty of spying for Russia; and several hard-right German members of the Bundestag are known to have close ties to Moscow. Even the democracies have to be cautious about vetting information from one another. Take the relationship between the United States and Pakistan, which underscores the reality that nations can have mixed agendas. In recent years, Pakistan was helpful in some instances in providing intelligence to Washington about Al Qaeda and Taliban activities in the mountainous border in nearby Afghanistan. Yet the Pakistani intelligence service, Inter-Services Intelligence (ISI), has also attempted to run double agents against the United States; and some ISI officers are known to have close friendships and ideological ties with the Taliban and perhaps other extremist groups.[73]

Of concern, too, in liaison relationships is a reliance on foreign-partner paramilitary forces for irregular warfare carried out by the Pentagon and the CIA (taken up in detail in the next chapter of this book). In such locations as Niger and Somalia, the United States has teamed up with sometimes questionable foreign liaison groups for sabotage, computer hacking, propaganda campaigns, and other secret operations – even assassination plots – often without any consultation with the State Department. Some of these foreign groups have proven to be extremely bad actors engaged in serious human rights violations, including rape, torture, and extrajudicial killings (recall the Blackwater example). The good name of the United States is significantly stained when such liaison partnerships come to light. Several intelligence experts and members of Congress have called for the tightening of laws related to the use of proxy forces.

In frustration over the embarrassing Curveball episode, DCI Porter J. Goss vowed after 9/11 never again to rely on foreign liaison relationships – with Germany or anyone else outside the Five Eyes. And even within the Five Eyes, the history of Soviet success in penetrating MI6 with moles was (and remains) a sobering consideration – just as it was for the British with respect to moles uncovered over the years within America's spy agencies (see Chapter 5 on counterintelligence). Goss's stance against intelligence liaison relationships didn't last long, though, as he realized how important these ties with other open societies can be. As Maria Langan-Riekhof, director of the NIC, has pointed out, "Challenges aren't going to stay within the borders of a single country anymore, and we're going to feel them globally much faster."[74]

Despite the need for caution, the United States and the other democracies have much to gain from sharing their intelligence findings with one another other. The common foes of Russian imperialism (as manifested most recently in its invasion of Ukraine); unfair Chinese trade; ongoing terrorism; illegal drug dealing, sex trafficking, and other forms of international crime; and the continued worldwide proliferation of WMDs should provide adequate incentives for open societies to share their collection-and-analysis capabilities.

This book turns next to a darker side of intelligence activities: the use of secret power to manipulate – even overthrow – foreign regimes in an effort to advance the interests of one's own country, or (stated more laudably) in the interests of protecting and advancing democratic governments and principles around the world. In the adoption of "covert actions," the open societies have sometimes taken drastic steps, using their secret agencies to defend democracy in a hostile world. In the process, they have on occasion unacceptably crossed important legal and moral boundaries and stained the very principles they hoped to protect.

4

Covert Action:
Secret Attempts to Shape History

In 1960, during its final months in office, the Eisenhower Administration approved – in opaque, circumlocutional language – a CIA assassination plot against an African leader.[1] The decision was a drastic step that crossed the long-held sacrosanct line that state killings by the United States should be confined to military actions on authorized battlefields, not directed against overseas civilian officials. Murder attempts aimed at foreign heads-of-state would have the effect of opening a Pandora's box of horrors, out of which might fly a retaliatory plot against leaders in Washington, DC. This decision in the waning months of the Eisenhower Administration was a disturbing turn of events in this nation's foreign policy, and an unexpected (and highly secretive) decision from an American president.

The target was Prime Minister Patrice Lumumba, the freely elected leader of the Congo, who made a fatal error in approaching the Soviet Union for economic and military assistance – a step practically guaranteed to place the African leader on America's list of targets for a CIA-directed coup d'état, however limited and driven by national self-interest the Congo's new "friendship" with Moscow might have been. Earlier, the United States had rejected Lumumba's request for similar aid, forcing him in desperation to make his pitch for aid from the Soviet Union as an alternative.

The Kremlin jumped at the opportunity for a strategic opening in the heart of Africa, and soon, at Lumumba's invitation, ten small Soviet aircraft landed in the Congo as part of a new bilateral agreement between Moscow and Léopoldville. Though he remained an independent nationalist skillfully playing off the Kremlin against Washington, Lumumba's indiscretion placed him firmly in the CIA's crosshairs. In 1961, DCI Allen Dulles sent a cable to the Agency's COS in the Congo, with this message all in capital letters:

> IN HIGH QUARTERS HERE IT IS THE CLEAR-CUT CONCLUSION THAT IF [LUMUMBA] CONTINUES TO HOLD HIGH OFFICE, THE INEVITABLE RESULT WILL AT BEST BE CHAOS AND AT WORST PAVE THE WAY TO COMMUNIST TAKEOVER OF THE CONGO WITH DISASTROUS CONSEQUENCES FOR THE PRESTIGE OF THE UN AND FOR THE INTERESTS OF THE FREE WORLD GENERALLY. CONSEQUENTLY WE CONCLUDE THAT HIS REMOVAL MUST BE AN URGENT AND PRIME

OBJECTIVE AND THAT UNDER EXISTING CONDITIONS THIS SHOULD BE
A HIGH PRIORITY OF OUR COVERT ACTION.[2]

Concocted specially for Lumumba's lips, a powerful poison in a secret satchel
traveled from DS&T labs at Langley to the Agency's COS in the Congo. The
accompanying instructions advised that the material should be injected into
the Congo President's food, toothpaste, or whatever else might reach his
mouth.

So well-guarded was Lumumba, however, that it proved impossible for
the CIA's assets to gain direct access in the presidential palace – either to
him, his food, or his toothpaste. Unable to consummate the plot, at least
directly, the Agency nonetheless continued to pour money into the Congo,
lining the pockets of anti-Lumumba politicians. The most notably recipient
of this largess was Joseph Mobutu, who soon agreed to lead a coup against
the government as urged by the COS. The insurgency succeeded and the
United States immediately recognized the Mobutu regime. The new government quickly apprehended Lumumba and placed him under house arrest,
which at least shielded him from another CIA poisoning attempt, since the
UN provided guards for their high-level prisoner while he was held captive.
Lumumba managed to escape his confinement, but he was soon recaptured,
jailed in a military prison, and beaten regularly by Mobutu's henchmen.

When the CIA's own assassination efforts against Lumumba ground to a
halt through lack of access, the COS in Leopoldville – with the "roguery of
an old elephant" (in a Graham Greene phrase for overly adventurous spies) –
proved more successful in working with the Belgian intelligence service, the
Sûreté de l'état, toward the same objective. The government of Belgium also
wanted Lumumba out of the picture and, with the help of local "cut-outs"
(intermediary assets), the Agency and Sûreté de l'état managed between them
to maneuver the deposed president into a meeting held in the countryside
with another Congolese faction that opposed him. The pretext was to seek
a negotiated settlement of their disputes. As anticipated by the CIA and its
Belgian cohort, as well as by the Mobutu regime, in a succession of deteriorat-
ing circumstances this rival group apprehended Lumumba, beat him almost
to death, then placed him before a firing squad in a remote savanna on the
outskirts of Elisabethville.

However indirectly, and thanks largely to the local experience and contacts
of the Belgian spy service, the CIA had achieved the goal of the Eisenhower
Administration to eliminate Patrice Lumumba from the scene. Was his death
necessary for the security of the United States? The incoming Administration,
led by President John F. Kennedy, didn't think so; and the Agency's own director at the time, Allen Dulles, subsequently viewed the Congolese covert action
as superfluous and the danger that Lumumba posed "overrated."[3]

Covert action as an intelligence mission

Legal underpinnings

In the United States, covert action (CA) is sometimes referred to as the "quiet option" by officials inside the CIA, the organization normally called upon to plan and implement this approach to solving America's problems abroad through secret operations. The phrase is drawn from the questionable assumption that covert action is likely to be less noisy and obtrusive than sending in a Marine brigade. While sometimes this is the case, there was nothing quiet about covert action at the Bay of Pigs in 1961, or against the Taliban regime in Afghanistan after the 9/11 attacks. Another label is the "third option," pointing to CA as a choice that lies somewhere between diplomacy and overt warfare. As explained by Henry Kissinger, Secretary of State during the Nixon Administration: "We need an intelligence community that, in certain complicated situations, can defend the American national interest in the gray areas where military operations are not suitable and diplomacy cannot operate."[4] A favorite euphemism for CA in more recent years, beginning with the Carter Administration, is the anodyne phrase "special activities."

In 1990, Congress provided, for the first time, a formal statutory definition of this heavily veiled side of American foreign policy: "An activity or activities of the United States Government to influence political, economic, or military conditions abroad, where it is intended that the role of the United States Government will not be apparent or acknowledged publicly."[5] Specifically excluded from the definition were intelligence collection and counterintelligence operations; traditional diplomatic, military, and law enforcement activities; or routine support to overt U.S. activities aboard. Stripped down further to the basics, CA may be thought of as "those activities CIA undertakes to influence events overseas that are intended not to be attributable to this country."[6] Simpler still: "Covert action is influence."[7] Prior to detailed legislative authority for CA enacted by Congress in 1992, presidents relied on a boilerplate clause in the National Security Act of 1947 for its legal justification. This founding statute for modern U.S. intelligence focused almost exclusively on the collection-and-analysis mission. Then, in a final section, the law (drafted mainly by one of President Truman's top national security aides, Clark Clifford) provided gauzy authority for the new DCI and the Agency to perform "such other functions and duties related to intelligence affecting the national security as the President or the National Security Council may direct."[8]

Rationale

Behind this spongy legal language lies the reality that covert action is nothing less than a nation's attempt to change the course of history through the

Photo 4.1: DCI Colby
DCI William E. Colby at a National Security Council meeting in the White House, 1975.
Source: Gerald R. Ford White House Photographs, National Archives.

use of secret operations against other nations, terrorist groups, or factions – "giving history a push," as a senior CIA operative has put it.[9] Throughout the course of World War II, the Special Operations Executive (SOE) in Britain and the Office of Strategic Services (OSS, its U.S. counterpart) were influential forerunners in the uses of covert action, with the Third Reich serving as the enemy target. Both organizations relied on the courage of men and women in their ranks to, as Churchill urged at the time, "set Europe ablaze" by blowing up bridges and railroads, while inciting internal opposition inside Hitler's Germany.

Subsequently, during the Cold War, the main concern of the Agency's Covert Action Staff within the Operations Directorate (the CAS, now known as the Special Activities or SA Division) was, according to one of its leaders, "the global challenge of communism ... to be confronted whenever and wherever it seemed to threaten our interests."[10]

A Cold War DCI, William E. Colby (1973–6), reasoned that CA was vital to counteract the political and subversive threat posed by the secret operations of the Soviet intelligence services (the KGB and the GRU) in Europe and around the world – just as NATO provided a critical line of military defense in Western Europe and the Marshall Plan erected a bulwark of foreign aid to counter Soviet economic encroachments. When threats arise to America's interests in the world, "it is better that we have the ability to help people in these countries where that will happen, quietly and secretly," Colby advised, "and not wait until we are faced with a military threat that has to be met by armed force."[11]

Thus, taking a stand against communism became the primary *raison d'être* for covert action during the Cold War. Whether such targets as Iran (1953), Guatemala (1954), Angola (1975), and Chile (1964–72) qualified as "truly important" (in Colby's phrase) is a matter of dispute. With respect to Angola, a CIA official maintained that, "ultimately, the purpose was to throw the Soviets out, at which point we would leave, too." Critics, though, find these arguments unpersuasive. For example, with respect to CIA covert actions against Nicaragua during the 1980s, the German Nobel laureate in literature, Günter Grass, asked plaintively: "How impoverished must a country be before it is not a threat to the U.S. government?"[12] Senator Frank Church, who led a Senate inquiry into the subject of CA in 1975, concluded that "our targets were leaders of small, weak countries that could not possibly threaten the United States."[13]

The implementation of covert action

The CIA is almost always the organization called upon by the President and the NSC to conduct covert actions. The Agency's infrastructure for this purpose ("the plumbing," in CIA-speak) consists of the DO; the Special Activities (SA) Division, along with its paramilitary wing, the Special Operations Group (SOG); overseas stations and bases; personnel on loan from the military; and civilian contractors. For much of the Agency's early history, the role of the President in the approval of a CA was meant to be tightly concealed, through the practice of "plausible deniability." According to this "doctrine," presidents should be as pure as Caesar's wife; the reputation of the United States had to be protected if a CA ran amok and ended up on the front pages of the world's newspapers. Keeping the White House at a distance from unsavory activities would allow the President to say publicly: "I never authorized that inappropriate secret operation, and I am taking measures to punish those who carried it out."

Yet when the President is kept at arm's length from covert actions as they are carried out overseas, the operations lack the proper accountability that comes with explicit White House approval. With no paper trail leading to the Oval Office and the operations surrounded in darkness, the danger arises that a CA may be pursued even without the President's imprimatur – or even knowledge. President Eisenhower rejected the plausible denial approach in 1960, when the Soviets shot down a CIA U-2 spy plane over their territory on the eve of a Washington–Moscow summit. He chose to acknowledge responsibility publicly for the risky reconnaissance mission. The U-2 flight was a collection operation, not a covert action; nonetheless, for the first time, accountability had overruled plausible denial with respect to an intelligence activity. The implication was that presidents might henceforth take direct responsibility for covert actions, as well. The doctrine of plausible deniability proved more enduring than some anticipated, however. Not until the mid-1970s, in the midst of a spy scandal in the United States, did Congress at last decide to bury the doctrine of plausible deniability. With the Hughes–Ryan Act of 1974, lawmakers enacted legislation that required explicit presidential approval for all important CAs. Such operations would now have to be more clearly authorized from the top – indeed, explicitly signed off by the nation's chief executive. Further, in an even greater departure from tradition, any important CA approved by the President would have to be reported to special panels of accountability in Congress. In an unprecedented move, lawmakers would now be part of the covert action decision process.

In the aftermath of the 9/11 attacks and America's involvement in wars in Iraq and Afghanistan, another serious question arose about the challenge of maintaining accountability in the implementation of covert actions. This new concern came about as a result of the Pentagon's Special Forces and CIA private contractors edging their way into this domain.[14] The questionable use of organizations in addition to the Agency for covert action had already produced a scandal of major proportions during the Reagan Administration: the Iran–*contra* affair. These covert actions, which involved a secret arms sale to Iran and escalating CA activities in Nicaragua, were never properly reported to Congress, as required by the Hughes–Ryan Amendment and the even more strongly worded Intelligence Oversight Act of 1980.[15] Further, the Reagan Administration violated the Boland Amendments – a series of increasingly restrictive laws, named after their chief sponsor, the Chair of the House Permanent Select Committee on Intelligence Edward P. Boland (D, Massachusetts), and passed in the early 1980s. These amendments expressly prohibited covert actions in support of the *contras* in Nicaragua, who were attempting to overthrow the democratically elected, left-leaning Sandinista regime. The Carter Administration had previously recognized the Sandinistas as Nicaragua's legitimate government.

Staff on the NSC, including two consecutive National Security Advisors, schemed to bypass the Boland restrictions and the other statutory limitations on covert action that dealt with its approval and reporting requirements. NSC staff established their own secret organization outside government, called "The Enterprise," and launched privately funded CAs in support of the Nicaraguan *contras*. When this subterfuge eventually leaked to a Middle East newspaper in 1986 and played back into the United States, lawmakers realized Congress had been duped and, in 1987, they undertook a full-scale investigation into the scandal. Lawmakers instituted new legislative limits related to covert action, including a more precise definition of its boundaries. The new law, the Intelligence Oversight Act of 1991, emphasized again that the President had to formally sign a covert action approval – not just say "yes," or offer a nod and a wink, by way of approval.[16]

The methods of covert action

During the Cold War and since, covert action has taken four different forms, although they are often used together. The broad categories are: propaganda, political activities, economic disruptions, and paramilitary operations (PM ops).

Propaganda

The most frequent form of covert action conducted by the United States has been various forms of propaganda, known more euphemistically as "perception management" by Agency insiders. Or what Russian intelligence officers refer to as "agitprop" – one arrow in their quiver of CAs (or "active measures," in their terminology). Nations have overt channels of information dissemination, of course, such as the United States Information Agency (USIA) or the White House use of press releases about presidential decisions; but governments frequently seek, as well, to reinforce these messages through hidden channels of communications that reach around the world. These channels are often accepted by local citizens overseas as more credible than a U.S. government agency. One example is Hans Beidenhofer (a fictional name used here for purposes of illustration), who writes op-eds for *Der Spiegel* in Hamburg and is widely read and trusted by Germans. If Herr Beidenhofer wrote during the Cold War that he endorsed the idea of U.S. intermediate nuclear missiles on German soil as a deterrent against a Soviet invasion through the Fulga Gap, that might have carried more weight with local readers than if the same idea were advocated by the U.S. secretary of defense. Foreigners who are employed as newspaper reporters, magazine editors, television producers, or talk show hosts – any "influencer" in a position to express a public point of view favorable to the United States as if it were their own – become fair game for recruitment by the CIA as a "media asset."

Whatever foreign policies or slogans an administration in Washington might be touting in public – perhaps the danger of renegade nuclear aspirations pursued by Iran – the CIA pushes the same themes through its hundreds of covert media channels around the world. This network is like a vast, interwoven fabric. During the Cold War, some seventy to eighty secret media insertions were made each day by the Agency into different parts of its global propaganda system – a "Mighty Wurlitzer," as it was referred to proudly inside the Agency's Covert Action Staff.[17] Once released, however, propaganda can drift here and there, possibly back to the United States – a phenomenon known as "blow-back" or "replay." When this occurs, information originally meant for the eyes and ears of audiences overseas (friend or foe) finds its way back home to influence – and perhaps inadvertently deceive – America's own citizens. Most of America's covert propaganda, though, is truthful, a repeat of what officials are saying publicly in Washington. Yet sometimes, in 1–2 percent of the cases, Agency propaganda is false ("black" or "disinformation") and these media placements abroad become a particularly disquieting form of blow-back. A senior Agency official, Dr. Ray Cline, conceded once that "it used to worry him a lot" that false CIA propaganda about mainland China might fool China experts in the Department of State, skewing their analyses.[18]

The most significant difference between secretive global propaganda operations carried out by the United States, on the one hand, and China and Russia, on the other, is the high disinformation content adopted by the dictatorial nations in the propaganda operations. Their digital authoritarianism relies on trying to manipulate worldwide media channels, both traditional and new social, by way of an army of bots and trolls that disseminate fake "news" stories across every global time zone. An example: the claim emanating from Moscow and Beijing that Ukraine has operated secret biological warfare laboratories throughout the Russian-Ukrainian war. Increasingly, China has played the role of echo chamber for each Russian fabrication, resonating President Putin's false claims – a one–two punch from the world's autocratic giants.

An example of CIA covert propaganda operations during the Cold War was its concealed sponsorship, until revealed by a leak in the early 1970s, of Radio Free Europe (RFE) and Radio Liberty (RL). These stations broadcast programming into the Soviet Union and its satellite nations in an effort to break the biased and often dishonest grip of the communist government on news, entertainment, and culture, as well as to inculcate in listeners a favorable (and at least reasonably objective) view of life in the United States and its fellow democracies. Similarly, the CIA routinely attempted to infiltrate Western literature (books by Soviet dissenters and others, along with magazines and newspapers from the West) into the communist world. A high-ranking CIA official offers this assessment of the Agency's propaganda program aimed at the Soviet Union and its puppet allies: "This has maintained several independent thinkers in the Soviet bloc, has encouraged the distribution of ideas, and has increased the pressures on totalitarian regimes."[19] Even among more neutral observers, the Agency's propaganda activities are generally credited with helping to sustain dissident movements behind the Iron Curtain and subtly contributing to the eventual fall of the Soviet empire – although the effects of this propaganda defy precise measurement.

Of greater controversy during the Cold War was the Agency's use of propaganda against the democratic republic of Chile. In 1964, at the direction of the Johnson Administration, the CIA spent $3 million to blacken the name of

Photo 4.2: Salvador Allende
President Salvador Allende Gossens of Chile, a prime CIA covert action focus during the presidencies of Lyndon B. Johnson and, especially, Richard M. Nixon.
Source: Biblioteca del Congreso Nacional, Chile.

presidential candidate Salvador Allende Gossens in an effort to prevent his election for fear that he was a socialist with ties to Moscow. An expenditure of this magnitude in the Chilean election was equivalent at that time, on a per capita basis, to about $60 million in a U.S. presidential campaign – a staggering sum at the time. Although defeated in the 1960s, Allende persevered and eventually won the Chilean presidency in 1970.

Under orders from the Nixon Administration, the CIA then ratcheted up its propaganda operations to undermine the Allende government, spending an additional $3 million between 1970 and 1973 in negative publicity against the regime. President Nixon and his top aides feared that the Soviet Union might use Chile as a base to spread communism throughout the Western Hemisphere. They worried that Allende might become the next Fidel Castro in Latin America. To help protect their own interests in Chile, the International Telephone and Telegraph (ITT) Corporation and other American businesses secretly offered the Nixon Administration $1.5 million to aid the anti-Allende CAs, out of a concern that the Chilean President might decide to nationalize their holdings in Chile. According to Church Committee investigators in

1975, the forms of propaganda used by the CIA against Allende included press releases, radio commentary, films, pamphlets, posters, leaflets, direct mailings, paper streamers, and wall paintings. The Agency relied heavily on images of communist tanks and firing squads; and it paid for the distribution of hundreds of thousands of copies, in this Catholic country, of an anti-communist pastoral letter written years earlier by Pope Pius XI. The Allende government was overthrown in 1973.

Sometimes propaganda planners at the CIA seemed to be writing for the theater of the absurd. For example, one head-scratching CIA scheme hatched in the early 1960s envisioned the incitement of a coup against the Cuban regime, spurred by a flamboyant propaganda campaign. The idea was to have American submarines surface off the coast of Havana and fire starshells from their decks that would attract the attention of the islanders. Agency assets inside Cuba would then spread the word: "Christ has come! Rise up against the anti-Christ!" Leaflets dropped at night from CIA aircraft would carry a similar message. A DO officer explained to an investigative committee: "And this would be the manifestation of the Second Coming and Castro would be overthrown."[20] The CAS dubbed the plan "Elimination by Illumination." The Kennedy Administration had the good sense to reject the proposal before it went forward.

One of the most successful CIA propaganda operations took place in Central America in 1954. The purposes in this instance were twofold: first, to protect the investments in Guatemala of the United Fruit Company, an American firm with a lucrative banana monopoly in Central America (America's spy chief, Allen Dulles, and his brother, the Secretary of State, John Foster Dulles, had both served on the board of directors for the United Fruit Company); and, second, to exhibit for world consumption the determination of the Eisenhower Administration to thwart any leader who might have some affiliation, however weak (or imagined), with the Soviet Union.[21] The Agency set up a radio station in the mountains of Guatemala, where local CIA assets began broadcasting the fiction that a full-fledged revolution was taking place, and that the masses were rising up against the supposedly pro-communist dictator Jacobo Árbenz. The skillful broadcasts, augmented with modest paramilitary operations against the regime guided by U.S.-funded insurrectionists, led a nervous Arbenz to resign, in the belief that a mythical people's army of 5,000 was marching toward the capital.[22]

Today, a CIA propaganda media insertion might inveigh, for example, against Russia's development of destabilizing "supersonic" missiles; attempt to educate the world about who Putin really is, revealing the atrocities his armies have perpetrated in Ukraine; or excoriate the Chinese for having unsafe "wet markets" that may be the source of zoonotic diseases that have germinated pandemics like the Covert-19 virus. On their side of world affairs, the autocrats – most notably, Russia, China, Iran, and North Korea – will continue to pollute the world's air waves with their own forms of propaganda, which are chiefly fabrications designed to undermine freedom and open elections in the democracies. Lies, manipulation, and deceit are the main currencies in their approaches to intelligence propaganda. In the United States, the RAND think-tank has referred to "the firehose of falsehoods" that routinely spread around the world from Russia's intelligence apparatus. Over the years, Moscow has relied on its secret media channels across the latitudes to falsely castigate the United States for everything from plots to assassinate the pope and supporting extremist attacks against Saudi Arabia's Grand Mosque (which led Pakistani protestors to burn down the American embassy in Islamabad), to spreading the AIDS virus in Africa and Covid-19 throughout the world.

Closed societies like Russia are also expert at disseminating "deepfakes" – highly realistic audio, video, and photography that make someone seem to be doing and saying things they never did. On rare occasions, the CIA has engaged in this form of propaganda, too, as when it distributed through its hidden communication and media channels fabricated videos of Saddam Hussein during America's Persian Gulf Wars against Iraq in 1990–1 and then again in 2003. These videos portrayed him as even more duplicitous than he actually was (quite a trick). In contrast, for the dictatorships in the world, this is standard fare designed to sow confusion and unrest in the open societies. With both the democracies and the dictatorships – not to mention private-sector groups and individuals – now so skillful at manipulating information, it becomes harder and harder to discern what is real and what is fake. This state of affairs is of particular concern for the free nations, since truth is the very anchor of democracy, and is likely to be exacerbated by the introduction of artificial intelligence methods into these deception practices.

Political activities

The quiet option sometimes takes the form of financial aid to friendly politicians and bureaucrats abroad – bribes, if one wishes to put a harsh light on the practice, or stipends for the advancement of democracy if one prefers a rosier interpretation. Whatever one chooses to call this form of assistance ("King George's cavalry" is the amusing British MI6 expression), the record is clear that, throughout the Cold War, the CIA secretly provided substantial sums of cash to a number of political groups and individuals overseas, including a host of pro-Western parties and factions in West Germany, Greece, Egypt, the Philippines, and Chile, to mention just some examples that have made their way into the public record. During the Cold War, an important part of political covert action – the bone and sinew of CA – was funding for anti-communist labor unions in Europe, an objective of high priority soon after the end of World War II. One well-publicized case involved support for the Christian Democratic Party in Italy during the 1960s against its principal opponent, the Italian Communist Party. Providing money to the Christian Democratic Party openly may well have discredited its reputation, causing Italian voters to conclude that the party was just a puppet of the United States; therefore, the White House turned to covert funding as a means of avoiding this taint.

The CIA maintains a stable of "agents of influence" around the world: individuals, from valets and chauffeurs to personal secretaries and key ministerial aides, who presumably have sufficient access to high-ranking political figures to influence their decisions. The purpose, as with propaganda, is to convince important foreign officials to lean toward the United States and its allied democracies and away from the Soviet Union – or, these days, Russia; China; Iraqi insurgents; extremists among the Taliban, Al Qaeda, and ISIS; the government of Iran; and other antidemocracy adversaries in the Middle East, Southwest Asia, and anywhere else in the world. As is the case with humint operations generally, the Agency seeks to expand its global corps of agents of influence (a goal made more difficult to achieve with the short tours of its operations officers and their limited foreign-language capabilities).

Since 1983, a nongovernment National Endowment for Democracy (NED) based in Washington, DC has served as a nonprofit foundation devoted to the strengthening of democratic institutions around the world. According to its website, "NED is dedicated to fostering the growth of a wide range of democratic institutions abroad, including political parties, trade unions, free markets and business organizations, as well as the many elements of a vibrant civil society that ensure human rights, an independent media, and the rule of law." Some critics of the CIA suggest that the Agency ought to move out of the way and let this more open organization serve as America's arm in helping democracies flourish abroad; others argue back that, however helpful NED's activities might be, the CIA still has a role in assisting this worthy goal in places too dangerous or closed off for NED officials to operate.

Economic disruptions

The CIA has also attempted to slow or even destroy the economies of adversaries. In one instance during the Kennedy Administration, Agency operatives planned to spoil Cuban–Soviet relations by lacing sugar bound from Havana to Moscow with an unpalatable, though harmless, chemical substance. At the eleventh hour, a White House aide discovered the scheme and had the 14,125 bags of sugar confiscated before they were shipped to the Soviet Union. The aide had concluded that the United States should not tamper with another nation's food supplies.[23] Other methods of secret economic disruption have reportedly included efforts to incite labor unrest; smuggle counterfeit currencies into target nations to cause inflationary pressures; depress the world price of agricultural products grown by adversaries (such as Cuban sugar cane); sneak defective components into the construction materials for a foreign nuclear reactor; contaminate foreign oil supplies or computer parts; and – upping the ante – dynamite electrical power lines and oil-storage tanks, as well as mine an enemy's harbors with explosive charges to harm ships and undermine the target nation's international trade relations.

In the realm of economic activities, CA presents a much nastier portrait of America's secret foreign policy. Additional examples include efforts to incite labor strikes; instigate power blackouts; turn oil refineries into smoke; severing telephone lines; blow up electrical power grids, bus depots, and bridges; and contaminate lubricants to bring about a breakdown of machinery in an adversary's industrial plants. An NSC memo from the Johnson Administration reviewed plans to harm the Cuban economy. These included a commando sabotage operation against a wharf site, along with sabotage activities aimed at disabling a fuel barge steaming through coastal waters. In more recent years, the Trump Administration ordered the U.S. Cyber Command to carry out online cyberattacks against an Iranian intelligence organization involved in operations against American tankers in the Persian Gulf.[24]

In response to a White House request during the Johnson years for new ideas on how to deal with Cuban leader Fidel Castro, the Pentagon proposed "Operation SQUARE DANCE": the destruction of the Cuban economy by dropping from the cargo hatches of aircraft under the darkness of night a parasite known as Bunga, which would attack the island's sugar cane plants. "The economic and political disturbances caused by this attack could be exacerbated and exploited," claimed a DoD memo, "by such measures as spreading hoof-and-mouth disease among draft animals, controlling rainfall by cloud seeding, mining cane fields, burning cane, and directing other acts of conventional sabotage against the cane milling and transportation system." The hoped-for end result, concluded the memo, would be "the collapse of the Castro regime." The military planners conceded that adoption of SQUARE DANCE "would introduce a new dimension into Cold War methods and would require a major change in national policy."[25] They were ready to carry out these measures anyway, though, if the White House so desired. The National Security Advisor at the time, McGeorge Bundy (a former Harvard University professor and liberal arts dean), was troubled by such extreme options – even against the likes of the Cuban dictator – and he rejected the proposal. The DoD memo provides startling insight into America's capacity and, evidently at some levels of government, its willingness to engage in radical covert economic operations to achieve U.S. foreign policy goals.

As part and parcel of the attempts to undermine Allende before and after his run for the presidency, the CIA adopted various covert measures to undermine the Chilean economy. By heightening the level of economic dislocation and social unrest in Chile, the Nixon Administration, whose initial covert actions had failed to prevent Allende's victory in the presidential election, hoped that local military forces would decide to strip Allende of his powers. According to the Church Committee's investigation, the DCI at the time, Richard Helms, took handwritten notes at a White House meeting on September 15, 1970, about what could be done if Allende were to win. Huddled in the Oval Office with President Nixon, Secretary of State Henry Kissinger, and Attorney General John Mitchell, Helms jotted in his notebook: "Make the economy scream." One method adopted for this purpose by the Agency was to disrupt the nation's trucking industry, a ploy that dramatically impeded the flow of commerce from town to town throughout Chile. A decade later, attempts by the Reagan Administration to topple the Sandinista regime in Nicaragua would again turn to economic covert actions, including the mining of the nation's harbors and the blowing up of power lines across the countryside.

Paramilitary operations

Secret warlike activities, known as paramilitary (PM) covert actions, are yet another arrow in the CIA's quiver – the most lethal of all. No CAs have held higher risk or generated more criticism than large- and small-scale "covert" wars (as if wars can be kept secret for long). From 1950 to 1953, the Agency's covert action capabilities attracted high funding to support America's overt warfare on the Korean Peninsula – the first major use of this foreign policy tool by the United States. Henceforth, whenever the United States was involved in overt warfare somewhere in the world, the Agency would be there as well to support the military with PM covert actions. Then, in 1953, the CIA provided support to pro-American factions that brought down the Iranian Prime Minister, Mohammed Mossadeqh, and replaced him with someone more pliable, the Shah of Iran, Mohammed Reza Shah Pahlavi. The following year, the Agency succeeded with its plan to frighten the democratically elected Arbenz government out of office in Guatemala by a combination of chiefly spreading CA propaganda that inaccurately labeled Arbenz as a Moscow puppet, but also political, economic, and small-scale PM operations. Over the next two decades, the Agency mobilized its paramilitary capabilities for several secret military attacks against foreign governments, offering support (with mixed degrees of success) for anti-communist insurgents in such places as Ukraine, Poland, Albania, Hungary, Indonesia, Oman, Laos, Vietnam, Malaysia, Iraq, the Dominican Republic, Venezuela, Thailand, Haiti, Greece, Turkey, and Cuba.

While the Bay of Pigs venture in Cuba exploded in the face of DO planners, several other schemes experienced some degree of success – at least over the short run. For example, from 1962 to 1968, the CIA backed the Hmung tribesmen (pronounced with a silent "h"), sometimes referred to as the Meo tribesmen. The Hmung fought a war in North Laos against North Vietnamese puppets known as the Communist Pathet Lao. This war kept the Pathet Lao occupied and away from killing U.S. troops fighting next door in South Vietnam. The Hmung and the Pathet Lao struggled to a draw in Laos, until the United States withdrew from the ring to concentrate its efforts in Vietnam. Following this withdrawal, the Hmung lacked U.S. arms and advisors; they were soon routed by the Pathet Lao, with only some fortunate Hmung fighters exfiltrated by the CIA for resettlement in the United States. During this time, the Agency also conducted extensive covert action operations in Cambodia, as well as against the North Vietnamese and their Viet Cong allies in South Vietnam, until the U.S. military retreated from Indochina in 1973.

Under President Ronald Reagan, the Agency pursued major paramilitary operations in a number of locations around the world, but with special emphasis in Nicaragua and Afghanistan. The operations in these two countries combined represented the second most extensive use of covert action in the nation's history at the time (slightly surpassing its emphasis in the Korean War; see Figure 4.1 below). While the Nicaragua involvement had an ugly ending with the Iran–*contra* scandal, the Administration's covert support of *mujahideen* fighters against Soviet invaders in Afghanistan is considered one of the glory moments in the CIA's history. The Agency provided Stinger missiles to the *mujahideen*, which helped turn the tide of the war and sent the Red Army into retreat. Also, the Reagan Administration chalked up another major covert action success in Poland by secretly helping that nation free itself from communist control. In the case of support to the *mujahideen*, who later morphed into the Taliban regime in Afghanistan and provided a safe haven for Al Qaeda, the joy of members of the Reagan Administration who supported these atavistic warriors would turn to woodworm and gall with the events of 9/11. The very group they had helped in the 1980s, the Taliban, had aided and abetted the worst attack ever against the United States.

After 9/11, covert action reached another high point in terms of emphasis by the United States – in fact, the beginning of the nation's most pronounced use of this approach to foreign policy, eclipsing (albeit by a narrow margin) the adoption of "special activities" in both the Korean War and the Reagan Administration's covert wars in Afghanistan, Nicaragua, and Poland. In the aftermath of the 9/11 attacks, the purpose was to support America's overt wars in Iraq and Afghanistan, along with operations directed against Al Qaeda, ISIS, and other terrorist organizations, as well as (most recently) behind-the-scenes supplies not only of intelligence reports but weaponry and training to Ukrainian freedom fighters struggling against the Russian invasion of Ukraine in 2022.

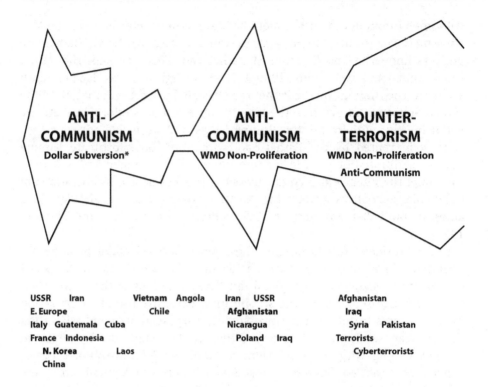

USSR   Iran   Vietnam   Angola   Iran   USSR   Afghanistan
E. Europe   Chile   Afghanistan   Iraq
Italy   Guatemala   Cuba   Nicaragua   Syria   Pakistan
France   Indonesia   Poland   Iraq   Terrorists
      N. Korea   Laos   Cyberterrorists
      China

'47–'52 '53–'60 '61–'63 '64–'68 '69–'76 '77–'80 '81–'88 '89–'92 '93–'00 '01–'08 '09–'16 '17–'20 '21–'24

Figure 4.1: The ebb and flow of U.S. covert actions, 1947–2024.

This figure provides an approximation of the emphasis placed by the United States on the Third Option in the modern era; the wider the "river", the greater the emphasis. It also depicts the major motivations or "currents" driving the river: chiefly anti-communism (especially in the early years of the Cold War and during the Reagan Administration) and, more recently, counterterrorism, with "dollar subversion" (see below), and WMD non-proliferation notable influences as well.

*The CIA analog of "dollar diplomacy," an approach to foreign policy based on advancing private U.S. commercial interests (see Loch K. Johnson, *American Foreign Policy and the Challenges of World Leadership: Power, Principle, and the Constitution* (New York: Oxford University Press, 2015): 119).

Source: Based on Loch K. Johnson, *The Third Option: Covert Action and American Foreign Policy* (New York: Oxford University Press, 2022), p. 159. Used with permission.

The assassination option

This chapter began with a look at the CIA's efforts to kill the African leader Patrice Lumumba at the beginning of the 1960s. Perhaps the most controversial form of PM covert action has been the use of assassination as a method to eliminate dangerous, or sometimes just annoying, foreign leaders. The Soviets referred to this option as "wet affairs," a method they adopted in 1940 to dispatch regime critic, fellow communist Leon Trotsky, whom a Soviet intelligence operative murdered with an ice pick during Trotsky's exile in Mexico. In the modern era, Russia has resorted to dispatching a number of regime critics – especially former intelligence officers who have moved to the West – with poisoning as a favorite method. The CIA's involvement in death plots came to light in 1975. In files discovered by presidential and congressional investigators (the Rockefeller Commission and the Church Committee, respectively), the DO referred to its attempts at assassinating selected foreign leaders with such euphemisms as "termination with extreme prejudice" or "neutralization." At one time the Agency established a special (and aptly named) panel – the "Health Alteration Committee" – to screen assassination proposals. The CIA also developed a tiny dart the size of a sewing needle (a "nondiscernible microbioinoculator," in fanciful DS&T terminology), which could be silently propelled toward an unsuspecting target from the barrel of an oversized .45 pistol equipped with a telescopic sight. Agency scientists considered the dart gun, which was accurate up to 250 feet and would leave no trace in the victim's body, the perfect murder weapon.

Fidel Castro attracted the full attention of the CIA's Covert Action Staff and its Special Operations Group during the Kennedy and Johnson Administrations. The Agency emptied its medicine cabinet of drugs and poisons in various attempts to kill, or at least debilitate, the Cuban leader. In one operation, the CIA placed depilatory powder in Castro's shoes when he traveled abroad; the substance was meant to enter his bloodstream through his feet and cause his famously charismatic beard to fall off his chin. The Agency also impregnated Castro's cigars with the hallucinatory drug LSD, as well as with a deadly botulinum toxin; dusted his underwater diving suit with Madura foot fungus; sneaked an agent into his kitchen, who tried (but failed) to place a poison capsule in his soup; and attempted to find someone with access to Castro who could inject the highly poisonous substance Blackleaf-40 into his skin, using a needle-tipped ballpoint pen. In this last plot, the CIA made contact with a promising agent in Paris on November 22, 1963, ironically the very same day that America's own president was assassinated.

All these efforts failed, for Castro was elusive and well-protected by an elite security guard trained by the KGB. (Today's Russian Foreign Intelligence Service is known by the acronym SVR – one of six spy organizations to emerge in Moscow from the shadow of the KGB after the collapse of the Soviet Union.) So the Agency turned to the Mafia for assistance: a Chicago gangster, Sam Giancana; the former Cosa Nostra chief for Cuba, Santo Trafficante; and the mobster John Rosselli. These men still had contacts on the island from pre-Castro days when Havana was a world gambling mecca. No doubt assuming the U.S. government would back away from Mafia prosecutions in return for help against Castro, the crime figures volunteered to assemble assassination teams of Cuban exiles and other hitmen, then infiltrate them into Cuba. None of these plots succeeded. Soon after the Church Committee called Giancana and Roselli as witnesses to testify in its assassination inquiry, both men were murdered, in crimes that remain unsolved.

Rafael Trujillo of the Dominican Republic, Ngo Dinh Diem of South Vietnam, and General René Schneider of Chile were other national leaders killed by factions that periodically had connections with the CIA; however, the Church Committee concluded that at the time when each of these individuals was murdered, the Agency no longer had control over the assassins. The CIA also gave weapons to dissidents intent on eliminating President Sukarno of Indonesia and François President "Papa Doc" Duvalier of Haiti. Both managed, nonetheless, to survive into old age. In Duvalier's case, the failed assassination plans seem once again to have gone forward without the Agency's direct involvement – although it is unlikely that officials at Langley or the White House would have shed many tears had the plotters succeeded.

The CIA has also been implicated in the incapacitation or death of lower-level officials. The most well-known operation of this kind was the Agency's Phoenix Program, carried out in South Vietnam as part of the U.S. war effort to subdue the influence of communists in the countryside (known as the Viet Cong or VC). According to William Colby, who led the program for a time (and was later appointed DCI), some 20,000 VC leaders and sympathizers were killed – though 85 percent of these victims were engaged in military or paramilitary combat against South Vietnamese or American soldiers. The other deaths remain under an ethical cloud.

In 1976, soon after Congress revealed the CIA's involvement in international murder plots, President Gerald R. Ford signed an executive order against this practice. The wording of the order, endorsed by his successors, reads: "No person employed by or acting on behalf of the United States Government, shall engage in, or conspire to engage in assassination."[26] While honored most of the time, situations have occurred where administrations have bent this language to suit their own needs. For example, President Reagan ordered the bombing of President Muammar Qaddafi's house in 1986 as part of an air raid against Libya, on grounds that he had been aiding and abetting terrorism (the Libya leader was unharmed); and President George H.W. Bush ordered the bombing of Baghdad – including the palaces of Iraqi leader Saddam Hussein – during the first Persian Gulf War (1990–1). Indeed, the first Bush White House "lit a candle every night hoping Saddam Hussein would be killed in a bunker" during these bombings, recalls a former DCI.[27] In these instances, the United States was involved in overt warfare against Libya and Iraq; under such conditions (ideally, authorized by Congress, although the attacks against Libya were not), the executive order on assassination is suspended.

More recently, as authorized by Congress, the United State became involved in overt warfare in Iraq and Afghanistan, and against ISIS (as well as continuing its retaliation against Al Qaeda and its supporters – most visibly, the Taliban in Afghanistan and Pakistan). In these struggles too, the executive order against assassination was lifted, or at least loosely applied. Saddam was again regularly a target in the Second Persian Gulf War that began in 2003; but, as in the First Persian Gulf War, he proved to be highly elusive. Eventually, though, in December 2003, U.S. troops discovered him hiding in a hole in the ground near his hometown in Iraq. He was arrested, tried in an Iraqi court, then hanged when found guilty of war crimes – all with the strong encouragement of the United States under President George W. Bush. (Saddam had ordered an assassination attempt against the President's father and mother – former President George H.W. Bush and Barbara Bush – soon after Iraq's defeat in the First Persian Gulf War, when the Bushes were visiting Kuwait to celebrate the victory. This fact was not lost on Bush the son.) In the aftermath of the Bush II years in the White House, the Obama Administration added Afghan narcotics dealers to the drone target list, along with ISIS members in the Middle East and North Africa.

Since the end of the Cold War, the CIA (in tandem with the U.S. Air Force) has developed and deployed its most lethal paramilitary weapon: the armed drone, such as the Predator and its more muscular brother, the Reaper. Both forms of UAV are armed with Hellfire missiles and can quickly fly across national boundaries. For their takeoffs and landings, these systems are controlled remotely from sites in the Middle East, Southwest Asia, and North Africa (among other locations around the world), while the targeting and firing phases of flight are guided from Langley, as well as from bases in Nevada and other locations in the United States. Critics maintain that these remote "pilots" are too distant from their targets to feel any sense of concern about the carnage they have wrought. Cruising at relatively low altitudes, the drones are equipped with sophisticated cameras that help operators in the United States confirm the identity of a target before the UAV missiles are released in such remote places as the Sahel region of Niger, Chad, and Mali, as well as Somalia on the Horn of Africa.

Targeting mistakes are made from time to time, unfortunately, as terrorists hide out in mosques and other locations where civilians too may be inadvertently struck by the Hellfire missiles. The CIA and the military go to great lengths to avoid this "collateral damage." They check the validity of the targets time and again before releasing the missiles; but PM operations by drone is a form of warfare, and, historically, innocents have always paid part of the price along with targeted combatants – one of many good reasons for favoring the negotiated settlement of international disputes through diplomacy rather than taking up arms (overtly or covertly).

With respect to civilian casualties, the Obama Administration claimed on NBC News in 2016 that "only" 100 civilians had died in the course of nearly 500 U.S. drone strikes since 2009. Later that same year, the Administration clarified the numbers: between 64 and 116 civilians had died in 473 drone strikes. Independent groups countered, however, that the actual number of

Photo 4.3: Reaper Drone
MQ-9 Reaper drone at a U.S. Army airfield in New York, 2012.
Source: United States Air Force.

civilian deaths exceeded 1,000.[28] More recently, drone assassination initiatives have been vetted by lawyers on the NSC working with their counterparts in the Intelligence Community. The initial step is a targeting recommendation prepared by attorneys in the IC or the Department of Defense. Next, the NSC Deputies Committee (consisting of those second in command at the recommending agency or the DoD), gives the proposal a thorough scrub, before passing it along to the DNI, D/CIA, and the SecDef on the Principals Committee. If the potential target is a U.S. citizen, the President must sign off as well, and the congressional oversight committees (SSCI and HPSCI) are informed. In extraordinary cases, these steps can be short-circuited, with the President alone providing authorization for the attack. Beyond these tightened procedures, the Obama Administration redoubled its efforts to avoid casualties among innocent civilians by improving intelligence reconnaissance before giving the go-ahead for a drone attack to take place. Moreover, the guidelines fashioned by the Obama Administration require that drone assassinations can go forward only if the targeted individual poses a grave threat to the United States, and if there is a "near certainty" that no civilian casualties will result from the attack – a standard relaxed during the Trump Administration.

Despite improvements in the care of drone targeting selections, several top officials at the Agency began to express their view publicly that covert action – especially drone attacks – had become too dominant in the CIA's global operations, with intelligence analysts focused more and more on establishing GPS drone-targeting coordinates than they were on the production of assessments about world affairs.[29] At Langley, D/CIA John O. Brennan urged the restoration of analysis as the top priority in the Agency's portfolio of responsibilities, with the CIA involved in drone strikes only in limited instances. (Oddly, along with Robert M. Gates, Brennan was only the second CIA leader to have had prior service as an Agency analyst – in an organization that prides itself on its analytic role in the shaping of American foreign policy.) In its final years, the Obama Administration started to shift more of the responsibility for counterterrorist drone attacks to the Pentagon and away from the CIA, in part because D/CIA Brennan strongly opposed the idea of the Agency as a "killing machine" rather than an organization engaged chiefly in its primary mission of collection and analysis. Presidents Trump and Biden continued this trend toward shifting most drone killing assignments to the DoD, but the Agency still remains deeply involved in UAV warfare against terrorist targets in the Middle East and North Africa.

At the highest level of government, ethical considerations have sometimes entered into covert action decisions related to drone warfare. For example, during the Clinton Administration, the President called off two counterterrorist attacks by cruise missiles just as they were ready to be fired from U.S. destroyers in the Red Sea against Osama bin Laden. In one instance, Bin Laden was surrounded by his wives and children in a village; and, in another, by princes from the United Arab Emirates (UAE, an American ally – of sorts) on a bird-hunting expedition. On another occasion, bad luck thwarted a drone strike aimed at Bin Laden. In that instance, President Clinton approved the firing of missiles from a U.S. Navy cruiser in the Red Sea at a suspected Al Qaeda gathering in the desert near the town of Khost in Paktia Province, Afghanistan, but a lucky Bin Laden had already departed before the warheads struck the encampment.

The Al Qaeda leader continued to evade U.S. assassination attempts, lying low somewhere in the mountains of Pakistan. He eventually moved under the cover of darkness to a walled compound in Abbottabad, just thirty-five miles from the Pakistani capital of Islamabad. President Obama deployed a Navy Seal team that landed helicopters inside the grounds of this hideaway in 2011 and, in a chaotic gunfight in the main house, a Seal member shot Bin Laden to death in his quarters. In 2022, a DoD drone passed over downtown Kabul and killed his successor, Ayman al-Zawahiri, who had also been a key figure in the 9/11 attacks against the United States.

Exactly who should be on the "kill" list has been a controversial subject. Originally, the Patriot Act of 2001 stipulated that only those enemies involved in the 9/11 attacks were legitimate targets for retaliation. Since then – and without further legislative guidelines – the target list has widened. For example, a U.S. citizen hiding out in Yemen by the name of Anwar al-Awlaki was placed for consideration on an assassination list generated by the Obama Administration, even though it was never demonstrated to the public that he had actually been involved in plots against the United States. If he had been, al-Awlaki could be considered a legitimate target; however, if he had limited himself to making speeches against the United States, he would have been just one of hundreds of radicals in the Middle East and Southwest Asia who have advocated *jihad* against the West in recent years. Behind closed doors, attorneys in the Obama Administration eventually decided that there was enough evidence to show that Awlaki had participated in terrorist activities for him to qualify as a legitimate assassination target. The President signed the death warrant and the Yemeni iman was blown to pieces by Hellfire missiles in 2011.[30] He was not the first U.S. citizen to be killed by CIA drones. In 2002, a Predator fired a missile at an automobile crossing a Yemeni desert with six passengers suspected to be Al Qaeda members. All six were inciner-ated. One turned out to be an American citizen. Each of these events, and there have been others (including, by accident, the killing of Awlaki's son by yet another U.S. drone), raises serious questions about the relationship between due process and assassination.

At present, the procedures for developing assassination lists continue to lack sufficient clarity and oversight. Reportedly, the decision to kill requires the approval of the U.S. ambassador to the target country, as well as the CIA chief of station, the DO director, the D/CIA, and the DNI. As noted earlier, if the target is an American citizen, like al-Awlaki, attorneys in the Justice Department and the President must also approve. Further, at least a few of the members of the congressional intelligence committees (SSCI and HPSCI) are briefed on the targeting, and some of their staff are invited to the White House Situation Room from time to time to follow the videos of the drone attacks. The idea is to demonstrate to overseers the care being taken by the Administration to avoid civilian casualties.

Despite some efforts to reassure congressional supervisors that the IC is doing its best to act prudently, the U.S. spy agencies have often drawn the ire of lawmakers who have viewed some post-9/11 secret operations as excessive. Examples include the use of harsh interrogation methods during the Bush II Administration, as well as the use of extraordinary renditions (subjects explored in more depth in Chapter 6). With these excesses in mind, critics have argued that a more formal congressional review should take place when it comes to drone assassinations. Critics have suggested further that the courts should also be part of this decision-making process, with the establishment of a new court to issue warrants for assassinations, after a careful judicial review of the evidence for and against the potential targeting. A precedent for special intelligence courts is the panel set up by the Foreign Intelligence Surveillance Act of 1978, a major initiative advanced by the Church Committee inquiry. Under FISA procedures, executive officials are supposed to seek warrants from a panel of judges before engaging in telephone wiretaps and other clandestine surveillance methods against American citizens suspected of involvement in activities that threaten national security.[31]

In recent years, the CIA has flown no drone missile attacks against ISIS targets in Iraq and Syria, leaving this particular terrain to the Pentagon's UAV pilots. A new debate began in Washington about the CIA's remit. Should it step out of the Murder, Inc. business altogether, handing over drone warfare exclusively to the Pentagon? A group of vocal dissenters opposed the views of President Obama and D/CIA Brennan on shelving the Agency's drone capabilities. For one thing, argued top SSCI leaders Chairman Richard Burr (R, N. Carolina) and Ranking Minority Member Dianne Feinstein (D, California), sometimes the Pentagon was too slow in sending drones against known terrorist targets in Iraq and Syria, leading to "missed opportunities" once the CIA had spotted ISIS fighters. The CIA's drone commanders should be allowed to pull the trigger in those circumstances, they maintained.

Hiding behind this reasoning were even stronger concerns on Capitol Hill. First, SSCI's leaders rightly believe that the CIA is subject to greater congressional accountability than the Pentagon. This is true because of the Hughes–Ryan requirements that require prior notice to SSCI and HPSCI of all important covert actions (established and refined by the Intelligence Oversight Acts of 1980 and 1991). Further, ISIS was beginning to operate increasingly outside the officially authorized DoD theaters of war – traditionally Agency/DO territory. Thus, maintained the SSCI leadership, the CIA should remain in charge of those drone attacks outside formal war zones. Finally, continuation of CIA drone warfare provided SSCI and HPSCI members with ongoing access to the high circles of policymaking in the White House. Opponents of these views continued to reason, however, that Pentagon drone attacks have in fact been more accountable than the Agency's, because DoD operations do not have to be clothed in as much secrecy as CIA operations. This debate continues (and is examined further in Chapter 5).

Even when the United States has decided to assassinate an ISIS member or other vetted target overseas, the task has proved difficult to carry out. Castro reportedly survived thirty-two attempts on his life attempted by the Agency.[32] Efforts to take out the warlord Mohamed Ali Farrah Aidid of Somalia failed during America's brief involvement in fighting on the African Horn in 1993; Saddam Hussein proved impossible to locate inside Iraq during the 1990s; and Bin Laden evaded detection for almost a decade after 9/11. Dictators are paranoid, well guarded, and elusive, as are high-ranking members of ISIS, Al Qaeda, and their terrorist brethren. Anwar al-Awlaki also proved elusive for years. Troubling, too, is the thought that assassinations carried out by the United States may encourage others to retaliate against the U.S. president and other officials in Washington when they travel overseas – or even inside the American homeland.

In the future, drones may be increasingly guided by sophisticated AI methods, which could make these aircraft autonomous. Without a trained human at the controls on a minute-to-minute basis, would an AI drone be able to distinguish a terrorist from an innocent girl carrying water from a well to her parents' hut in Mali? Would a free-will flying robot understand what was legal and moral? Critics of this trend toward autonomous war-fighting machines also wonder if AI paramilitary drones would be susceptible to computer hacking by foreign intelligence services, with data alterations that could change – even reverse – their flight coordinates. Scientists have expressed concern that humans could lose control altogether of the algorithms that would guide autonomous UAVs. In March 2019, UN Secretary General António Guterres stated: "Machines with the power and discretion to take lives without human involvement are politically unacceptable, morally repugnant, and should be prohibited by international law." A special treaty signed by all nations seemed imperative to halt the potential dangers of what have become known as "free will" weaponry.

The ebb and flow of covert action

Although out of favor with some administrations in the United States, others have spent enormous sums of money on covert action. Support for these operations during the Cold War accelerated from the very beginning of the CIA's history, moving from nonexistence in 1947 to high prominence during the Korean War in 1950–3, an intense time of battle and blood. Support for CA then fell back to much lower levels until a new spurt of major funding kicked in during the height of the Vietnam War in 1968–71; support then declined again for a decade before a dramatic resurgence during the Reagan years (see Figure 4.1).

The war in Korea dramatically boosted the CA mission in the Agency's infant days. As John Ranelagh reports, funding "increased sixteen-fold between January 1951 and January 1953," and personnel assigned to the mission doubled.[33] During this period, the CA budget "skyrocketed," according to the Church Committee.[34] Tails were up at Langley and bottles of Pol Roger made their rounds on the seventh floor. Successes in Iran (1953) and Guatemala (1954) further encouraged the Eisenhower and Kennedy Administrations to rely on the Agency's Covert Action Staff to achieve American foreign policy victories. William J. Daugherty notes that the outcomes in Iran and Guatemala "left in their wake an attitude of hubris" at Langley and with the members of the Eisenhower Administration's national security team.[35] Using the cover of darkness that covert action provided, this approach to American foreign policy suddenly seemed densely studded with numerous inviting possibilities and, within the boiler-room of the DO, engines began snorting and bellowing.

Even the Bay of Pigs fiasco in 1961 – initially a heavy millstone weighing on the breast of the Kennedy Administration – proved to be only a small and short-lived blip of skepticism about the use of covert action, before President Kennedy turned again to the Agency for assistance in the resolution of international headaches. Throughout the 1960s and early 1970s, the DO and its allied mercenaries abroad waged a subterranean World War III against communist forces – most notably in the jungles of Indochina. At times, covert actions absorbed up to 60 percent of the CIA's annual budget.[36]

A precipitous slide downward for the "quiet option" occurred in the early 1970s, induced by a growing disillusionment over the war in Vietnam, government spending cuts pursued by the Nixon Administration, tentative overtures of détente with the Soviet Union, and a domestic spy scandal in 1975 that was accompanied by revelations about CIA assassination plots and attacks against the democratically elected government of Chile (the Allende regime). The CA revelations, especially from the Church Committee, raised doubts among the American people and their representatives in Congress about the ethics and the value of "special activities." Public reaction brought covert action "to a screeching halt," recalls a senior CIA official.[37] Interest in the "third option" would resume during the presidency of Jimmy Carter – which was ironic given that he had campaigned in 1976 against the use of CA "dirty tricks" by the Agency. The most important catalyst for Carter's turn-around was the Soviet invasion of Afghanistan in 1979. The United States would have to fight back, the President decided (with strong nudging from his hawkish National Security Advisor, Zbigniew Brzezinski); and secret CIA operations would have to be the instrument of retaliation – since it would be mutually suicidal to initiate an overt war with the USSR, with its thousands of nuclear warheads atop ICBMs that could streak across the vast expanse of the northern polar region to strike cities from Los Angeles to New York City in less than a half-hour.

During the following decade – the 1980s – covert action entered a Golden Age, surpassing even the burst of America's secret interventions abroad during the 1950s, when CA first became a major claimant for intelligence funding. At the time, the Reagan Administration recorded the historical high point of U.S. support for secret interventions abroad since 1947, although a more recent emphasis on covert operations – especially paramilitary activities with UAVs in the Middle East and Southwest Asia – would surpass this record during the Obama and Trump years. The 1980s were also the only time major attention was given to CA by the United States without an accompanying involvement by the nation in a major overt war. The more normal pattern is for CA high points to occur within the framework of support to military operations (SMOs) during significant U.S. military interventions abroad: Korea, Vietnam, and, more recently, Iraq, Afghanistan, and the struggles against ISIS, Al Qaeda, and Taliban insurgents. The Reagan years demonstrated that, if an administration so chooses, it could commit to high levels of emphasis on covert action even when the United States was not involved in overt wars abroad.

Thus, during the 1980s, the CIA's Operations Directorate would become the chief instrument for advancing the ideologically driven "Reagan Doctrine" of opposing communist-backed wars of liberation in the developing world, from El Salvador to Cambodia. The primary targets for the Reagan Administration were the Sandinistas in Nicaragua and the Red Army in Afghanistan. Funding poured into both operations, illegally in the case of Nicaragua (and thus the Iran–*contra* scandal). The Nicaraguan intervention cast upon the CIA the darkest mark in the history of its use of CA – worse even than the debacle at the Bay of Pigs. This scandal represented a fundamental assault on the U.S. Constitution and violated as well the landmark Intelligence Oversight Act of 1980 (examined in Chapter 6), as the Reagan Administration – specifically, NSC staff and elements of the CIA – attempted to bypass Congress and raise funds privately to advance covert actions against Nicaragua, even though these operations were explicitly prohibited by Congress (the Boland Amendments). In addition to its violations of U.S. law, the scheme also failed to topple the Sandinistas, whose leader, Daniel Ortega, continued to rule Nicaragua off and on in competitive elections (and is once again the President of Nicaragua today). In contrast, the Afghan intervention by the Reagan Administration followed proper authorization, with lawful adherence to the Hughes–Ryan reporting procedures for covert actions. Moreover, this use of the third option succeeded in helping to drive the Soviet military out of Afghanistan. The Administration's covert actions in Poland also adhered to U.S. laws and again had positive results in the nurturing of open electoral procedures and other democratic principles.[38]

President George H.W. Bush has noted that he found covert action a valuable option on occasion, but funding for special activities went into sharp decline during his years in the White House (1989–92), leveling out at around just below 1 percent of the U.S. intelligence budget – far below its heyday during the Reagan years.[39] From a place of prominence in the U.S.-led anticommunist crusades of the Cold War, the CA mission had fallen into a state of near disregard by 1991. A senior DO officer has looked back on these days ruefully:

> I feel that a lot more could be done in the broad area of covert action in support of policy with the proper resources allocated to the mission. I am not thinking in terms of going back to the days when CA was 60 percent of the CIA budget; but I do feel that less than 1 percent is below minimum. It is a mission that is legally and properly assigned to the Agency and, once we can get better understanding of it and clear up some of the controversies that surround it, I think it should have additional people if we are to carry out effectively what is the mission assigned to us by the president.[40]

Similarly, during the Clinton Administration, DCI John Deutch observed: "Since the public controversies of the eighties over Iran–*contra* and activities in Central America, we have greatly reduced our capability to engage in covert action."[41] Throughout the years of his tenure (1995–7), funding for covert action began to turn modestly upward, as a means for helping new democratic regimes deal with hostile forces (as in Haiti, for instance), as well as for thwarting the machinations of terrorists, drug dealers, and weapons proliferators. These latter targets rose to the level of a Tier 1A threat-assessment during the Clinton years when covert actions became more narrowly tailored, less global in nature, than during the Cold War.

With the election of George W. Bush, covert action at first remained at a modest level – until the 9/11 attacks. Then, with three wars fought simultaneously by the United States (in Iraq and Afghanistan, as well as against global terrorists), the third option underwent a renaissance, directed against targets chiefly in the Middle East and Southwest Asia. This rejuvenation brought the use, and the status, of CA up to – and soon beyond – levels comparable to the earlier historical high points: those special activities that had supported the war in Korea, followed by the Reagan Administration's use of this approach to foreign policy during its involvement in Nicaragua, Afghanistan, and Poland.

At first, President Barack Obama maintained the already high level of interest in covert action in America's national security apparatus established by the second Bush Administration; then he began to use this approach even more earnestly in Afghanistan and Pakistan. The Obama Administration rapidly reached the record highs of emphasis on CA mentioned earlier. In 2011, President Obama also authorized CA support to rebels fighting against the Qaddafi regime in Libya and, when that regime crumbled and Qaddafi was killed, against the new ISIS insurgency in this troubled North African nation. More recently, President Trump further increased CIA drone attacks against suspected terrorists around the world. For President Biden, the center piece of covert action has been the paramilitary provision of weapons and training support to Ukraine troops in their life-or-death struggle to repel Russian invaders.

A ladder of escalation for covert action

In 1965, strategist Herman Kahn of the Hudson Institute published an influential volume in which he offered an "escalation-ladder metaphor" for understanding the coercive features of international affairs. Kahn described his ladder as a "convenient list of the many options facing the strategist in a two-sided confrontation."[42] In a comparable ladder of escalation for covert actions (see Figure 4.2), the underlying analytical dimension traveling

Threshold Four: Extreme Options
29 Use of WMDs
28 Major secret wars
27 Assassination
26 Small-scale coups d'état
25 Major economic dislocations; crop, livestock destruction
24 Environmental alterations
23 Pinpointed covert retaliations against non-combatants
22 Torture to gain compliance for a political deal
21 Extraordinary rendition for bartering
20 Major hostage-rescue attempts
19 Sophisticated arm supplies
Threshold Three: High-Risk Options
18 Massive increases of funding in democracies
17 Small-scale hostage rescue attempt
16 Training of foreign military forces for war
15 Limited arms supplies for offensive purposes
14 Limited arms supplies for balancing purposes
13 Economic disruption without loss of life
12 Modest funding in democracies
11 Massive increases of funding in autocracies
10 Large increases of funding in autocracies
 9 Disinformation against democratic regimes
 8 Disinformation against autocratic regimes
 7 Truthful but contentious propaganda in democracies
 6 Truthful but contentious propaganda in autocracies
Threshold Two: Modest Intrusions
 5 Low-level funding of friendly groups
 4 Truthful, benign propaganda in democracies
Threshold One: Routine Operations
 3 Truthful, benign propaganda in autocracies
 2 Recruitment of covert action assets
 1 Support for intelligence collection

Figure 4.2: A partial, heuristic "ladder of escalation" for covert actions.

Source: The author's estimates, based on interviews with intelligence managers and officers over the years, along with a study of the literature cited in the notes of this chapter. For a more elaborate depiction and discussion of this CA ladder, see Loch K. Johnson, *The Third Option: Covert Action and American Foreign Policy* (New York: Oxford University Press, 2022).

upward is the extent to which the options are increasingly harsh violations of international law and deep intrusions against the sovereignty of another nation. As the examples in Figure 4.2 illustrate, CAs can run the gamut from the routine on the lower rungs of the ladder to the extreme at the higher rungs.[43]

The lines of demarcation between high- and low-threshold covert actions can be indistinct, subject to debate and disagreement. Some members of the UN General Assembly's Special Committee on Friendly Relations argued in 1967, for instance, that covert propaganda and the secret financing of political parties represented "acts of lesser gravity than those directed towards the violent overthrow of the host government."[44] Other Assembly members rejected this perspective, especially those who wished to avoid legitimizing any form of CA. As a result of the divided opinion, the Special Committee equivocated, neither supporting nor prohibiting covert propaganda and secret political funding. A perspicacious observer of the committee's work concluded: "The texts that the General Assembly approved represent compromise formulations that are open to multiple interpretations."[45] What follows, and is shown in Figure 4.2, is also open to many interpretations, but the ladder metaphor does at least provide the reader with a sense of the rising levels of severity that the adoption of covert actions can entail.

Threshold One: Routine options

At the lower end of the ladder for covert actions – Threshold One – are arrayed such relatively benign activities as the limited dissemination of truthful, noncontroversial propaganda themes (Rung 1) directed against closed, authoritarian societies (such as extolling to Yugoslavians the benefits of trade with the West in the early years of the CIA's covert propaganda programs soon after the end of World War II). These low-rung activities are commonplace for most nations engaged in international affairs.[46]

Threshold Two: Modest intrusions

With Threshold Two, the degree of intrusiveness against another country or group begins to escalate beyond the routine, and the risks increase. This category would include the insertion of truthful, noncontroversial propaganda material into the media outlets of democratic regimes with a free press. Here, covert action is aimed at like-minded governments – for example mutually advancing opposition to human trafficking (Rung 5).

Threshold Three: High-risk options

Threshold Three consists of controversial steps that could trigger within the target nation a response significantly damaging to international comity. Here, propaganda operations remain truthful and compatible with overt policy statements, but now the themes are contentious (Rung 7) – say, reporting truthfully that Taliban soldiers have sprayed acid into the faces of young girls on their way to school in Afghanistan or killed international health-aid workers in Pakistan. At Rungs 8 and 9 (maintaining the distinction between nondemocratic and democratic regimes), propaganda activities take a nastier turn, employing deception and disinformation against the world's close societies – say, falsely blaming an adversary for an assassination attempt or fabricating documents to stain an adversary's reputation. Even propaganda operations against a nation without a free media are of concern here, because of the way in which blow-back can deceive citizens in the democratic regimes. Rung 12 stands for an escalation based on relatively modest levels of secret funding to affect elections, but this time within a democratic regime – a much more questionable step. Damrosch underscores the distinction: "A political system that denies basic political rights is in my view no longer a strictly internal affair," but rather one properly subject to international interventions.[47]

At Rung 13, the use of covert action involves attacks against economic entities within a target nation. A power line is destroyed here, an oil depot contaminated there; a virus or "worm" is inserted into the computer infrastructures of a foreign government; labor strikes are encouraged within an adversary's major cities. The measures are carefully planned to remain at the level of harassment operations, with a low probability that lives will be lost; nonetheless, a nation at this rung on the ladder has entered into a realm of more forceful operations.

A nation resorts to paramilitary operations at Rung 14, supplying arms to counter weapons previously introduced into the target nation by an adversary. Secret military training may accompany the arms transfers. This is a major step upward, for now an intelligence service has brought weapons into the equation. A modest arsenal of unsophisticated, but nonetheless deadly, arms might be provided to a favored rebel faction as a means for balancing the correlation of forces in a civil war. At Rung 16, a hostage rescue attempt is envisioned, one that could well lead to the loss of life even though it is designed to be small in scale so as to limit the potential for losses.

At Rung 17, massive expenditures are dedicated to improve the political fortunes of friendly parties within a democratic regime – perhaps $40 million in a small democracy and $100 million or more in a larger one. The objective is to support the emergence of a foreign faction into power that is the friendliest toward the United States. For some critics, this amounts to a troubling attempt to tamper with electoral outcomes in free societies; for proponents, it is simply an effort to make the world a better place by aligning nations along a compatible democratic axis. Attempts at covert influence against truly democratic elections – those in which the rights of political dissent and opposition are genuinely honored – represent a clear-cut violation of the noninterventionist norm (and related rules of international law) and have little claim to legitimacy, in contrast to lower-rung operations directed against self-interested autocratic regimes.

Threshold Four: Extreme options

With Threshold Four, a nation enters an especially dangerous and controversial portal of covert action: the "hot zone" of America's secret foreign policy. Here is where the lives of innocent people may be placed in extreme jeopardy.

At Rung 18, the types of weapons provided to a friendly faction are more potent than at earlier rungs – say, Stinger and Blowpipe anti-aircraft missiles, or UAVs armed with Hellfire missiles that enable the faction to take the offensive against a common adversary. At Rung 19, a nation might attempt an elaborate hostage-rescue operation that could well entail extensive casualties, even if that was not the intention. Skipping to Rung 21, a prisoner might be tortured in an attempt to gain intelligence about future terrorist plans for an attack against the United States or one of its allies; and, in the case of rendition, forceful abduction is intended, carefully planned, and directed against a specific person, perhaps with the intention of using the hostage as a pawn in secret negotiations toward some policy objective. Acts of brutality can occur at this level in retaliation for a hostile intelligence operation – say, the torture of a terrorist's relative as an act of revenge (said to be a Russian specialty).

On the highest rungs, covert action escalates dramatically to include violence-laden environmental or economic operations, as well as paramilitary activities against targets of wider scope than is the case at lower levels on the ladder. Large numbers of noncombatants in the civilian population may become targets, whether planned or inadvertent. For example, the CA may try to bring about major environmental alterations (Rung 24), from the defoliation or burning of forests to the contamination of lakes and rivers, the creation of floods through the destruction of dams, and operations designed to control weather conditions through cloud seeding in hopes of ruining crops and bringing about mass starvation. At this rung, too, the covert action aggressor attempts to wreak major economic dislocations within the target nation by engaging in the widespread counterfeiting of local currencies to fuel inflation and financial ruin; by sabotaging industrial facilities; destroying crops through the introduction of agricultural parasites (like Bunga) into the fields; or by spreading hoof-and-mouth disease or African swine fever among livestock. Rung 25 has the covert action aggressor adopting even higher-stake operations: overthrowing a foreign regime, though with minimal intended bloodshed (as in Iran in 1953 or Guatemala in 1954). The next step, Rung 26, arrives at the level of assassination plots against specific foreign leaders or terrorists and includes, in recent years, the use of Predators and Reapers as the instruments of murder – with all the risks these operations carry of incurring civilian casualties, not to mention the real possibility of retaliation against one's own democratically elected leaders.

Near the top of the escalation ladder (Rung 27) is a form of secret warfare that inevitably affects large numbers of combatants and noncombatants: the launching of protracted, full-blown paramilitary warfare against an inimical regime, comparable in scope to the CIA's "secret" war in Laos during the 1960s. At Rung 28, one's own democracy is assaulted from within, by wrong-minded leaders who flaunt law and the Constitution in the relentless pursuit of their policy goals (as with the Iran-*contra* affair in the United

States). Finally, at Rung 29, a nation introduces extreme WMDs into the CA calculus – nuclear, biological, chemical, or radiological arms – meant to inflict widespread death in the population of the target nation and that could lead to the disintegration of entire civilizations, democratic and authoritarian alike, as the deterrent doctrine of mutual assured destruction (MAD) reaches its logically existential conclusion.

Evaluating covert action

As the ladder of escalation suggests, covert action raises profound legal and ethical questions about what kinds of operations should be acceptable and what should be beyond the pale of consideration. How one assesses these questions will depend on how one views the place of law and morality in the conduct of a nation's foreign policy. "Do no evil though the world shall perish," admonished the eighteenth-century German philosopher Immanuel Kant. Taken to the extreme for CA, a devotee of the Kantian school might well reject all but the very lowest rungs on the ladder of escalation. In this spirit, a U.S. Undersecretary of State during the Cold War argued:

> [America] ought to discourage the idea of fighting secret wars or even initiating most covert operations [because] when . . . we mine harbors in Nicaragua . . . we fuzz the difference between ourselves and the Soviet Union. We act out of character . . . When we yield to what is, in my judgment, a childish temptation to fight the Russians on their own terms and in their own gutter, we make a major mistake and throw away one of our great assets.[48]

At the other end of the ethical spectrum is a point of view so nationalistic that the use of almost any form of CA might be considered acceptable by some, if it would serve the national interest. The specific consequences (the ends) of a covert action – the protection and advancement of the state – become more important than the means one adopts. According to this "consequentialist" perspective, in light of the anarchic and hostile world environment in which we live, a nation must defend itself in every possible way, including the full range of dark arts available through the auspices of a nation's secret services. As the Hoover Commission advised America's leaders in 1954: "We must learn to subvert, sabotage, and destroy our enemies by more clever, more sophisticated and more effective methods than those used against us."[49]

Two former CIA officials have extolled this realist approach to CA in the context of the Cold War (with logic that presumably applies to terrorists, Russia, and China today). "The United States is faced with a situation in which the major world power opposing our system of government is trying to expand its power by using covert methods of warfare," argued Ray Cline, a senior CIA analyst, referring to the Soviet Union. "Must the United States respond like a man in a barroom brawl who will fight only according to Marquis of Queensberry rules?"[50] G. Gordon Liddy, an Agency operative (and later a Watergate conspirator), stated the case more bluntly: "The world isn't Beverly Hills; it's a bad neighborhood at two o'clock in the morning."[51] The CIA would have to act accordingly.

One thing is certain: covert action is tricky in more than one sense of the word. For example, certain conditions must be present for success, such as an indigenous resistance movement supported by the CIA against an outside invader, as in the Afghanistan model during the 1980s. It helps, also, to have a willing partner in the region, as was Pakistan during the CA in Afghanistan at the time of the Reagan Administration; or, in another example, the Northern Alliance of local anti-Taliban Afghanis, who joined with the CIA soon after 9/11 in attacking the regime in Afghanistan, which had provided a safe haven for Bin Laden and other Al Qaeda leaders. Further, the more allies the better. Britain, China, Egypt, and Saudi Arabia helpfully joined with Pakistan and the United States in support of the *mujahideen*'s struggle against the Soviet invaders during the 1980s.[52]

Moreover, covert action outcomes can be highly unpredictable, for history is known to push back. Often there are long-range unanticipated, and detrimental, consequences that result from secret interventions. In the Guatemalan coup of 1954, for instance, the United Fruit Company was no doubt pleased at the outcome at the time (a result also sought by the U.S. Congress), but the impoverished citizens of that nation had to endure repressive regimes after the CIA intervention. As journalist Anthony Lewis writes: "The coup began a long national descent into savagery."[53] Not until 1986 did Guatemala enjoy a civilian government, in yet another change aided by the Agency. Moreover, following twenty-six years of repressive rule by the Shah of Iran (placed in power by the United States and the United Kingdom in 1953), the people of that nation rose up in revolt in 1979 and threw their support behind the nation's mullahs and a fundamentalist religious regime – one that remains at odds with the democracies today.

Even the celebrated ousting of the Soviets from Afghanistan during the 1980s, which one experienced CIA operative has referred to as "the most effective [covert action] in the spy agency's history,"[54] had a downside. The Soviet defeat set the stage for the rise of the fundamentalist Taliban regime and its support for Al Qaeda during the buildup for the terrorist attacks against New York City and Washington, DC, in 2001. Moreover, the Stinger missiles and other CIA weaponry were never returned to Langley; they remained in the hands of Al Qaeda terrorists, Taliban extremists, and Iranians, who purchased them on the open market from *mujahideen* warriors after the Soviets fled Afghanistan. "You get all steamed up backing a rebel group for reasons that are yours and not theirs," President Kennedy's National Security Advisor

McGeorge Bundy once cautioned. "Your reasons run out of steam and theirs do not."[55]

The CIA's assassination plots against foreign heads of state eventually became known to the world and left an impression of the United States as a global Godfather. This was hardly the image most Americans desired in a Cold War contest with the communist nations to win the allegiance of people around the world. Moreover, what if Castro had been killed during the Kennedy years? He would have been replaced by his brother, Raoul, who was equally truculent toward the United States. Furthermore, as periodically stressed in this book, to order the killing of foreign leaders is to invite retaliation against one's own chief of state – and leaders in the democracies are much more accessible and vulnerable. Assassination plots open a Pandora's box. As a Yale University School of Law professor has written: "Assassination in any form presents a cascading threat to world order."[56] Such has been the history of assassinations between Israelis and Palestinians, with murder plots see-sawing back and forth endlessly between the two without any resolution to the major policy differences that divide them.

Of course, one person's perception of long-term negative effects may be countered by another's delight over short-term gains. Looking back on the Iranian coup, for example, DCI Colby argued that "the assistance to the Shah to return in 1953 was an extremely good move which gave Iran twenty-five years of progress before he was overthrown. Twenty-five years is no small thing."[57] He might have added that neither is a quarter-century of low prices for Americans at their gas pumps, which this allegiance with the Shah assisted.[58]

For Daugherty, the CIA's "finest hour" of covert action occurred in Poland near the end of the Cold War, when the Agency helped to prevent a Soviet invasion of that nation and aided its movement toward democracy, setting an example for the rest of Central Europe.[59] Another former DCI, Stansfield Turner (1977–80), points to the CIA's covert propaganda program aimed at communist regimes during the Cold War as a particularly effective use of CA. "Certainly one thinks that the book programs [smuggling behind the Iron Curtain books and other reading materials that were critical of communism in general and the Soviet regime in particular, the broadcast programs, the information programs do good," he has said. "When you get facts into a country where the truth is not a common commodity, you're doing some good."[60]

Guidelines for covert action

As these illustrations suggest, special activities can be useful. This fact was demonstrated by the U.S. rout of the Taliban in Afghanistan immediately following the 9/11 attacks. The first U.S. casualty in that counterattack against

Al Qaeda and its Taliban hosts was Johnny Michael "Mike" Spann of Winfield, Alabama, an Auburn University graduate and CIA/SOG officer. America's combination of Special Forces, B-52 bombing, CIA paramilitary operations, and assistance from the local Northern Alliance in Afghanistan during 2001–2 provides a model of how covert action and overt force can be effectively intertwined to defeat enemies of democracy. Yet we know that the use of CA can also be acutely embarrassing and damaging to a nation's reputation: witness the Iran–*contra* scandal, the Bay of Pigs fiasco, and America's assassination plots in the 1960s.[61]

Hoping to avoid potential embarrassments caused by inappropriate CA operations, William H. Webster (the only person to have headed both the FBI and then the CIA) crafted a set of questions that he posed to the Operations Directorate throughout his tenure as DCI (1987–91) each time its officers brought him a CA proposal:

- Is it legal? [with respect to U.S. law, not necessarily international law]
- Is it consistent with American foreign policy and, if not, why not?
- Is it consistent with American values?
- If it becomes public, will it make sense to the American people?[62]

These questions make good sense and carry with them a set of principles that should be remembered by all CA planners. Insightful, too, are the observations of DCI John Deutch (1995–7). In a discussion he had with a predecessor, Richard Helms (1966–73), Deutch developed a two-item checklist that he suggested should be imposed by the CIA's DDO before approval of a CA. Beginning with the fourth litmus test on Webster's list above (regarding the potential of embarrassment from public disclosure), the key questions for Deutch were: "Will the American people support you if it shows up on the front page of the paper?" and – pointing to the important matter related to the odds of success – "Do you have confidence that you can do it effectively and completely?" When President Obama ordered the capture or (if he resisted arrest) the killing of Bin Laden in 2011, he estimated that the chances for success were only about fifty-fifty. Some of the planners in the IC believed the odds were even less than that. Such disagreements underline the uncertain chances for a good outcome that often accompany a covert action – even over the short haul (as in this case), let along the long-term consequences of an operation like the one during the Reagan years that supported the Taliban regime in Afghanistan against Soviet invaders (before the Taliban cozied up to Al Qaeda). Deutch was correct, though: responsible CA planners should do their best to estimate the chances of success. And, one might add, adopt a robust skeptical stance when the odds appear low. As the national security journalist Dexter Filkins once put it a *New Yorker* article: "There is no moral case for doing something you're not able to do."[63]

Useful to consider, as well, is the admonition of Clark Clifford, former presidential advisor and Secretary of Defense in the final year of the Lyndon Johnson presidency. In his testimony before the Church Committee in 1975, Clifford stressed that special activities should be adopted only in circumstances that "truly affect our national security." Cyrus Vance, who would become Secretary of State in the Carter Administration, advanced a similar thesis before the committee. Covert action, he emphasized, should be used only when "absolutely essential."[64]

Finally, decision-makers in Washington, DC should constantly keep in mind the constitutionally based framework by which policy choices are made in the United States. A central legal and ethical question that should always guide America's resort to a CA is: has the proposed initiative been approved by the President and carefully reviewed by SSCI and HPSCI lawmakers? After all, congressional checks and balances of executive branch activities are the lynchpin of America's democracy. Further, this intelligence accountability has been explicitly embedded in U.S. law since 1975 (a topic closely examined in Chapter 6). In light of these important standards, the planting of propaganda in the media of fellow democracies, or the tampering with democratic elections (as occurred in Chile, for instance), hardly seem to qualify as acceptable practices. And the Iran-*contra* affair is so far beyond the pale of legal and moral acceptability as to be immediately recognized as a shameful blow against democratic principles. The bottom line: one should be wary of all covert actions designed to manipulate fellow democratic regimes – or one's own legal procedures.

Further, CA planners in the democracies would do well to keep in mind a cautionary note from Professor Roger Fisher of Harvard University's School of Law. "To join some adversaries in the grotesque world of poison dart-guns and covert operations," he reasoned, "is to give up the most powerful weapons we have: idealism, morality, due process of law, and belief in the freedom to disagree, including the right of other countries to disagree with ours."[65] One should also reject "special activities" that target any nation's environment or food supplies; or those CAs that involve lethal targeting against individuals – except in the case of terrorist leaders wanted for murder who resist arrest for purposes of a fair trial. On September 11, 2001, Al Qaeda was responsible for the death of nearly 3,000 people on American soil, with additional killings in Iraq, Afghanistan, Syria, and elsewhere thereafter. Like ISIS, it hopes to bring about even larger casualties in the West. These terrorist groups are worthy targets for many of the CA options presented in the ladder of escalation. The democracies of the world should coordinate their special activities against the enemies of open societies, just as they do some of their intelligence collection operations. Terrorists – with their agenda of suicide bombings, beheadings, mass executions, and savage attacks against schoolgirls, aid workers, and other innocents – have revealed themselves as barbarians. Even against such brutal adversaries, however, the West must avoid abandoning its own moral values by adopting the indiscriminate use of CAs that reach beyond a pinpointed targeting of Al Qaeda, ISIS, and related terrorist organizations, and deterring Russian and Chinese territorial expansion. In the practice of these dark arts, the democracies risk adopting the behavior of the very adversaries they oppose. Therefore, CA options must be used sparingly and cast narrowly; they must honor the law and ethical principles, and be submitted to close supervision by presidents and lawmakers, prime ministers and parliamentarians.

If covert actions are meant to secretly advance a nation's interests abroad, counterintelligence – thwarting hostile acts by authoritarian regimes and terrorist factions against the open societies – is also a matter of great importance for the survival of the world's open societies. The next chapter turns to this subject, widely considered to be a perplexing "wilderness of mirrors."

5

Counterintelligence:
Guarding the Democracies

In October and November 1969, the antiwar movement brought thousands of protesters to Washington, DC, in the largest mass demonstrations ever in the history of the United States. Not only the draft-age youth of America, but practically the entire nation was obsessed with the war in Vietnam. In turn, the Nixon Administration became increasingly focused on the rising tide of protests that ebbed and flowed along the Mall to within a stone's throw of the West Wing. At one point, presidential aides ordered the encirclement of the White House grounds with D.C. Metro buses, as if the protesters were Apaches and the Oval Office an imperiled wagon train in the western territories. As historian Theodore H. White recalled: "Perplexed by a street madness which seemed beyond the control of either his staff, his own efforts, or the FBI, [President Nixon] groped for solutions."[1]

President Richard M. Nixon was unwilling to face the possibility that he could be so unpopular on the nation's campuses; there had to be a sinister foreign hand involved behind the scenes, inciting college radicals to turn against their own country by paying them off or perhaps by brainwashing them – maybe both. John Ehrlichman, one of the President's top aides, turned to the Intelligence Community for answers, but the IC rejected the hypothesis of foreign involvement. There was simply no evidence to support that allegation. These were "credit card revolutionaries," as one intelligence officer put it, using their parents' credit cards to travel around the country demonstrating against a war they found illegitimate and unworthy of America's involvement.[2] Nixon and Ehrlichman remained skeptical of this argument.

In June 1969, Ehrlichman heard about a young aide on the White House speech-writing staff, a 29-year-old by the name of Tom Charles Huston. As a Republican activist and head of the Young Americans for Freedom (YAF, a right-leaning student association) while an undergraduate at Indiana University, he had gained first-hand experience in confronting antiwar campus protesters. Moreover, he was bright, articulate, and impassioned about their lack of patriotism. Another plus: he had become an Army veteran. After college, Huston had joined the Army as an intelligence officer and was assigned to the Pentagon. During off-hours, he engaged in volunteer work for the Nixon presidential campaign. Intelligent and hard-working, he soon attracted attention among Nixon's senior assistants and, when his military tour came to an end, he had a job waiting for him in the White House. His immediate supervisor suggested to Ehrlichman that Huston could conduct for the President a study of the antiwar protest movement. Ehrlichman followed up and asked Huston to investigate the sources of funding for the student protests. After a brief pep talk in "the Oval" (White House slang for the Oval Office) from President Nixon himself, the young staffer – with little experience in Washington – suddenly found himself in a commanding position to examine more closely the "hippies" who (he had been long convinced) were undermining American society.

With a sense of zeal, Huston set out from the Oval for the office of William C. Sullivan, assistant director for domestic intelligence at the FBI – the number three official in the Bureau beneath the legendary J. Edgar Hoover and his deputy and personal companion Clyde Tolson. Sullivan was the government's top counterintelligence officer, responsible for discovering and foiling threats to America from home-grown subversives, as well as from hostile intelligence services operating inside the United States – especially the Soviet KGB. It was in his office that Huston started work on efforts to curb alleged foreign intelligence support of student antiwar protests aimed at the Nixon White House.

Huston informed Sullivan about his orders from the President and Ehrlichman. They wanted to know everything about the antiwar movement, "especially," Sullivan remembers the youthful White House aide emphasizing, "all information possible relating to foreign influences and the financing of the New Left." Further, the White House sought advice on what steps could be taken to provide the maximum possible intelligence coverage of these "radicals." By courier, Huston sent a similar message to the leaders of the CIA (DCI Richard Helms), the NSA (Admiral Noel Gayler), and the DIA (General Donald Bennett) – all with a June 31, 1970, deadline for a written response back to the White House. Sullivan kept Director Hoover informed of these activities. When the responses came back to Huston, Sullivan's advice resonated well with the White House concern about a covert sponsorship by the Soviet Union of the protests in the United States. Together, he and Sullivan then worked out a plan to convince Hoover and the other three intelligence chiefs to lower the legal barriers that barred espionage operations by the IC against domestic protesters inside the United States.[3]

In early June 1970, the President personally met with Helms, Hoover, Gayler, and Bennett in the Oval Office. Nixon told them that the demonstrators were "reaching out for the support – ideological and otherwise – of foreign powers," and that the radicals were trying to "destroy their country." He ordered the group to "insure that the fullest possible inter-agency cooperation is being realized and that all our resources are being utilized to gather the types of information which will enable us to halt the spread of this terrorism before it gets completely out of hand."[4] On June 25, the four intelligence chiefs met again, this time in Hoover's office at FBI Headquarters in downtown Washington. They had gathered to sign a top secret (since declassified) forty-three-page "Special Report" that became known eponymously in the White House as "the Huston Plan." The report provided a list of existing restraints on collection that the President could – and should – lift, thus enabling the Intelligence Community to spy on the war dissenters (see the examples in Table 5.1). On July 14, President Nixon signed his approval of the recommendations. In a chilling turn of history, the Huston Plan was now secret presidential policy.

As historian White has observed, the methods proposed in the Huston Plan reached "all the way to every mailbox, every college campus, every telephone, every home" in America.[5] Huston had emphasized to the President that these methods would have advantages that far "outweigh the risks."[6] Moreover, they would provide the White House "with the type of intelligence which cannot be obtained in any other fashion."[7]

The Huston Plan proved short-lived, however. Attorney General John Mitchell urged Nixon to reconsider his decision, on grounds (as Nixon recalled) that the "risk of public disclosure . . . was greater than the possible benefits to be derived."[8] Hoover, too, began to have second thoughts and withdrew his support. Absent Hoover's imprimatur, the Huston Plan quickly collapsed and the President rescinded his initial approval. The broad attack on American civil liberties, directed toward the antiwar movement, had been stopped short.

Or so it seemed. Five years later, Church Committee investigators discovered that the nation's intelligence agencies had been involved in improper domestic spying both *before* the Huston Plan and even *after* its supposed rescission by President Nixon. The IC pursued these illegal self-initiatives – outside the ambit of presidential approval – all in the name of counterintelligence. Ostensibly, the spy agencies claimed they were protecting the nation against hostile (and, it turned out, virtually nonexistent) Soviet influences on America's youth. In reality, though, they already knew from earlier surveillance the false nature of that hypothesis, but argument provided good cover for carrying out – and gaining additional funding for – counterintelligence operations more generally against the KGB.[9]

In 1975, the Church Committee called Huston as its main witness for public hearings into this startling domestic spy proposal. He expressed remorse for the plan that bore his name:

> The risk was that you would get people who would be susceptible to political considerations as opposed to national security considerations. Or would construe political considerations to be national security considerations, to move from the kid with the bomb to the kid with a picket sign, and from the kid with the picket sign to the kid with the bumper sticker of the opposing candidate. And you just keep going down the line.[10]

Table 5.1: Key intelligence recommendations proposed by the Huston Plan, 1970

	RECOMMENDATION
Communications intelligence	• Present interpretation should be broadened to permit and [*sic*] program for coverage by NSA of the communications of U.S. citizens using international facilities.
Electronic surveillances and penetrations	• Present procedures should be changed to permit intensification of coverage of individuals and groups in the United States who pose a major threat to the internal security. • ALSO, present procedures should be changed to permit intensification of coverage of foreign nations. [The rest of this paragraph remains classified]
Mail coverage	• Restrictions on legal coverage [that is, examining the writing and postmarks on the outside of envelopes] should be removed. • ALSO, present restrictions on covert coverage [that is, reading the message inside] should be relaxed on selected targets of priority foreign intelligence and internal security interest.
Surreptitious entry [that is, the break-in option]	• Present restrictions should be modified to permit procurement of vitally needed foreign [a still classified section] material. • ALSO, present restrictions should be modified to permit selective use of this technique against other urgent and high priority internal security targets.
Development of campus sources	• Present restrictions should be relaxed to permit expanded coverage of violence- prone campus and student-related groups. • ALSO, CIA coverage of American students (and others) traveling or living abroad should be increased.
Use of military undercover agents	• Present restrictions should be retained.

The Huston Plan episode provides an important, indeed fundamental, lesson in counterintelligence. However vital this intelligence mission is – and there should be no doubt the democracies have genuine enemies who must be identified and resisted by a well-trained counterintelligence corps – a democracy has to be on guard against the use of this tradecraft to spy against its own law-abiding citizens. Sound security measures against genuine threats at home and abroad, yes; turning the open societies into Orwellian "Counterintelligence States" like North Korea, no.

The proper focus of counterintelligence

In the United States, an executive order offers this definition of counterintelligence (CI):

> Counterintelligence means information gathered and activities conducted to identify, deceive, exploit, disrupt or protect against espionage, other intelligence activities, sabotage or assassination conducted for or on behalf of foreign powers, organizations or persons or their agents, or international terrorist organizations or activities.[11]

Stated simply, the task of CI is to thwart hostile acts that might be perpetrated against one's nation by different kinds of groups and individuals – for example: homegrown extremists, international terrorists, hostile foreign intelligence services, criminal organizations, reckless leakers, and careless handlers of classified materials. The increased spying against the democracies by Russian's SVR and China's MSS, accompanied by expanded threats against the U.S. government posted on the Internet by domestic hard-right nihilists and anarchists, have led to a more concerted focus by the IC on counterintelligence defenses. This reemphasis on counterintelligence has occurred in all the world's democracies, largely as a result of stepped-up efforts by the Chinese and the Russians to secretly manipulate world affairs.

Homegrown extremism: The Oklahoma City bombing

On April 19, 1995, the United States suffered an assault from inside the nation by an extreme rightwing American citizen. On that terrible morning, a rental truck sat parked at a curb downtown in Oklahoma's state capital, near the entrance to the Alfred P. Murrah Federal Building. In the truck's storage space, a homemade bomb made of combustible fuels in fifty-five-gallon drums suddenly erupted in a powerful blast of ammonium nitrate and nitromethane. The wave of destruction tore into the building. The date marked the second anniversary of a fatal assault by the FBI on the Branch Davidian sect near Waco, Texas, which resulted in the death of seventy-six people. The Waco massacre had become a symbol for some right-leaning "patriot" groups in the United States of the growing danger posed by the federal government in Washington – a theme that would again motivate insurrectionists who stormed the U.S. Capitol on January 6, 2021, urged on by President Trump.

The Oklahoma City explosion, triggered by an alienated young veteran, Timothy McVeigh, was the worst terrorist attack in the United States since a bomb detonated in front of the Morgan Bank on Wall Street, September 16, 1920, killing thirty-eight men and women.[12] In a letter written shortly before the bombing of the Murrah Building, McVeigh said that he had shifted from being an "intellectual" in the anti-government movement to being an "animal" determined to shed blood in honor of his cause.[13] The bombing left 168 people dead, including 19 children, and injured more than 500 other individuals.[14] Careless in his escape plans (his car license plate was out of date, for instance), McVeigh was soon captured as he fled Oklahoma City. Conviction and a death sentence followed.

One of the many questions raised by the Oklahoma City bombing was the extent to which the FBI had failed in placing counterintelligence informants inside patriot groups of the kind to which McVeigh had belonged. A well-placed informant – a "mole," in CI spytalk – could have alerted the Bureau to the planned attack.[15] This history also pointed to a larger concern: the growing danger of homegrown extremism, whether on the left or the right. In 2023, Secretary of Homeland Security Alejandro Mayorkas told a television audience that the most significant terrorist threat to the U.S. homeland was domestic extremism.[16] CI officers and academic experts pointed especially to the increasing number of online threats expressed by alienated groups and individuals on the hard-right.

International terrorism

Ambush at the Agency

The dangers to the free societies from hostile regimes and terrorists are palpable – everything from attacks against computers in the democracies (potentially an electronic Pearl Harbor, as some specialists envision a modern-day and massive cyberattack) to the "lone wolf" murdering of citizens like those in Oklahoma City in 1995. With respect to the targeting of civilians, here is another example, this one from a dreadful January day in 1993 and involving a foreign terrorist inside the United States. At 8:00 a.m. on what seemed to be a normal day, a long line of CIA employees sat in their automobiles, queued up at a traffic signal on Dolly Madison Highway as they waited to make a turn into the main entrance of the Agency's forested compound at Langley. Just a typical morning for Agency commuters – until suddenly a strange noise became audible to those waiting in their cars at the stop light. Perhaps a fender bender had occurred somewhere at the front of the queue; yet the noise grew louder and sounded more like firecrackers popping on the 4th of July. Then the source of the noise became all too clear.

Carrying an AK-47, a dark-haired man of stocky, medium build, his face stone cold, his eyes unblinking, had walked up to the first of the idling cars, a Volkswagen, and fired into the open window, striking the driver in the back as he tried to lean away from the barrel. The assailant then trotted toward the next car, then the next, spraying bullets into the windows at close range – some seventy rounds in all. As witnesses recalled, glass shattered, car horns blared, and people screamed or prayed that the weapon would run out of ammunition.[17] The killer, a Pakistani national by the name of Mir Aimal Kansi, raced back to the first car and finished off the driver as the wife of the dying Agency officer jerked open the door on the passenger side and safely ducked for cover. Kansi then ran to his station wagon parked nearby and sped away from the scene. Two Agency employees slumped against their steering wheels, blood seeping from gaping bullet holes in their bodies. Down the line of cars, others moaned from the agony of their wounds.

Kansi escaped back to Pakistan, flying out of the United States that same day. His expired passport went unnoticed by airport security. It took four-and-a-half years for a joint team of CIA and the FBI counterintelligence officers to track him down at a small village in his homeland, where he was captured and returned to the United States for trial. A day after his conviction in 1997, four American oil executives were killed in Karachi, Pakistan, in apparent retaliation. In 2002, Kansi was put to death by lethal injection at the Greensville Correctional Center in Jarratt, Virginia. Hours before his death, Kansi said he had carried out his attack to protest U.S. policies toward Muslim countries.

The 9/11 attacks

The most fateful collapse of CI defenses in U.S. history, though, came in the form of a more ambitious attack by international terrorists: Al Qaeda's devastating assault against two major cities within the American homeland on September 11, 2001. Several opportunities arose for blocking this attack. Recall from Chapter 1 that, as early as 1995, the CIA's Counterterrorism Center (CTC) warned the White House and other high government offices that "aerial terrorism" could strike inside the United States, with terrorists hijacking commercial aircraft and flying them into skyscrapers – precisely what happened six years later on that heart-wrenching day.[18] Yet missing in the CTC's early alert were any specifics about when and where such an event might occur – *actionable* intelligence. Moreover, the warning was part of a CTC list of many other potential perils that faced the nation, including the targeting of urban areas by terrorists flying crop-duster airplanes filled with anthrax or deadly biological agents in their spray tanks; the contamination of U.S. city water supplies with lethal toxins; and the smuggling of timed explosives into America's nuclear-reactor sites.

This lengthy and disquieting catalogue seemed to have the effect of paralyzing officials, preventing them from addressing any specific one among the litany of unsettling possibilities, even from sharing the aerial terrorism warning with the Department of Transportation (responsible for airport security) or the American Pilots Association. Another obstacle to action was no doubt the costs involved in defending against terrorism from the skies, such as strengthening airport security to carrying out more thorough security checks on boarding passengers, sealing cockpit doors, and hiring sky marshals – although each of these measures would have summed to a minuscule expense compared to the loss of life and property that resulted from the 9/11 attacks. Wishful thinking that aerial terrorism would never happen inside the United States proved more palatable to decision-makers than the political risks of advocating the expenditure of finite resources on events that might never take place. The press of distracting daily events, along with the numbing effect that accompanied the thought of a wide range of other possible terrorist disasters – all costly to deter – caused both the Clinton and the second Bush Administrations to dither in response to the red flags raised by the CTC regarding the threat of attacks from the skies.

The nation's experience with the devastation of Hurricane Katrina in 2005 points to a similar scenario. If the political leaders and citizens of New Orleans had been willing to pay the billions of dollars necessary to strengthen the surrounding levees to withstand a Category Five hurricane, the people of that great city would have been spared the catastrophic flooding that occurred, along with the immense costs and tragic deaths that accompanied this weather-induced crisis. Both the 9/11 attacks and the Katrina event raise a vexing public policy challenge: what should political leaders do when it comes to high-cost and high-danger, but low-probability, contingencies? With respect to the 9/11 attacks, better surveillance in California of two suspected Saudi terrorists who entered that state (and would soon participate in the airplane hijacking) might have unraveled the plot as well. Instead, both the CIA and the FBI fumbled this assignment and worked together with all the good will and liaison camaraderie of Kilkenny cats.

Recall, too, that Bureau headquarters personnel failed as well to respond to alerts from their own agents in the field that suspicious flight-training activity was taking place in Phoenix and Minneapolis, with foreign-born men wanting to know less about how to take off and land a commercial airliner and more about how to fly it once in the air. In the context of the aerial terrorism report on 1995, these field reports should have set off alarms at the FBI Building in downtown Washington – especially the case of a suspicious figure in Minneapolis, Zacarias Moussaoui. He had known connections to terrorists abroad and, as it was subsequently discovered, knew about the impending 9/11 plans.[19] A warrant to search his home computer (as recommended by the FBI's chief agent in Minneapolis) would have revealed the plan, but no such warrant was sought by Bureau Headquarters personnel from the Foreign Intelligence Surveillance Count in Washington. Adding to the failures of these and other CI defenses, from 1995 to 2001 members of Congress had held few hearings on terrorism, counterintelligence, or the quality of CIA–FBI liaison relationships.

Despite all of these mistakes, in January 2001 the top aide for counterterrorism in the Clinton White House, Richard A. Clarke, had the prescience of mind to warn the new National Security Advisor in the Bush Administration, Condoleezza Rice, that the NSC should act immediately to guard against a major Al Qaeda attack aimed at the United States. But even after these urgent warnings, it took Rice until September 4, 2001, to convene the first Council meeting of principals to discuss this topic.[20] The counterintelligence errors seemed to metastasize like a terrible cancer within the IC during the decade that preceded 9/11. Above all, America's spy agencies lacked a mole inside Al Qaeda, or even much understanding among IC analysts of the plans and capabilities of the terrorist organization to carry out attacks beyond the Middle East and Africa.

Hostile foreign intelligence services

Sometimes America's counterintelligence setbacks result not in the death of U.S. citizens at home, but in the targeting by foreign intelligence services of America's own intelligence officers or their recruited agents abroad, accompanied by a rolling up of valuable CIA operations in foreign lands. A result of this first approach is treason inside the U.S. spy agencies – "a hole in the bucket," in German CI lingo. The cases of Aldrich "Rick" Hazen Ames of the CIA and Robert Hanssen of the FBI, turncoats who both began their spying for the Soviet Union at about the same time in 1984, are prime illustrations of Moscow's successful efforts to infiltrate America's intelligence services during and after the Cold War.[21]

Aldrich Hazen Ames

Aldrich Ames was a senior CI officer within the CIA who had responsibilities for the Soviet Union. From that perch, he knew the identities of most of the Agency's assets in the USSR and had knowledge of the IC's collection activities, covert actions, and counterintelligence operations directed toward this most important of the West's Cold War targets. A senior CIA counterintelligence officer who helped uncover Ames's treachery told the Aspin–Brown Commission in 1995 that the traitor had essentially ruined the Agency's ability to spy against the Soviets during the final years of the Cold War.[22]

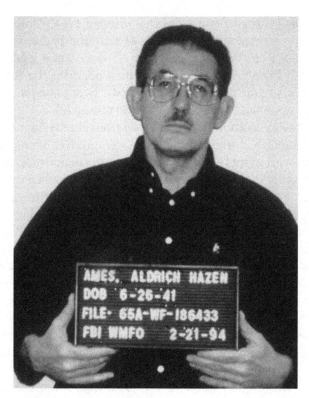

Photo 5.1: Aldrich Ames
CIA traitor Aldrich Hazen Ames, mugshot, 1994.
Source: Federal Bureau of Investigation.

Ames had engaged in espionage for the Soviets and then the Russians from 1984 to 1994, when his deceit was finally uncovered. Clues to his treasonous behavior had been there all along: questionable responses to the periodic polygraph tests given to all Agency employees (although he was given a pass by the examiners anyway); the absence of a mortgage on his $540,000 home in Arlington, Virginia; the purchase of a pricey new Jaguar automobile; expensive cosmetic dental work; a new wardrobe; increased foreign travel – all on a modest government salary. Yet Ames was hardly the only person at Langley to have a fancy house and car; the Agency has a number of well-to-do officers, individuals of independent wealth drawn by a sense of patriotism or a quest for adventure to a life of international sleuthing on behalf of the United States.

Ames, though, stood out in other ways as well. The "corridor file" (rumors at Agency Headquarters or, in slang, "rumint") about him had been negative long before his misdeeds were uncovered. He was widely known as a drunkard. This fact, plus his surplus of disposable income, raised questions among some colleagues. When they inquired about the fancy home and the new Jag, however, Ames brushed them off with stories of his Colombian wife (who was his partner in espionage). He claimed that she had recently inherited a pile of money from her family. Moreover, since Ames's father had been a well-regarded DO officer for decades (which provided the son with a halo effect), and because drunkenness was not exactly page-one news at Langley, his colleagues accepted the explanations and moved on.

For Ames, the motivation for treason had been chiefly financial. An earlier divorce settlement had drained his bank account. His handlers in Moscow provided him with more than $4.6 million for his handiwork. Moreover, the challenge of evading detection by U.S. counterintelligence officers became something of a fascinating game for him. The Aspin–Brown Commission probed into how Ames was finally uncovered by painstaking CI detective work (known as "walking back the cat," in CI terminology). It was an example of the CIA and the FBI effectively working together, which (as the reader of this book has seen) is not always the case. The damage assessment of Ames's spying revealed substantial setbacks for the United States. His sale of secrets to the KGB and its successor, the SVR, had led to the execution of at least ten Agency assets operating inside the government in Moscow. Further, based in part on Ames's tipoffs, the SVR's counterintelligence unit succeeded in rolling up more than 200 CIA intelligence operations aimed at the Kremlin.

No one in Washington knew at the time that while the Aspin–Brown Commission was investigating the Ames case, his foul work was being complemented by another major Soviet asset inside the U.S. government: FBI agent Robert Hanssen, who had been working off and on for the Soviets and Russians throughout the previous two decades. Not until 2001 was the Bureau able to track down its own internal Moscow mole – thanks to a CIA agent inside the SVR who helped tag Hanssen and Ames (neither of whom knew about this particular Agency asset inside the Kremlin).

Robert Hanssen

With a job high up in the FBI's Soviet counterintelligence division, Hanssen – like Ames – was well placed to inform the Kremlin about U.S. espionage activities against the Soviet Union and, subsequently, Russia. Hanssen began selling secrets to the Soviets in 1979 and wasn't apprehended until 2001. After their 180-degree turn away from loyalty to the United States, Ames and Hanssen together managed to finger almost all CIA and FBI assets working against Soviet and Russian targets. In addition to confirming many of the secrets that Ames had provided to his Moscow spymasters, Hanssen further revealed in-depth intelligence regarding U.S. nuclear war preparations and how Washington would respond to a first strike by the Soviet Union, then Russia; on the location of listening devises planted by the CIA and the NSA throughout the Soviet Embassy as it was being construction on Wisconsin Avenue in Washington; and more than 6,000 pages of classified documents from the IC. In addition, he informed the SVR about America's highly classified underwater sigint capabilities for tracking Russian submarines.[23]

In Hanssen's case, the motivation for treason was less financial than had been true with Ames, although he did request some payment in gems that were valued at $1.4 million (roughly a fourth of the total payoff to Ames). Hanssen lavished these profits on a friend, an attractive stripper in Washington whom he had met at a bar. Professing to be a deeply religious Catholic, he spent little of these ill-gotten gains on himself and seemed primarily interested (again, like Ames) in a game of counterintelligence cat-and-mouse. When caught, Hanssen's response to authorities who asked him why he had become a traitor was: "Fear and rage. Fear of being a failure and rage at not being able to provide for my family."

Careless tradecraft on their parts, coupled with clues from the CIA's mole in Moscow, eventually gave both Ames and Hanssen away. Ames is currently serving a life sentence in a U.S. federal penitentiary. While in prison, Hanssen "commuted" his life sentence by dying in June 2023. As a means for assuring improved attention to counterintelligence responsibilities at the highest levels of the Agency following the unmasking of Ames, DCI John Deutch established a special position of Associate Deputy Director of Operations for Counterintelligence.

The unauthorized disclosure of classified information

The Snowden leaks

In 2013, Edward J. Snowden was a young computer expert at a private consulting firm, Booz Allen Hamilton. One of his assignments was to assist with a project at the National Security Agency. While at the NSA in Ft. Meade, Maryland, he downloaded and stole more than a million documents from its computers. He fled the United States with these papers stored in his hard drive, then moved on to Russia. In the name of whistleblowing, he sent – "leaked" – these highly classified papers to newspapers in the United Kingdom and the United States: the *Guardian* and the *Washington Post*. His avowed purpose was to bring to the public's attention an NSA domestic "metadata" program that was inappropriately gathering – in a fever dream of counterintelligence ubiquity – data on the communication patterns (though not the message content) of millions of American citizens across the nation. He seemed to view himself as a courageous idealist fighting against what was – and he was correct about this conclusion – a massive violation of civil liberties by the U.S. government. He became an overnight hero to many in the United States and other democracies.

His actions, though, soon became more ambiguous. At the same time he revealed the NSA's improper adoption of the metadata program and related transgressions against U.S. citizen communications (which violated the Foreign Intelligence Surveillance Act of 1978), he also released detailed budgets of the agencies within the IC, as well as other extremely sensitive, highly classified information. These disclosures went far beyond his understandable concern about the NSA's metadata program; these leaks gave to America's adversaries precise information about U.S. intelligence priorities, not to mention specific tradecraft. It was, in the view of some experts, the most egregious leak of classification information in American history.

Further, as more information about the Snowden computer heist became available, his critics began to raise reasonable queries about his behavior. Why hadn't he gone through established procedures for whistleblowing, taking his case against the metadata program to Booz Allen Hamilton directors, to the Intelligence Oversight Board in the White House, or to staff on the House and Senate Intelligence Committees on Capitol Hill? He failed to contact any of these officials. Moreover, why did he flee to Russia – of all places – rather than patriotically stand his ground at home against the NSA's clear overreach of its authorities? And a question of great importance: why did he leak so many other documents regarding entirely legal and highly classified intelligence activities – an act that could have (and secretly may have) caused serious damage to the security of the United States?

Further leaks

The Snowden leak came on the heels of another infamous unauthorized flood of top-secret intelligence to a social media outlet. This leak came from an Army intelligence analyst by the name of Bradley (now Chelsea) Manning, who in 2010 provided an outside group ("WikiLeaks") with 1.6 gigabytes of classified data. Among further examples of unauthorized disclosures of classified intelligence was a leak in 2017 by a CIA software engineer, Joshua Schulte. He provided WikiLeaks with information on hacking tools used by the Agency against foreign intelligence services; it was the largest theft ever of classified documents from the CIA. Both individuals were convicted and sentenced to prison for their disclosures.

Then, in 2023, an Air Force National Guard technology support staffer – 21-year-old Jack Teixeira of Massachusetts – sent hundreds of highly classified documents, meant strictly for senior U.S. military and intelligence officials, to a circle of online friends. These papers soon emerged more widely on the Internet, revealing to the world weaknesses (for example) in Ukraine's air defense system, thereby allowing Russia to adjust its own combat operations against that nation. Reportedly, Teixeira was just showing off to his chat group about all the secrets he knew. His actions remain under judicial review; if convicted, he faces a significant term of incarceration.

The irresponsible handling of classified documents: Presidential abuse

Although less damaging because the papers were never made public, or (as far as is known) never made available to a foreign power or terrorist organization, FBI investigators found that a former president, a former vice president, and an incumbent president all had classified government documents in their homes. In the initial case, the Bureau followed up on tips about top-secret papers reportedly stored at former President Donald Trump's lavish estate in Mar-a-Lago, Florida. After acquiring a search warrant from the DoJ, Bureau agents respectfully searched the premises and indeed discovered a large number of highly classified documents on the premises. Subsequently, the FBI conducted another warrant-based search of President Joe Biden's home in Delaware and found additional (though far fewer) classified papers. Biden immediately said he was unaware they were in his possession, and that they had no doubt been misplaced through staff packing mistakes when he departed the Office of the Vice President at the end of the Obama Administration. The Bureau also found a small number of classified papers at former Vice President Mike Pence's home. He, too, expressed surprise that the documents were among the possessions that came with him in boxes when he retired after the Trump Administration lost the 2020 election. Biden apologized and cooperated with a wider FBI search of his residences, which uncovered no additional documents. The small volume of classified papers found in Biden's two homes were immediately delivered to their proper location, in Washington, DC secure storage vaults. Pence also apologized and immediately returned his papers.

In sharp contrast, Trump railed against the FBI "raid" (his term) as a political stunt waged against him by the Biden Administration. Further, he balked at returning any of the papers (the Bureau took the ones it initially found anyway back to Washington for proper storage), and refused to allow further searching of his many homes. A special prosecutor looking into this matter viewed Trump's refusals to cooperate as a clear case of illegal obstruction of justice. The former president and his GOP followers in Congress responded that the FBI, the Justice Department, and the special prosecutor were all merely engaged in a political "witch-hunt" against Trump and his chiefly Republican supporters. In their delusional view, the Biden Administration had "weaponized" the Bureau and other agencies in the executive branch for President Biden's own political purposes – above all, so he could retain control of the White House in 2024. It was a low point in the history of relations between the two major U.S. political parties, Republicans and Democrats.

Officials in the DoJ, as well as media, the special prosecutor, journalists, and GOP-led congressional committees in the House of Representatives, vowed to probe further into these charges and countercharges. In the summer of 2023, one of four indictments and ninety-one criminal counts brought against former President Trump revolved around his efforts to obstruct federal agents from retrieving classified documents from Mar-a-Largo and his other domiciles. In the meantime, one conclusion was self-evident: the United States had some significant problems in its chain-of-custody for keeping classified documents secure in government safes. No security personnel in charge of these papers should ever have let anyone – even presidents and vice presidents – fail to return sensitive papers to their proper government safes at the end of each day, to be checked out the next day if still needed by authorized officials. Those procedures are Counterintelligence 101.

A parade of traitors

While these cases are some of the most well-known counterintelligence and counterterrorism stumbles for the United States in recent years, they are hardly the only ones. Even during World War II, the United States was dealing with Soviet moles in the Manhattan Project. According to an authoritative study undertaken by John Haynes, Harvey Klehr, and Alexander Vassiliev, the British scientist Klaus Fuchs worked secretly for the Soviets and managed to steal from the Manhattan Project enough secrets about the construction of nuclear weaponry to save the Kremlin years of delay and millions of rubles in acquiring the atomic bomb – which it managed to finish constructing by 1949, much more quickly than anticipated by the CIA.[24]

Haynes and his colleagues found that the Soviets had recruited other "atomic spies," too, including David Greenglass, Russell McNutt, and Ethel Rosenberg – all part of the Julius Rosenberg spy ring – and, in the collection discipline of signals intelligence, the NSA's William Weisband, who informed the Soviets about America's ability to eavesdrop on their military communications (the Venona program). The KGB was successful, moreover, in suborning the influential left-leaning journalist I.F. Stone; plus, Soviet military intelligence – the GRU – proved able to attract the services of a well-placed senior State Department official, Alger Hiss, a Georgetown social fixture with vaunted academic credentials. The study by Haynes and colleagues calculated that, from the end of World War II through the 1950s, the Soviets had been able to entice some 500 Americans to spy on their behalf – chiefly private-sector engineers, not government officials. Many of these "spies" caused little damage to U.S. security and, to keep the cash payments flowing their way from Moscow, they probably fooled their Kremlin handlers into thinking they were more valuable than they really were (a chronic problem for those in the business of recruiting assets for counterintelligence or intelligence collection). Clearly, though, a few individuals – Fuchs and Weisband stand out among them were significant Soviet CI coups.

In another example of successful espionage by the Soviet Union against the United States later in the Cold War, the Walker family pedaled U.S. Navy communications intelligence to Moscow during the 1960s. Among the items sold by the Walkers to the KGB was top-secret information about America's underwater listening grid in the Atlantic Ocean that was able to track the movement of Soviet submarines, intelligence later augmented by Hanssen. The Walkers also provided their Moscow handlers with data on the firing codes for U.S. submarine-launched ballistic missiles (SLBMs), which in time of war would have given the Kremlin an opportunity to neutralize this important sea leg of America's nuclear deterrence. Had war erupted between the superpowers, the espionage carried out by the Walker family could have had much greater consequences than even the documents turned over to the Kremlin by Ames and Hanssen. In 1985, Barbara Walker, divorced and vengeful after being denied alimony payments, finally blew the whistle to the FBI on her former husband John, the leader of the spy ring.

The types of people who turn against their own country, and their motives, have varied over the years.[25] Here are a few other examples:

- Jack E. Dunlap, who worked at the NSA in the 1960s, turned over reams of useful sigint data to his Soviet handlers.[26]
- Clyde Conrad, a U.S. Army noncommissioned officer, gave the KGB information from 1975 to 1985 about Army operational plans and communications procedures if war were to break out between the United States and the Soviet Union on the battlefields of Western Europe.[27]
- William Kampiles, a first-year CIA officer, sold the Soviets a manual on U.S. surveillance satellites for a pittance in 1977, hoping evidently – with wild reasoning (or simply an incredulous alibi) – that the Agency would then use him as a double agent once he had developed his Soviet contacts.[28]
- Edward Lee Howard of the CIA signed up with the KGB in 1983 to sell secrets about the Agency's Moscow operations; he then escaped to the Soviet Union when the FBI attempted to nab him.[29]
- Jonathan Jay Pollard and his wife, unmasked in 1985, gave U.S. Navy intelligence data to the Israeli government, because of their attraction to Zionism (although they didn't say no to the $30,000 yearly stipend they were provided by Israel for their ongoing kindnesses).[30]
- Harold J. Nicolson, the highest-ranking CIA officer ever to be charged with treason, was busy spying for the Russians at the same time as Ames, Hanssen, and Howard, until he was caught in 1996 – thanks in part to the

new, post-Ames procedures that required intelligence officers to disclose detailed information to their supervisors at Langley about their personal finances.[31]

- Robert C. Kim pled guilty to spying on behalf of South Korea in 1997.[32]
- Brian P. Regan, an Air Force master sergeant assigned as an analyst to the NRO, attempted to sell surveillance satellite data to the Iraqis, Libyans, and Chinese, but was discovered and sentenced to life in prison in 2003.
- A spate of American citizens of Chinese birth have either spied or offered to spy for China, including Larry Wu-tai Chin, a "sleeper agent" at the CIA – a mole-in-waiting, biding his time before he began to steal secrets for China (and who, like Ames, passed his polygraph tests before being caught in 1985); and Dongfan (Greg) Chung and Chi Mak, both California engineers working for defense contractors. Chung was arrested in 1979, and Mak in 2005. In 2023, Jinchao Wei and Wenheng Zhao, two U.S. Navy sailors in Southern California, were arrested for providing military secrets to Chinese intelligence officers. Spying for Beijing was hardly just a result of ethnic ties, though; also in 2023, Joseph D. Schmidt, a former NCO who took classified information with him upon retirement from the U.S. Army, contacted the Ministry of State Security (MMS) while visiting Hong Kong with offers to provide national security secrets.[33]

Counterintelligence officials – like every other fair and sensible person – must be careful not to lump together whole ethnic groups as disloyal citizens just because of the behavior of a few. Needless to say, the overwhelming majority of Asian-Americans – and individuals of every other ethnic background – who work in the IC are completely loyal to the United States. The great shame of the Franklin D. Roosevelt Administration was its decision to force Japanese American citizens living in the United States to abandon their homes and move to guarded military camps in Utah and elsewhere during World War II – not because of evidence against them, but simply because they had a Japanese heritage. Such stereotyping is anathema to democratic principles. A dark irony from these days was the fact that, at the time of these internments, many Americans of Japanese descent were fighting for the United States against the Japanese in the Pacific Islands and on the high seas. Many lost their lives in World War II as U.S. sailors, soldiers, and airmen.

Several of the genuine traitors listed above, and others, were discovered during the 1980s, a period that is sometimes referred to as "The Decade of the Spy." A high point in the number of captured moles in the United States during that decade was 1985, remembered by experts as "The Year of the Spy." Over the years since World War II, this rogues gallery adds up to a depressing list of CI setbacks. In light of the long periods in which Soviet, Russian, and Chinese moles have remained hidden, a former CIA/CI officer concedes that "the overall record of United States counterintelligence at catching spies is not good."[34] Yet, as the Ames, Hanssen, and several other high-profile cases attest, U.S. counterintelligence officials have had many successes in stopping threats against the nation, too, and capturing those who have turned their coats. Further, America has hardly been alone in suffering from CI vulnerabilities. Though of small comfort, Great Britain, France, and Germany (for instance) experienced Soviet penetrations during the Cold War at even higher levels of their governments than occurred in Washington, DC.

Of some additional succor is the fact that the West has had its share of successes in espionage operations against the Soviet empire, as well as present-day Russia, that have never been uncovered by Moscow's counterintelligence defenses.[35] Moreover, it should be underscored that those American who have violated their trust by misusing classified information represent a tiny fraction among the millions of federal employees who have held sensitive positions in government over the years and honored the public trust placed in them.

Motivations for treason

A central CI question is: why do citizens betray their country? Journalist Scott Shane has noted that the mnemonic MICE – for money, ideology, compromise (that is, being blackmailed after one is caught in a compromising circumstance), and ego (an "I can beat the system" mentality, exhibited by Ames and Hanssen, among others) – sums up the standard answers from experts. He suggests this rule of thumb should be updated with a new mnemonic: MINCES, adding to the mix the phenomenon among some immigrants of a continuing devotion to their place of birth ("N" for nationalism) that can lead them to spy for the "old country," plus "S" to capture the reality that the lure of sex – "honeytraps," in Russian intelligence lingo – can sometimes corrupt individuals who have access to classified information.[36] Political scientists Stan Taylor and Daniel Snow examined reasons why Americans during the Cold War committed treason. They place the lures that attracted these traitors into several categories.[37] Greed (money) tops their list at 53.4 percent, followed by ideology at 23.7 percent (say, pro-communism over pro-democracy). Much further down this hierarchy of motivations is ingratiation (5.8 percent) – that is, efforts to fulfill a friendship or love obligation, or seduce a sexual partner; and disgruntlement (2.9 percent) – typically on-the-job anger over failure to advance in one's career. A final "other" category accounted for 12.2 percent and includes individuals who fantasized about possible James Bond adventurers for themselves that might derive from flirting with the Russian, Chinese, or some other foreign intelligence service (a feature of the "E" or ego dimension in MICE).

The relatively recent discovery of several American citizens of Chinese heritage acting for Beijing as moles points to a change in motivations for treason in the United States, at least as discerned in a study by Katherine L. Herbig, a Defense Department contractor.[38] Ideological causes were the driving influence for most traitors in the 1940s and during the early stages of the Cold War, according to her analysis. For example, with astounding naivety about the dark intentions of Joseph Stalin, Klaus Fuchs thought the Soviets would be able to advance world peace more effectively if the U.S.S.R. could match the United States in atomic weaponry. Herbig (like Taylor and Snow) found, however, that, after the atomic spy cases of the 1940s and 1950s, greed began to dominate the explanations for treachery throughout the Cold War. In more recent years, she (as was true with journalist Scott Shane) detected a trend toward naturalized Americans becoming spies for their previous place of citizenship (China or South Korea, for example), out of a sense of devotion to their heritage. Many of these individuals have proclaimed loyalty to America, but to their nation of heritage as well – a duality that is obviously unacceptable when it leads to the unauthorized disclosure to the old homeland of sensitive national security information pilfered from the vaults of intelligence agencies in the United States.

China is currently involved in highly aggressive intelligence operations against the world's democracies. They take the form of expanded attempts to penetrate U.S military bases at home and overseas, including about a dozen attempts at sneaking onto these bases between mid-2022 and mid-2023. The purpose is to take photographs and steal documents, along with a similar targeting of civilian government offices in Washington and even in the various state capitals. Additional methods have included cyberattacks, improved satellite surveillance and spy plane reconnaissance, increasingly sophisticated uses of AI in global influence operations, and the stepped up tracking of Western spies inside China. Operatives directed by the Chinese Ministry of State Security routinely probe social media, such as LinkedIn, to see who in the United States has accepted a publicly disclosed intelligence job, in hopes of perhaps recruiting some of them; and Chinese operatives also regularly try to penetrate Microsoft's cloud computing platform. In 2016, China even brazenly sought to recruit R. James Woolsey, a former CIA Director, who was considered as a possible Trump Administration appointee. This accelerated aggressiveness has led to a new form of Red Scare inside the United States and other open societies: a concern that government officials in the democracies may have been recruited by China's Ministry of State Security.[39]

Catching spies

Catching spies is not easy. Even super sleuth James J. Angleton, Chief of CIA Counterintelligence from 1954 to 1974, was taken in by the Soviets in

Photo 5.2: James Angleton
A scan of James Angleton's passport stamped between 1953 and 1956. Angleton was the CIA Chief of Counterintelligence from 1954 to 1974.
Source: Central Intelligence Agency.

at least one significant instance.[40] British MI6 liaison officer Harold A. R. "Kim" Philby befriended him in Washington, DC while stationed there in the 1960s. The two met frequently for Georgetown lunches and other social events, and often compared notes on their counterintelligence experiences in the underground struggle against Soviet intelligence operations aimed at the democracies. Both were well educated (Yale and Harvard Universities for Angleton, Cambridge University for Philby), cultured, debonair, and seasoned CI specialists. Yet, all along, Philby was a Soviet mole, working with a number of other well-placed British intelligence officers who had been students with him at university (the so-called "Cambridge Spy Ring") and chose in the 1940s to spy against their own country for perverted ideological ends – namely, to advance the glories of global communism. When investigators came close to uncovering his true loyalties, Philby fled to Moscow in 1991. Angleton had already begun to have suspicions about his British lunch-mate and was starting his own inquiries; nonetheless, his long previous ties with the MI6 officer were clearly a profound embarrassment to the Agency's CI Chief when Philby's true allegiances became known.[41]

Thereafter, Angleton turned even more paranoid, a natural occupational hazard to begin with for all CI officers. He redoubled his mole-hunting efforts inside the CIA, perhaps to compensate for his humiliation over the Philby shock. Critics inside the Agency protested to the CIA's leadership that Angleton had begun to point the finger of guilt indiscriminately at colleagues, claiming they were possible Soviet agents – all without proper evidence to substantiate this serious charge. Critics viewed his approach as a form of McCarthyism inside the Langley compound. They complained, as well, that he had been far too passive in his attempts to penetrate the governments in the Warsaw Pact (the Soviet satellites in Eastern Europe). This assertion had some truth to it; Angleton had started to reason – again without convincing evidence – that such operations were futile, because of probable existing penetrations within the Agency by KGB agents who would immediately tip off the Kremlin.[42]

Angleton supporters retorted that he was just doing his job as a determined and indefatigable CI professional, one who would have caught Ames had he still been CI Chief during the Decade of the Spy. Moreover, they argued, Angleton was hardly passive – indeed, he was the most energetic CI Chief the Agency had ever had, even running penetration and disinformation operations out of the CI Staff offices in the DO that sometimes looked more like covert action than counterintelligence and with little supervision from the seventh floor DCI suite of offices at Langley. In one widely reported example, Angleton is said to have doctored the famous "secret speech" delivered in 1956 by Soviet President Nikita Khrushchev following the death of his predecessor Joseph Stalin. By adding deceptive paragraphs to the document and circulating it in Eastern Europe, Angleton apparently hoped to stimulate uprisings against the Soviet regime by painting an even more venal portrait of the Stalinist era than the damning, unadulterated speech delivered by Khrushchev himself.[43]

In 1974, as the accusations about Angleton's excesses swirled through the hallways at Langley, DCI William E. Colby fired him as CI Chief. The ostensible grounds were that Angleton had acquired too much control over the Agency's relations with Israeli intelligence; the real reason, though, was the rising number of complaints about his overzealous activities inside the CIA as Counterintelligence Chief. Some even leveled the farfetched allegation that Angleton was himself a Soviet mole, trying to wreak havoc from within the Agency's Headquarters Building. Others, just as recklessly, thought that of Colby too. No wonder Angleton often referred to his discipline of counterintelligence as a "wilderness of mirrors."[44] It was sometimes hard to know in this surreal realm – where the caverns of secrecy were even deeper and darker than for covert action – who was telling the truth and who was lying.

A British journalist captured part of the reason for the controversy over Angleton's tenure as CI Chief at Langley. Counterintelligence is "a murky world," he wrote, "full of risks, dangers, personal jealousies and never-ceasing suspicions that the man in the office next to yours may be a Soviet agent. It is a situation that creates paranoia, corroding men's characters."[45] Political scientist Robert Jervis added this astute observation about CI tradecraft: "There is no easy answer to the question of how much paranoia is enough."[46]

A seasoned CI officer has written: "Except temporarily in the aftermath of spy scandals and major operational failures, the CIA historically has put less emphasis on CI."[47] The judgment of a presidential commission was more blunt in 2005: "U.S. counterintelligence efforts have remained fractured, myopic, and only marginally effective."[48] One conclusion held by almost every expert is that, just as with the other intelligence missions, America's counterspy operations are far too decentralized ("stovepiped") and lacking in cohesive leadership – a central finding of the Church Committee in 1975 that is still valid today. At least, though, the 2004 Intelligence Reform and Terrorism Prevention Act created a National Counterterrorism Center, with reporting lines to both the White House and the DNI. The NCTC has helped to coordinate America's counterterrorism efforts against global terrorist factions. Most observers, though, still view the Center as only partially successful in its attempts to bring all-source fusion into the counterintelligence domain, with all the agencies in the IC working closely together to prevent future breaches of U.S. security interests – especially by China, Russia, and global terrorist organizations.

Moles of the intelligence variety are a species that are unlikely to become extinct. In 1995, a senior Agency CI officer warned the Aspin–Brown Commission that "we're never going to stop people from 'volunteering' [that is, spying for the enemy]. We just have to learn how to catch them earlier, and to encourage people to report on those engaged in suspicious activities."[49] Catching spies relies on good CI tradecraft – the methods of mole-hunting – to which we turn next.

CI tradecraft: Security and counterespionage

Counterintelligence tradecraft consists of two complementary halves: security and counterespionage (CE). The former is the passive or defensive side of CI, while the latter is the offensive or aggressive side.

Security

In Renaissance Venice, a method of security used by the all-mighty Council of Ten was the Lions' Mouths. Marble lions were placed throughout the city with their mouths agape, so "Venetians could inform the Council anonymously of their suspicions of their neighbors" by simply stuffing an accusatory hand-written note into the mouth of the beast to finger the local threat to society.[50] There were no public trials and no appeals. A favorite punishment was to bury the accused upside-down in a central piazza, legs protruding. Happily, those days are passed – although ISIS has its own medieval forms of counterintelligence. In 2016, when one of its senior leaders was killed by a U.S. drone strike in northern Syria, the ISIS CI unit conducted a witch-hunt in an attempt to find informants within the ranks of the terrorist organization. The possession of a mobile phone or an Internet connection could be enough to have a suspected Western mole beheaded, burned alive, or lowered into a vat of acid. In the more humane democratic societies, CI relies instead on the maintenance of good security at an intelligence agency, which entails putting in place static defenses against hostile operations aimed at one's home country. Such defenses include the screening and clearance of personnel, along with the establishment of programs to safeguard sensitive information, such as extensive investigations into the backgrounds of job candidates.

Other security checks come into play. Polygraph ("lie-detector") examinations are administered to all new recruits at the CIA, for example, and periodically for those intelligence officers who are already employed. The polygraph is hardly foolproof, though, as the Ames example illustrates: he routinely passed his tests. Even before the Ames era, several traitors at the NSA underwent periodic polygraph tests, but their spying for the Soviet Union never came to light.[51] On the flipside, the unreliability of the polygraph can sometimes ruin the reputations of individuals who are innocent, but who react with some anxiety when wired up to the machine. In the words of a three-time COS officer at Langley: "[The polygraph] has done great harm to our personnel system and agent base."[52] On occasion, however, lie-detector probes can disclose genuinely suspicious behavior. For instance, one prospective Agency employee blurted out during a polygraph "flutter" (CIA slang for the test) that he had murdered his wife and buried her in their backyard – a definite disqualification for a security clearance. On the whole, however, given their history of errors, polygraph tests should be weighed with some degree of skepticism.

Additional security measures adopted by intelligence agencies and other governmental national security buildings include electric fences; armed guards accompanied by fierce dogs; Jersey barriers, razor wire, and bollards; locks on vaults and doors; ID badges; education sessions on how to maintain security; a close accounting of sensitive documents by way of sign-in and sign-out systems (a method sometimes poorly practiced, as underscored by Snowden and others discussed earlier); computer, email, fax, and telephone monitoring by internal security officers; a censorship of materials written by intelligence officers for public consumption; camouflage; and the use of encoded messages.

Security concerns extend overseas, too. Embassies must protect their personnel and classified documents, for instance. In addition, U.S. intelligence officers often find themselves in hostile regions of the world. In 1983, a hashish-drugged terrorist drove a truck filled with explosives into the entrance of the American embassy in Beirut, killing hundreds of Marines and several intelligence officers. In 2000, Al Qaeda terrorists in Yemen attacked the Navy destroyer USS *Cole* moored in the harbor of the capital city, Aden. Seventeen American sailors died in that suicide bombing. In 2009, a double agent – a Jordanian physician by the name of Humam Khali Abu-Mulal al-Balawi, pretending to work for the CIA against Al Qaeda – detonated a bomb concealed beneath a suicide vest he was wearing while standing near a cluster of Agency officers who had gathered to meet with him for a strategy session in Khost, Afghanistan. Among the CIA officers who perished was the COS for Afghanistan, Jennifer Matthews. In each of these instances, tighter security could have prevented the tragedies. For example, at a minimum, prior to the Khost attack, al-Balawi's bona fides should have been more completely vetted and updated by CI specialists (who erred in trusting him too much); and, as a matter of routine, he should have been thoroughly searched before the meeting took place.[53]

The cyber dimension

Also vulnerable to hostile assault in recent years are computer systems in democratic regimes, doubly so since the 9/11 attacks and ensuing efforts by the United States and others to share information more effectively via computers that connect their intelligence services in the greater IC and, to some extent, foreign intelligence liaison computers. In the United States, attempts are underway to link up computers throughout the Community, as well as those used by state and local counterterrorism authorities at IC fusion centers. While improved sharing is vital, it creates a counterintelligence nightmare, with the possibility of a future Ames or Hanssen not only stealing from their own organizations but having access to the IC's full computer network. "Even as we've greatly expanded information sharing since 9/11," warns a U.S. counterterrorism official, "you still have to think about security and the sensitivity of certain data."[54] This realm of CI concern is often referred to as covert information operations or, more formally, Computer Network Operations (CNOs).

An illustration from 2023 involves Microsoft security personnel, who reported that China was engaged in electronic spying against a wide range of U.S. infrastructure targets, including communications facilities as well as electric and gas utilities, maritime operations, and transportation hubs. The residual digital "dust" emitted by public (and private) computers is increasingly being swept up by foreign hackers around the globe. Experts believed that it would be simple for the Chinese to move from this form of spying (intelligence collection) into destructive covert action attacks, such as disrupting communications between the United States and fellow democracies around the world. Given the frequency of this active "cyberespionage" and a potential upward turn toward even more aggressive "cyberwarfare" (including disinformation and sabotage) – along with the prospect of advanced cyber intrusions spearheaded by AI – the dangers that loom ahead in cyberspace are alarming.

As discussed throughout this book, disinformation alone has become a massive CI challenge, since social media now allows a lie manufactured by Russian, Chinese, or other hostile foreign intelligence services to disseminate around the world with unprecedented reach and alacrity – and with little to no filtering. When a devastating wildfire broke out on the Hawaiian island of Maui in 2023, for instance, China's disinformation machine claimed that the conflagration was in reality the result of a secret "weather weapon" being tested by U.S. intelligence agencies. This absurd disinformation campaign was bolstered by fake photographs generated by AI techniques – all designed to discredit the reputation of the United States at home and abroad as an irresponsible militaristic nation.[55] Here is a glimpse into the future of global fakery – malevolent AI fairy tales – that will further complicate the affairs of nations.

The worry is accompanied by another set of existing CI challenges posed by adversarial spying from space, as demonstrated vividly by a Chinese Army high-altitude spy-balloon intrusion in near space (11–62 miles above the Earth's surface, and just below orbiting satellites) over U.S. territory in February 2023. The United States shot down the 200-foot-tall balloon, just as China had brought down an American spy balloon floating above its mainland borders decades earlier, in 1974. By all accounts, though, the Chinese balloon turned out to be a tempest in a teapot. In a CBS television interview, General Mark Milley, the Chair of the Joint Chiefs of Staff in the Pentagon, said the balloon was actually carrying no operating spy equipment. Launched from China's Hainan Island, it had been accidentally blown off course by strong winds over the Pacific Ocean, probably as it was attempting to surveil U.S. military bases in Guam and Hawaii. This possibility of an unintended and feckless spy balloon drifting over the continental United States, fully tracked by the NSA and NGA, was lost on some lawmakers and State Department officials, who took a shrill Chicken Little stance and demanded the shootdown. Even President Biden briefly fell prey to the hysteria, stating in public that the balloon "was carrying two freight cars worth" of spy gear. The most serious aspect of this charade was the IC's apparent inability to provide even America's top leader with accurate information about the nonthreatening nature of the balloon.[56] The imbroglio led to the cancellation by the United States of a long-scheduled diplomatic meeting between Secretary of State Anthony Blinken and the Chinese leader Xi Jinping, further souring relations between the two superpowers. Subsequent reporting indicated that Xi himself had known nothing about the wayward balloon, as embarrassed Chinese military leaders kept the information from him. Xi halted the use of balloon surveillance, although this moratorium was likely to be short-lived.

Also violating U.S. airspace are foreign quadcopter surveillance drones; and troubling, too, for CI practitioners, is the difficulty of breaking the computer codes of hostile intelligence services and their governments in antidemocratic enclaves around the world as data encryption techniques grow in sophistication. Again, China excels in computer advances, making it a leading global threat in U.S. intelligence assessments and stimulating the recent creation of a CIA Mission Center at Langley to focus on the Asian superpower. China and Russia are not alone, though, in constituting threats to American society from the cyber domain. Cyberespionage and cyberwarfare capabilities are spreading to smaller nations (Iran and North Korea are prime examples), as well as drug cartels and other international crime organizations – not to mention even small terrorist factions. In the democracies, experts in the intelligence agencies and outside IT consultants are working intensively together to establish reliable firewalls that can shield against a foreign espionage feast at the expense of the democracies in the computer domain – an "all-source Ames." As Magda Long at King's College London emphasizes, government CI specialists will have to pursue "a multi-pronged approach through public–private partnerships as the technology evolves."[57] In the United States, Silicon Valley and D.C. experts in the Intelligence Community are developing closer partnership ties in combating these various electronic global threats.

Soon after the end of the Cold War, senior CIA/CI manager Paul Redmond referred to the problem of countering cyberattacks as the number one challenge facing CI officers.[58] Since then, DNI James R. Clapper (2010–17) and several other intelligence officials have often referred to cybersecurity as America's foremost intelligence challenge. Clapper remains convinced that Russian cyber interventions during America's 2016 presidential election helped to discredit the Democratic candidate Hilary Clinton and catapulted the outsider Donald Trump into the White House.[59] In 2019, a study by the SSCI found that Russia had targeted the voting systems of all fifty American states during the 2016 presidential election.

More recently, incumbent DNI Avril D. Haines has noted how the advent of the Covid-19 pandemic (2019–22) enhanced the ability of governments around the world – both open and closed – to track citizens more closely and accumulate large amounts of data on them.[60] She argues that dictatorships have used these advanced surveillance tools to tighten their repressive grip at home, but also to expand their capacities for spying on and manipulating democratic regimes from afar – Chinese and Russian specialties, respectively. The Chinese have been preoccupied with recruiting moles in U.S. industries who are often Chinese-born American citizens. Their orders are to steal secrets on everything from military systems (fighter-jet and rocket technology, for instance) to proprietary corn seeds, toothpaste whitener, locomotive engineering, semiconductors, and solar panels.[61]

Not that the Russians have been slouches at sleuthing against the democracies. In 2022, for example, Moscow's cyberespionage against software manufactured by a U.S.-based management company called SolarWinds gave Russia access to about 18,000 private and government networks. Another illustration of the cyber threat is Iran's Islamic Revolutionary Guards Corps, which has launched cyberattacks against dozens of U.S. banks – and even attempted to take control of a small dam in a New York suburb.[62]

As the Covid-ridden year of 2020 came to an end, the Russians began to mount even more aggressive cyberespionage against the United States and other democratic nations, along with cyber covert actions aimed at fomenting disbelief around the globe about the value and the future of open societies and democratic principles. This widespread hacking by Moscow's intelligence assets, as well as Ransomware gangs, would take much of 2021–3 to unravel and establish defenses against. In 2021 alone, according to a PBS Television assessment, foreign cyber hacking cost the United States some $109 billion in lost revenue. The aggressive approach used by Russia in their cyberattacks against the pro-democracy nations signaled the future possibilities of an escalation that could include electronic attacks against energy grids, along with the infrastructure of stock exchanges, hospitals, air-traffic control, nuclear reactors, and schools (among many other possible – and unnerving – targets).

The democracies will continue to ramp up their cyber defenses, as well as their capacity to repay in kind not only cyberespionage attacks, but – if necessary – cyberwarfare perpetrated by authoritarian adversaries. The discipline of cyber-deterrence strategy has gone into overdrive. Until officials in Washington established a unifying United States Cyber Command (USCYBERCOM) in 2017, America's reaction to these kinds of threats had been fragmented and lacking in coordination – the old "stovepipe" problem in a new setting. With USCYBERCOM in place as one of the eleven unified combatant commands under the umbrella of the DoD, the response capabilities have improved dramatically. It works closely with the NSA, and the director of that agency is dual-hatted, serving as commander of both organizations. The purpose of USCYBERCOM's various "Mission Teams" is to coordinate all DoD cyberspace resources. Increasingly, it is vigorously pursuing both cyber-defense objectives and a capacity for cyber offensive as well – that is, America's evolving instruments of covert action *qua* electronic sabotage.

Former DNI Clapper takes an aggressive stance on the pursuit of cyber covert actions. "You could do a lot of damage to the Russian economy if you essentially cut them off from the world financial system," he has remarked.[63] Already, by 2023, about $300 billion in Russian central bank assets had been frozen by Western governments. Some insiders at the Agency go further, arguing that Russian President Putin's personal financial holdings should be the focus of pinpointed targeting. A career CIA/DO officer, Paul R. Kolbe, put it this way: the United States should, "when needed, quietly bloody a few noses."[64] While the methods of hidden electronic warfare continue between the democracies and their foes, some still hold out hope for a cyber "arms control" accord among the nations of the world. Even Kolbe advocates "small steps" for nations that just might lead to "some degree of cooperation and, in time, a foundation for eventually regulating norms and behavior" related to cyberspace. The alternative is clear: all nations, regardless of their forms of government, will witness firsthand the electronic disintegration of the world's computers and all the activities they facilitate. The danger here is great.

Problems continue to exist in coordinating and consolidating the work of the various counterintelligence organizations in the United States. Every government agency dealing with national security policy has a CI wing, but the "big ones" like USCYBERCOM and NSA have a responsibility for reaching out to them with a helping hand on the complex cyber front. This can become a major and ongoing management challenge in knocking down institutional "stovepipes" within the IC. Some reformers believe that the United States should have a stand-alone counterintelligence agency, along the lines of Britain's MI5, with all the U.S. counterintelligence entities working together under the same roof. Civil libertarians worry about this possibility, though; too much domestic surveillance capabilities all located under one director – say, another J. Edgar Hoover – is understandably unsettling to them. Others suggest that, on the contrary, CI should be kept decentralized within the different agencies and departments that deal with national security policy. This would allow individual CI units to keep a closer eye on just their own employees, guarding against activities that might run counter to each agency's established security procedures.

Counterespionage

The identification of specific adversaries and the development of detailed knowledge about the operations they are planning, or already conducting, against one's own country are the starting points for successful counterespionage, which former CIA/CI Chief Redmond defines as "the detection and neutralization of human spies."[65] Personnel engaged in CE attempt to block such operations by infiltrating the hostile service or terrorist faction with a mole of their own, an operation known as a "penetration," as well as – alternatively or jointly – by using sundry forms of manipulation to mislead the adversary, a practice known as "deception".

Infiltrating the enemy camp

The *penetration agent* transcends all other counterintelligence tradecraft in its potential value.[66] Since the primary goal of CI is to contain the enemy's intelligence services and saboteurs, it is desirable to know the intentions and capabilities of that adversary in advance, and in as much detail as possible. The best way to achieve this objective is through a highly placed infiltrator – a mole – inside the opposition's intelligence service or government; or, in the case of counterterrorism, within a terrorist cell. In the words of John A. McCone, a DCI from the eras of Presidents Kennedy and Johnson: "Experience has shown penetration to be the most effective response to Soviet and Bloc [intelligence] services."[67] More recently, DNI Dennis C. Blair observed in 2009 that "the primary way" the IC determines which terrorist organizations pose a direct threat to the nation is "to penetrate them and learn whether they're talking about making attacks against the United States."[68] Furthermore, a well-placed mole may be better able than anyone else to determine whether one's own service has been infiltrated by an outsider. Recall, that Ames and Hanssen may have escaped detection for much longer if the CIA had not had the benefit of its own mole inside the Kremlin, unbeknownst to the two traitors, who helped pinpoint their identities.

The methods used for penetrating (infiltrating) an opposition's intelligence service take several forms. Usually the most effective and desirable penetration is the recruitment of an *agent-in-place*, sometimes called a defector-in-place. He or she is already in the employment of an enemy intelligence service or a terrorist organization and, therefore, as an insider, close at hand to information the United States would like to steal.

The *double agent* is another standard method of infiltration, whereby an individual overseas pretends to spy for the intelligence service of his or her own country, but in fact is working all along for the United States or some other nation. This approach, in which some genuine documents need to be given to the agent for passage to the target intelligence service as a means for supporting his or her bona fides, is risky; the loyalty of the agent is often ambiguous and double-crosses are commonplace. Is the double agent really working for the United States, or still for the other side? Or perhaps playing both sides for twice the profit? Further complicating matters in the double-agent business is the fact that they can become triple agents. Welcome to Angleton's dizzying maze of mirrors.

Almost as good as the agent-in-place, and less troublesome to manage than the double agent, is the *defector*, who can bring along with him or her a deep knowledge of an enemy's intelligence service or the internal operations of a terrorist group. An agent-in-place is ultimately preferable to the defector, though, because of the former's continuing access to useful information from inside the enemy's camp about the latest plans and capabilities.

Many of the best assets acquired by the United States, such as Oleg Penkovsky, have been agents-in-place; others have been genuine, not fake, defectors who initially contacted a U.S. embassy overseas as "walk- ins." They either literally walk into the embassy and volunteer as spies, or perhaps toss classified documents over an embassy wall to make contact with someone inside (as did Penkovsky, though as an agent-in-place, not a defector).

Soon after the assassination of President Kennedy, the CIA granted asylum to a Soviet apostate by the name of Yuri Nosenko, who proffered a central message in his debriefings once inside the United States: the Soviets had nothing to do with the assassination of the President – even though the accused murderer, Lee Harvey Oswald, had temporarily defected to the USSR before the assassination. After an extensive questioning of Nosenko, the FBI concluded that his story was true and signed off on his bona fides. CIA/ CI Chief Angleton, however, refused to side with the Bureau's judgment after extensive interrogation sessions with Nosenko at the Agency's training facility in rural Virginia (conducted by the Agency's Office of Security, not Angleton – although he was kept closely informed). The Office of Security held Nosenko for 1,277 days at the facility, in spartan conditions. Eventually, most of the IC – including most of his Agency interrogators – accepted Nosenko as a dependable ally in the struggle against the Soviet Union. He resettled in the Washington, DC area and served as a CIA consultant. Angleton and his staff at Langley never believed in him, though, or in his core message. Four decades later, DCI George Tenet would refer to poor CIA–FBI relations – part of which involves deciding together on the bona fides of defectors – as the most serious weakness in the U.S. counterintelligence shield in the lead-up to the 9/11 attacks.[69]

Deception and disinformation

Another CE method is to give the enemy a false impression about something, causing him to take actions contrary to his own best interests. As Jervis observes: "Counterintelligence and deception are closely intertwined. Most obviously, the state must fear that the other side is using its agents to convey a false picture. The other side of this coin is that the state can use the other's intelligence service in order to propagate its own deceptions."[70] More mirrors with multiple images and reflections.

Fooling the Germans into believing that D-Day landings would occur in the Pas de Calais, rather than at Normandy, is a classic example of a successful joint American and British deception operation during a turning point of World War II. Jervis emphasizes the potential importance of this deception: "Had [Hitler] known that the landings were coming at Normandy, or had he released his reserve divisions as soon as the Allied troops hit the beaches, he could have pushed the invaders into the sea."[71]

Surreptitious surveillance and provocations

CE practitioners are also expert in tracking suspected moles through the use of audio, mail, physical, and "optical" (photographic, imint, or geoint) surveillance techniques. In 1975, a local terrorist group known as September 17th gunned down a CIA chief of station in Athens, Greece. When his body was flown home for burial at Arlington National Cemetery, East European "diplomats" (actually CI officers) slipped into the throng of media attending the service and began taking pictures of CIA officers in attendance, as well as recording their automobile license-plate numbers.

Since the focus of offensive CI is the disruption of the enemy service, provocation operations can be an important element of counterespionage. Here the objective is to harass an adversary, perhaps by suppressing or jamming broadcasts emitting from enemy radio and television stations, or by interrupting social media communications. Other methods involve the public disclosure of the names of an enemy's agents, or by sending a trouble-making false defector – a "dangle" – into an adversary's midst – someone who is in reality an *agent provocateur* on a short-term mission to sow confusion and dissension, then escape. Some CI specialists thought this was exactly the mission of SVR Colonel Vitaliy Sergeyevich Yurchenko, who "defected" to the United States in 1985, only three months later to jump up from his table while at a Georgetown restaurant with his CIA handler and race up Wisconsin Avenue to the Soviet embassy, where he re-defected (as do about half of all defectors). The embassy held a press conference to welcome him back. Postmortems on this case remain torn over whether Yurchenko was a dangle all along, or whether he became fearful that Russian intelligence officers would harm his family in Russia and decided to return home and cooperate with authorities. Others say he hoped for a reunion with his Russian lover.

Often the Soviet and Russian response to a defector is to issue a death warrant. One of the favorite methods involves coating with novichok food or surfaces the subject is apt to encounter, reputedly the most poisonous substance ever invented. The fact that Yurchenko was never killed, or even imprisoned, by the Russians lends credence to the hypothesis that he was in fact a false defector engaged in finding out what he could about Agency CI methods (although while in the hands of the CIA he did give up some useful information about Russian spy operations against the United States).

Renditions and interrogations

Perhaps the most controversial forms of counterintelligence tradecraft since the Huston Plan – ones that straddle the boundaries of covert action – have been the use of extraordinary renditions and harsh interrogations by the CIA. During the Administration of President George W. Bush, it came to light that the Agency had "rendered" (kidnaped) suspected terrorists in Europe and flown them in CIA aircraft to foreign locations – Cairo was a favorite or the Agency's own secret prisons ("black sites") in Central Europe and elsewhere – where they could be interrogated, and sometimes tortured, in an attempt to learn more about the activities of Al Qaeda. These renditions, ordered by the Bush II Administration and accompanied by loose guidelines from the Justice Department, led to intelligence excesses. By allowing detainees to be taken to another country that has no concerns about U.S. constitutional protections, government officials delude themselves into believing that America has thereby evaded culpability for any unethical activities that might occur during the interrogations. After all, the reasoning ran during the Bush II Administration, it was not the Agency itself applying electrodes to the bodies of the victims. Sometimes mistaken identities led to the rendering of the wrong individuals; other times, victims told their tormentors whatever they thought they wanted to hear – anything to stop the pain – then they later recanted.

In 2003, for instance, the CIA captured Khalid Sheikh Mohammed (given the acronym KSM for short by his Agency handlers) in Pakistan. He was the suspected, and later confirmed, mastermind of the 9/11 attacks against the World Trade Center and the Pentagon. When KSM was captured, the media speculated that he might be mistreated, even tortured, by his Agency interrogators. Officials at Langley responded that no brutal force would be used, not least because psychological pressure was considered more effective than physical pain. He might be subjected to sleep deprivation, perhaps; but, if he cooperated, he would be given rewards: good food, cigarettes, books, rest, a television set. Agency officials conceded, though, that the captured terrorist might be forced to sit or stand in stressful positions for hours at a time – but there would be no stretching on the rack. Only subsequently did it become known that KSM was waterboarded 183 times, in a form of torture that simulates drowning.

A report on CIA torture practices, issued by SSCI's Democrats in 2015, further indicates that Al Qaeda members were chained, naked and hooded, to the ceiling of interrogation rooms; routinely kicked to keep them awake; and shackled so tightly that blood flow to their limbs was halted. Two prisoners identified as Al Qaeda members were killed during interrogations at a U.S. military base in Afghanistan, beaten to death with blunt instruments.[72] It remains a matter of dispute as to whether such methods produced valuable intelligence gains (most experts say no), but one conclusion is widely accepted: in the court of world opinion, the use of torture has harmed American's reputation for fair play and ethical behavior – a significant attribute in the global contest for the allegiance of other nations and their citizens.[73]

In the wake of the 2001 terrorist attacks against the United States, Cofer Black, the head of the CIA's Counterterrorism Center (CTC), declared: "There was a before 9/11 and there was an after 9/11. After 9/11, the gloves came off."[74] When the gloves come off, though, all too often fundamental democratic values are thrown out of the window.

Secrecy and the state

Executive privilege

In the eyes of some executive branch officials, a central attraction of America's secret agencies has been the opportunity they afford to chart a foreign policy course with little or no public debate. In its covert shipment of arms to Iran in 1985–6, for example, the Reagan Administration carried the goal of exclusion to an extreme, not only refusing to inform Congress but keeping the operation strictly within the limited confines of a few NSC staffers, some field operatives, and a narrow slice of the CIA (including DCI William J. Casey) – beyond the purview of even the President and the NSC's other principal members, let alone lawmakers.

Often this goal of exclusion is achieved through the proclamation of executive privilege – an assertion by the President of constitutional authority to withhold information from the legislative and judicial branches of government. Appearing before the Ervin Committee, established by the Senate in 1973 to investigate the Watergate scandal and chaired by Sam Ervin, Jr. (D, North Carolina), President Nixon's Attorney General, Richard Kleindienst, claimed that "the constitutional authority of the President in his discretion" allowed the White House to withhold information in the President's possession "or in the possession of the executive branch" if the President concluded that disclosure "would impair the proper exercise of his constitutional functions." This implied that Congress could be prohibited from speaking to any of the millions of employees in the executive branch, if the White House so decreed.

President Nixon went even further, claiming that not only could current members of his staff refuse to appear before congressional committees, including the Ervin panel, but so too could past members – an unprecedented expansion of the executive privilege doctrine, which some senators immediately labeled "the doctrine of eternal privilege." Nixon claimed, too, that his "presidential papers," which he defined magisterially as "all documents, produced or received by the President or any member of the White House staff in connection with his official duties," were immune from congressional probes. Conveniently for the White House, this definition included White House tape-recordings sought by Ervin Committee investigators to see if they contained conversations about the Watergate scandal (which, indeed, they did – the "smoking gun" that led to the impeachment proceedings against President Nixon and his resignation from office). "What do they eat that makes them grow so great?" a droll Senator Ervin asked during Senate hearings into this matter, referring to the President and his staff. Ervin continued: "I am not willing to elevate them to a position above the great mass of the American people. I don't think we have any such thing as royalty or nobility to let anybody come down at night like Nicodemus and whisper something in my ear that no one else can hear." He concluded: "This is not executive privilege. It is executive poppycock." In 1974, the Supreme Court also disagreed with the President's broad interpretation of executive privilege and, in *United States* v. *Nixon* (418 U.S. 683), a majority of the judges required that the tape-recordings be turned over to Senator Ervin.

Subsequently, the Ford Administration stretched the cloak of executive privilege to another extravagant length. At issue was Operation SHAMROCK, a secret NSA program designed to intercept cables and telegrams sent abroad or received by Americans – a significant violation of civil liberties in the United States. Initially at the request of the Truman Administration, the corporations RCA, Global, and ITT World Communications began to store their international paid message traffic on magnetic tapes. They would then turn these messages over to the NSA. Concerned that the operation may have been in violation of a federal law that protects the privacy of communications, a House subcommittee decided in 1976 to investigate the matter and called the corporation presidents to testify as witnesses. The CEOs turned to the White House for guidance and President Ford, through his Attorney General, Edward H. Levi (former dean of the Law School at the University of Chicago), claimed that the corporations were immune from congressional appearances in this case, because SHAMROCK was a sensitive, top-secret project ordered by the White House. The doctrine of executive privilege had now been extended to the private sector, this time with respect to an improper intelligence operation.

Members of the House subcommittee were dismayed by this White House response. "The Attorney General is without any authority," declared Representative John E. Moss (D, Utah), a respected, long-serving lawmaker. "It is the most outrageous assumption, the most arrogant display by the Attorney General I have seen. Some damn two-bit appointee of the President is not the law-making body of this country."[75] The subcommittee voted for a contempt of Congress citation against any witness who failed to appear for the hearings. When the gavel came down to begin the hearings a few days later, all three CEOs – now having second thoughts about following Attorney General Levi's recommendation to stay at home – were in their assigned chairs in front of the subcommittee members, ready to answer questions. The hearing proceeded without sensitive NSA methods being discussed, but still with a proper probe into the White House and corporate violations of U.S. privacy laws.

Delay and deceit

Such major confrontations between the branches over secrecy provisions are rare. More commonly, as a form of resistance the executive branch simply resorts to "stonewalling" and "slow-rolling" – attempts to avoid sharing information with lawmakers by various methods of delay. Professor Raoul Berger of Harvard University's School of Law, an expert on executive privilege, observed that "bureaucrats engage in interminable stalling when asked for information." He spelled out the implications:

> At bottom, the issue concerns the right of Congress and the people to participate in making the fateful decisions that affect the fortunes of the nation. Claims of presidential power to bar such participation, or to withhold on one ground or another the information that is indispensable for intelligent participation undermine this right, sap the very foundations of democratic government.[76]

Prior restraint

In a further attempt to bottle up information within the executive branch despite the right of the people in a democracy to know about almost all of their government's activities (with the exception of a few matters, such as the names of CIA spy recruits overseas, that it would be foolish and harmful to reveal), officials sometimes try to curb the publication of materials deemed sensitive. This withholding by the government of the media or a citizen's right to publish information is often referred to as "prior restraint." Understanding that truth and transparency are the *sine qua non* for successful democracy, courts in the United States have been loath for the most part to permit the enforcement of prior restraints. "Any system of prior restraints of expression comes to this Court bearing a heavy presumption against its constitutional validity," declared the Supreme Court in the celebrated case *New York Times* v. *United States* (1971), better known as the Pentagon Papers case.

In this Court decision, the Nixon Administration failed to convince a majority of justices that prior restraint was necessary to prevent publication of a secret DoD history of the Vietnam War. Administration lawyers maintained that publication would be harmful to U.S. foreign policy. The man responsible for the leaking of this classified history, DoD analyst Daniel Ellsberg, believed, on the contrary, that Americans deserved to know the facts about their nation's combat involvement in Indochina. This knowledge would make the national debate over further warfare in that remote part of the world more meaningful and based on facts. Ellsberg was convinced that no secrets of real significance were in the documents; rather, the materials were being kept secret because officials wished to hide from the public a record of various mistakes that had been made, leading the United States deeper into the war. In sharp contrast, Ellsberg's critics saw his decision as being close to treason, because he had revealed classified information without proper authorization – a major counterintelligence taboo.

After trying unsuccessfully to convince some members of Congress to reveal the report in a congressional floor debate (immune from court action), a frustrated Ellsberg took the fateful step of leaking the Pentagon Papers to the *New York Times* and the *Washington Post*. In response, the White House moved to stop further publication of the papers by bringing an injunction against the *Times*, which was the first paper to print excerpts from the history. Given the great importance of the issue and the key figures involved, the case moved quickly to the nation's highest court. Mr. Justice Potter Stewart expressed the majority view in the six-to-three decision against the government's attempt to exercise prior restraint:

> We are asked, quite simply, to prevent the publication by two newspapers of material that the Executive Branch insists should not, in the national interest, be published. I am convinced that the Executive is correct with respect to some of the documents involved. But *I cannot say that disclosure of any of them will surely result in direct, immediate, and irreparable damage to the Nation or its people*. That being so, there can under the First Amendment be but one judicial resolution of the issues before us. I join the judgments of the Court. [77]

The public's right to know in a democracy

A proper counterintelligence concern for the protection of certain information within the executive branch makes sense. No American wants to endanger the lives of public servants in the U.S. intelligence agencies, the assets they recruit overseas, or the FBI's informants at home; and no thoughtful person would countenance the revealing of other "good" secrets, such as the specifications of the nation's weaponry or the timetable for U.S. troop deployments overseas. The record indicates that these secrets have been fairly well contained. Former Secretary of State Dean Rusk often said, from the vantage point of retirement after decades of service in the Kennedy and Johnson Administrations, that he "knew of no national security leak that truly damaged America's major interests."[78] Similarly, according to a prominent senator in 1976:

> Secrets that ought to be kept are being kept. For example, with the single exception of the book by Philip Agee [a CIA officer who defected and wrote an account of his experiences inside the Agency, which revealed the names of some of his fellow officers overseas] . . . there has been little or no disclosure of CIA sources or methods, or of the confidentiality of sensitive negotiations, such as preceded the partial test ban treaty, SALT

I, and the release of the Pueblo crew [a U.S. spy ship captured by North Korea during the Cold War].[79]

Some of the most egregious security breaches have come from within the executive branch itself, not from the media, lawmakers, or other "outsiders." For example, the Department of State leaked highly classified information to a writer preparing a favorable profile on then-Secretary of State Henry Kissinger, with no legal action taken against the leaker or the Secretary. Further, as this chapter has documented, the CIA and other intelligence agencies have had personnel who provided secrets to America's enemies, such as Edward Lee Howard, the Walker family, Ames, and Hanssen. Added to this list are outside intelligence contractors, like Edward Snowden. Then there is the matter of former President Trump's possession of large numbers of highly classified documents that he took with him into retirement – and refused to return to the government when they were discovered. In most cases, improved counterintelligence procedures within the IC and other agencies in the executive branch (including the White House) would do more to protect the "good" secrets than repressive measures of prior restraint taken against the First Amendment rights of journalists and other outside scribblers.

In those instances when America's secret agencies have overreached in their counterintelligence operations (as with the Huston Plan), the nation has been reminded again of James Madison's warning, now etched in marble on a wall at the Library of Congress: "Power, lodged as it must be in the hands of human beings, is ever liable to abuse." A free society cannot remain free for long without a reliable counterintelligence capability; yet, nor can it remain free without effective accountability over CI and other secret intelligence activities. This is the topic addressed in Chapter 6.

6

Safeguards against the Abuse of Secret Power

On December 6, 1977, the House Permanent Select Committee on Intelligence (HPSCI) convened to hear Admiral Stansfield Turner, DCI for President Jimmy Carter, present his first briefing on a presidential covert action approval. The committee had only recently come into existence in response to congressional investigations in 1975–6 that revealed widespread violations of domestic law by the Intelligence Community, as well as controversial operations abroad (including assassination plots against foreign leaders). Moving more quickly, senators across the Hill had already put in place their own new intelligence oversight committee in 1976: the Senate Select Committee on Intelligence (SSCI). Comporting with congressional tradition, each panel was known informally by the name of its Chair: the Boland Committee in the House (after Edward P. "Eddie" Boland, D, Massachusetts) and the Inouye Committee in the Senate (after Daniel K. Inouye, D, Hawaii).

A 65-year-old bachelor with a legendary baritone singing voice that in Irish pubs in Boston softened his otherwise stern disposition, Chairman Boland was a force to be reckoned with in the House of Representatives. He was a former roommate and close confidant of the Speaker, Thomas "Tip" O'Neill (another Boston Democrat equally at home in Irish pubs), and a senior member of the almighty Appropriations Committee. Boland eschewed the arrogance of many of those in lofty positions in Washington, but he was in the habit of getting his way. On this December morning in HPSCI's suite of offices, nestled near the Rotunda and well-guarded by Capitol Hill police, Boland rose to greet Admiral Turner as he entered the low-ceiling, bunker-like hearing room. It was the DCI's first trip to the committee's hideaway quarters. Seven of the panel's thirteen members had shown up for the session, plus the three committee staffers allowed to attend this particularly sensitive meeting. All were curious to meet the President's spy chief. The other six members of the panel evidently had duties they deemed more pressing than this opportunity to participate in the new committee's first top-secret covert action briefing.

Turner carried himself with an air of supreme confidence. Ruggedly handsome, stocky, and silver-haired, Turner had been a pugnacious middle guard on the Naval Academy football team and a Rhodes Scholar at the University of Oxford. Subsequently, he had raced through the naval ranks to an admiralty. The position of Chief of Naval Operations was said to be his prime objective,

Photo 6.1: DCI Turner
DCI Admiral Stansfield Turner (left) greets his former classmate at the Naval Academy,
President Jimmy Carter, during the Admiral's swearing in as DCI on March 9, 1977, at the CIA
Headquarters Building in Langley, Virginia.
Source: Central Intelligence Agency.

after this interlude at the CIA, a post for which he had been recruited by an
admiring classmate, President Jimmy Carter.

The DCI nodded cordially to the Chairman and the other committee members seated around a thick mahogany U-shaped bench whose prongs aimed
out toward a witness table that awaited the Admiral and his entourage. Turner
sat down, then pulled a prepared statement from his briefcase. He took less
than five minutes to present the basics to the committee about the President's
recent approval (a "finding") for a covert action – a briefing required by law
ever since the passage of the Hughes–Ryan Act in late December of 1974.

Once Turner had completed his short statement, silence filled the room,
disturbed only by the hum of neon lights behind a latticework of wooden
slats on the ceiling. The lawmakers at first assumed the DCI had just paused
for a sip of water, but instead Turner looked around the room at the members
and grinned. "That's it," he said. Representative Roman Mazzoli, a short,
feisty Democrat from Kentucky, cleared his throat and proceeded to pick
apart the covert action from A to Z. The target was an insignificant country;
the operation cost too much; the briefing had been vague. Turner stared
at the notebook on the table in front of him. He clenched his teeth and flexed
the muscles that lined his jaw. When Mazzoli finished, the DCI offered a spir-

ited defense of the operation. The Kentuckian remained skeptical, however, and presented another round of objections.

Chairman Boland interceded. "I'd like to have a serious debate," he said, "but this is not the place." As a committee staffer in the room would later remember, one could only wonder why this was not the place. After all, it was a closed meeting within the inner sanctum of the HPSCI offices, guarded by Capitol Hill's finest and periodically "swept" to ensure that no listening devices had been planted by foreign spies. Was it not the duty of the new committee to review the activities of the nation's secret espionage organizations, perhaps especially when it came to covert actions?

"I don't want any adversary proceedings between this committee and the intelligence agencies," Boland continued, with furrowed eyebrows and the implicit suggestion that the Admiral had done his duty and could now depart. A lowly junior member of the Congress, Mazzoli sank back into his chair, with a mixture of shock and vexation registered on his face. A few of the Committee members looked at Boland in dismay, but none came to Mazzoli's rescue. This was, after all, Edward P. Boland, a man who could make or break a career for anyone who sought funding for their district from the House Appropriations Committee – in other words, every member of Congress. Boland adjourned the session and Admiral Turner left the room wreathed in smiles.

Boland's philosophy was about to be tested more energetically, though, by a few young members of his committee. Admiral Turner returned to the HPSCI hearing room a few weeks later with another covert action finding signed by Carter. On this occasion, the DCI found a stenographer seated near the witness table. This individual, carefully screened by the FBI and holding a top-secret clearance, was in attendance to keep a verbatim record of what was said by the DCI and his aides during the briefing, as well as by the lawmakers in attendance. Turner began his presentation hesitantly as he kept an eye on the stenographer. After only two minutes, the Admiral abruptly halted his review of the covert action, having concluded – as he told Boland and the rest of the committee (eleven members strong this time) – that, after further thought, he had decided that to allow a verbatim record of the CA briefing would be a breach of national security. The Admiral said he would discontinue his presentation until the stenographer had departed the room.

For a full minute, only the hum of the neon lights softly buzzed in the tomb-like quiet of the HPSCI hearings room as committee members pondered the Admiral's request. Boland finally interrupted the silence. "All right," he said, "we'll dispense with the stenographer."

As the stenographer gathered his equipment for an exit, one of the HPSCI aides slipped a note to Les Aspin (D, Wisconsin), another junior member of the committee like Mazzoli. "We *must* have a record of these briefings,"

Box 6.1: The *contra* section of the Iran–*contra* finding, 1981

I hereby find that the following operations in foreign countries (including all support necessary to such operations) are important to the national security of the United States, and direct the Director of Central Intelligence, or his designee, to report this finding to the concern committee of the Congress pursuant to law, and to provide such briefings as necessary.

SCOPE	PURPOSE
Central America	Provide all forms of training, equipment, and related assistance to cooperating government throughout Central America in order to counter foreign-sponsored subversion and terrorism. [Still-classified section omitted here.]
	Encourage and influence foreign governments around the world to support all of the above objectives.

Source: "Presidential Finding on Central America, N16574," *Public Papers of the President: Ronald Reagan* (Washington, DC: U.S. Government Printing Office, 1986). The President approved the finding on March 9, 1981. Originally top secret, it was partially declassified during congressional hearings into the Iran–*contra* scandal in 1987. The "purpose" section is succinct, leaving considerable leeway for the CIA to fill in the details during implementation. When Congress passed the Boland Amendments to prohibit further covert actions in Nicaragua, the Reagan Administration moved underground and created "The Enterprise" to carry on these operations without the knowledge of Congress.

---

emphasized the note. "How else are we going to have any memory of what the DCI said, and whether – a year from now – the CIA is living up to his assurances? It'll be the Agency's recollection against ours." The aide was suggesting nothing less than having Aspin walk the plank, with Captain Boland glowering from the bridge. Aspin, though, understood the importance of a written record for holding officials to account, and he also had something of a swashbuckling streak. He spoke up immediately against dismissing the stenographer. Boland stared down the table in Aspin's direction with a scowl on his face. When Mazzoli seconded Aspin's request, Boland's countenance grew darker still.

With the grim look of a headmaster about to frog-march two recalcitrant schoolboys from the classroom, Boland repeated that a verbatim record of the closed hearing was unnecessary for these proceedings. In support of the Chairman, Admiral Turner said that he would leave behind a copy of the short presidential statement of approval. Aspin insisted, though, that the finding itself – a highly abbreviated synopsis of the target and the scope of the covert action – was insufficient. (For an example of a rare declassified presidential finding, see Box 6.1.) Far more important was the DCI's follow-up explanation during the committee's Q&A about the operation's specific goals, methods, costs, and risks. Unimpressed by the young upstarts Aspin and Mazzoli, Chairman Boland again ordered the hapless stenographer, caught in the middle of this exchange, to leave the premises.

At this point, Aspin thrust his head and shoulders across the green-baize bench top in front of him and stared along its curvature toward Boland. "I call for a vote on this matter, Mr. Chairman," he said coldly. A crisp "second" came from Mazzoli. Boland's face changed color from a dark hue to crimson as he shoved his chair back from the bench in anger and disgust. He ordered the committee clerk to call the roll. In the boxing ring of House politics, Les Aspin and his sidekick Roman Mazzoli had just bloodied the nose of a House heavyweight champion.

The committee clerk slowly read the names of those committee members present. When the tally came to an end, by a margin of a single vote – six to five – Aspin and Mazzoli had won the right for HPSCI to have a verbatim record of the full DCI briefing on a covert action proposal. It was a still point in a turning world, an instant in which an element of representative democracy edged its way into one of the most remote and hidden chambers in the government of the United States. By implication, this principle would apply as well to any other briefing the committee deemed important enough to require an accurate, written account. Against his will, Chairman Eddie Boland had been forced into a more serious form of intelligence oversight, one that would allow HPSCI lawmakers and their staff to monitor the ongoing performance of the secret agencies in light of promises made by the DCI during committee hearings. Word of this confrontation quickly made its way to the other side of the Hill and SSCI members demanded to have their own stenographer present, thenceforth, to ensure a reliable memory for senators about assurances from the nation's spy chief during briefings.

The evolution of safeguards against intelligence abuse in the United States

The era of trust (1787–1974)

A later HPSCI Chair, Lee H. Hamilton (D), often pointed out to his constituents in Indiana that Congress had to do much more than write laws. First, its members had to study hard in advance to make sure proposed laws were carefully drafted; and then they had to follow up to ensure the laws were working properly. This is what is meant by "accountability" or "oversight" on Capitol Hill. Another member of Congress (first in the House, then in the Senate), Wyche Fowler (D, Georgia) had a simpler definition: "Oversight keeps bureaucrats from doing something stupid."

Figure 6.1: Auth on the lack of meaningful congressional oversight of intelligence prior to 1975.

Source: Auth, *Philadelphia Inquirer* (1976). Used with permission.

The approach of the United States toward intelligence accountability chosen by Boland in his early years as HPSCI Chairman – that is, a posture of benign neglect – had prevailed throughout the long sweep of American history until the domestic spy scandals of 1974, a stretch of almost 200 years. Cartoonist Auth of the *Philadelphia Inquirer* depicted the "footsie" relationship between the CIA and lawmakers during the early decades of the Cold War (see Figure 6.1). Throughout this era of trust between America's secret agencies and their overseers, intelligence was set apart from the rest of the government. The dominant attitude among members of Congress was that the honorable men and women in the intelligence agencies would have to be trusted to protect the United States against dangerous and unscrupulous forces at home and abroad. "No, no, my boy, don't tell me," a leading Senator, John Stennis (D, Mississippi), told DCI James R. Schlesinger in 1973 when the Director attempted to provide a full accounting of the CIA's operations abroad. "Just go ahead and do it, but I don't want to know."[1]

While most of the nation's intelligence officers have indeed been honorable men and women, the writers of the Constitution could have predicted that eventually power – perhaps especially secret power – would be misused. Resonating a bedrock principle of government accountability, Justice Louis Brandeis reminded Americans in a 1926 Supreme Court opinion that the

purpose of the Constitution had been "not to promote efficiency but to pre-
clude the exercise of arbitrary power. The purpose was not to avoid friction,
but, by means of the inevitable friction incident to the distribution of the
governmental powers among three departments, to save the people from
autocracy."[2]

Yet this sound philosophy often gave way to the exigencies of fighting
against unprincipled enemies of the United States, whether the Barbary
pirates of yore, communists of the Cold War, terrorists, or the ongoing threats
of Russian and Chinese truculence in the contemporary setting. America,
the world's oldest democracy, would follow the practice of regimes around
the world and throughout history: it would set its secret agencies outside the
framework of checks-and-balances that is the hallmark of free societies. A
hostile world demanded no less than a doctrine of intelligence exceptionalism. For the sake of the nation's safety from hostile foreign powers, efficiency
would have to take pride of place over civil liberties.

This is not to say that the U.S. intelligence agencies were devoid of all
vestiges of accountability. During the Cold War and since, most of their
activities were and continue to be approved by officials in the White House
and the National Security Council. Further, from time to time, the CIA would
report (or at least try to report) to lawmakers – though often only to find deaf
ears like those of Senator Stennis. Now and then, as in the aftermath of the
Bay of Pigs fiasco, the embarrassing U-2 shoot-down over the Soviet Union
in 1960, and the controversy surrounding CIA subsidies for the National
Student Association in 1967, a few lawmakers would call for inquiries and
intelligence reform; but there were never enough reformers in Congress to
bring about significant change. While David M. Barrett correctly maintains
that the devotion of lawmakers to intelligence oversight has been underrated
in the scholarly and popular literature, congressional approval of intelligence
programs seems nonetheless to have been highly discretionary during the era
of trust. For the most part, presidents and lawmakers provided DCIs and other
intelligence managers with broad authority to conduct secret operations at
home and abroad – largely as they saw fit.[3]

In the autumn of 1974, this neglect of adequate intelligence supervision
would change dramatically, beginning with a spy scandal and accelerating
into the most thorough investigation ever made of America's secret agencies.
Soon, 1975 would become known as the "Year of Intelligence."

The era of uneasy partnership (1975–86)

Belief in intelligence exceptionalism underwent radical revision in the United
States when the *New York Times* reported in 1974 that the Agency had been
engaged in domestic espionage – CIA spying on American citizens.[4] The Bay
of Pigs, the U-2 shoot-down, and CIA student subsidies were one thing, but

Photo 6.2: Senator Frank Church
Seated on the left of Senator and Vice Chairman John Tower (R, Texas), the Chairman of
the Church Committee – Senator Frank Church (D, Idaho) – displays a CIA poison dart gun
during public hearings into covert action, held in the Senate's Russell Building on Capitol Hill,
September 17, 1995.
Source: Henry Griffin, U.S. Capital.

spying on voters back home was quite another matter. In the context of this
stunning revelation, concurrent *Times* reporting on Agency covert actions
against the Allende regime in Chile – a democratically elected government
– took on added weight and drew further criticism of the CIA's secret operations. Reacting with rare alacrity, Congress set up panels of inquiry in January
1975: first the Church Committee in the Senate and then the Pike Committee
in the House. Not to be left behind, the Ford Administration established a
presidential investigative commission, led by and named after Vice President
Nelson Rockefeller (R, New York).

The Church Committee dug deeper than the other panels, spending sixteen
months on its investigation and issuing a set of public reports that stood more
than six feet high (as well as other reports measuring another six feet high
that still remain classified).[5] The panel confirmed the *Times* had been correct
about improper CIA surveillance within the United States, as well as covert
action against the democratic government of Chile; but it quickly discovered
the newspaper accounts had only scratched the surface of wrongdoing by
America's secret agencies. The investigative findings demonstrated that the
CIA had opened the mail to and from selected U.S. citizens, which generated

1.5 million names stored in the Agency's computer bank (Operation CHAOS). But it found, too, that Army intelligence units had compiled dossiers on 100,000 American citizens during the Vietnam War era, and that the vast computer facilities of the NSA had monitored every cable sent overseas, or received from overseas, by Americans between 1947 and 1975 (Operation SHAMROCK). The NSA had also engaged in questionable wiretapping within the United States (Operation MINARET).

Among the Church Committee findings emerged – demon-like, from the vaults of the FBI – what proved to be the most stunning misuse of intelligence authority of all: Operation COINTELPRO. The Bureau had created files on more than one million Americans, and carried out more than 500,000 investigations of "subversives" from 1960 to 1974 – all without a single court conviction. As Senator Walter Mondale (D, Minnesota), a senior member of the Church Committee, recalled: "No meeting was too small, no group too insignificant" to escape the FBI's attention.[6] From 1956 to 1971, Bureau agents had engaged in secret smear campaigns against thousands of groups and individuals, simply because they had expressed opposition to the war in Vietnam or criticized the slow pace of the civil rights movement. The Ku Klux Klan made the Bureau's enemies list as well – as did seemingly any group that failed to fit into Director J. Edgar Hoover's image of a loyal American. Target Number One for Hoover, though, was the civil rights leader Martin Luther King, Jr., the victim of many campaigns of lies and innuendo perpetrated by the FBI. The Bureau even attempted to blackmail Dr. King into taking his own life in 1964, on the eve of his acceptance speech for the Nobel Peace Prize.

As historian Henry Steele Commager correctly observed, "perhaps the most threatening of all the evidence that [stemmed] from the findings of the Church Committee" was "the indifference of the intelligence agencies to constitutional restraint."[7] As a result of the *Times* reporting, along with the two congressional and the Rockefeller inquiries, lawmakers vowed to correct this attitude of indifference through the institution of laws, regulations, and, above all, a new philosophy of meaningful and consistent legislative review of intelligence activities by Congress. It was time to say goodbye to the earlier era of benign neglect and the doctrine of intelligence exceptionalism. *The law works* – that was the central conclusion reached by the Church Committee. Each of the security objectives sought by presidents and their aides during the Cold War could have been achieved without descending into the muck of COINTELPRO, CHAOS, SHAMROCK, MINARET, and other questionable operations adopted by the nation's spy agencies. The United States could fight the totalitarian states without becoming one itself. Liberty and security had to be kept in balance if America were to stay true to its democratic values and traditions.

The *Times* reporting and the investigations of 1975 led to a sea change in attitudes within the United States about the need for better supervision of the Intelligence Community. Soon thereafter, other democracies around the world would follow suit by establishing stronger guardrails against the abuse of power by their secret agencies. Even before the establishment of the Church and Pike Committees, in response to the *Times* reporting, Congress had passed the Hughes–Ryan Act near the end of December 1974. This law was revolutionary in concept. It required the President to explicitly approve ("find" – the reason why this White House approval step is called a "finding") all important covert actions. By legally mandating a presidential statement of purpose about a proposed CA, clearly authorized by the signature of the commander-in-chief, this first step effectively ended the doctrine of "plausible deniability." Next, the finding had to be reported to Congress in a "timely manner," soon defined to mean within a couple of days. Since 1976 and 1977, the reports have been presented orally in executive sessions to both SSCI and HPSCI (as illustrated by the HPSCI example that began this chapter).

The Hughes–Ryan law did not go so far as to require congressional *approval* of covert actions – which would have raised tangled separation-of-powers issues in the American constitutional system of government – but it did set up a meaningful opportunity for lawmakers to influence these operations. After a CA briefing, nothing would stop members of SSCI and HPSCI (meeting separately for the briefings) from expressing their opposition – or even calling for a committee vote on the merits of the covert action. Neither the views nor the vote would be legally binding on the President, but a House or Senate Committee that was riled up enough over what members considered an ill-advised intelligence operation could only be ignored at political risk by the White House and the CIA. The precise nature of the opposition would matter. If it were only a junior member or two on SSCI or HPSCI, the President might choose to ignore the criticism. If the opponents included powerful members of SSCI and HPSCI – say, the Chairs – that would be a different story and the White House would probably want to reconsider going forward with the covert action. Backing away altogether from the CA might be prudent, as well, for a president who faced majority opposition in both committees. So while Hughes–Ryan provided no formal legal authority for Congress to stop a covert action in its tracks, it did require reporting on these operations to legislative overseers. That reality sets the stage for the expression of political opposition within the sheltered confines of SSCI and HPSCI, which – if members were so disposed – could gel into widespread opposition to a White House proposal.

Further, if SSCI and HPSCI opposed a covert action, but the President ignored this "recommendation," members of the two committees could convene a secret session of Congress and formally vote up or down on the floor to shut off money for the operation – an extreme contingency, but exactly what Congress did with the Boland Amendments to stop covert action in Nicaragua during the 1980s (named after their sponsor, HPSCI Chair Boland – no longer a pushover for the CIA at this later stage in his House career). Constitutionally, an irate set of lawmakers could (but never have so far) even bring impeachment proceedings against a president considered out of control in his or her conduct of a particularly questionable CA or other intelligence activity.

Short of these more extreme responses, members of Congress could vote against replenishment of the CIA's Reserve for Contingency Fund, through which lawmakers annually provide readily available seed money for CAs so the White House can move swiftly (if necessary) in ordering the use of the "third option" during emergency situations. Just as one should think twice about pulling on the tail of a tiger, so does a president, as well as a DNI or D/CIA, think twice about entering into a dispute with members of SSCI or HPSCI – the funders of intelligence operations. This intangible sense of prudence by presidents and their aides gives to the reporting provision of the Hughes–Ryan Act an added unwritten dimension of power, even if the law is devoid of explicit authority for lawmakers to formally approve or disapprove covert actions. Currently, SSCI's high credibility as the only fully functioning bipartisan committee on Capitol Hill gives this panel special clout in the White House and within the IC.

A continuing problem of this findings process, though, has been the occasional authorization from the President of so-called "generic" or "worldwide" findings – broad statements that endorse vague covert action initiatives. For example, without elaboration, the wording of the finding might read: "The President finds in favor of using lethal force against terrorists worldwide." This could be an ambiguous prescription for unleashing assassins and drones against any number of targets abroad, including other nations – or even American citizens who may be preaching *jihad* against the West from Yemen (as in the case of Anwar al-Awlaki, killed by a U.S. drone in 2011). Especially when assassination is involved, critics advocate the use of more specific findings for each target, so that lawmakers and others in the CA decision loop can review the merits of each case.

Other statutes designed to define the boundaries of probity for the secret agencies were soon passed in the wake of Hughes–Ryan, such as the important Foreign Intelligence Surveillance Act (FISA) in 1978, which banned warrantless national security wiretaps. Wiretap surveillance powers had been misused within the executive branch over the years for political gain by Democrats and Republicans alike. In the context of the nation's experiences during the Year of Intelligence investigations (1975), the intent to weed out inappropriate intelligence practices was still strong enough to carry on the work of the Church Committee. Lopsided majorities in both chambers of Congress voted in favor of the FISA reform. The new law required a "prior judicial warrant [involving] all electronic surveillance for foreign intelligence or counterintelligence purposes in the United States in which communications of U.S. persons might be intercepted" (50 U.S.C. 1801–1911). In the mid-1980s,

FISA was amended to authorize the issuance of warrants for FBI physical searches ("black-bag jobs") as well – a supplement to the law's initial focus on electronic surveillance. The original 1978 statute also established a special FIS Court whose temporary rotating judges (drawn by the Supreme Court's Chief Justice from districts throughout the nation) would review surveillance warrant applications from the FBI, the CIA, the NSA, and occasionally other intelligence agencies. The third branch of government in the United States – the judiciary – was now involved in the accountability procedures for intelligence activities.

Two years later, Congress enacted another far-reaching law to further tighten supervision over America's secret agencies. Although only two pages in length, this Intelligence Oversight Act of 1980 bore sharp teeth, requiring *prior* (not just "timely") notice to SSCI and HPSCI, and on *all* (not just CIA) important intelligence operations – collection and counterintelligence, too, in addition to covert action.

Beginning with the Hughes–Ryan Act and carrying on until the Iran–*contra* scandal of 1987, lawmakers, presidents, and DCIs attempted during this experimental era of uneasy partnership to fashion a workable relationship between democratic openness, on the one hand, and effective secret intelligence operations, on the other – that is, between liberty and security. The result was a dramatic increase in attention on Capitol Hill to the nation's spy agencies. When it came to intelligence supervision by lawmakers and their staff, the difference between pre-1975 and post-1975 was as stark a difference as night is to day. To some extent, at least, democracy had entered the hidden side of America's government – a development unprecedented in world history. The Iran–*contra* affair would demonstrate, however, that this New Oversight was far from foolproof.

An interlude of distrust (1986–91)

Efforts by the NSC staff and a few CIA officers (led by DCI Casey) during the Reagan years to bypass Congress and conduct covert actions against the Sandinista regime in Nicaragua – even though prohibited by the Boland Amendments – displayed a sobering failure of the New Oversight that had been established in the years between 1974 and 1980.[8] Even when SSCI and HPSCI leaders directly questioned NSC staffers, including National Security Advisors Robert C. McFarlane and his successor Vice Admiral John M. Poindexter, about the rumored clandestine organization named "The Enterprise" (a super-secret entity created by the NSC staff to carry out the CAs), the lawmakers were deceived. The NSC's top staff simply lied to members of Congress about these illicit operations.

Following an investigation into the scandal, lawmakers enacted two new laws that further tightened executive and legislative supervision over the

Intelligence Community. The Inspector General Act of 1989 established a more meaningful IG office at the Agency, confirmed by the Senate and with a mandate to keep members of both SSCI and HPSCI regularly and fully informed of any improper activities at Langley. Within government agencies, IG offices consolidate authority over audits and investigations within the various government agencies. IGs are expected to keep their agency leaders and lawmakers well apprised of any unlawful or unethical activities that have taken place within their agency's walls. In addition to providing detailed reports from time to time, they must also periodically testify at SSCI and HPSCI oversight hearings. While based within their own agency, each IG has considerable independence to investigate allegations of wrongdoing and, if serious improprieties are uncovered, they are expected to report them to the congressional intelligence panels. Frequently, though, this reporting has failed to happen, because such criticism could mar the reputation of the agency in question and ruin the IG's relationship with the senior management team inside the agency, which could be harmful to an officer's career. It takes courage and integrity to faithfully fulfill the IG job description; the best of them, though, have honored their oaths of office. In addition, the Intelligence Oversight Act of 1991 clarified the definition and the limits of covert action. It also underscored the necessity of – indeed, the *required* – formal *written* approval by the President as part of a CA finding, not just a slippery verbal assent. With these measures, the government would be attempting once more to make the experiment in intelligence accountability work.

The era of partisan advocacy (1991–2001)

A product chiefly of a harsh take-no-prisoners form of political rhetoric advocated by a new GOP Speaker, Newt Gingrich (Georgia), the post-Iran–*contra*, post-Reagan Administration atmosphere in Washington proved poisonous to constructive bipartisan support for intelligence within SSCI and HPSCI – and almost every other issue brought before lawmakers. This sudden partisan divide on the intelligence oversight panels and throughout the Congress was a startling departure from the past. Partisan cooperation with respect to intelligence activities reached its apotheosis in the late 1970s, at which point SSCI and HPSCI members began to divide along party lines, a fault that widened dramatically in the 1990s and the years since then – at least until very recently when SSCI began to show signs of a return to a spirit of bipartisanship in its ranks, thanks to the calming, fair leadership of Chairman Mark Warner (D, Virginia). Except for some acrimony and split voting generated by disagreements over whether to allow CIA covert actions in Nicaragua during the Reagan years, prior to the ascendance of Speaker Gingrich to power the two Congressional Intelligence Committees had almost always registered unanimous, bipartisan votes as they decided on intelligence policies. In the early years following the start of New Oversight in 1975, members of Congress from both parties had been guided by a sense that intelligence matters were especially sensitive and ought to be placed above the normal partisan fray in Washington.[9]

Yet, in the period after the Republican takeover of Capitol Hill in the 1990s, notes Joel Aberbach, a new mood emerged, one that was "hostile not only to the intent and behavior of political appointees, but to the missions of many federal programs and agencies."[10] Both HPSCI and SSCI proved vulnerable to this rising partisan storm. Stephen Knott attributes the growing polarization, in part, to a Republican wariness toward President Bill Clinton's foreign policy, as well as to a "simple partisan payback for years of perceived Democratic hectoring of Republican presidents."[11] Acrimonious partisan politics swirled around the nomination of Robert M. Gates for DCI in 1991 – his second try, this time successful but by the narrowest vote margin of any DCI nominee. Unfortunately, by 1997, the politics of intelligence had become as vituperative as practically every other policy domain. In 1996, the candidacy of Anthony Lake, the Clinton Administration's National Security Advisor, for DCI led to a deeply bitter struggle between Democrats and Republicans in Congress, with Lake finally withdrawing his name from consideration. Intelligence had become a political football. The hearings, described by an observer as "vitriolic," were punctuated by the most heated public exchanges across the aisle in SSCI's history.[12]

In a continuation of the political in-fighting, SSCI – under the leadership of Senator Pat Roberts (R, Kansas) from 2003 to 2006 – would soon vote strictly along party lines in rejecting a proposed investigation into the Bush II Administration's decision in the aftermath of the 9/11 attacks to bypass the procedures of FISA and engage in the warrantless surveillance of the international communications of American citizens. The SSCI Vice Chairman, John D. Rockefeller IV (D, West Virginia), pronounced the panel "basically under the control of the White House, through its chairman [Roberts]." In return, Chairman Roberts was equally adamant that the committee's Democrats were merely trying to score points against President Bush.[13] "Got'ya oversight" became the standard practice for both parties on each of the two intelligence oversight panels. The Church Committee model of bipartisan accord on intelligence matters in 1975–6 had fallen by the wayside

The era of mass surveillance (2001–12)

Partisan squabbling over intelligence continued to roil both SSCI and HPSCI long after the Al Qaeda attacks against the United States in 2001. Indeed, according to a close observer of Congress, the bickering grew even more heated. "One could only marvel at the degree to which partisanship had come to infect the work of the two committees," writes L. Britt Snider, former SSCI counsel (as well as a former CIA inspector general). "Once held up as models of how congressional committees should work," he further observed, "they now seemed no different from the rest."[14] Added to this internal political stress on the Intelligence Committees was a new ambivalence among their members toward the nation's secret agencies, displayed when House and Senate lawmakers merged temporarily into a Joint Committee to probe the tragic intelligence and policy failures leading up to 9/11. Some members of this Joint Committee scolded the intelligence agencies for their errors; even SSCI's Chair, Senator Roberts, usually an arch-defender of the CIA, bemoaned in 2004 that not a single official in the Intelligence Community had been "disciplined, let alone fired" for the mistakes related to the surprise terrorist attacks against the United States, or for its faulty prognosis about WMDs in Iraq. In dismay, he concluded that the "Community is in denial over the full extent of the shortcomings of its work."[15]

While Senator Roberts and a few other once reliable champions of the intelligence agencies occasionally displayed flashes of ambivalence and rebellion, for the most part SSCI and HPSCI members fell into an oversight stupor. They forgot the warnings of Madison and the wisdom of the Constitution, as well as the abuses uncovered by the Church Committee in 1975. Oversight came to mean rallying behind the President and the Intelligence Community to support the fighting that had ensued in Iraq, Afghanistan, and against global terrorism. This was an amplification of a trend visible even before 9/11. Prior to the terrorist attacks on the American homeland that day, SSCI had held only a couple of hearings on the subject of Al Qaeda. On the House side, the oversight record was just as dismal. Members of HPSCI held only two hearings on terrorism between 1998 and 2001 – the fewest of any conducted by a security or foreign affairs panel on Capitol Hill in the period leading up to the 9/11 attacks.[16] In another measure of their torpid existence, between 1976 and 1990 the two Intelligence Committees averaged fewer than two public hearings a year. Amy Zegart found a low number of intelligence hearings in later sessions of Congress as well.[17] Even when hearings are held by SSCI and HPSCI, the attendance can be poor.

"We really don't have, still don't have, meaningful congressional oversight [of the Intelligence Community]," observed a GOP leader, Senator John McCain (R, Arizona), in 2004.[18] That same year, the 9/11 Commission concluded that "congressional oversight for intelligence – and counterterrorism – is now dysfunctional."[19] A former staff aide on the Church Committee noted further in 2009 that, "unfortunately, the process of congressional oversight of intelligence, including covert action, so carefully crafted in the 1970s, is now regarded as something of a joke in Washington."[20] The horrors of Operations CHAOS and COINTELPRO seemed to have faded from memory – at least for the time being. When news broke in December 2005 about the warrantless wiretaps secretly carried out by the second Bush Administration, some SSCI and HPSCI members complained publicly about the FISA violations, but they never did much about it. According to a seasoned reporter with an intelligence beat, the relationship between the congressional oversight committees and the IC had "degenerated into a mutual admiration society for secret agencies."[21] Lawmakers seemed to have concluded that it was time to rally behind the spy organizations, even if some (like Roberts) felt occasional twinges of ambivalence toward the IC because of its disturbing failures between 2001 and 2003.

The era of rebalancing (2013–24)

The NSA metadata program

In 2013, a controversial "metadata" surveillance program was disclosed through the most significant breach of classified information in American history. That year, recall, the NSA temporarily hired from the private sector (the Booz Allen Hamilton corporation) a computer expert by the name of Edward J. Snowden, who had also worked for the CIA. Snowden was appalled by what he viewed as an excessive gathering of information by the NSA about the communication patterns of American citizens, including the names and contact numbers of anyone in the United States using a telephone or social media (though not the actual content of their communications). Snowden leaked information to the media (the *Washington Post* and the *Guardian*) about this program, codenamed "215." Further, the NSA had engaged in Operation PRISM, which targeted the actual content of sigint communications without first obtaining a FIS Court warrant (a violation of FISA revealed by the *New York Times* in December 2005). He also provided the media with thousands of other secret documents that included highly classified, detailed budget data for America's intelligence agencies. Snowden fled overseas and, in an odd landing for someone professing devotion to democratic principles, he took up residence in Russia.[22]

The Snowden documents on the NSA's metadata program, along with the FISA violations disclosed earlier by the *Times*, vividly revealed how the fear and anger generated by the September 2001 terrorist attacks had caused the United States to turn rapidly toward an overemphasis on security at the expense of American liberties. As a result of the public's reaction to the Snowden revelations about the NSA's intelligence fishing expedition, this tilt toward unfettered intelligence-collection operations – even at home – underwent a reversal. Serious questions arose as to whether the second Bush Administration and the NSA had gone too far in targeting the communications logs of American citizens (almost all of whom had nothing to do with global terrorism), as well as ignoring the FISA warrant requirement for wiretaps. Citizens properly feared that liberty in the United States could be crushed in the name of security.

This concern about warrants arose from Section 702 of FISA. That passage of the law had allowed the NSA to collect messages of foreigners abroad even when they were interacting with American citizens within the United States – all facilitated by the cooperation of U.S. communications companies like Google and AT&T. This led to the creation of a vast database of possible terrorists, chiefly comprising electronic communications (such as email and other digital messaging). These communications were compiled and stored by the NSA in guarded vaults located in Utah. The program was meant to ferret out bad actors in the United States – citizens and others operating within the homeland – who might be connected to foreign intelligence services, terrorist organizations, or organized crime syndicates.

On the surface, this approach appeared sensible, but the NSA and the FBI were accused by critics of overreaching. The collection operations were, they argued, cast too widely – and without individual warrants. The result: an undermining of the privacy of Americans, with scant or no compelling evidence for the need to target those individuals, store data on them, or have the right to sift through this data in subsequent months and even years. Reformers insisted in 2013 that the government should be required to obtain a warrant before carrying out such activities. The proper filters, based on evidence of tangible foreign intelligence or criminal contacts by those targeted for surveillance, were often set aside under Section 702, as the NSA and the FBI threw an indiscriminate electronic net across the United States. The Snowden disclosures had revealed that the NSA had carried out surveillance *on the entire American population* – as if that agency had learned nothing from the Church Committee's discovery in 1975 of its shameful SHAMROCK and MINERET surveillance misadventures.

Yet even in the face of a strong public reaction to the NSA's bulk collection activities, only two SSCI members voted against its continuation: Ron Wyden (D, Washington) and Mark Udall (D, Colorado). They joined forces in a failed attempt to declassify the program. "What happens when you get on [the SSCI]," Wyden has observed, "right away the Intelligence Community sweeps in and basically starts the process of trying to kind of say, 'Well, these are tough issues.' And, in effect, only one point of view gets conveyed." He continued: "It's our job to do vigorous oversight and not just get caught up in the culture that makes you, in effect, something more like an ambassador [for the IC] than a vigorous overseer."[23] For another leading Republican Senator, John McCain, what happened in the metadata case was simple: "Clearly, [the members of SSCI] have been co-opted. There's no doubt about that."[24] A study by the Brookings Institution (a think-tank in Washington, DC) found that "the Snowden revelations exposed a profound failure by Congress to understand and deliberate about the government's massive collection of phone and email records. It dealt with the need for secrecy by leaving the decisions entirely to the president or the intelligence agencies themselves, while pretending to maintain statutory standards."[25]

The number of SSCI and HPSCI members in support of the metadata program started to shrink, though, as more details came to light – especially when an Obama-appointed study panel (the President's Review Group), led by Professor Geoffrey Stone of the University of Chicago Law School, issued a strongly critical analysis.[26] Another prominent law professor, Jack Goldsmith at Harvard University, said that "the program was an example of the Administration going it alone, in secret, based on inadequate legal reasoning and flawed legal opinions."[27] With the criticism mounting, President Obama started to have second thoughts about his unquestioning support for the Bush Administration's electronic surveillance programs.

For critics of the metadata program, the demand from the Bush and Obama Administrations for actionable intelligence about terrorism had unfortunately cast aside basic American values of privacy and liberty. Shock, fear, uncertainty, and revenge had comingled to erase the established legal standards for surveillance, especially as embodied in the Foreign Intelligence Surveillance Act of 1978. In the wake of 9/11, the Bush Administration had adopted a vacuum-cleaner approach to electronic surveillance, rather than (as advocated by civil libertarians) a more pinpointed targeting of individuals based on a warrant procedure and a standard of reasonable suspicion that a suspect might be involved in terrorist or other criminal activities.

As the public debate continued to fester in the United States over the metadata program, Congress passed the USA Freedom Act. This bill, designed to overhaul the Patriot Act of 2001 (which was about to expire), passed in 2015 with overwhelming majorities. The new law sought to trim back the reach of the Patriot Act and the NSA's metadata activities. In the same month, the U.S. Court of Appeals for the Second Circuit in New York declared metadata collection illegal, a judicial decision that bolstered the efforts of privacy-oriented lawmakers on Capitol Hill to rebalance the equilibrium between security and liberty.

President Obama continued to endorse some aspects of the NSA's metadata program, but he instituted improved safeguards; and since the USA Freedom Act adopted his proposed added privacy protections, he signed the bill. The key provisions of the new law and the President's new approach included an emphasis on limiting metadata collection to just two communications linkages from an initial terrorist suspect, along with the storage of this more constricted data in the files of the telephone companies – rather than within massive NSA computer storage banks in Utah. Further, the data could be kept for no more than five years. Only when armed with a proper FISA warrant could the NSA (or any other of the spy agencies) access these files to examine the intelligence as it related to terrorist suspects. In addition, the FIS Court would be encouraged to have a public interest attorney present during its hearings about IC warrant requests for wiretaps, or for access to the metadata held by private telephone companies (such as Verizon).

The decision of the New York federal court and the enactment of the USA Freedom Act strongly signaled a change in attitudes about the proper balance between national security and individual privacy – both vital for any viable democracy. "I'm not going to vote for an extension of a law [the Patriot Act] that has recently been declared illegal by a federal circuit court," declared liberal Senator Chris Coons (D, Delaware); and conservative Senator Rand Paul (R, Kentucky) asked his colleagues on the Senate floor: "Are you really willing to give up your liberty for security?"[28] Now, the pendulum was swinging back against the nation's national security hawks and toward its civil liberty doves. As *New York Times* analysts put it, in motion on Capitol Hill was a shift away "from a singular focus on national security at the expense of civil liberties to a new balance in the post-Snowden era."[29] The coalition in favor of an intelligence rebalancing was made up of progressive Democrats and libertarian Republicans who brought about, the *Times* reported, "a changing tide in post-Sept. 11 America, where privacy concerns have become as important as national security interests for many people."[30]

Further complicating this ongoing debate between proponents of security and defenders of civil liberties was a ruling by the FIS Court in the summer of 2015 that the NSA did indeed have a right to continue its metadata program, regardless of the New York Second Circuit opinion – at least until Congress made clear exactly what the boundaries were going to be for the NSA's surveillance practices. "Second Circuit rulings are not binding" on this panel, declared Michael W. Mosman, a FIS Court judge.[31] Judge Mosman had become persuaded that a metadata program, had one existed in 2001, might well have prevented the 9/11 attacks; however, other reports pointed to the fact that the CIA had lots of information about two of the eventual terrorists hiding out in San Diego fully two years before the attack, but never shared this information effectively with the FBI, which is responsible for domestic counterintelligence. "There was no need for a metadata collection program," concluded a thoughtful commentator. "What was needed was [CIA] cooperation with other federal agencies."[32]

Congress continued to deliberate on the long-term fate of the NSA's collection operations involving American citizens as targets. The uses of FISA Section 702 remained unresolved, even as this provision of the law was set to expire at the end of 2023. Had these controversial NSA intelligence collection operations led unequivocally to successes in curbing terrorist attacks, the argument in favor of their continuation would have been persuasive; in fact, though, the NSA, the FBI, and the White House were unable to offer examples that were sufficiently convincing to quell the defenders of civil liberties – just as was the case with the CIA's use of torture against suspected terrorists in the wake of 9/11. As 2023 came to an end, Republicans in the GOP-controlled

House could not agree on whether to renew Section 702. As a result, they postponed a decision until the next session of Congress in 2024, relying on an obscure provision in the surveillance law that allowed 702 in its present ambiguous state to continue into April. The fate of the main question – whether or not all surveillance activities aimed at American citizens ought to require a judicial warrant – remained in limbo.

The Senate Torture Report

Immediately after the 9/11 attacks, President Bush II gave the CIA the authority to capture, detain, and, when necessary, kill Al Qaeda operatives around the world. Then, the following year, he waived Common Article 3 of the Geneva Conventions that prohibited "cruel treatment and torture" (even though the United States had ratified an international Convention Against Torture in 1988, signed by President Ronald Reagan). Further, in 2002, the head of Justice's Office of Legal Counsel (OLC) provided the CIA with additional after-the-fact authority to engage in harsh interrogation techniques.[33] Journalist Jane Mayer remarks that "unthinkable cruelty" was becoming official U.S. policy.[34]

The CIA reacts to 9/11

In September 2002, the CIA finally briefed a few members of HPSCI and SSCI about its interrogation activities. At the time, the Chair of the Senate Committee, Bob Graham (D, Florida), requested additional information. The Agency slow-rolled and stonewalled him, however, knowing that he was about to retire from the Senate in a few months. One nonpartisan outside observer concluded that the Agency's approach to SSCI and HPSCI during this time was one of "disdain and evasiveness."[35]

In 2005, however, the Agency's interrogation program began to unravel. During November of that year, reporter Dana Priest of the *Washington Post* revealed the existence of CIA prisons located aboard; and, soon afterward, the Deputy Director of Operations (the Agency's top CA officer), destroyed videotapes of the CIA's torture sessions, despite earlier admonitions from SSCI and HPSCI that these tapes had to be preserved.[36] It took two years, though, before the *New York Times* learned about and reported on the destruction of the torture tapes. "There is only one reason why [the videotapes] were destroyed: because certain people wanted that information never to be available," concluded SSCI Chairwoman Dianne Feinstein (D, California), who had expressed support for the NSA's controversial sigint operations as a counterterrorism tool but now decidedly did not approve of torture. She believed the destruction of the torture tapes had all the earmarks of a CIA cover-up.[37]

During the fall of 2006, the plenary SSCI membership was briefed on the interrogation program for the first time, five years after its initiation. General Michael V. Hayden, the CIA's Director (and the former NSA Director who had initiated the metadata program), gave the briefing in his typically self-assured and pugnacious manner. He vouched for the effectiveness of the interrogation methods and, in one of his more egregious moments of peddling fiction on Capitol Hill, he claimed with Delphic assurance that the CIA's methods were actually quite benign: merely "tummy slapping," as Senator Feinstein recalls him saying in macho posturing.[38] Feinstein later remembered that Hayden had presented "the entire set of techniques as minimally harmful and applied in a highly clinical and professional manner. They were not."[39] D/CIA General Hayden, whose skill in the art form of cozening members of Congress is widely acknowledged, seemed to have an elasticity of moral vision, as if the line of accountability for intelligence was a large, gray space wide enough for both the CIA and the NSA to get lost in.

While these events were evolving, SSCI decided in March 2009 – at long last, critics would complain – to initiate a staff investigation into the Agency's interrogation practices. Prodded by public calls for a "truth commission" to examine "torture" and other rumored harsh treatment of detainees, as well as still angered over the unauthorized destruction of the interrogation videotapes, the SSCI voted in a bipartisan manner – fourteen to one – in favor of a formal inquiry. The lone holdout was GOP Senator Saxby Chambliss (Georgia), the committee's Vice Chairman.[40]

The rest of the Republican members soon had second thoughts, though, and joined Chambliss in an abandonment of the SSCI's torture inquiry, on grounds that it had become politicized. It had; they made it so. The Democrats pressed on and, after more than five years of research, writing, and wrangling with the Agency and SSCI Republicans, they sent a draft report to Langley and the White House for a classification review. Several more months passed. Finally, a fatigued SSCI voted by a margin of eleven to three (with one abstention) to give up on publication of the full report and settle for the release of just an executive summary – if it could achieve at least that much. The three senators who voted no, all Republicans, opposed the public release of even a declassified executive summary.

After an agonizing eight additional months of tug-of-war over declassification decisions, SSCI finally gained permission from the Obama Administration near the end of 2014 to publish the executive summary. (At no point during or after this process did President Obama ever discuss the committee's findings with Senator Feinstein.) Even in its truncated form, the executive summary of the report was a lengthy and searing document: 499 pages long and with 2,725 footnotes. Its influence was enormous, despite all these efforts by the CIA, the Obama Administration, and SSCI Republicans to deep-six the torture findings.

Reaction to the Torture Report

When the GOP members of SSCI bailed out of the torture inquiry, the Democratic members authorized six of their professional staffers to move forward nonetheless to try and determine the precise source of authorization in the Bush II Administration for the Agency's use of torture. The staff also examined the nature of the around-the-clock interrogation techniques, which ran from rectal feeding and waterboarding three detainees (183 times, in the instance of Khalid Sheikh Mohammed, the suspected mastermind of the 9/11 attacks, known by Agency interrogators as KSM), to mock executions and sleep deprivation lasting for days – fully seven-and-a-half days in one instance. Some of the detainees were confined to cramped, coffin-like boxes, sometimes with insects thrown in with them for added torment. According to the SSCI report, one of the waterboarded detainees, Abu Zubaydah, "became completely unresponsive, with bubbles rising through his open, full mouth."[41] The report said that one ploy used by the CIA was the "hard takedown," whereby five brawny Agency officers would jump a detainee, hood him, cut away his clothing, punch him, and drag him down a hallway.

The D/CIA at the time of the SSCI torture inquiry, John Brennan, has said that the Senate report is full of exaggerations and errors – an incomplete and selective picture of what occurred, in his view. Republicans on SSCI echoed this judgment in a minority report. Yet, in 2016, the chief military prosecutor at Guantánamo (where 9/11 detainees had been imprisoned), General Mark Martins, read the full classified document and commented publicly that the facts were accurate, based on his knowledge of the interrogation program.[42]

The SSCI staff investigators also studied the question of whether these methods had elicited useful information that shielded the United States from further terrorist attacks. According to some accounts, Brennan is said eventually to have acknowledged: "We have not concluded that it was the EITs ['enhanced interrogation techniques' – that is, torture in euphemistic CIA-talk] within that program that allowed us to obtain useful information from the detainees subjected to them." Other reporters, though, have quoted him as saying that the EITs "did produce intelligence that helped thwart attack plans, capture terrorists, and save lives." Brennan views this latter statement as a misquote by the media and has clarified his view with this observation: "The detention and interrogation program – not the techniques – produced such intelligence." He also referred to the torture methods as "abhorrent," and concluded that the question of whether torture had been useful was ultimately "unknowable."[43]

In contrast, the conclusions reached by SSCI investigators were that the methods used by the CIA to extract information from detainees had been far more barbaric than the Agency had claimed (for example, one partially naked detainee, who had been apprehended in a case of mistaken identity, died of hypothermia in 2002); and that the effectiveness of this approach had been grossly exaggerated by General Hayden and everyone else at Langley, the White House, and the Justice Department.

Many observers of this debate pointed out that the more important matter had to do with the damage the use of torture had done to America's reputation around the world for fair play and dedication to human rights. As President Obama said about the SSCI report (despite his unwillingness to release the full report and his delay after delay in even declassifying the executive summary): "[It] reinforces my long-held view that these harsh methods were not only inconsistent with our values as a nation, they did not serve our broader counterterrorism efforts or our national security interests . . . upholding the values we profess doesn't make us weaker, it makes us stronger."[44] The Senate Torture Report had clearly raised vital questions about whether America's spy agencies had overreached in the direction of security by adopting counterterrorism measures alien to the nation's fundamental ethical principles.

The CIA attacks SSCI staff

Also in 2014, in the context of the SSCI torture investigation, the Agency further contributed to the growing sense in the United States that the time had come to rebalance the security–liberty equation. In a move that set a new standard of brazenness and disdain toward congressional overseers, CIA officers hacked into computers – four times – that the SSCI staff had used during its investigation into Agency torture activities. The CIA's cyber-warriors removed 870 documents during one hit, and 50 on another occasion.[45] Director Brennan claimed – falsely, it turned out, although perhaps he thought his statement was correct at the time – that SSCI staffers had first hacked into the Agency's computers. In fact, the Agency had accidentally sent to the SSCI staff computers used in the CIA's own internal examination of its interrogation practices – the so-called Panetta Review, named after then D/CIA Leon Panetta, who had ordered an internal review into the Agency's adoption of torture techniques. Amazed and pleased to stumble across this unknown study on the Agency computers provided to the SSCI staff, which the CIA should have shared with SSCI in the first place, the staffers were gratified to find that this in-house study closely paralleled their own findings.

Unhappy that the Senate investigators now had inadvertently been provided with the Panetta Report, some people in the Agency, including Brennan, tried to turn the tables on their Hill tormentors by claiming that the SSCI staff had stolen the Report by way of illegal hacking. The tradecraft of the CIA abroad often includes the use of deception and manipulation; these dark arts were now turned against "Sissystan," as Agency officers had disdainfully nicknamed SSCI. The Senate Select Committee on Intelligence had become, for the CIA, essentially just another foreign country targeted for covert action. Even Senator Chambliss, one of the Agency's premier advocates in Congress, blanched at these accusations from the D/CIA. "John [Brennan] didn't handle that right," Chambliss managed to say in mild rebuke.[46] A SSCI member observed more bluntly at the time: "It's WWIII between the CIA and Senate."[47]

The SSCI Chair Dianne Feinstein (who passed away in 2023 after a long and distinguished career in the Senate) wrote to Brennan, reprimanding the Agency for its search into the computers it had loaned to SSCI. She said that this intervention might well have violated the separation of powers doctrine that lay at the heart of the Constitution (not to mention the CIA's founding law in 1947, which clearly prohibited Agency operations inside the United States). The computers did belong to the CIA but, at the time, they had been given clearance by the Agency for use by SSCI and, therefore, should have been off limits to Langley until officially returned to the CIA by the Senate Committee. Instead, the CIA – astonishingly – had begun to spy on the SSCI staff. The D/CIA, Brennan, took weeks to respond to Feinstein's reprimand. A Senate colleague of Feinstein's warned her that Brennan's intentions on behalf of the Agency were "to intimidate, deflect, and thwart legitimate oversight."[48] Subsequently, the CIA Director would concede in testimony before the full committee that a "trust deficit" had opened up between SSCI and the Agency, and he finally apologized to Feinstein and Chambliss for the hacking transgression.

The CIA engaged in other forms of harassment against the committee's investigators, too. The Agency's Acting Chief Counsel went after the SSCI staff with a vengeance, perhaps distressed by the fact that his name appeared more than 1,600 times in the committee's Torture Report – each of which he managed to have deleted during the White House declassification wars. He referred the names of the SSCI staffers who wrote the Torture Report to the Justice Department for investigation.

In the light of these activities, the CIA's understanding of and allegiance to the existing laws and rules on accountability became a subject of deep concern on Capitol Hill and in the media. Senate Majority Leader Harry Reed (D, Nevada) warned Feinstein: "Look, you can't stand by anymore! The CIA is leaking stuff. They're making your staff out to be the bad guys!"[49] The Agency's efforts to spy on SSCI staffers were an unprecedented violation of the oversight relationship – an operation carried out with impunity, despite a strong, even angry, complaint delivered by Senator Feinstein during a press conference.

Brennan appointed a panel to look into the charges. Three of the five members of this group were CIA officers; the other two were outside individuals known to be friendly toward the Agency. After a brief "investigation," the CIA absolved itself of any blame and announced, with its practiced skills of *agitprop*, that the whole episode had been just a "misunderstanding."[50] In sharp contrast, the CIA's own Inspector General had reported earlier that the Agency's hacking into SSCI computers was improper, as was the effort by the CIA Acting General Counsel to file a crimes report with the DoJ against the committee's staffers. The Agency's IG, David Buckley, who had been critical of the CIA's treatment of the SSCI staff, soon found himself discredited and ostracized inside the Agency. He resigned, as his own organization closed ranks against him – sometimes a regrettable occupational hazard for honest IGs at Langley and elsewhere in the executive branch.

Despite this opposition from the CIA, in 2015 the findings of the SSCI Torture Report significantly influenced the Senate vote of 71–21 in favor of banning America's use of any interrogation techniques in the future that were not specifically authorized in the list of less draconian methods provided in the *U.S. Army Field Manual*. No more waterboarding or other forms of torture.

A mixed record

A former SSCI Chair, Jay Rockefeller (D, West Virginia), summed up the CIA's response to the interrogation inquiry as an "active subversion of meaningful congressional oversight."[51] To some degree, however, SSCI and HPSCI both bear some blame for allowing the CIA torture and the NSA metadata programs to move forward for so long before they took a closer look at them. The acceptance at face value of Hayden's misleading "tummy slapping" remarks (as happened, too, with National Security Advisor Robert McFarlane's assurances in the 1980s about the alleged nonexistence of "the Enterprise" during the Iran–*contra* episode) proved to be a painful mistake. Overseers must learn to be more skeptical and tenacious – using hearings to dig for the truth, swearing in witnesses under oath and, when necessary, resorting to subpoena powers to obtain access to key documents and witnesses – until they are reasonably sure that all the facts are on the table.

Further, as several CIA directors noted in an op-ed, once the congressional overseers were finally informed by the executive branch about the Agency's interrogation activities, SSCI and HPSCI "missed a chance to help shape the program – they couldn't reach a consensus. The executive branch was left to proceed alone, merely keeping the committees informed."[52] Journalist David Ignatius concurs. He accepted the SSCI report as "immensely valuable," but tagged the oversight committee for never properly addressing "Congress's own failure to oversee these activities more effectively." Ignatius wondered: "Did the members of Congress push back hard, as we now realize they should have? Did they demand more information and set stricter limits? Did they question details about the interrogation techniques that were being used?" His correct response: "They did not."[53] Legal scholar Michael Glennon has asked: "Where was SSCI while all this was going on?"[54] He might have added: "And where was HPSCI?" Neither committee inspected, for example, any of the CIA's controversial "black sites" (detainee prisons) overseas where many of the torture practices were taking place.

At the same time, SSCI earns high marks in persevering with its inquiry into the interrogation program, despite great adversity and insufficient cooperation from the executive branch. (An example: the Obama White House, at the CIA's instigation, blocked 9,000 pages of documents requested by SSCI during its probe, on grounds of executive privilege). The Torture Report is no doubt flawed. It would have been especially good to have had more bipartisan participation, at the staff and member levels. The Republicans could have made this happen, but deserted the project in an effort to slow down and discredit the probe. The GOP members would have had plenty of opportunities along the way to insert their dissenting views into the report, setting the record straight as they saw it when they believed the Democrats were off-mark. In this sense, the Republican strategy did the CIA a great disservice. Among Republicans, only Olympia Snowe (New Hampshire) at least occasionally displayed a bipartisan spirit on SSCI and a willingness to search for the truth about CIA torture with her colleagues across the aisle.

Critics have charged the Democratic staff who worked on the report with allowing their ethical objections against torture to outweigh a dispassionate evaluation of the program's effectiveness. The staffers – each of whom had strong professional credentials for investigating – deny this allegation, arguing that their purpose was to lay out the facts, which is exactly how they proceeded.[55] At any rate, the facts clearly indicated that the CIA's resort to torture was not very effective, just as the value of the NSA's controversial sigint metadata programs were routinely exaggerated by intelligence officials (and even at times by Senator Feinstein, who knew less about, and was less interested in, the NSA than she was in the CIA).[56]

Senator Feinstein, the accountability hero throughout the doleful episode of the SSCI inquiry into CIA torture practices, had taken on President Obama and D/CIA Brennan. In the end, she well captured the normative findings of the committee's Torture Report. "We're not Nazi Germany," she concluded. "We don't torture people. We don't waterboard them 183 times until they nearly stop breathing. We don't put them in coffins and attach them to walls for, like, 100 hours."[57] Hayden dismissed her views as too "emotional," but she was not alone in her outrage. Senator McCain for one, himself a victim of torture at the hands of ruthless North Vietnamese interrogators during the war in Vietnam, observed that "this question is not about our enemies; it's about us."[58]

A shock theory of intelligence accountability

As this look at the different phases of intelligence accountability suggests, the intelligence oversight performance of Congress fluctuated widely during the Cold War and has continued to do so ever since. Several observers have commented on these ups and downs. Writing in the years before the Church Committee investigation, for example, the distinguished Intelligence Studies scholar Harry Howe Ransom noted that intelligence accountability had been "sporadic, spotty, and essentially uncritical."[59] Even after the introduction of the

New Intelligence Oversight procedures in 1975 during the Church Committee inquiry, students of the subject have discerned inadequate attention to this responsibility in recent years.[60] The chief cause of this inattentiveness by lawmakers derives from the nature of Congress: its members seek re-election as their primary objective. As a result, they usually conclude that passing spending bills for local projects and raising campaign funds is a better use of their time than the often tedious review of executive branch programs. This is especially true for intelligence accountability. The examination of secret operations must take place in closed committee sanctuaries on Capitol Hill, outside of public view. Absent public awareness, the chances for credit-claiming – important to a lawmaker's re-election prospects – are remote.[61]

An examination of intelligence accountability in the United States since the Year of Intelligence in 1975 indicates a cyclical pattern of stimulus and response. A major spy scandal or failure – a "shock" – transforms the perfunctory performance of intelligence oversight into a burst of intense program scrutiny. This burst is followed by a period of reasonably attentive oversight activities that yield remedial legislation or other reforms designed to curb inappropriate intelligence operations in the future. Then comes the third phase of the shock cycle: backsliding into a middling practice of oversight.

Political scientists McCubbins and Schwartz offer the useful metaphor of "police patrolling" and "firefighting" to highlight differences in commitment by lawmakers to oversight responsibilities.[62] Patrolling consists (metaphorically) of steadily checking up on the executive bureaucracy by shining a flashlight into darkened windows, jiggling the lock on the door, walking the streets with a keen eye. In contrast, firefighting requires an emergency reaction to a calamity after it occurs. Lawmakers *qua* firefighters jump on the fire truck when the alarm sounds and try to put out the conflagration – that is, resolve the scandal or failure. This pattern is depicted in Figure 6.2. A prominent member of Congress has evoked the policing analogy. "There has been no cop on the beat," said Representative Henry A. Waxman (D, California), Chair of the House Oversight and Government Reform Committee, who accused Republicans of abandoning their oversight responsibilities. Waxman continued: "And when there is no cop on the beat, criminals are more willing to engage in crimes."[63]

To reach the level of a shock (or "fire alarm"), an allegation of intelligence failure or impropriety has to have sustained media coverage, with at least a few front-page stories. In 1974, for example, in the run-up to the creation of the Church Committee the *New York Times* had an unusually high coverage of reporting on the CIA from June through December: some 200 articles. In December alone, nine stories on the Agency made the front page – unprecedented at the time. Here was a steady drumbeat of chiefly negative reporting, setting the stage for a strong public – and, therefore, congressional and presidential – reaction to the most explosive of these news

The Patterns

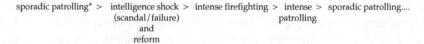

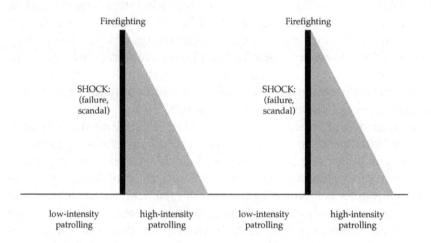

* A result of insufficient opportunities for credit-claiming and the enhancement of re-election prospects, which in turn produce an inattentiveness to oversight duties and a concomitant ripening of conditions for scandal or failure.

Figure 6.2: A cycle of intelligence shock and reaction by congressional overseers since 1975.

Source: Initially presented in Loch K. Johnson, "A Shock Theory of Congressional Accountability for Intelligence," Loch K. Johnson, ed., *Handbook of Intelligence Studies* (New York: Routledge, 2007), pp. 343–360; figure at p. 344.

items: Operation CHAOS, the CIA domestic spy scandal. On the eve of the next major intelligence scandal, the Iran–*contra* affair during the Reagan Administration, the *Times* carried eleven front-page stories in both October and November 1986 about possible intelligence abuses related to a rogue covert war in Nicaragua. The number jumped to eighteen front-page stories in December, setting the stage for the Joint Committee investigation into the scandal in 1987.

Congress has greater authority than the media to investigate intelligence operations – from the power of the purse to the power of the subpoena and, ultimately, impeachment. The media, though, seem to have more willpower to conduct oversight, driven in part at the management level by a profit motive to sell newspapers through the exposure of government scandals and failures. Or, at the reporter's level, to garner professional esteem, prizes for outstanding investigative journalism, and a sense of self-accomplishment. Yet even intense media coverage may not be enough in itself to bring out the "firefighters" on Capitol Hill. The warrantless wiretaps and the CIA torture practices during the second Bush Administration, for instance, attracted considerable media attention, but no major congressional inquiry (beyond the report on torture prepared behind the scenes by Democratic staff members on SSCI). The nation continued to feel under the threat of possible terrorist attacks and, in this climate of fear, investigations into those shocking revelations were never pursued with the ardor warranted by the NSA and CIA violations. Such considerations as the personalities of congressional overseers – especially the attitudes of the SSCI and HPSCI Chairs (the soft-pedaling of Agency torture by SSCI's Chair, Saxby Chambliss, for instance) – can play a role, too, in determining whether an intelligence shock leads to a major fire-fighting response by lawmakers.[64] In addition, when the congressional chambers and the White House are held by different parties (a situation referred to as "divided government" by political scientists and journalists in the United States), bipartisan cooperation can become more challenging.

Intelligence shocks

After Congress began to take intelligence oversight seriously toward the end of 1974, lawmakers devoted about six years to intensive investigating (fire-fighting), stimulated by the five major intelligence controversies or shocks (triggering alarms) presented in what follows and in Table 6.1. The rest – the vast majority of the time – has been spent in police patrolling. Sometimes this patrolling has been vigorous (the influential Senate Torture Report is a conspicuous example, at least for the Democrats on SSCI); but, for the most part this "checking up" has been carried out in a perfunctory manner.

Major alarm no. 1: The domestic spy scandal (1974)

As discussed earlier, the government of the United States responded to news allegations of CIA domestic spying (Operation CHAOS) with the Church, Pike, and Rockefeller inquiries. The findings of these panels led to the creation of SSCI and HPSCI, the FIS Court warrant requirements of 1978, and the Intelligence Oversight Act of 1980, with its dramatic requirement of prior notice to Congress for all important intelligence operations.[65]

Major alarm no. 2: The Iran–contra scandal (1986)

The Inouye–Hamilton Committee, which examined the Iran–*contra* allegations, revealed unlawful intelligence operations carried out by NSC staff and a few CIA officials.[66] Its findings led to enactment of the CIA Inspector General Act of 1989, creating an IG with responsibilities to keep Congress informed of Agency improprieties; and the Intelligence Oversight Act of 1991, which clarified covert action definitions and tightened its approval procedures.

Major alarm no. 3: The Ames counterintelligence failure (1994)

In response to the discovery of Aldrich Ames's treachery, Congress created a presidential–congressional panel of inquiry, known as the Aspin–Brown

Table 6.1: Types of stimuli and key oversight responses by lawmakers since 1974

Year	Stimulus	Oversight response	Purpose of response
1974	FA (#1)	Hughes–Ryan Act	Controls over covert action
1976–7	FA (#1)	Est. SSCI, HPSCI; critical reports	More robust accountability
1978	FA (#1)	FISA	Warrants for electronic surveillance
1980	FA (#1)	Intel. Oversight Act	Tightening oversight rules
1980	P	Intel. Information Procedures Act	Improvements in intel. judicial proceedings
1982	P	Intel. Identities Act	Protect intel. officers/agents
1984	P	CIA Information Act	Limits on FOIA requests
1987	FA (#2)	Critical report	Improve intelligence oversight
1989	FA (#2)	CIA Inspector General Act	Improve internal CIA oversight
1991	FA (#2)	Intel. Oversight Act	Further tightening oversight rules; defining covert action
1996	FA (#3)	Est. DCI assistants; critical reports	IC management improvements; strengthening CI
1997	P	Intel. Authorization Act provision	Controls on CIA use of journalists
1998	P	Whistleblowers Protection Act	Improving procedures for whistleblowing
2001	FA (#4)	USA Patriot Act; authorization of war against Al Qaeda and Taliban regime, AUMF; increases in counterterrorism funding	Reaffirm FISA surveillance warrant procedures for suspected terrorists; institute formal authorization for paramilitary counterattacks against Al Qaeda and Taliban
2004	FA (#4)	Critical reports	Improving humint and analysis
2004	FA (#4, #5)	Intel. Reform & Terrorism Prevention Act (IRTPA)	Strengthening CT, IC coordination, est. ODNI
2008	P	FISA Amendments Act	Supporting NSA metadata program
2015	P	USA FREEDOM Act	Safeguards against excesses in NSA operations
2023	P	Wrangling over FISA's Section 702	Tighter FISA/NSA/FBI surveillance rules

Abbreviations:
FA = fire alarm (#1 = domestic spying; #2 = Iran-*contra*; #3 = Ames/Somalia; #4 = 9/11; #5 = WMD in Iraq)
P = patrolling
humint = human intelligence
IC = Intelligence Community
FISA = Foreign Intelligence Surveillance Act [P.L. 95-511; 92 Stat. 1783 (Oct. 25, 1978)]
DCI = Director of Central Intelligence
DNI = Director of National Intelligence; ODNI = Office, Director of National Intelligence
CI, CT = counterintelligence, counterterrorism
AUMF = authorization of the use of military force

Commission and led by former Secretaries of Defense Les Aspin and Harold Brown. A U.S. intelligence failure on the Horn of Africa, leading to the deaths of several American soldiers, contributed to the sense in Washington that a major investigation into intelligence practices was warranted. The Commission published a report calling for reforms across the board of intelligence activities, but with special emphasis on the need for a stronger DCI and for revealing to the public the annual aggregate intelligence budget figure so that taxpayers would know how much they are spending on these government programs.[67]

Major alarm no. 4: The 9/11 attacks (2001)

The failure of the intelligence agencies to warn the nation about the catastrophic terrorist attacks against the American homeland in 2001 led Congress to form a joint committee of inquiry (the Graham–Goss Committee) and, subsequently, to urge the creation of an even more comprehensive presidential investigative panel (the Kean Commission) to probe further into the disaster.[68] Moreover, HPSCI released to the public a critical evaluation of the CIA's humint activities around the world, stressing the lack of good assets in key locations.[69]

Major alarm no. 5: The absence of WMDs in Iraq (2003)

In light of an incorrect intelligence judgment about the likely presence of WMDs in Iraq, expressed in a National Intelligence Estimate of October 2002, Congress supported the creation of a presidential commission on intelligence (the Silberman–Robb Commission) to investigate this analytic failure.[70] Moreover, SSCI undertook a parallel but separate probe into the faulty WMDs estimate, focusing on the CIA's errors, but electing not to examine questions about the poor policy use of warning intelligence that was provided by the IC to the Clinton and Bush II White Houses.[71]

Muted alarms nos. 6 and 7: NSA metadata (2013) and CIA torture programs (2013)

Full blast alarms might have sounded and ensured a major investigation by Congress in the wake of the NSA sigint collection controversies (the metadata program and the Section 702 warrantless wiretaps), as well as after exposure of the CIA'S use of torture. The impulses toward serious intelligence inquiries (fire-fighting) by lawmakers and the White House were dampened down, however, by the ongoing potential danger of future terrorist attacks. A sense prevailed among many (although by no means all) key officials in Washington that security considerations would have to supersede matters of liberty and privacy – at least for the time being.

Happily, there have been no major intelligence "alarms" or even significant-but-muted "alarms" since the metadata and torture controversies, unless one were to count the attempts by rightwing lawmakers in the House GOP to claim that the FBI has been "weaponized" to destroy Donald Trump and his MAGA ("Make America Great Again") populist movement. House hearings on this subject have uncovered no persuasive evidence to this effect, although these Republican-propelled inquiries are clearly ongoing. Neither SSCI nor HPSCI have bothered to probe these allegations, which simply have not risen to the level of earlier and more legitimate (empirically grounded, credible) "alarm" levels.

Key issues of intelligence accountability

Who should be informed?

Several prominent issues have dominated the ongoing debate over how legislative oversight should be conducted with respect to the intelligence agencies. The first is *who* should be kept informed on Capitol Hill. Before 1974, the answer was just a few lawmakers on the small intelligence subcommittees of the Armed Services and Appropriations Committees – if indeed the DCI deigned to tell them anything at all, or if the lawmakers were (unlike Senator John Stennis) willing to listen. Today the "witting circle" of those lawmakers kept informed of intelligence activities has widened to include members of SSCI and HPSCI, as well as (on some topics) selected members on these two panels who also serve on the Appropriations, Armed Services, Foreign Affairs, and Judiciary Committees. The top four leaders of Congress – two from each party – are also informed on some emergency occasions. Intelligence officials, though, are not beyond playing games with these reporting rules, sometimes attempting to whisper only into the ear of a committee Chair – DCI Turner's ploy with Eddie Boland early in their relationship, until Boland began to wonder how much he could critically peer into the activities of the intelligence agencies while locked in a bear hug by the DCI.

On other occasions, intelligence managers may seek to limit their briefings on a finding, or some other key intelligence decision, to only a "Gang of Eight" (the top four congressional leaders and the top four SSCI and HPSCI leaders from both parties); or even a "Gang of Four," by limiting the witting circle to only the GOP and Democratic leaders of the two Intelligence Committees (or sometimes the phrase is used to refer to the four top congressional leaders).[72] The Gang of Four concept is strictly an invention of the executive branch, used from time to time by presidents of both parties since 1980, as during the attempts by the second Bush Administration to inform only a few lawmakers about the NSA metadata program and the CIA's adoption of torture. Nowhere is the Gang of Four provision allowed by statute; and the Gang of Eight is a group (first mentioned in the Intelligence Oversight Act of 1980) that, it should be emphasized, was supposed to be resorted to only in times of emergency. Yet, in 2002, the second Bush Administration briefed – all too briefly, according to recipients – just the Gang of Eight during its questionable use of warrantless wiretaps, as revealed by the *New York Times* in 2005.

Worst of all, sometimes the favorite number of lawmakers the executive branch sees fit to brief on Capitol Hill has been zero – the "Gang of None" – as was clearly the case with Operations CHAOS, COINTELPRO, SHAMROCK, and MINARET, and the CIA assassination plots. The longest-serving DCI, Allen Dulles (1953–61), once said that he felt obliged to tell the truth only to one person: the President – if he asked.[73] On another occasion Dulles widened the circle by one. "I'll fudge the truth to the Oversight Committee," he stunningly admitted to a journalist, "but I'll tell the chairman the truth – that is, if he wants to know."[74] In bold contrast, the intent of the 1980 and 1991 Intelligence Oversight Acts was to have *all* the members of SSCI and HPSCI briefed (along with a few senior staff in attendance), not just some subset. The only exception: grave emergencies, when – even then – the Gang of Eight must be soon informed. The committees, though, must insist on this approach or IC managers will sidestep the full-briefing rule.[75] Certainly the two Oversight Committees have demonstrated their trustworthiness over the years, with virtually no major leaks from them.

Another central issue has been the question of *when* intelligence managers ought to inform lawmakers about their activities. Prior to 1974, the answer was whenever the IC managers felt like it, if at all. With respect to the Hughes–Ryan Act, the answer concerning covert actions evolved into an understanding that the briefing would take place "in a timely fashion," defined during the floor colloquy in Congress that preceded the vote on this law to mean within twenty-four hours. The 1980 Intelligence Oversight Act – short in length, but long in reach – changed the formula powerfully to mean "prior notice" (except in an emergency, which allowed reporting – recall – to just the Gang of Eight for a couple of days, after which full briefings to SSCI and HPSCI were expected). Of great importance, this concept of *ante facto* reporting had won out over *ex post facto* reporting and, in the process, intelligence oversight acquired much greater strength. Lawmakers were now in a position to object to an operation *before* it was already under way – *before* the horse was out of the barn. For example, HPSCI chairman Peter Hoekstra (R, Michigan) once protested to President George W. Bush directly about a specific CA immediately after the briefing on the finding and the President reportedly modified the operation based on this criticism.[76] During confirmation hearings, the (successful) DCI nominee Robert M. Gates testified that he would strongly consider resigning from office if a delay in reporting to Congress went beyond just a few days at the most.[77]

An unspoken, but important, side benefit often results from the Hughes–Ryan briefings on covert action. As former Secretary of State Dean Rusk observed at an International Studies Association, South, meeting at the University of Georgia on October 5, 1979, "regular discussions are beneficial between Congress and the executive, even when they are 'pointless'" (by which he meant: even when talks might not resolve a policy issue at that moment). Why? Because dialogue that transcends party differences can be vital for building trust and rapport between the branches – the establishment of personal relations that is so useful as a lubricant to ease the friction in the sometimes sputtering institutional engines of democracy.

What information should be reported?

The question of *what* kind of information should be reported is obviously important, too. Again, before 1974, this decision was left to the discretion of the DCI. The Hughes–Ryan Act then set a new standard by requiring a report to the congressional oversight committees on important CAs. The far-reaching Intelligence Oversight Act of 1980 made it clear that Congress wished to be kept informed of "all" important intelligence activities, not just covert actions. This remains the gold standard, although one the executive branch has periodically sidestepped.

Which agencies are expected to report?

Further debate has surrounded the topic of *which* of the eighteen agencies must report to lawmakers. Before 1974, the answer was that the reporting, however infrequent, would be carried out by the CIA, since the DCI was housed in its Headquarters Building at Langley. Then the 1980 Oversight Act stressed that *all* IC agencies, as well as other "entities" if they were engaged in intelligence activities, would be expected to keep the oversight panels on Capitol Hill informed. This broad language included NSC staff, a matter that became controversial during the Reagan Administration when that staff chose to ignore this provision as it launched its illegal, super-secret Iran–*contra* covert actions.

The roles played by lawmakers as intelligence supervisors

In dealing with their intelligence oversight duties since 1974 – facing the who, when, what, and which challenges discussed above – members of Congress have adopted one of four major roles: the ostrich, the cheerleader, the lemon-sucker, or the guardian, with fluctuations by some lawmakers between the different roles according to personalities and the circumstances of the time. These roles suggest a range of oversight involvement that members of SSCI and HPSCI have tended to display.

The ostrich

The first type of intelligence overseer is the "ostrich." Here is the member of SSCI or HPSCI who embraces a philosophy of benign neglect toward the intelligence agencies (see Figure 6.3). This view characterized almost all members of Congress before the domestic spy scandal of 1974 (Operation CHAOS). A classic illustration of the ostrich is Senator Barry Goldwater (R, Arizona), who became chairman of SSCI in 1981. He had previously served as a member of the Church Committee. While on that committee, Goldwater voted in 1976 against the creation of SSCI on grounds that it was unnecessary – the very panel that, ironically, he would come to lead. He also opposed most of the other ninety-eight reforms recommended by the Church Committee, including closer judicial scrutiny of wiretapping operations inside the United States and more extensive congressional hearings on CIA covert actions. Goldwater was content with the system of oversight that existed before 1975: an occasional, desultory review of spy activities by a few largely ceremonial subcommittees on intelligence housed within the Armed Services and the Appropriations Committees.[78]

The cheerleader

The second type of intelligence overseer is the "cheerleader." In this instance, the member of Congress has removed his or her head from the sand, but only for the purpose of cheering more loudly on behalf of the intelligence agencies. The cheerleader is interested primarily in the advocacy of spy activities, the support of intelligence budgets, and the advancement of clandestine operations at home and abroad against suspected enemies of the United States. During oversight hearings, the cheerleader specializes in "softball" pitches – easy questions gently tossed so that intelligence managers called as witnesses can belt them over the center-field fence.[79] In press conferences, the cheerleader acts as a defense attorney for America's secret agencies, hinting at their behind-the-scenes, "if you only knew" successes; lauding the heroism of intelligence officers and agents; castigating journalists for printing leaked secrets that imperil the nation; and warning of threats at home and abroad that could lead to another 9/11 if the intelligence agencies are hamstrung or left unfunded by kibitzing lawmakers and their staffs. Such statements by cheerleaders are often true: intelligence officers do have successes, and sometimes they are heroes. But they are one-sided in their perspective, lacking a critical eye for intelligence inadequacies that cry out for reform. Recall how Representative Boland assumed the role of cheerleader when he became the first chair of HPSCI in 1977. He often swallowed his personal skepticism about specific covert operations and expressed his full support for the government's secret bureaucracy, determined to show that his committee could be trusted as a responsible supervisor of intelligence operations on Capitol Hill. His dealing with the irascible DCI William Casey – a much more ideological and volatile personality than DCI Adm. Turner – would soon lead him away from this role-type and toward that of "guardian" (see below).

The lemon-sucker

A third role type is the "lemon-sucker" – a term used by President Bill Clinton to describe those economists who displayed a sour disposition toward a proposed government policy. This approach is as one-sided as the cheerleader, only at the opposite extreme. For the lemon-sucker, nothing undertaken by the intelligence agencies is likely to be worthwhile. From this point of view, the secret agencies are inherently immoral: opening and reading other people's mail; eavesdropping on telephone conversations and social media; stealing documents; overthrowing governments; perhaps even killing people with drone missiles or poisons. The skeptical lemon-suckers also charge the spy agencies with incompetence. Recall how, in 1996, a well-regarded member of SSCI, Senator Daniel Patrick Moynihan (D, New York), dismayed by what he wrongly perceived as the CIA's inability to anticipate the collapse of the Soviet empire, called for the abolition of the Agency.[80]

The guardian

The fourth type of intelligence overseer is the "guardian." This role conforms best with the hopes expressed by legislative reformers during the Year of Intelligence in 1975. Representative Lee H. Hamilton (D, Indiana), HPSCI chair from 1985 to 1987, has argued that the ideal intelligence overseers are both "partners and critics" of the secret agencies.[81] Another HPSCI member, Norm Dicks (D, Washington), observed that "overseeing the intelligence community is like being a good parent: you have to encourage and discipline."[82]

| | | *Responsibility for intelligence support* | |
		Low	High
Responsibility for intelligence evaluation	Low	1 The ostrich	2 The cheerleader
	High	3 The lemon-sucker	4 The guardian

Figure 6.3: A typology of roles assumed by intelligence overseers in the U.S. Congress.

Photo 6.3: Representative Lee Hamilton
9/11 Vice Chair Lee Hamilton.
Source: 9/11 Commission.

As intelligence "partners," lawmakers must educate the American people on the virtues of maintaining an effective intelligence capability for the sake of America's security. Without defenders on Capitol Hill, the spy agencies – given the secrecy of their programs – are at a major disadvantage in gaining public support for their activities and sizable budgets. Yet, to be an effective overseer, a lawmaker must also be a fair critic: someone who searches for, acknowledges, and corrects programmatic flaws. This challenging role requires the ability, above all, to be objective and to speak out against questionable activities (in closed hearings on those occasions when the operations in question are too sensitive for public review).

Representative Hamilton has come as close to this ideal as any member of SSCI or HPSCI. When he was head of HPSCI, he regularly convened committee meetings, paid close attention to memos and reports from his staff and the intelligence agencies, followed up on media allegations of intelligence wrongdoing and mistakes, traveled to U.S. spy bases abroad to review programs in the field, and spent long hours combing through intelligence budgets and talking to IC professionals at Langley and other spy agency headquarters buildings. Yet even he was initially fooled by the Iran–*contra* conspirators (see Chapter 4).

The dynamic nature of intelligence accountability

Casey once explained his "theory" of intelligence oversight in this manner: "The job of Congress is to stay the f– out of my business."[83] Pursuing this "philosophy" Casey managed to do the seemingly impossible: he single-handedly turned SSCI's most reliable ostrich, Goldwater, into one of its most vocal lemon-suckers in Congress. The catalyst in this dramatic transformation was Casey's misleading testimony during an appearance before SSCI when Goldwater was its chairman. When asked by a committee member whether the CIA was mining harbors in Nicaragua, the DCI offered an adamant "no" in response. Only later did it become clear that Casey was relying on a technical point: the Agency was not mining *harbors*; it was mining *piers* within the harbors. This attempt to toy with the SSCI angered its leader, as Goldwater's institutional pride overruled his former feelings of blind deference toward the IC – at least temporarily. Goldwater fired off a letter to one of the best venues in the nation's capital for venting: the *Washington Post*. Castigating Casey for his attempts at legerdemain on Capitol Hill, the letter said in part: "It gets down to one, little, simple phrase: I am pissed off!"[84] As Goldwater's ire over Casey receded, however, the chairman drifted into a cheerleading role for the remainder of his tenure on SSCI through 1985 (though at least he was no longer merely an ostrich).

In search of guardians

The role of guardian was widely accepted by intelligence reformers on Capitol Hill in 1975 as the ideal, because it balanced support for intelligence with a determination through persistent program review to avoid future agency failures and scandals. No more Operations CHAOS and COINTELPRO, no more Huston Plans. Since then, former DCI Robert M. Gates convincingly stated the case for intelligence oversight on Capitol Hill. "Some awfully crazy schemes might well have been approved," he said, "had everyone present [in the White House] not known and expected hard questions, debate, and criticism from the Hill. And when, on a few occasions, Congress was left in the dark, and such schemes did proceed, it was nearly always to the lasting regret of the presidents involved."[85]

Regardless of these compelling reasons for a lawmaker to assume the guardian role of a dedicated intelligence overseer, most observers agree that members of Congress continue to perform far below their potential when it comes to the supervision of America's spy agencies. The cheerleader remains the default role on Capitol Hill. This phenomenon was demonstrated for the public vividly when, in 2022, a House Republican majority banished two of the most energetic and highly regarded guardians from continuing their HPSCI membership: Adam Schiff (D, California) and Eric Swalwell

(D, California). Rather than attacking oversight guardians, whether Democrats or Republicans, the single most important intelligence oversight responsibility facing the United States is to select SSCI and HPSCI members of both parties who will work diligently all year round as guardians to improve intelligence performance and strengthen accountability. Citizens in the United States and the other open societies must engage in conversations about the importance of integrity and the rule of law within their secret agencies. Only when that happens will representatives of the people devote more attention to the vital duty of intelligence accountability in all nations that aspire to keep their liberty.

The final chapter that follows summarizes the key themes of this book and examines some recent developments related to U.S. intelligence activities. These contemporary years witnessed an astonishing falling out between the agencies of the Intelligence Community and their most important consumer: Donald J. Trump, when he was President of the United States from 2017 to 2021.

7

National Security Intelligence:
Hidden Shield and Sword of the Democracies

This book has examined the three core dimensions of national security intelligence, or NSI: organization; its three primary missions (collection and analysis, covert action, and counterintelligence); and accountability. Each is vital to the success of the democracies in their ongoing struggle against global forces that are anathema to the principles of free and open societies.

NSI is by no means the only, or even the most important, ingredient for success in this struggle. That distinction would go to the armed might of the democracies: the possession of weaponry – firepower[1] – capable of repelling the dark forces arrayed against freedom, be they the Barbary pirates in America's early history; autocrats and monarchs from the 1600s to the 1900s; the totalitarian threat posed by Germany, Italy, and Japan during the first half of the twentieth century; the communist challenge of the Cold War; modern-day terrorists; or Russian and Chinese muscle-flexing in current times – most notably, manifested in Moscow's invasion of Ukraine.

Important, as well, in the defense of the democracies is an effective program of public diplomacy. Here is the "soft power" that can exert an attraction on would-be democracies in the world drawn to the idea of a free press, just trials, and competitive elections, as well as fair play in foreign affairs and the practice of empathy toward people everywhere. Accompanying the basic requirement of setting a good example as a world power is the need to help the less well-off nations develop economically, through foreign aid, joint ventures, fair trade agreements, and the sharing of technological know-how. Important, too, is the complete rejection of torture, extraordinary rendition, secret prisons, and illegal or unsavory intelligence operations that erase the distinction between the democracies and their adversaries.[2]

Along with these other attributes of good representative government and global citizenship, NIS also has a significant role to play as both a shield for the democracies and, in their further defense, a hidden sword in the form of covert action and counterespionage. The proper use of NSI can provide information to improve the chances of victory on the battlefield against anti-democratic forces, as at Midway during World War II, in the more recent Persian Gulf wars, or NATO's assistance to Ukraine. It can detect moles burrowing inside the open societies, as with Ames and Hanssen in the United States (though, one can hope, with a more rapid detection of traitors in the future). In time of war, it can also help fool enemies, as with the deception operations that preceded the Allied invasion of Europe at Normandy. It can offer insights that smooth the way to more effective diplomacy and more equitable trade relations. It can discover and prove with clear evidence human rights violations, from the horror of mass graves spotted by satellites during NATO's war in Serbia during the 1990s to the secret reports from assets who have infiltrated human-trafficking organizations, drug cartels, and international crime syndicates. New uses of NSI promise better surveillance of worldwide environmental and pandemic threats as well.

Often referred to as the "first line of defense," NIS is all this and more. Beyond the eyes and ears of the democracies, it is a measure of their hearts, a test of whether open societies can stand up effectively to the enemies of freedom and yet still keep their constitutional principles intact – the accountability side of the NSI equation. This closing chapter offers an overview of these core dimensions. It also highlights the central challenges that lie ahead to ensure the intelligence shield and sword serve as a reliable complement to armed defense, public diplomacy, and economic statecraft in the preservation and advancement of free governments around the world. Lastly, it brings the NSI story up to date by briefly examining recent trials and tribulations – the setbacks and successes – of intelligence in the United States.

National security intelligence as organization

The democracies have no use for an intelligence service that is splintered into separate baronies and fails to provide policymakers with the holistic "all-source fusion" of information so necessary for successful, fact-based, comprehensive decision-making. Nor do they want an all-powerful intelligence czar who stifles competitive intelligence and dissent, or rises above the reach of overseers – as did the FBI's Director J. Edgar Hoover. The organizational goal in the United States and the other democracies is a well-integrated intelligence service with a chief able to hire and fire, and to coordinate community-wide budgets and programs; but, at the same time, a spymaster who is appropriately held in check by the internal guardrails of serious-minded accountability carried out by intelligence overseers. In the United States, this would be the profile of an ideal Director of National Intelligence in the executive branch and a set of dedicated intelligence "guardians" on Capitol Hill.

A cosmetic DNI

The American model falls far short of this ideal. Its DNI is weak, with limited authority over the nation's eighteen secret services – a "leader" in name,

Photo 7.1: DNI Clapper
In the Oval Office for the *President's Daily Brief*, the longest serving DNI Gen. James R. Clapper
meets with President Barack Obama to discuss developments in North Korea, November 23,
2010.
Source: The White House.

but one without sufficient personnel or budget controls to truly integrate
the workings of the wide Intelligence Community. Other than improving
accountability practices by having more guardians in Congress, no reform
measure in the United States is more pressing than the pursuit of more effective cooperation among the nation's spy agencies. This would require the
establishment of a genuine DNI to replace the cardboard cut-out fashioned for
the nation by misguided lawmakers during the halting intelligence reform
movement of 2004.

Only one DNI has been able to compensate for this lack of formal authority:
General James R. Clapper, by virtue of his management skills, his experience
(fifty years of service in the intelligence business), and his wide circle of contacts throughout the IC. The current DNI, Avril D. Haines – the first woman
to hold this position – is new to the office, but displays all the skills necessary
for success. She may be able to pick up where Clapper left off in the pursuit of
a more complete organizational integration of the IC that is so critical to the
steady achievement of all-source intelligence.

Photo 7.2: DNI Haines
Avril D. Haines, the first woman to serve as DNI, speaks at the Office of the Director of National Intelligence in McLean, Virginia, on July 18, 2022.
Source: U.S. Department of State.

Horizontal and vertical integration

An additional organizational challenge in the democracies is to carry forward the integration of their national intelligence agencies not only "horizontally" – that is, melding the training, the computers, and the sharing of findings among the intelligence agencies in the service of the federal government – but "vertically" as well, downward from the federal government to the states and localities. At these lower levels of governance, counterterrorist and law enforcement officers (as well as other public officials) are on the front lines of likely targets for terrorist and violence-prone domestic extremists: the cities and towns, transportation facilities, and local government facilities within the world's democracies. Yet, presently in the United States, these state and city officials are rarely provided with the timely, high-quality intelligence they need, even though tentative steps have been taken toward developing "intelligence fusion centers" in America's major metropolitan areas. These centers are locations where federal and local analysts can gather together to share data and insights on potential threats at the grassroots.[3]

Liaison relationships

Challenging, as well, is the development of better liaison connections of two kinds: the first is internal to each democracy, and the second is among the open societies. One sense of the term "internal liaison" refers to the crafting of improved professional (nonpolitical) ties between decision-makers in the policy departments and the analysts in the intelligence services who provide them with timely and relevant information and insight. Frequently, the left hand (decision-makers) lacks coordination with the right hand (information-providers in the IC) – the consumers and producers of intelligence. An expanded program of placing intelligence liaison officers inside government policy departments and agencies would allow them to provide their IC collectors and analysts each day with an accurate, up-to-date understanding of what information needs are of highest priority among decision-makers. Otherwise, an intelligence officer tethered to his or her desk risks becoming irrelevant, instead of a valuable partner in decision-making who can bring reliable facts and assessments to the table in a policy agency. Recall the earlier example in this book of the CIA's success in initiating a productive liaison relationship with the International Affairs Division of the Environmental Protection Agency (EPA).[4]

A second meaning of internal liaison is the goal of improving the communication between the intelligence agencies themselves, encouraging them to share collection-and-analysis responsibilities – the Holy Grail of IC institutional integration. The failure of the CIA and the FBI to speak regularly and cooperatively with one another over the years – most conspicuously during the months preceding the 9/11 attacks – is a legendary and tragic illustration of the results that poor liaison can yield. The sharing of intelligence across IC institutional boundaries is mandatory for successful NSI outcomes and should always be a major focus of intelligence managers and their overseers.

A third form of liaison – among the intelligence services of the world's democracies – poses an even more difficult challenge, since it must overcome security and cultural barriers inherent in relations between nations. The principle of "foreign liaison" or "burden-sharing" is compelling, though. The world has changed in important ways that can be summed up with the term "globalization" – an unparalleled integration of nations around the globe, brought about by new communications and transportation technologies. Along with this globalization has come the potential rapid spread of threats that can have an effect far beyond their local origins: crime from Nigeria; heroin from Afghanistan, and fentanyl from Mexico and China; weapons proliferation from Iran and North Korea; terrorism from hideouts in the Middle East and Southwest Asia; pathogens of pandemic scale from the wet markets of China and the jungles of Africa; ecological changes caused by fossil-fuel consumption and acid rain in the regions of Europe, Asia, and the United States. What was once someone else's problem is now everybody's problem. No single country has all the answers, all the information, or all the resources to respond to these global challenges to freedom and security. By working together, however, and sharing intelligence as well as participating in the more aggressive intelligence operations – covert action and counterespionage – against the world's dark authoritarian forces, the democracies can improve their chances for a more peaceful planet.

This is the *raison d'être* behind the effective Five Eyes intelligence alignment. Australia, Canada, New Zealand, the United Kingdom, and the United States have demonstrated that intelligence can be shared effectively and securely. So have improved intelligence liaison practices within the framework of the United Nations and NATO.[5] Further, Europe has exhibited some success in its ongoing experiment to develop a Euro intelligence service. These are hopeful signs that the secret services can help unite the democracies through a carefully controlled expansion of intelligence-sharing, in their common quest to subdue the world's violence-oriented and antidemocratic forces – be they war-prone nations like Russia under Vladimir Putin, drug dealers, human traffickers, environmental polluters, or terrorist organizations. A next-step worthy of serious consideration: an expansion of the Five Eyes liaison to include Germany and Japan.

Security intelligence as a set of missions

Planning and direction

As discussed in Chapter 2, intelligence producers are frequently left in the dark about what sort of intelligence those in high office need in order to address more effectively the problems they confront in their in-boxes each day. The organizational remedy of improved internal liaison ties – the building of information bridges between the policy and the spy agencies – is a necessary condition for a better understanding between the two camps, but it is not sufficient. One must also have much better direct dialogue between the consumers and producers of intelligence, with more frequent threat-assessment meetings devoted to the discussion of the nation's intelligence collection-and-analysis priorities. Valuable, as well, would be regular, informal get-togethers to nurture the ties of trust and rapport that are essential for a smooth working relationship between decision-makers and intelligence officers – although (it bears repeating) each side must strictly maintain objectivity in dealing with facts and assessments related to world threats and opportunities, eschewing politics at every turn.

Collection

Too often the techint side of tradecraft, with its dazzling spy satellites and eye-catching photographs (geoint), attracts a preponderance of resources from budget planners – prodded by the lobbying efforts of satellite and drone manufacturers (now part of the military-industrial complex that President Eisenhower warned of in his celebrated "Farewell Address" of 1959). This focus on technical intelligence often comes at the expensive of humint and osint. Yet the array of world targets demands adequate funding for every one of the "ints." The idea is to have synergistic, all-source fusion, to meet the goal of acquiring as complete a portrait of world events as possible each day, derived from all the secret agencies employing their specialized disciplines in close coordination with one another and with the important contribution of osint always in mind. Each of the ints and each of the IC agencies can bring to the table important pieces of the global jigsaw puzzle. Within humint, more resources are clearly needed for nonofficial cover (NOC) positions overseas, which provide a better opportunity for meeting and recruiting the nontraditional enemies of the democracies – terrorists in particular – than do government-hosted cocktail parties in foreign capitals.

Processing

Perhaps no feature of intelligence in the democracies is more conspicuous than the outpacing of data collection over what the secret agencies are able to absorb, translate, and understand. One expert estimated in 2009 that, every four to six hours, the NSA was collecting a volume of material equivalent to the entire holdings of the Library of Congress.[6] That deluge has increased significantly since then. The democracies face the proverbial search for the needle in the haystack, with the needles and the haystacks growing exponentially in number. The solution will come only with breakthroughs in information sifting, as the democracies become smarter about what to collect and faster at finding the needles (the "signals" rather than the "noise"). These advances depend on improvements in information technology, abetted by new breakthroughs in AI, as well as better methods for faster and more accurate foreign-language translations of sigint interceptions and messages embedded in social media.

Analysis

As examined in Chapter 3, vital to better performance in the cerebral domain of analysis is the recruitment to the intelligence services of the best brain-power the democracies can muster. What is needed are men and women well trained in the array of university curricula relevant to understanding world affairs, which today includes courses in just about every academic discipline. As with CIA case officers responsible for asset recruitment and handling, especially valuable will be individuals proficient in the world's so-called "strategic languages" spoken in hot spots around the world – such as Arabic, Farsi, Urdu, and Pashtun. And, of course, Russian and Chinese language abilities will always be much valued as the intelligence agencies enlist new officers to their ranks.

As a way of encouraging all-source fusion, a greater commitment to the joint training of analysts from different agencies will help to engender the kinds of lasting collegial bonds that result in better interagency communications and data-sharing throughout the entire IC. So will more regular transfers of personnel between agencies – circulating the intelligence workforce around the IC – as a part of any successful officer's career advancement. While these steps have already been initiated, they remain too limited in their outreach. Further, within agencies, "co-location" deserves more support (as the CIA has understood and moved to adopt): knocking down the barriers between operatives and analysts so they can work more closely together as they prepare accurate assessments of foreign events and conditions that draw upon both the "ground truth" of case officers and the "library" knowledge of analysts.

Also of high priority must be the encouragement of critical reviews of intelligence draft reports, through the use of "Team A–Team B" exercises. This approach to "competitive analysis" can provide an acid bath for data interpretations by encouraging dialogue between CIA analysts (Team A) and outside experts on the nation's academic campuses and think-tanks (Team B). Moreover, when it does arise, analytic dissent needs to be clearly flagged for the attention of decision-makers. As the "slam dunk" experience with George Tenet and George W. Bush illustrates during the rush to war against Iraq in 2003 (when the DCI assured the President that the existence of WMDs in Iraq was as guaranteed as this sure-shot in basketball), the virtues of dissent are sometimes displaced in Washington in deference to good news and group consensus – however delusional.

Dissemination

Then comes one of the toughest assignments of all for the intelligence officer: in the midst of building the rapport so necessary for gaining access to policy-makers and enhancing the flow of information from the field into the mind of the decision-maker, the analyst, the liaison officer, the *PDB* and NIE briefer, the D/CIA, the DNI – whatever the form of intelligence – must remain absolutely neutral in providing data and insights. Rapport and trust, yes, even a degree of friendship, but the intelligence officer must maintain a professional ability to step back from Washington politics, to understand the importance of the bright line of honesty and neutrality that should exist between the producer and the consumer of intelligence. Crossing that line can transport the intelligence officer into the domain of politicization – the "cooking" of intelligence to please the political objectives of an administration. Staying on the proper (nonpolicy) side of this demilitarized zone is the cardinal rule of intelligence. When that line is crossed, the guilty intelligence officer becomes simply another policy advocate – of which there is already an abundance (and properly so) in the democratic capitals of the world.

Covert action

As American decision-makers ponder the possible adoption of a CA, they should keep former DCI William H. Webster's set of guidelines close at hand. In Judge Webster's prescriptions (see Chapter 4), these controversial secret operations should adhere to U.S. law; remain consistent with ongoing foreign policy objectives and traditional values; and – should they become public – the operation should strike the American public as sensible and supportable. Covert actions pursued by the United States should also honor the procedures that require explicit and written presidential approval, followed by reporting to Congress prior to the implementation of a proposed operation (under the provisions of the Hughes–Ryan Act of 1974 and the Intelligence Oversight Acts of 1980 and 1991). Relevant, too, are the anticipated odds of success. If a CA is too much of a long shot, as calculated by leading policymakers and analysts, it should be abandoned; sending intelligence personnel, whether CIA officers or their assets, into a likely losing situation (particularly in especially dangerous circumstances) is patently improper.

Further, in congruence with the spirit of a democratic alliance against the enemies of open societies, covert actions should not be directed against fellow democratic regimes. In the same spirit, the democracies should join together whenever possible in conducting CAs directed against common threats. Above all, the democracies should move up the ladder of CA escalation – whether separately or together – toward highly intrusive operations only with the greatest circumspection, mindful that wise observers over the years have counseled that the "third option" should be adopted only when absolutely essential – as a last measure when all other overt policy options have been found lacking.

Leaders in the democracies should be sensitive to the fact, too, that the highest rungs on the ladder are anathema to the values extolled by the open societies. They run contrary to the great moral advantage enjoyed by the democracies over the "anything goes" attitude of terrorists and dictators who fear the ethical standards raised high by the free nations. Only terrorist organizations, international crime syndicates, and foreign armies that violate established international boundaries should be targets of high-rung CAs. Even then, the democracies should reject operations that risk the death of innocent civilians; destroy animal and plant life; alter the environment;

cause Western intelligence officers – whether interrogators or paramilitary soldiers – to descend into the kind of barbaric behavior displayed by the 9/11 terrorists, or the Russian Army in Ukraine. Vital, too, is the honoring of a nation's constitutional boundaries and the rule of law.[7]

Counterintelligence

Success in the world of counterintelligence depends on the vigilance of co-workers inside democracy's secret agencies. Intelligence officers and their managers can best spot furtive activities, excessive drinking, or lavish life-styles among their colleagues that might be a tip-off to outside funding by a foreign intelligence or terrorist organization. Americans and Europeans have learned a great deal from CI failures over the past several decades and have taken steps to tighten their defenses, such as a more careful monitoring of employee bank accounts in the aftermath of the Ames treachery at the CIA. Moreover, a closer watch is necessary over outside contract officers (like Edward Snowden) who are employed only temporarily by the U.S. intelligence agencies and may not have the proper training for, and appreciation of, intelligence accountability and whistleblower procedures, as well as legal and moral boundaries that have been set in place in recent decades. Although no doubt there will be future Hanssens and Philbys, what one hopes for – as a result of greater attention to security concerns and counterespionage practices – is their more rapid detection and arrest.

National security intelligence and the importance of accountability

The experiment in intelligence accountability is here to stay in most, if not all, democracies; but it has periodically displayed unsettling signs of backsliding. In the United States, one could see this most obviously in the Iran–*contra* affair of the mid-1980s; in the failure of Congress to examine the preparedness of the IC to discover and thwart a terrorist attack against the homeland in the years leading up to 9/11 (2001); in the warrantless wiretapping, metadata collection, and torture techniques adopted by the second Bush Administration and the CIA after those terrorist attacks; and in the lethargy that settled for a time over the SSCI and HPSCI oversight panels during the opening decades of the twenty-first century. The cycle of intelligence "shock" (scandals and failures) and congressional reaction has repeated itself time and again, without sufficient attention being paid by members of Congress to the value of dedicated, high-intensity police patrolling on Capitol Hill as a means of preventing an intelligence shock in the first place. Nevertheless, even though the New Intelligence Oversight that began in 1975 in the United States has sometimes proved disappointing in practice, the level of congressional (as well as executive and judicial) accountability over America's secret operations still remains vastly superior to what existed prior to the Year of Intelligence.

In the United States, a starting place to correct a drift backwards toward weak intelligence accountability is to straighten out the tangled lines of jurisdictional responsibility among the oversight panels on Capitol Hill. The Judiciary, Foreign Relations, Armed Services, and Appropriations Committees already have full plates; SSCI and HPSCI should be given sole jurisdiction for almost all intelligence activities, with the Judiciary Committees assisting with the FBI and the FIS Court. The outcome would be clearer lines of responsibility and improved accountability.

The greatest challenge, though, as discussed in Chapter 6, is to bring out the guardian instincts of lawmakers serving on SSCI and HPSCI – indeed, throughout the chambers of Congress and in the parliaments of democracies around the globe. This feat will require a fresh set of incentives in the democracies that reward the serious practice of guardianship with the perks of office (improved parking and office space for star award-winning overseers, for example). The public, however, will be the ultimate arbiter of whether lawmakers pay attention to intelligence oversight duties. If citizens direct their votes toward candidates who are dedicated to the guardian role and take accountability seriously, for intelligence and all their other substantive responsibilities; if journalists cover and report on sterling acts of oversight by lawmakers; if academicians teach about the central place of government accountability in America's form of government, as spelled out in the Constitution and the *Federalist Papers*; if presidents, IC agency chiefs, and DNIs explain how accountability actually strengthens NSI by encouraging debate about intelligence options within the hidden councils of government; and if those with executive authority share the burdens of intelligence accountability with lawmakers (as former DCIs Colby and Gates often encouraged) – only then will members of Congress be more likely to gravitate toward the guardian role.

Several accountability and reform proposals that continue to warrant closer attention in the United States are presented in Table 7.1. These steps toward a more effective IC management and genuine intelligence oversight may prove quixotic. Perhaps there is just not enough gumption on Capitol Hill to make the necessary changes. Perhaps money has such a grip on the American system of government that fundraising for re-election, along with lobbying by the military-industrial-intelligence complex, will keep lawmakers frozen in the posture of uncaring "ostriches" or uncritical "cheerleaders." Perhaps a cycle of feckless police patrolling, followed by vigorous firefighting, is the fate of the United States and the other democracies. Ultimately, as Chapter 6 emphasized, it is up to citizens in the open societies to demand a more serious exercise of accountability by their elected representatives.

Table 7.1: National security intelligence: A reform agenda for the United States

Focus	*Primary proposals*
Organization	• Provide the DNI with full budget and appointment powers • Expand internal intelligence liaison services • Expand bilateral and multilateral liaison among the democracies • Expand "co-location" practices inside IC agencies
Mission: Collection and analysis	
Planning	• Improve formal and informal dialogue (liaison) between the producers and consumers of intelligence
Collection	• Expand humint, especially NOCs
Processing	• Improve "horizontal" interagency computer compatibility in the IC, as well as "vertical" connections to state and local law enforcement and intelligence officials – although with reliable firewalls against hostile entry • Improve data sifting, and increase the speed of foreign language translations of intercepted data
Analysis	• Establish more competitive analysis • Highlight dissent (including within the executive summaries or Key Judgments) • Increase production of research intelligence
Dissemination	• Market intelligence more effectively • Focus on "niche intelligence," that is, responding to the specific informational in-box needs of policymakers • Educate analysts and managers about the dangers of politicization and call attention to its practice wherever spotted
Mission: Covert action	• Practice greater discrimination, adopting this approach only when absolutely essential • Avoid operations against fellow democracies • Reject extreme options • Honor constitution procedures, plus all U.S. laws regarding written presidential authority for a CA and substantive prior briefings to SSCI and HPSCI's full membership
Mission: Counterintelligence	• Pay more attention to this neglected mission • Redouble emphasis on training, at the time of recruitment and steadily thereafter • Constantly upgrade computer firewalls against cyberattacks

Table 7.1: (*continued*)

Focus	Primary proposals
	• Tighten security checks for all personnel • Monitor the access of contract workers to classified intelligence, as thoroughly as if they were full-time IC employees
Accountability	• Improve incentives for "guardians" engaged in intensive "patrolling" • Insist on a full and timely (except in extreme emergencies) *ante factum* report to SSCI and HPSCI on *all* important intelligence activities (as stipulated in the 1980 and 1991 Intelligence Oversight Acts)

The future of national security intelligence

What major challenges have arisen for the practice of NSI in the democracies since the second edition of this book appeared in 2017? In the United States, the most conspicuous event related to NSI proved to be the election of President Donald J. Trump in 2016. He had never served as a state governor or lawmaker, as a member of the U.S. House of Representatives or Senate, as Vice President, or as a decorated military leader – the training grounds for previous incumbents holding the nation's highest political office. The outcome of their selection of a neophyte politician to the presidency had a profound effect on the IC for two main reasons.

First, during the Trump Administration, the IC experienced its worst relationship with the White House in modern U.S. history. President John F. Kennedy had his private moment of anger toward the CIA in the wake of the Bay of Pigs disaster; Lyndon B. Johnson was periodically miffed by the Agency's negative assessments of U.S. progress during the Vietnam war; Richard M. Nixon frequently expressed to his top aides a distrust of Langley as an enclave of Ivy League liberals; and Bill Clinton had little interest in NSI. (Illustrations: he skipped the memorial service honoring the victims of the Mir Kansi attack against the CIA – a perceived slight that harmed his relationship with the Agency; and he largely ignored the final report of his own presidential inquiry into the state of post-Cold War intelligence, the Aspin–Brown Commission.) With Trump, though, attacks against the IC took the form of frequent, personal, and open verbal warfare throughout the four years of his tenure. The IC agencies – and the CIA and FBI in particular – became the vortex of quarrels and endless recriminations directed their way from the White House and (increasingly) the ODNI. Intelligence officials worried on a daily basis about the future of their ties with their most important consumer, the White House.

A second effect was the rise of rightwing extremist in support of Trump's challenge to the 2020 presidential election results that had placed Democrat Joe Biden ahead of him in the victory column. This domestic extremism manifested itself most visibly in the insurrection against Capitol Hill that took place on January 6, 2021. On that day, violence-prone "election deniers," as those who believed the 2020 election results were rigged are known, stormed the Congress as lawmakers carried out their constitutional duty to officially count the Electoral College votes (which had gone against Trump). The actions of the pro-Trump rioters had been encouraged and inflamed by public statements made by President Trump in preceding days and that morning. Capitol Hill police managed to subdue the insurrectionists – with significant injuries to the police force, including three deaths – but the danger of extremist behavior in support of Trump was now self-evident and feared by counterintelligence officers throughout the IC and by law enforcement officers across the country.

Would the pro-Trump MAGA movement spawn further violence by the right against a broad range of their perceived enemies, not only in Washington but in the fifty state capitals? Potential targets could include U.S. government buildings from Maine to Hawaii, along with elected officials affiliated with the Democratic Party from Biden to local public figures in every council in cities, towns, and villages throughout the nation. As discussed in Chapter 5, most CI experts believed this anticipated domestic violence was more likely to take the form of a lone-wolf attack against a government building, in the style of Timothy McVeigh against the Murray Federal Building in Oklahoma City in 1995. Yet social media chatrooms frequented by extremists boiled, too, with talk of a nationwide revolution against "the Establishment" (the Democratic "elites") and what President Trump had routinely referred to as the "Deep State" – supposedly the CIA, FBI, NSA, and other members of the secret bureaucracy in Washington, which (in an act of vaporous ideology) the hard right decided had been "weaponized" by President Biden to destroy MAGA populists and white America. As Pushkin understood in the poem "The Hero" (1830): "Uplifting illusion is dearer to us than a host of truths." Or at least it can be for some arrant extremists.

Donald J. Trump and the Intelligence Community

The relationship between President Trump and America's spy agencies – a four-year-long battle – grew so bizarre that it warrants examination here. Throughout Trump's presidency, the IC was tossed and turned as if its agencies were so many rafts on a tempestuous sea. Trump, whose views on presidential power leaned strongly toward the extravagant, accused the IC – and especially the CIA and FBI – of a wide assortment of transgressions, from too much independence and allegedly spying against him to a steady barrage of criticism aimed at its analytic reporting.

In December 2016, a CIA Acting Director Michael Morell told *Politico* that Russian meddling in the recent presidential election was "the political equivalent of 9/11." Trump dismissed similar findings of Russian manipulation reported by a special prosecutor, Robert S. Mueller III, as well as by a special SSCI investigation. The President was particularly infuriated by these charges because he believed the intelligence agencies were leaking rumors to the American media, based on IC humint and techint sources, that indicated Moscow's operations to manipulate the 2016 election were the reason why Trump had narrowly defeated his Democratic opponent, Hillary Clinton. Neither Mueller nor SSCI accused the Trump team of collusion with the Russian government, but both inquiries discovered an unusual set of interactions between Trump campaign aides and Moscow officials, including Russian intelligence officers. Former DIA chief General Michael Flynn, for example, was even seated at a table with Russian President Putin and top SVR officers in Moscow – not the usual dining partners of a former U.S. intelligence agency director. As criticism of these relationships mounted and became a subject of FBI counterintelligence concern, President Trump steadily berated FBI Director John B. Comey as disloyal, and often expressed cutting remarks about other intelligence agency directors, too. In response, Comey, John Brennan at the CIA, and DNI James R. Clapper complained aloud when queried by the media that the President was trying to "delegitimize" the nation's intelligence agencies.[8] President Trump also attempted to place barriers between the Special Forces branch of the Defense Department and its important relationship with the CIA's paramilitary operatives.

To help solidify his control over the IC, President Trump successfully nominated John Ratcliffe for the DNI position. Ratcliffe was a former Republican member of Congress from Texas who had remained loyal to the President during his two impeachment proceedings in the House. His qualifications for office were close to zero. While a HPSCI member, he had one of the worst records for attendance in that panel's history. Even when present, he stayed only a short time at committee hearings and rarely posed any questions. At the time of his nomination, a former high-ranking intelligence official in Washington said privately to the author that the former House member "didn't have a clue about what ODNI does or why . . . this will be like a pig looking at a wrist watch." As with Trump's earlier nomination for D/CIA, Mike Pompeo, political loyalty once again overrode professional preparation for a high-level intelligence job. The important consideration for the White House was to ensure that no DNI – or D/CIA – would upset the President. Further, with respect to intelligence accountability, the Trump Administration often refused to comply with SSCI and HPSCI document requests and regularly blocked witnesses from testifying on the Hill.

As this unfortunate situation continued to unfold, Trump threatened to strip away the security clearances of those intelligence directors who had publicly commented on the importance of Russian "active measures" against Hillary Clinton as a key reason for Trump's presidential victory. He eventually did take away Brennan's clearances after the D/CIA retired, preventing him from serving as a government consultant. The reason: Brennan had said on air, as a CNN consultant, that Trump's face-value acceptance of Russian President Putin's denial of 2016 Russian election manipulation against the United States was nothing less than "traitorous." Most outside observers viewed the presidential retaliation against Brennan and other intelligence officers as an excessive measure taken to silence critics.

An always hoped-for harmonious (though never political) relationship between the producers of intelligence (the IC) and their No. 1 consumer (the President) had clearly ruptured. While this unprecedented public wrangling went on, the spy agencies pursued their duties to provide government officials with accurate, timely, and objective intelligence – although several media reports surfaced that charged intelligence personnel with avoiding the delivery of possibly contentious reports to the White House, for fear of further agitating the mercurial President and his aides. The order of the day from the Oval Office seemed to be only for airbrushed intelligence; so, unless one wanted a public squabble with the President of the United States, it was better to avoid carrying bad news to the White House. Here was a form of politicization: never tell the President and his aides something that might make them unhappy. Even this unprofessional selective reporting by some intelligence officials failed, however, to mollify Trump. His disdain for the IC had manifested itself early on. During the 2016 election campaign, he had rejected the normal briefings on international affairs that have traditionally been provided by the CIA to presidential candidates since 1960 based on the idea that the winner of a presidential campaign ought to arrive at 1600 Pennsylvania Avenue (the White House) with reliable current knowledge about world affairs. Once elected, Trump continued to find these briefings a waste of his time.

Intelligence briefings do sometimes repeat things that one can learn from the newspapers or CNN, but they usually include helpful additional information as well, derived from clandestine sources. For a while, the new President even banned the DNI, the D/CIA, and other leading intelligence officials from attending meetings of the National Security Council. Trump failed to understand the wise recommendation offered by Richard Helms (see Chapter 3) that the President needs someone present in the high councils of government who will focus strictly on the facts, without any policy axes to grind.

Once in the White House, Trump also took the surprising step of choosing as D/CIA an individual with minimal intelligence experience: Mike Pompeo, a GOP member of the House from Kansas and the fiercest Capitol Hill critic of Hillary Clinton when she had served as Secretary of State. Traditionally, the Agency has usually been known for its objectivity, standing above the political fray, providing facts and unbiased analysis to presidents; yet now it was going to be led by an avowed far-right politician. The President even sent D/CIA Pompeo, who had become his Polonius, to North Korea in 2018 to prepare for a U.S. summit meeting with that country – clearly a task alien to the Agency's long-standing tradition of policy neutrality and better left to the Department of State. Before long, Trump placed Pompeo in a more suitable position for this kind of policymaking; he became the Administration's Secretary of State.

Meanwhile, Trump's diatribe against the IC rolled on. He claimed that his predecessor, President Barack Obama, had ordered the FBI to conduct illegal surveillance against him during the 2016 campaign; and he maintained, further, that the IC was involved in behind-the-scenes plotting against him that was reminiscent (he averred while visiting the CIA one day for a media "happening") of Adolf Hitler's methods of defaming adversaries during the Third Reich. This comparison did not play well at Langley or the rest of the IC, leaving intelligence officers astonished and dismayed by the President's disrespect for their public service. President Trump began to reject out of hand several of the Agency's core reports to the White House, including the IC's widely supported conclusion that the Crown Prince of Saudi Arabia had arranged the barbaric murder (the dismemberment) of *Washington Post* journalist Jamal Khashoggi.

As well, Trump initially stiff-armed the scheduling each morning in the Oval Office of the usual presentation to the nation's chief executive on the *President's Daily Brief*. He later relented, but insisted on just an oral briefing, rather than his personal reading of the latest intelligence findings in the *PDB* from around the world. As a result, he missed important details that presidents and other national security officials benefit from knowing about evolving global events and conditions. Now and again, he skipped the *PDB* sessions altogether in favor of consulting with his top aides, none of whom had any intelligence experience (other than Ratcliffe and Pompeo, with their limited exposures to the IC).

President Trump had set a record in his dealings with the IC: no other U.S. chief executive had consistently behaved in such a publicly anti-intelligence manner. Nor was he friendly toward leading military figures. He often complained about the Chair of the Joint Chiefs of Staff, General Mark Milley (whom he had personally selected for that job). In retirement, the former President publicly said in September 2023 – in a jaw-dropping suggestion – that Milley ought to be executed. His crime? Milley had telephoned his Chinese counterparts during the January 6, 2021, insurrection to assure Beijing that the Pentagon would not act irrationally during the Trump-inspired uprising – even if friends of the White House marauding on Capitol Hill were doing so. This was a standard operating procedure, an act of responsibility taken by military officials to make sure that aberrant domestic events were not misconstrued abroad as an indication that the United States was unraveling. When General Milley retired a few days after the former President's staggering remark – as had long been scheduled after an illustrious four-year term as JCS Chief – his response was to say in a farewell speech that American soldiers take an oath to the Constitution, not to a "wannabe dictator" – a biting reference to the former President.

Ironically, though, while President Trump constantly berated the CIA and the Pentagon, he did find beguiling their instruments of secret power. Adopting a John Wayne tough guy demeanor, he advocated the further use of waterboarding by the CIA, for instance, just as Congress and the public were turning against the use of torture methods. In fact, the President said he would "bring back a hell of a lot worse than waterboarding."[9] Further, Trump sent increasing numbers of suspected terrorists to prison cells in Guantánamo without due process; and he also loosened President Obama's accountability restrictions on the use of drone killings abroad – in Somalia, northeastern Niger, southern Libya, Yemen, and elsewhere. White House permission had been required during the Obama years as President; now the DoD and the CIA could decide themselves who should be taken out by Hellfire missiles fired by MQ-9 Reaper drones.

Trump also accelerated the use of drone attacks and, during his waning days in the White House, ordered the drone killing of the Iranian official Qasem Soleimani, despite a long-time (since 1976) U.S. executive order prohibiting such actions. The argument for the hit was that "targeting killings" of military personnel are allowed under the law. Yet, at the time of his assassination, Soleimani was a high-ranking member of the Iranian government's inner circle of policymakers (though he had once been a military figure). One of the most vocal critics of the Soleimani targeting was former D/CIA John Brennan. He recalled that, in his experience during the Bush II and Obama Administrations, there was no "consideration given to targeting for assassination an official of a sovereign state."[10] Under Trump, democratic institutions and principles in the United States began to look increasingly fragile.

The misuse of democratic procedures by the White House spilled over from the Trump Administration into the Congress. During the Trump presidency, the GOP chair of HPSCI – Devin Nunes (California) – became a lacky for the Administration, a fifth column acting more as a senior aide to the President than a constitutionally envisioned legislative check against the misuse of power at the highest levels of the executive branch. According to media reports, Nunes met regularly with White House staff to plan how he might best divert the attention of HPSCI Chairman Adam Schiff (D, California) and his Democratic colleagues away from a thorough investigation into possible collusion by Trump with the Russians in derailing Hillary Clinton's presidential campaign in 2016.

When the GOP took over the House in 2020, Republican members removed guardian overseers Schiff and the equally indefatigable Eric Swalwell (D, California) from HPSCI membership – both being punished for their criticism of President Trump's run-ins with the IC. Subsequently, in 2023, the House GOP voted to censure Schiff for his leadership role in the impeachment proceedings against Trump during his presidency. According to the lead sponsor of the resolution, Representative Anna Paulina Luna (R, Florida), "Mr. Schiff exploited his position as chair of Intel Committee and every opportunity possible threatening national security, undermining our duly elect president [Trump] and bringing dishonor upon the institution" [*sic*]. In the rowdy session in which the voting split along party lines, House Speaker Kevin McCarthy (R, California) read the rare censure resolution out loud to shame Schiff, as, in return, Democrats in the chamber booed the Speaker. It was the lowest point in the post-1975 history of the New Intelligence Oversight, with HPSCI (like the House itself) now torn apart at the chamber's party seams. Fortunately for the concept of intelligence accountability, SSCI continued to carry out its oversight duties under the level-headed and largely bipartisan leadership of Chairman John Warner (D, Virginia). In October 2023, McCarthy would become the first Speaker of the House ousted by his own party. In the perception of a small number of GOP diehard rightwingers, their Speaker had become too moderate for their tastes.

It is too early to provide a balanced appraisal of national security intelligence during the Biden years, but – with the exception of an ongoing discussion between SSCI and the White House over full committee access to evidence regarding the classified documents discovered at the homes of Biden, Pence, and Trump – the relationship between the Oval Office, the Congress, and the IC seemed to have returned almost to a normal, civil level of discourse. This rebalancing was a function in part, no doubt, because of Biden's experience in dealing with intelligence as Vice President in the Obama Administration and as a long-serving member of the Senate. Moreover, he benefited from two first-rate leaders in the IC: Avril Haines as DNI and William J. Burns (a career State Department diplomat and former U.S. ambassador to Russia) as D/CIA. Early in his term at Langley, Burns pursued greater diversity in the Agency's workforce and, overseas, he guided the dissemination of U.S. intelligence to Ukraine on such topics as the locations of the invading Russian Army and its generals, as well as the nature of Moscow's widespread disinformation activities related to the war. The Administration was fortunate, too, in having one of the best SSCI chairmen ever in Senator Warner.

Despite some signs of normalcy in intelligence relationships between the executive and legislative branches of government, there was one deeply unsettling development. As discussed in Chapter 5, in the aftermath of

President Trump's defeat in his 2020 bid for re-election, hard-right members of Congress and MAGA adherents across the country began to accuse the Biden Administration of "weaponizing" the DoJ and the FBI (among other components of their "Deep State" bogeyman) against the Trump camp. Those endorsing this view pointed to the Bureau's "raid" – which was actually a respectful search based on a warrant – of the former President's home at Mar-a-Lago. During this search, FBI agents discovered a sizable cache of highly classified intelligence documents from the Trump years, including nuclear-weapons data, classified maps, and DoD war plans to invade Iran if necessary (among other highly sensitive papers). That these documents contained intelligence sources and methods (details on U.S. spying abroad via techint and humint) was enormously troubling to the Intelligence Community, not to mention America's allies and assets overseas. When the Bureau uncovered the documents (based on an inside tip), recall that Trump refused to return them to the government. This led to his indictment by the DoJ both for their illegal possession and for the obstruction of justice inherent in the former President's refusal to return the papers to their proper location in secure government vaults in Washington, DC.

GOP election deniers and Deep-Staters in Congress called for a Church Committee-like investigation into the DoJ and the FBI as possible secret political arms of the Biden presidency. Once the Trump wing of the Republican Party had gained a sufficient number of new seats during the 2020 elections to take control of the House of Representatives, several such inquiries were launched. Critics of this spate of inquiries into the Biden Administration and the IC maintained that, whereas the Church Committee was known for its fact-based investigation, bipartisanship, and insistence on following the rule of law, the House GOP approach was quite the opposite. The House in 2023 seemed to be engaged in a pro-MAGA political exercise, fueled by partisan attacks from Republican leaders against Democrats and anything to do with the Biden Administration, with a disregard for the legal violations displayed by Trump's possession and ongoing retention of sensitive, highly classified intelligence documents at Mar-a-Lago.[11]

In the middle of these inquiries and accompanying hearings on Capitol Hill, the Republicans went further into the domain of performance art. The Chair of the House Judiciary Committee, Jim Jordan (Ohio) and his conservative allies in the "Freedom Caucus" launched impeachment proceedings against Biden, on alleged grounds that he may have improperly assisted his son, Hunter Biden, to secure business deals at home and abroad. The circus that the House of Representatives had become continued, as the GOP majority failed to enact a budgetary resolution that, left unresolved, would have led to a government shutdown and the cancellation of pay checks for the military and many other citizens; promulgated a shrill rebellion against their own Speaker with no clear successor; pursued with high vitriol a war against the

FBI and America's other intelligence agencies; and remained unbending in their allegiance to Donald Trump, despite four indictments and ninety-one criminal counts levied against him in various judicial circuits. As the end of 2023 grew near, the GOP finally selected a new Speaker and, with the help of Democrats, at last passed a budget resolution. Whether or not Speaker Mike Johnson of Louisiana could manage to tame the House into becoming a reliably functioning part of America's federal government in 2024 remained a troubling question.

The threats on the horizon

Beyond America's shores, the IC faces – along with allied services in the world's fellow democracies – a series of additionally daunting developments. These include a growing superpower belligerence on the world stage, most notably displayed by Russia's invasion of Ukraine, but also China's more aggressive foreign policy stances. In particular, the Intelligence Community will be called upon for continued support to Ukraine forces in their resistance to a takeover by the Russian Army. On the new threat agenda, too, is an increase in the danger of WMDs, with Russia developing supersonic ICBMs and cruise missiles, China rapidly expanding its nuclear-weapons arsenal and its navy, and North Korea testing long-range nuclear missiles capable of striking the homeland of the United States and all the other democracies. In addition, advances in surveillance technologies continue to race forward, including the ability of antidemocracy regimes around the world to manipulate with new methodologies the media and social communications of citizens in the open societies – hostile tradecraft that includes ever more sophisticated means. Among these new approaches is the use of AI, with its unnerving possibilities for ever more sophisticated cyberespionage and cyberattacks aimed at a multitude of targets inside the democracies. A challenge, too, has become how to improve the capabilities of the open societies to anticipate developments related to "softer" global intelligence priorities, such as tracking deadly weather and other environmental conditions. On this environmental front, with the use of satellites and other intelligence sensors, spy agencies in the democracies are in a position to help scientific communities around the world monitor such concerns as vanishing rainforests and coral reefs, melting ice floes, diminishing rivers, and rising temperatures. The intelligence agencies can also assist the early detection of pandemics that threaten all of humanity.

America's intelligence services, like those of its allies, have found themselves facing a storm of expanding intelligence requirements ("tasking") by their governments. In 1995, as director of DIA, the future DNI James Clapper commented on the seemingly endless list of targeting requirements that had been placed upon the IC by policymakers since the end of the Cold War. "I'd welcome the day when someone tells us what we can quit doing but it doesn't happen," he lamented. "Tasking is addictive."[12] By 2023, the list of intelligence collection objectives had grown like Topsy – with no end in sight. President Trump may not have appreciated the IC, but most U.S. presidents – as well as foreign presidents and prime ministers in other democracies – have turned with increasing frequency to their intelligence agencies for information that might aid them in coping with a world whose complications seem only to multiply.

Citizen responsibilities

Some citizens in the democracies say, "I don't care if the government spies on me; I have nothing to hide." They – and everyone lucky enough to live in an open society – need to re-evaluate that philosophy of governance, so anathema to the antipower founding principles of the U.S Constitution and the guiding documents of other democratic societies. All of us need to remain mindful of the American experiences with Operations CHAOS, COINTELPRO, SHAMROCK, and MINARET, along with the more recent examples of intelligence overreach displayed in post-9/11 warrantless wiretapping and metadata operations of the NSA, as well as the CIA's embrace of harsh interrogation methods. These overzealous intelligence initiatives should impress upon every American, and citizens of democracies throughout the world, that even freely elected governments have in the past, and could in the future, use their spy agencies to counter law-abiding protests. Spy agencies have the capacity to ruin the lives of citizens because some bureaucrat (in the case of COINTELPRO, Director Hoover) doesn't like the color of their skin, what they may have said or written, or their political beliefs, moving – as Tom Charles Huston of the Nixon Administration put it – "from the kid with the bomb to the kid with a picket sign, and from the kid with the picket sign to the kid with the bumper sticker of the opposing candidate."

Part of the responsibility of living in a democracy is to take an active role in demanding the protection of fundamental constitutional freedoms, electing only those presidents and prime ministers, senators and representatives, governors, parliamentarians, state legislators, and mayors who vow to take seriously the principles of liberty and privacy. As the founders of the United States well understood, those blessed with living in open societies would have either to fight for their liberty or see it vanish. This fact of life applies to every democracy across the meridians. It is incumbent upon the leaders of the free nations to embrace the concept of intelligence accountability, even in – *particularly in* – the darkest corridors of secret power. For this to happen, it is equally incumbent on citizens in the democracies to insist on this unyielding vigilance of their government's secret agencies.

Notes

PREFACE TO THE THIRD EDITION: ROADMAP TO A HIDDEN WORLD

1 See Richard W. Aldrich, *The Hidden Hand: Britain, America and Cold War Secret Intelligence* (London: John Murray, 2001), p. 5.

2 For the 2009 survey, see Peter Monaghan, "Intelligence Studies," *Chronicle of Higher Education* (March 20, 2009), pp. B4–B5. For the more recent appraisal that found a dramatic growth in the discipline since the survey, see Loch K. Johnson, "The Development of Intelligence Studies," in Robert Dover, Michael S. Goodman, and Claudia Hillebrand, eds., *Routledge Companion to Intelligence Studies* (New York: Routledge, 2014), pp. 3–22.

3 See Peter Gill, Stephen Marrin, and Mark Phythian, eds., *Intelligence Theory: Key Questions and Debates* (New York: Routledge, 2009). See also Peter Gill and Mark Phythian, "What Is Intelligence Studies?" *International Journal of Intelligence, Security and Public Affairs* 18/1 (2016), pp. 5–19; Loch K. Johnson and Allison M. Shelton, "Thoughts on the State of Intelligence Studies: A Survey Report," *Intelligence and National Security* 28 (February 2013), pp. 109–20; Stephen Marrin, "Improving Intelligence Studies as an Academic Discipline," *Intelligence and National Security* 31/2 (March 2016), pp. 266–79; and Damien Van Puyvelde and Sean Curtis, "'Standing on the Shoulders of Giants': Diversity and Scholarship in Intelligence Studies," *Intelligence and National Security* 32/1 (February 2017).

4 See R. Gerald Hughes, Peter Jackson, and Len Scott, eds., *Exploring Intelligence Archives: Enquiries into the Secret State* (New York: Routledge, 2008).

5 Frank Church, "Meet the Press," NBC Television (August 17, 1975).

CHAPTER 1: NATIONAL SECURITY INTELLIGENCE: THE FIRST LINE OF DEFENSE

1 This reconstruction by the author is based on the evidence presented in *The 9/11 Commission Report: Final Report of the National Commission on Terrorist Attacks Upon the United States* (New York: Norton, 2004) – the Kean Commission, led by Thomas H. Kean, Chair, and Lee H. Hamilton, Vice Chair.

2 Carl von Clausewitz, *On War*, trans. Michael Howard and Peter Paret (Princeton, NJ: Princeton University Press, 1989), p. 117.

3 Letter from John Emerich Edward Dalberg-Acton (Lord Acton) to Bishop Mandell Creigton, dated April 5, 1887; quoted in John Bartlett, *Familiar Quotations*, 14th edn. (Boston: Little, Brown, 1968), p. 750a.

4 In a speech given on July 8, 1975, Senator Frank Church (D, Idaho; for whom the author served as a senior aide and speechwriter when he headed a major Senate investigation into the Intelligence Community that year) suggested that Lord Acton's famous admonition should be rephrased: "All secrecy corrupts. Absolute secrecy corrupts absolutely."

5 Merle Miller, *Plain Speaking: An Oral Biography of Harry S. Truman* (New York: Berkley Publishing, 1973), p. 420.

6 See Loch K. Johnson, ed., *The Oxford Handbook of National Security Intelligence* (New York: Oxford University Press, 2010), pp. 3–32.

7 For example, Hans Born, Loch K. Johnson, and Ian Leigh, eds., *Who's Watching the Spies? Establishing Intelligence Service Accountability* (Washington, DC: Potomac Books, 2005).

8 From a book review of Loch K. Johnson, ed., *Strategic Intelligence*, vols. 1–5 (Westport, CT: Praeger, 2007), in *Intelligence and National Security* 25 (April 2010), pp. 245–7; quote at p. 247.

9 *Fact Book on Intelligence*, Office of Public Affairs, CIA (September 1991), p. 13. An experienced foreign policy practitioner, Secretary of State Dean Rusk liked to think of the purpose of intelligence simply as "informing policymakers about what is going on in the world": see his *As I Saw It*, as told to Richard Rusk and edited by Daniel S. Papp (New York: Norton, 1990), p. 555.

10 The quote is from Peter Gill and Mark Phythian, *Intelligence in an Insecure World*, 2nd edn. (Cambridge: Polity, 2012), p. 19. On intelligence and the idea of decision advantage, see Jennifer E. Sims, "Decision Advantage and the Nature of Intelligence Analysis," in Loch K. Johnson, ed., *The Oxford Handbook of National Security Intelligence* (New York: Oxford University Press, 2010), pp. 389–403. A legendary British intelligence officer (and academician), R.V. Jones, explained intelligence simply by noting that "a sensible nation will seek to be as well informed as possible about its opponents, potential or otherwise, and – for that matter – about its friends. It will therefore set up an intelligence organization": "Intelligence in a Democracy," lecture, Department of State, Washington, DC (December 4, 1975), p. 8. Even seemingly small matters can be important when it comes to intelligence. The great American general George Marshall recalls this memory from the Normandy invasion during World War II: "[Army intelligence] never told me what I needed to know. They didn't tell me about the hedgerows, and it was not until later, after much bloodshed, that we were able to deal with them": quoted in Andrew Roberts, *Masters and Commander: How Four Titans Won the War in the West, 1941–1945* (New York: HarperCollins, 2009), p. 490.

11 Siobhan Gorman, "NSA Has Higher Profile, New Problems," *Baltimore Sun* (September 8, 2006), p. A1.

12 Both 85 percent figures are from *Preparing for the 21st Century: An Appraisal of U.S. Intelligence*, Report of the Commission on the Roles and Capabilities of the United States Intelligence Community (the Aspin–Brown Commission) (Washington, DC: Government Printing Office, March 1, 1996), p. 49. The $80 billion figure is based on a first-time disclosure by the government, in October 2010, as summarized by Walter Pincus, "Intelligence Spending at Record $80.1 Billion in First Disclosure of Overall Figure," *Washington Post* (October 28, 2010), p. A1. That spending was a record high at the time and represented a 7 percent increase over the year before, along with a doubling of the aggregate intelligence budget from pre-9/11 levels. Today, the budget is about $100 billion. In 2009, a DNI said publicly that the Intelligence Community in the United States employs 200,000 people: Dennis C. Blair, Director of National Intelligence, media round table, Washington, DC (September 15, 2009). For purposes of contrast, the British intelligence budget is reported to be about $3.6 billion a year: see Philip Johnston, "GCGH: Licensed to Eavesdrop," *Daily Telegraph*, London (August 27, 2010), p. A1.

13 Steven Aftergood, "DOD Releases Military Intel Program Budget Docs," *Secrecy New* 79 (October 5, 2009), p. 1. For a perspective on IC spending soon after the end of the Cold War, see the Report of the Commission on the Roles and Capabilities of the United States Intelligence Community (the Aspin–Brown Commission), *Preparing for the 21st Century: An Appraisal of U.S. Intelligence* (U.S. Government Printing Office: Washington, DC, March 1, 1996).

14 R. James Woolsey, interview with author, CIA Headquarters, Langley, VA (September 29, 1993).

15 Admiral Stansfield Turner, interview with author, McLean, VA (May 1, 1991). For a vivid description of the Admiral's difficulties in trying to manage the CIA, let alone the larger IC, see his *Secrecy and Democracy: The CIA in Transition* (Boston, MA: Houghton Mifflin, 1985). An example of cultural differences: it is unlikely that the following comment made by DO officer Cofer Black, the CIA's counterintelligence chief in the aftermath of the 9/11 attacks, would ever be uttered or looked upon favorably by an analyst in the DA. "Mr. President," Black said to President George W. Bush, "when we get through with these guys [Al Qaeda], they're going to have flies walking across their eyeballs"; quoted by Chris Wipple, "Four Horsemen of the Forever War," *Vanity Fair* (November 2021), p. 42.

16 See Loch K. Johnson, *Bombs, Bugs, Drugs, and Thugs: Intelligence and America's Quest for Security* (New York: New York University Press, 2000), Ch. 3.

17 Dana Priest and William M. Arkin, "A Hidden World, Growing Beyond Control," *Washington Post* (July 19, 2010), p. A1. On espionage outsourcing,

see Tim Shorrock, *Spies for Hire: The Secret World of Intelligence Outsourcing* (New York: Simon and Schuster, 2008); and Damien Van Puyvelde, *Outsourcing US Intelligence: Contractors and Government Accountability* (Edinburgh: Edinburgh University Press, 2019).

18 Cited in Miller, *Plain Speaking*, p. 420.

19 Ray S. Cline, *The CIA under Reagan, Bush, and Casey* (Washington, DC: Acropolis Books, 1981), p. 112.

20 Amy B. Zegart, *Flawed by Design: The Evolution of the CIA, JCS, and NSC* (Stanford, CA: Stanford University Press, 1999).

21 Michael Warner, "Central Intelligence: Origin and Evolution," in Michael Warner, ed., *Central Intelligence: Origin and Evolution* (Washington, DC: Center for the Study of Intelligence, CIA, 2001), p. 49.

22 Quoted by Mark Mazzetti, "Intelligence Chief Finds That Challenges Abound," *New York Times* (April 7, 2007), p. A10.

23 Bloomsberg News, "Director Wants More Authority in Intelligence," *New York Times* (April 5, 2007), p. A13.

24 Mark Mazzetti, "White House Sides with the CIA in a Spy Turf Battle," *New York Times* (November 13, 2009), p. A12.

CHAPTER 2: INTELLIGENCE COLLECTION: GLOBAL SPYING

1 Loch K. Johnson, *The Threat on the Horizon: An Inside Account of America's Search for Security after the Cold War* (New York: Oxford University Press, 2011), pp. 219–20. See also *Report of the Secretary of Defense to the President and the Congress* (Washington, DC: Government Printing Office, 1996).

2 Richard Helms, with William Hood, *A Look over My Shoulder: A Life in the Central Intelligence Agency* (New York: Random House, 2003), p. 234.

3 On the oversimplification of the cycle, see Arthur S. Hulnick, "What's Wrong with the Intelligence Cycle?" in Loch K. Johnson, ed., *Strategic Intelligence, Vol. 2: The Intelligence Cycle* (Westport, CT: Praeger, 2007), pp. 1–22; and for a series of useful essays that dissect "the cycle," see Mark Phythian, ed., *Understanding the Intelligence Cycle* (New York: Routledge, 2013).

4 R. James Woolsey, testimony, *Hearings*, Select Committee on Intelligence, U.S. Senate, 103rd Cong., 2nd Sess. (March 6, 1993).

5 Dean Rusk, remark to the author, Athens, GA (February 21, 1988).

6 Quoted by Adam Entous, "Stealth Mode," *The New Yorker* (May 31, 2021), p. 19.

7 Les Aspin, remark to the author, Washington, DC (July 14, 1994).

8 Mark M. Lowenthal, *Intelligence: From Secrets to Policy*, 6th edn (Washington, DC: CQ Press, 2014), p. 76.

9 Author's interview (August 28, 1984), Washington, DC.

10 See William J. Broad, "The Rocket Science of Missile Threats," *New York Times* (April 26, 2009), p. Wk. 3.

11 On the threat-assessment process, see Douglas F. Garthoff, *Directors of*

Central Intelligence as Leaders of the U.S. Intelligence Community, 1946–2005 (Washington, DC: Center for the Study of Intelligence, CIA, 2005), p. 240.

12 Johnson, *Threat on the Horizon*, p. 123.

13 Interview conducted by Loch K. Johnson, CIA (April 16, 1995), Langley, Virginia.

14 Loch K. Johnson, "Analysis for a New Age," *Intelligence and National Security* 11 (October 1996), pp. 657–71.

15 Loch K. Johnson, *Bombs, Bugs, Drugs, and Thugs: Intelligence and America's Quest for Security* (New York: New York University Press, 2002), pp. 60–9.

16 Quoted in Johnson, *Threat on the Horizon*, p. 135.

17 Johnson, *Threat on the Horizon*, p. 135.

18 Interview conducted by Loch K. Johnson, CIA (April 10, 1995), Langley, Virginia.

19 Interview conducted by Loch K. Johnson (July 15, 1994), Washington, DC.

20 Interview with senior intelligence official, conducted by Loch K. Johnson (June 6, 2023), Washington, DC.

21 William E. Colby, remark to the author, Washington, DC (January 22, 1991).

22 Joseph S. Nye, Jr., and William A. Owens, "America's Information Edge," *Foreign Affairs* (March/April 1996), p. 26.

23 Andrew Roberts, *Napoleon: A Life* (New York: Viking, 2014), pp. 108–9.

24 Office of the Director of National Intelligence, *The Inaugural Report of the Global Maritime and Air Communities of Interest Intelligence Enterprises* (November 2009), cited in "Federation of American Scientists Project on Government Secrecy," *Secrecy News* 89 (November 9, 2009), p. 2.

25 *Questions & Answers on the Intelligence Community post 9/11.* Office of the Director of National Intelligence (July 2010), p. 3.

26 Remarks to the Aspin–Brown Commission, author's notes (April 28, 1995). The author served as Aspin's assistant during the Commission's inquiries.

27 Remarks in a speech cited by intelligence scholar Richard L. Russell, "Low-Pressure System," *The American Interest* 2 (July/August 2007), pp. 119–23; quote at p. 120.

28 Michael Bronner, "When the War Ends, Start to Worry," *New York Times* (August 16, 2008), p. A27.

29 On the *Glomar Explorer*, see David H. Sharp, *The CIA's Greatest Covert Operation: Inside the Daring Mission to Recover a Nuclear-Armed Soviet Sub* (Lawrence: University Press of Kansas, 2012).

30 Both quoted in the *Boston Globe*, March 20, 1975. Generally on the "ints," see Mark M. Lowenthal and Robert M. Clark, eds., *The 5 Disciplines of Intelligence Collection* (Los Angeles, CA: Sage and CQ Press, 2016).

31 Douglas Jehl, "New Spy Plan Said to Involve Satellite System," *New York Times* (December 12, 2004), p. A1.

32 Steven Emerson, *Secret Warriors: Inside the Covet Military Operations of the Reagan Era* (New York: Putnam, 1988), p. 35.

33 *Organization and Management of Foreign Policy: 1977–80*, Department of State, vol. 28 (2016), document 63, p. 321. For the group of intelligence officers, see Richard Kerr, Thomas Wolfe, Rebecca Donegan, and Aris Pappas, "Collection and Analysis on Iraq: Issues for the US Intelligence Community," *Studies in Intelligence* 49 (2005), pp. 47–54; quote at p. 50.

34 Richard Barrett, "Time to Talk to the Taliban," *New York Times* (October 19, 2010), p. 25.

35 See John L. Millis, staff member, House Permanent Select Committee on Intelligence, "Our Spying Success Is No Secret," letter, *New York Times* (October 12, 1994), p. A27; and Steve Coll, *Ghost Wars: The Secret History of the CIA, Afghanistan, and Bin Laden, From the Soviet Invasion to September 10, 2001* (New York: Penguin, 2004), p. 317.

36 Interview conducted by Amy B. Zegart (June 2004), cited in her *Spying Blind: The CIA, the FBI, and the Origins of 9/11* (Princeton, NJ: Princeton University Press, 2007), p. 93.

37 See, for example, William Colby and Peter Forbath, *Honorable Men: My Life in the CIA* (New York: Simon & Schuster, 1978), p. 336; John Ranelagh, *The Agency: The Rise and Decline of the CIA* (New York: Simon and Schuster, 1987), p. 20; Lowenthal, *Intelligence: From Secrets to Policy*, 6th edn, p. 129; and Mark Mazzetti, "White House Sides With the CIA in a Spy Turf Battle," *New York Times* (November 13, 2009), p. A12, as well as his "Pakistan's Public Enemy," *New York Times Magazine* (April 14, 2013), p. 33.

38 See Robert M. Gates, *From the Shadows* (New York: Simon & Schuster, 1996), p. 560; and Bud Shuster, "HiTech vs. Human Spying," *Washington Times* (February 11, 1992), p. F3.

39 CBS News, "Faulty Intel Source 'Curve Ball' Revealed," *60 Minutes* (November 4, 2007).

40 See Joseph W. Wippl, "The CIA and Tolkachev vs. the KGB/SVR and Ames: A Comparison," *International Journal of Intelligence and Counterintelligence* 23 (Winter 2010–11), pp. 636–46; and a fictional account of the complicated relationship between assets and their handlers in Joseph Weisberg, *An Ordinary Spy* (New York: Bloomsbury, 2008), referred to in a blurb by a former DDO as "stunningly realistic."

41 See, respectively, the Kean Commission's report, entitled *The 9/11 Commission Report: Final Report of the National Commission on Terrorist Attacks upon the United States* (New York: Norton, 2004), p. 415; the Silberman–Robb Commission on the Intelligence Capabilities of the United States Regarding Weapons of Mass Destruction, *Final Report* (Washington, DC: Government Printing Office, 2005), pp. 410–11; and George Tenet, with Bill Harlow, *At the Center of the Storm: My Years at the CIA* (New York: HarperCollins, 2007), p. 24.

42 Author's interview with William E. Colby, Washington, DC (January 22, 1991).

43 See Dean Rusk, *As I Saw It* (New York: Norton, 1990), p. 560.

44 Author's interview with Robert M. Gates, Washington, DC (March 28, 1994).

45 John L. Millis, speech, Central Intelligence Retirees Association, Arlington, VA (October 5, 1998), p. 6.

46 Max Holland, "The 'Photo Gap' that Delayed Discovery of Missiles in Cuba," *Studies in Intelligence* 49 (2005), pp. 15–30; see especially p. 15.

47 On the U-2, see Gregory W. Pedlow and Donald E. Welzenbach, *The CIA and the U-2 Program, 1954–1975* (Washington, DC: Center for the Study of Intelligence, CIA, 1998), with a section on the aircraft's use during the Cuban missile crisis (at pp. 199–210).

48 Holland, "The 'Photo Gap.'"

49 John Lewis Gaddis, *We Now Know: Rethinking Cold War History* (New York: Oxford University Press, 1997), p. 262.

50 Sherman Kent, "A Crucial Estimate Relived," *Studies in Intelligence* (Spring 1964), pp. 1–18; quote at p. 15.

51 Gaddis, *We Now Know*, p. 267; James G. Blight and David A. Welch, eds., *Intelligence and the Cuban Missile Crisis* (London: Cass, 1998); and Raymond L. Garthoff, *Reflections on the Cuban Missile Crisis*, rev. edn (Washington, DC: Brookings Institution, 1989), pp. 35–6.

52 Author's interview with McNamara (January 24, 1985), Athens, GA. See also Sergey Radchenko and Vladislav Zubok, "Blundering on the Brink: The Secret History and Unlearned Lessons of the Cuban Missile Crisis," *Foreign Affairs Online* (April 3, 2023).

53 Dean Rusk, interview conducted by Professor Eric Goldman (January 12, 1964), Rusk Papers, Russell Library, University of Georgia, Athens, GA. See, also, Rusk, *As I Saw It*.

54 R. James Woolsey, author's interview, CIA Headquarters, Langley, VA (September 29, 1993).

55 Loch K. Johnson, "Evaluating 'Humint': The Role of Foreign Agents in U.S. Security," *Comparative Strategy* 29 (September–October 2010), pp. 308–33.

56 See Jeffrey T. Richelson, "The Technical Collection of Intelligence," in Loch K. Johnson, ed., *Handbook of Intelligence Studies* (New York: Routledge, 2007), pp. 105–17.

57 Respectively: Reuel Marc Gerecht, "A New Clandestine Service: The Case for Creative Destruction," in Peter Berkowitz, ed., *The Future of American Intelligence* (Stanford: Hoover Press, 2005), p. 128; and *Intelligence Authorization Act for Fiscal Year 2005*, Report 108–558, Permanent Select Committee on Intelligence (the Goss Committee), U.S. House of Representatives, 108th Cong., 2nd Sess. (June 21, 2004), p. 24.

58 "The CIA and the Media," *Hearings*, Subcommittee on Oversight, Permanent Select Committee on Intelligence, U.S. House of Representatives, 96th Cong., 1st Sess. (1979), p. 7.

59 Fewer than 10 percent of America's college students study a foreign language as part of their curriculum. An experienced former CIA officer notes: "CIA operatives are not particularly well prepared; they seldom speak foreign languages well and almost never know a line of business or a technical field": Michael Turner, *Why Secret Intelligence Fails* (Washington, DC: Potomac Books, 2005), p. 92.

60 See Robert Callum, "The Case for Cultural Diversity in the Intelligence Community," *International Journal of Intelligence and Counter-intelligence* 14 (Spring 2001), pp. 25–48.

61 On the FBI's failure to share counterterrorism data in the lead-up to 9/11, see Daniel Benjamin and Steven Simon, *The Age of Sacred Terror: Radical Islam's War against America* (New York: Random House, 2003), p. 304.

62 Foreign liaison can be tricky. Some of the liaison services abroad with which the United States has a relationship must be kept at arm's length, because they are embedded in authoritarian regimes with suspect motives and behavior; and even those that reside in friendly democracies must be dealt with gingerly, because they may have been compromised.

63 Author's interview with a senior NSA official who quoted the NSA Director, Washington, DC (July 14, 1994).

64 Bob Woodward, *Plan of Attack* (New York: Simon & Schuster, 2004), p. 215.

65 Millis, speech (see note 45).

66 Matthew M. Aid, "Prometheus Embattled: A Post-9/11 Report Card on the National Security Agency," in Loch K. Johnson, ed., *Essentials of Strategic Intelligence* (Santa Barbara, CA: Praeger, 2015), p. 436.

CHAPTER 3: INTELLIGENCE ANALYSIS: UNDERSTANDING WORLD AFFAIRS

1 Dana Priest and William M. Arkin, "A Hidden World, Growing Beyond Control," *Washington Post* (July 19, 2010), p. A1.

2 Richard K. Betts, "Analysis, War and Decision: Why Intelligence Failures Are Inevitable," *World Politics* 31/1 (1978), p. 89; see also his *Enemies of Intelligence: Knowledge & Power in American National Security* (New York: Columbia University Press, 2007).

3 Former Secretary of State Dean Rusk, *As I Saw It*, as told to Richard Rusk and edited by Daniel S. Papp (New York: Norton, 1990), p. 553; and the former intelligence officer, Beth Sanner, quoted in Julian E. Barnes, David E. Sanger, and Eric Schmidt, "Hamas Attack Raises Questions Over an Israeli Intelligence Failure," *New York Times* (October 8, 2023).

4 George Tenet, with Bill Harlow, *At the Center of the Storm: My Years at the CIA* (New York: HarperCollins, 2007), p. 30; the Kean quote is from Linton Weeks, "An Indelible Day," *Washington Post* (June 16, 2004), p. C1.

5 Interview with author (November 19, 1984), Washington, DC.
6 A DDI study during six months in 1994–5 indicated that policymakers had asked 1,300 follow-up questions after reading a *PDB*. In 57 percent of the cases, the questions were answered at the time of the briefing; in 43 percent of the cases, the CIA was queried later and provided answers within a day or two.
7 Author's interviews with Clinton Administration officials throughout 1992–7, Washington, DC.
8 Quoted in Loch K. Johnson, *America's Secret Power: The CIA in a Democratic Society* (New York: Oxford University Press, 1989), p. 90.
9 See John L. Helgerson, *Getting to Know the President: CIA Briefings of Presidential Candidates, 1952–1992* (Washington, DC: Center for the Study of Intelligence, CIA, undated – but apparently released in 1995 by the CIA).
10 Speech remarks, reported by Richard L. Russell, "Low-Pressure System," *The American Interest* 2 (July/August 2007), pp. 119–23; quote at p. 123.
11 Author's interview with George Tenet, Senior Director for Intelligence, NSC, Old Executive Office Building, Washington, DC (June 17, 1994).
12 See Tim Weiner, "C.I.A. Chief Defends Secrecy, in Spending and Spying, to Senate," *New York Times* (February 23, 1996), p. A5.
13 See Loch K. Johnson, *The Threat on the Horizon* (New York: Oxford University Press, 2011), pp. 168–72.
14 Lyman B. Kirkpatrick, "United States Intelligence," *Military Review* 41 (May 1961), pp. 18–22; quote at p. 20.
15 Stansfield Turner, *Secrecy and Democracy: The CIA in Transition* (Boston, MA: Houghton Mifflin, 1985), p. 243.
16 National Intelligence Council, National Intelligence Estimate, *Iran: Nuclear Intentions and Capabilities* (November 2007), cited by CNN News (December 2, 2007).
17 Sherman Kent, *Intelligence for American World Policy* (Princeton, NJ: Princeton University Press, 1949), pp. 64–5.
18 See Anne Hessing Cahn, *Killing Détente: The Right Attacks the CIA* (University Park: Pennsylvania State University Press, 1998).
19 Chester Cooper, retired CIA analyst, interviewed by Ron Nessen, "Intelligence Failure: From Pearl Harbor to 9/11 and Iraq" (television transcript), *America Abroad Media* (July 2004), p. 11.
20 For examples of DCI-penned NIEs, see the discussion of DCI Stansfield Turner in Douglas F. Garthoff, *Directors of Central Intelligence as Leaders of the U.S. Intelligence Community, 1946–2005* (Washington, DC: Center for the Study of Intelligence, CIA, 2005), p. 153.
21 Gregory F. Treverton, "Intelligence Analysis: Between 'Politicization' and Irrelevance," in Roger Z. George and James B. Bruce, eds., *Analyzing Intelligence: Origins, Obstacles, and Innovations* (Washington, DC: Georgetown University Press, 2008), p. 102.

22 Arthur S. Hulnick, review of Harold P. Ford's *Estimative Intelligence: The Purposes and Problems of National Intelligence Estimating* (New York: University Press of America, 1993), *Conflict Quarterly* 14 (Winter 1994), pp. 72–4; quote at p. 74.

23 Quoted by former DCI Robert M. Gates, *From the Shadows* (New York: Simon and Schuster, 1996), p. 566.

24 The metaphor comes from a CIA analyst, quoted in Johnson, *Threat on the Horizon*, p. 92. See also Johnson, "Analysis for a New Age," *Intelligence and National Security* 11 (October 1996), pp. 657–71. This article argues in favor of placing more intelligence liaison officers in policy departments so they can return to their agencies each day to inform analysts about what topics the departments are focused on – a vital method for making intelligence more relevant to the information needs of decision-makers. Sometimes those on the policy side of the government are inclined to discount the value of the IC and its products. Poking fun at this aspect of government – at the expense of an example drawn from the United Kingdom – a former Director of INR, Thomas Hughes, quotes an analyst in the Research Department of the British Foreign Office who served from 1903 to 1950. "Year after year the worriers and fretters would come to me with awful predictions of the outbreak of war," said the UK analyst. "I denied it each time. I was only wrong twice." Hughes observes that, using this cautious methodology, the analyst "can curl up in the luxury of a freebooting negativism. No reputation is staked, no career endangered." See Thomas L. Hughes. *The Fate of Facts in a World of Men: Foreign Policy and Intelligence Making.* Headline Series, No. 233 (Washington, DC: Foreign Policy Association, 1976), p. 48. Former Secretary of State Dean Rusk recalls that some U.S. intelligence officers dealt with the risk of intelligence failure with just the opposite strategy: by forecasting danger everywhere. "The CIA predicted eight out of the last three crises," recalled Rusk, looking back on his tenure as Secretary from 1961 to 1969; author's interview with Rusk (October 5, 1979), Athens, GA.

25 The author is grateful to the CIA for providing these statistics, which were compiled independently from two different sources within the Agency.

26 The data came to the author by year, not by DCI tenure; the decision rule here was to award all the NIEs in a given year to the Intelligence Director who served the most time in that particular year.

27 Letter from Sherman Kent to Frank Wisner (dated November 18, 1963), found by the author in the Sterling Library Collection, Yale University, Series I, Box 18, Folder 390.

28 Sherman Kent, "Estimates and Influence," *Foreign Service Journal* (April 1969), p. 17.

29 British intelligence came to the same conclusion. One of its leaders has written that "identifying Soviet strategic caution [was] perhaps the most

important single judgement of the [Cold War] period": Percy Cradock, *Know Your Enemy* (London: John Murray, 2002), p. 292.

30 In 1975, Senator Frank Church (D, Idaho) noted: "In the last twenty-five years, no important new Soviet weapons system, from the H-bomb to the most recent missiles, has appeared which had not been heralded in advance by NIEs": *Congressional Record* (November 11, 1975), p. S35787.

31 See Loch K. Johnson, *Secret Agencies: U.S. Intelligence in a Hostile World* (New Haven, CT: Yale University Press, 1996).

32 See George and Bruce, eds., *Analyzing Intelligence*; James P. Pfiffner and Mark Phythian, eds., *Intelligence and National Security Policymaking on Iraq: British and American Perspectives* (Manchester: Manchester University Press, 2008); and Robert M. Clark, *Intelligence Analysis: A Target-Centric Approach*, 3rd edn (Washington, DC: CQ Press, 2010), pp. 314–19.

33 Church (see note 30), p. S35786.

34 Hulnick, review of Ford, *Estimative Intelligence*, p. 74.

35 Harold P. Ford, *Estimative Intelligence: The Purposes and Problems of National Intelligence Estimating* (New York: University Press of America, 1993), p. 49.

36 William E. Odom, *Fixing Intelligence for a More Secure America*, 2nd edn (New Haven, CT: Yale University Press, 2004), p. 81. An added problem for analysts: the evidence may be clear, but the explanation less so.

37 Kent, "Estimates and Influence," p. 17.

38 Barton Gellman and Walter Pincus, "Depiction of Threat Outgrew Supporting Evidence," *Washington Post* (August 10, 2003), p. A1, quoting a senior intelligence official.

39 Gellman and Pincus, "Depiction of Threat Outgrew Supporting Evidence."

40 Tenet, with Harlow, *At the Center of the Storm*, pp. 321–2.

41 Tenet, with Harlow, *At the Center of the Storm*, pp. 322–3.

42 Senator Bob Graham, with Jeff Nussbaum, *Intelligence Matters: The CIA, the FBI, Saudi Arabia, and the Failure of America's War on Terror* (New York: Random House, 2004), p. 180.

43 Tim Weiner, *Legacy of Ashes: The History of the CIA* (New York: Doubleday, 2007), p. 487.

44 The NIE was entitled *Iraq's Continuing Program for Weapons of Mass Destruction* (NIE 2002–16HC). On the timing and Tenet's briefing, see Graham, with Nussbaum, *Intelligence Matters*, pp. 179–80.

45 Graham, with Nussbaum, *Intelligence Matters*, p. 187.

46 Graham, with Nussbaum, *Intelligence Matters*, pp. 185–9.

47 Interviewed by Wil S. Hylton, "The Angry One," *Gentleman's Quarterly* (January 2007), p. 21.

48 *Report on the U.S. Intelligence Community's Prewar Intelligence Assessments on Iraq*, Senate Select Committee on Intelligence (Washington, DC: Government Printing Office, July 7, 2004), p. 14.

49 Tenet, with Harlow, *At the Center of the Storm*, p. 338.
50 Author's notes on remarks by Mark M. Lowenthal, Canadian Association for Security and Intelligence Studies (CASIS) Conference, Ottawa (October 27, 2006).
51 The 80–90 percent figure comes from the author's interview with a senior CIA manager in the Agency's Intelligence Directorate, Washington, DC (August 28, 1997).
52 Lowenthal, CASIS Conference (see note 50).
53 John L. Helgerson, remarks to the author, International Symposium, The Hague, Holland (June 8, 2007).
54 Michael Bloch, *Ribbentrop* (London: Abacus, 2003), p. 167. At one point Ribbentrop vowed that he would personally shoot anyone who dissented from Hitler's worldview (p. xix).
55 See, respectively, Stansfield Turner, *Burn before Reading: Presidents, CIA Directors, and Secret Intelligence* (New York: Hyperion, 2005), p. 77; and Johnson, *America's Secret Power*, pp. 63–4. Mark Lowenthal, a former CIA analyst, notes that a "subtle and difficult skill to master is cultivating the intelligence consumer without politicizing the intelligence as a means of currying favor": *Intelligence: From Secrets to Policy*, 6th edn (Washington, DC: CQ Press, 2014), p. 161.
56 Richard Helms, with William Hood, *A Look over My Shoulder: A Life in the Central Intelligence Agency* (New York: Random House, 2003), p. 318.
57 On improving analysis, see Clark, *Intelligence Analysis*; George and Bruce, eds., *Analyzing Intelligence*; Robert Jervis, *Why Intelligence Fails* (Ithaca, NY: Cornell University Press, 2010); Loch K. Johnson, ed., *Strategic Intelligence, Vol. 2: The Intelligence Cycle* (Westport, CT: Praeger, 2007); Richard L. Russell, *Sharpening Strategic Intelligence* (New York: Cambridge University Press, 2007); and Timothy Walton, *Challenges in Intelligence Analysis* (New York: Cambridge University Press, 2010).
58 See Peter Wyden, *Bay of Pigs: The Untold Story* (New York: Simon & Schuster, 1979); and Arthur M. Schlesinger, Jr., *Robert Kennedy and His Times* (Boston, MA: Houghton Mifflin, 1978), p. 453.
59 Quoted by Greg Miller, "CIA to Station More Analysts Overseas as Part of its Strategy," *Washington Post* (April 30, 2010), p. A1.
60 Kimberly Dozier, "CIA Forms New Center to Combat Nukes, WMDs," Associated Press Report (August 18, 2010).
61 Joseph S. Nye, Jr., remarks, Commission of the Roles and Capabilities of the United States Intelligence Community, Washington, DC (June 1, 1995).
62 Richard K. Betts, "The New Politics of Intelligence: Will Reforms Work This Time?" *Foreign Affairs* 83 (May/June 2004), pp. 2–8; quote at p. 7.
63 Author's interview with Richard Helms, Washington, DC (December 12, 1990), in Loch K. Johnson, "Spymaster Richard Helms," *Intelligence and National Security* 18 (Autumn 2003), pp. 24–44; quote at p. 27.

64 See Willmoore Kendall, "The Function of Intelligence," *World Politics* 1 (1948–9), pp. 542–52.

65 William M. Nolte, remark, panel on intelligence analysis, International Studies Association annual meeting, San Francisco (March 2008).

66 See the findings of the Butler Report, discussed in R. Gerald Hughes, Peter Jackson, and Len Scott, eds., *Exploring Intelligence Archives: Enquiries into the Secret State* (New York: Routledge, 2008), Ch. 12.

67 Former U.S. diplomat Martin Hillenbrand, remarks to the author, Athens, GA (January 21, 1987). President Ronald Reagan's Secretary of State, George P. Shultz concluded acidly in his memoirs: "I had no confidence in the intelligence community . . . I had been misled, lied to, cut out." This reaction went beyond the Iran-*contra* scandal to include his view that "CIA analysis was distorted by strong views about policy": see George P. Shultz, *Turmoil and Triumph: My Years as Secretary of State* (New York: Scribner's, 1993), p. 864.

68 Daniel P. Moynihan, "Do We Still Need the CIA? The State Dept. Can Do the Job," *New York Times* (May 19, 1991), p. E17.

69 See *The 9/11 Commission Report* (New York: Norton, 2004), as well as Graham, with Nussbaum, *Intelligence Matters*; Jane Mayer, *The Dark Side* (New York: Doubleday, 2008); and Amy Zegart, *Spying Blind: The CIA, the FBI, and the Origins of 9/11* (Princeton, NJ: Princeton University Press, 2007).

70 See Hughes et al., *Exploring Intelligence Archives*; Jervis, *Why Intelligence Fails*; and Loch K. Johnson, "A Framework for Strengthening U.S. Intelligence," *Yale Journal of International Affairs* 2 (February 2006), pp. 116–31.

71 *Preparing for the 21st Century: An Appraisal of U.S. Intelligence*, Report of the Commission on the Roles and Capabilities of the United States Intelligence Community (Washington, DC: Government Printing Office, March 1, 1996).

72 Quoted in Julian E. Barnes and Adam Entous, "How the U.S. Adopted a New Intelligence Playbook to Expose Russia's War Plans," *New York Times* (February 23, 2023), p. A13.

73 On Pakistan–U.S. intelligence relationships, see, for example, Adam Goldman and Matt Apuzzo, "CIA and Pakistan Locked in Aggressive Spy Battles," *Associated Press* (July 6, 2010); and on America's resort to dubious proxy partnerships, see Charlie Savage and Eric Schmitt, "Rules for Pentagon Use of Proxy Forces Shed Light on a Shadowy War Power," *New York Times* (May 14, 2023), p. A13.

74 Quoted by Julian E. Barnes, "U.S. Intelligence Report Warns of Global Consequences of Social Fragmentation," *New York Times* (April 8, 2021), p. A15.

CHAPTER 4: COVERT ACTION: SECRET ATTEMPTS TO SHAPE HISTORY

1 This vignette is drawn from Loch K. Johnson, *The Third Option: Covert Action and American Foreign Policy* (New York: Oxford University Press, 2022).

2 The cable can be found in a declassified Church Committee document, entitled "Dulles Cable to Léopoldville," dated August 27, 1960, U.S. Government, Select Committee to Study Governmental Operations with Respect to Intelligence Activities, "The CIA Assassination Plot in the Congo, 1960–61," *Alleged Assassination Plots Involving Foreign Leaders: An Interim Report*, Senate, 94th Cong., 1st Sess. (November 1975), p. 15.

3 Stephen R. Weissman, *American Foreign Policy in the Congo 1960–1964* (Ithaca, NY: Cornell University Press, 1974), p. 280; see, also, his "An Extraordinary Rendition," *Intelligence and National Security* 25/2 (April 2010), pp. 198–222.

4 Henry Kissinger, remark, "Evening News," NBC Television Network (January 13, 1978).

5 The Intelligence Authorization Act of 1991 (50 U.S.C. 503 (e); Pub. L. No. 102–88, 105 Stat. 441, August 14, 1991); this statute amended the National Security Act of 1947, repealed the Hughes–Ryan Amendment of 1974, and was codified into law Executive Order 12333.

6 John Deutch, DCI, speech, National Press Club, Washington, DC (September 12, 1995).

7 William J. Daugherty, *Executive Secrets: Covert Action & the Presidency* (Lexington: University Press of Kentucky, 2004), p. 12. Even among intelligence professionals, sometimes there is confusion about the difference in meaning between "covert" and "clandestine." Kibbe offers this useful distinction: "Although [covert action] is often used interchangeably with the term 'clandestine,' the two are legally distinct: 'clandestine' refers to the tactical secrecy of the operation itself, while 'covert' refers to the secrecy of its sponsor"; see Jennifer D. Kibbe, "Covert Action, Pentagon Style," in Loch K. Johnson, ed., *The Oxford Handbook of National Security Intelligence* (New York: Oxford University Press, 2010), p. 170.

8 The National Security Act of 1947, Pub. L. No. 80–253, 61 Stat. 495; 50 U.S.C. 403–3(d)(5).

9 Author's interview with a senior CIA official in the Operations Directorate, Washington, DC (February 1986).

10 B. Hugh Tovar, "Strengths and Weaknesses in Past U.S. Covert Action," in Roy Godson, ed., *Intelligence Requirements for the 1980s: Covert Action* (Washington, DC: National Strategy Information Center, 1981), pp. 194–5.

11 William E. Colby, "Gesprach mit William E. Colby," *Der Spiegel* 4 (January 23, 1978), pp. 69–115; quote at p. 75; author's translation.

12 Quoted in *The Nation* (March 12, 1983), p. 301.

13 Frank Church, "Covert Action: Swampland of American Foreign Policy," *Bulletin of the Atomic Scientists* 32 (February 1976), pp. 7–11.

14 See Jennifer Kibbe, "Covert Action and the Pentagon," in Loch K. Johnson, ed., *Strategic Intelligence, Vol. 3: Covert Action* (Westport, CT: Praeger, 2007), pp. 145–56.

15 For Hughes-Ryan, see Section 662(a) of the Foreign Assistance Act of 1974; Section 662 of the Foreign Assistance Act of 1961 (22 U.S.C. 2422); and for the 1980 law: Title V, National Security Act of 1947, 50 USC 413.

16 Select Committee on Secret Military Assistance to Iran and the Nicaraguan Opposition, U.S. Senate, and House Select Committee to Investigate Covert Arms Transactions with Iran, U.S. House (the Inouye–Hamilton Committee), *Hearings and Final Report* (Washington, DC: Government Printing Office, 1987). The statutory responses came in the form chiefly of the 1991 Intelligence Authorization Act (see note 5). See also Malcolm Byrne, *Iran-Contra: Reagan's Scandal and the Unchecked Abuse of Presidential Power* (Lawrence: University Press of Kansas, 2014).

17 See Hugh Wilford, *The Mighty Wurlitzer: How the CIA Played America* (Cambridge, MA: Harvard University Press, 2008).

18 Dr. Ray S. Cline, testimony, "The CIA and the Media," *Hearings*, Subcommittee on Oversight, Permanent Select Committee on Intelligence, U.S. House of Representatives 95th Cong., 2nd Sess., 27 December 1977 (Washington, DC: Government Printing Office, 1978), p. 90.

19 Author's interview with a CAS officer, Washington, DC (February 21, 1976).

20 Senior DDO officer, testimony, *Hearings*, Select Committee to Study Governmental Operations with Respect to Intelligence Activities (the Church Committee), *Final Report*, 94th Cong., 2nd Sess., Sen. Rept. No. 94–465 (Washington, DC: Government Printing Office, 1976), p. 31; see, also, Church Committee, *Alleged Assassination Plots Involving Foreign Leaders*, Interim Rept., S. Rept. No. 94–465 (Washington, DC: Government Printing Office, November 20, 1975), p. 181n. During World War II, the OSS toyed with several ideas (also never executed) that were just as madcap, including an attempt to put estrogen into Hitler's bratwurst; dropping pornography by airplane into German foxholes as a means of driving the Wehrmacht mad; and spraying (again, from aircraft) tetrahydrocannabinol acetate on German field command tents to induce excessive chattiness and distract the Nazi brass from the war effort. The cupboard is full of cases that underscore the importance of accountability over some bureaucrats who, now and then, become overzealous and lose good judgment.

21 See Michael Grow, *U.S. Presidents and Latin American Interventions: Pressuring Regime Change in the Cold War* (Lawrence: University Press of Kansas, 2008).

22 David Wise and Thomas B. Ross, *The Invisible Government* (New York: Random House, 1964).

23 Tom Wicker et al., "CIA Operations: A Plot Scuttled," *New York Times* (April 28, 1966), p. A1.

24 Joint Chiefs of Staff, memo on SQUARE DANCE, dated October 30, 1964, and attached to a memo from R.C. Bowman to National Security Advisor

McGeorge Bundy, 1964 National Security Files (November 12, 1964), Lyndon Baines Johnson Presidential Library, Austin, TX. On the Trump cyberattacks, see Julian E. Barnes and Thomas Gibbons-Neff, "U.S. Carried Out Cyberattacks on Iran," *New York Times* (June 22, 2019), p. A1.

25 McGeorge Bundy, Memorandum to the President (January 9, 1964), p. 1, in *Miscellaneous Records of the Church Committee*, Senate Select Committee on Intelligence, Loch K. Johnson file on "LBJ Library National Security Papers Touching on Assass. and Covert Action in Cuba" (July 21, 1975), declassified on March 8, 2000, Record Number 157-10014-10096. Elsewhere in these Papers, a CIA operations officer underscored, in a letter for President Johnson's National Security Advisor Bundy, that the Agency possessed the "capacity, which is increasing, to sabotage Cuban merchant ships calling at foreign ports": "Des" – short for Desmond FitzGerald – to "Mac" Bundy (dated March 6, 1964), p. 2.

26 Executive Order 12333, Sec. 2.11.

27 Former DCI Robert M. Gates, quoted by Walter Pincus, "Saddam Hussein's Death Is a Goal," *Washington Post* (February 15, 1998), p. A36.

28 Unsigned editorial, "Lethal Force under Law," *New York Times* (October 10, 2010), Wk. 7. See also Ken Dilanian and Courtney Kube, "U.S. Report Will Say Drones Have Killed Just 100 Civilians," *NBC News* (June 24, 2016). For the corrected figure in 2016, see the unsigned editorial, "The Secret Rules of the Drone War," *New York Times* (July 10, 2016), p. SR8.

29 For accounts of U.S. drone attacks in the Middle East and Southwest Asia, see H. Gusterson, *Drone: Remote Control Warfare* (Boston: MIT Press, 2016); J. Kaag and Sarah S. Kreps, *Drone Warfare* (Cambridge: Polity, 2014); Jane Mayer, "The Predator War," *The New Yorker* (October 26, 2009), pp. 36–45; Mark Mazzetti, *The Way of the Knife: The CIA, a Secret Army, and a War at the Ends of the Earth* (New York: Penguin, 2013); Scott Shane, *Objective Troy: A Terrorist, a President, and the Rise of the Drone* (New York: Tim Duggan Books, 2015); and Chris Woods, *Sudden Justice: America's Secret Drone Wars* (New York: Oxford University Press, 2015). On the CIA rethinking the wisdom of its involvement in drone attacks, see Mark Mazzetti, "CIA to Focus More on Spying, a Difficult Shift," *New York Times* (May 24, 2013), p. A1.

30 On the drone murder of Awlaki, see Shane, *Objective Troy.*

31 "Lethal Force under Law" (see note 28).

32 Stansfield Turner, *Burn before Reading: Presidents, CIA Directors, and Secret Intelligence* (New York: Hyperion, 2005), p. 32.

33 John Ranelagh, *The Agency: The Rise and Decline of the CIA*, rev. edn (New York: Simon & Schuster, 1987), p. 220.

34 Church Committee, *Final Report*, p. 31.

35 Daugherty, *Executive Secrets*, p. 140.

36 Author's interview with senior DO manager, Washington, DC (February 18, 1980).

37 Author's interview with a senior DO officer, Washington, DC (October 10, 1980).

38 See Seth G. Jones, *A Covert Action: Reagan, the CIA, and the World War Struggle in Poland* (New York: Norton, 2018).

39 George H.W. Bush, letter to the author (January 23, 1994); and author's interview with DCI R. James Woolsey, Langley, Virginia (September 29, 1993).

40 Author's interview, Washington, DC (March 21, 1995).

41 Deutch, DCI speech (see note 6).

42 Herman Kahn, *On Escalation: Metaphors and Scenarios* (New York: Praeger, 1965), p. 37.

43 A CIA intelligence officer, James A. Barry, suggested to the author (who agrees) that the demarcation of broad thresholds on the ladder is more useful than the exact steps within each threshold, since it is difficult to agree exactly about whether some specific rungs should be higher or lower than other rungs. The key point, he argues, is that "there are degrees of damage – physical, economic and psychological/moral – and that these must be clearly articulated in a discussion of proposed covert actions" (letter to the author, dated May 18, 1992).

44 See Report of the Special Committee on Principles of International Law Concerning Friendly Relations and Co-operation among States, UN Doc. A/6799 (1967), p. 161.

45 Lori Fisler Damrosch, "Politics across Borders: Nonintervention and Nonforcible Influence over Domestic Affairs," *American Journal of International Law* 83 (January 1989), pp. 6–13; quote at p. 11.

46 On this norm, see Damrosch, "Politics across Borders," pp. 6–13. The Murphy Commission was known more formally as the Commission on the Organization of the Government for the Conduct of Foreign Policy; see its *Report to the President* (Washington, DC: Government Printing Office, June 1975).

47 Damrosch, "Politics across Borders," p. 36.

48 George Ball, "Should the CIA Fight Secret Wars?" *Harper's* (September 1984), pp. 27–44; quote at p. 37.

49 A top-secret recommendation (since declassified) of the General Doolittle Committee, a part of the Hoover Commission in 1954, cited in Church Committee, *Final Report*, p. 9.

50 Ray Cline, former DDI at the CIA, quoted by Ball, "Should the CIA Fight Secret Wars?" pp. 39, 44.

51 Remarks, public lecture, University of Georgia, Athens, GA (May 4, 1986), author's notes.

52 On these ingredients for success, see Milt Bearden, "Lessons from Afghanistan," *New York Times* (March 2, 1998), p. A19.

53 Anthony Lewis, "Costs of the CIA," *New York Times* (April 25, 1997), p. A19.

54 Bearden, "Lessons from Afghanistan."

55 McGeorge Bundy, remark to the author, Athens, GA (October 6, 1987). In 2016, the media revealed that CIA weapons shipped to Jordan, a U.S. ally, for dispersal to rebels opposing the Syrian regime of President Bashar al-Assad, were stolen by members of the Jordanian intelligence service (the GID, also known as the Mukhabarat). The theft included thousands of Kalashnikov (AK-47) assault rifles with millions of rounds, mortars, rocket-propelled grenades, and antitank guided missiles. In 2013, President Obama had approved the program (codenamed TIMBER), based on an apparently misplaced faith in the GID as a reliable intelligence liaison partner. In the past, though, Jordan had worked closely with the United States through a joint counterterrorism center in Jordan, as well as at a secret CIA prison outside of Amman where the Agency confined suspected terrorists. See Mark Mazzetti and Ali Younes, "Thefts Redirect Arms from C.I.A.," *New York Times* (June 27, 2016), p. A1.

56 W. Michael Reisman, remarks, "Covert Action," panel presentation, International Studies Association, annual meeting, Washington, DC (March 29, 1994).

57 Remarks, interview on "Larry King Live," CNN Television, Washington, DC (February 2, 1987).

58 Journalist Tom Friedman has observed that the United States treated the Arab world "as a collection of big, dumb gas stations, basically. We told them, 'Here's the deal. Keep your pumps open, your prices low, and be nice to the Jews. And you can do whatever you want out back'": Ian Parker, "The Bright Side," *The New Yorker* (November 10, 2008), pp. 52–65; quote at p. 61.

59 Daugherty, *Executive Secrets:* 201, 211; and, for a more detailed examination of this successful covert action, see Seth G. Jones, *A Covert Action: Reagan, the CIA, and the Cold War Struggle in Poland* (New York: Norton, 2018).

60 Stansfield Turner, author's interview, McLean, Virginia (May 1, 1991).

61 For an appraisal of the best and the worst of America's covert actions since 1947, see Johnson, *The Third Option* (Ch. 9).

62 Remarks, Aspin–Brown Commission staff interview (1996). Similarly, former National Security Advisor Bundy has said that "if you can't defend a covert action if it goes public, you'd better not do it at all – because it will go public usually within a fairly short time span": author's interview, Athens, GA (October 6, 1987). Stansfield Turner has also commented: "There is one overall test of the ethics of human intelligence activities. That is, whether those approving them feel they could defend their decisions before the public if their actions became public": *Secrecy and Democracy: The CIA in Transition* (Boston, MA: Houghton Mifflin, 1985), p. 178.

63 Dexter Filkins, "Damned if You Don't," *The New Yorker* (September 16, 2019), p. 24.

64 Testimony, Hearings: Covert Action, the Church Committee, vol. 7, pp. 50–5.
65 Roger Fisher, "The Fatal Flaw in Our Spy System," *Boston Globe* (February 1, 1976), p. A21.

CHAPTER 5: COUNTERINTELLIGENCE: GUARDING THE DEMOCRACIES

1 Theodore H. White, *Breach of Faith: The Fall of Richard Nixon* (New York: Atheneum, 1975), p. 133.
2 FBI counterintelligence officer, testimony, *Huston Plan Hearings*, Select Committee on Intelligence Activities (hereafter, Church Committee), U.S. Senate, 94th Cong., 1st Sess. (September 25, 1975), p. 137. Discussion of the Huston Plan here is based on the author's preparation of public hearings on the topic for the Church Committee in 1975.
3 Author's interview with William C. Sullivan, Boston, MA (June 10, 1975); the quote is from C. D. Brennan of the FBI Counterintelligence Branch to William C. Sullivan, memorandum (June 20, 1969), cited in the *Huston Plan Hearings*, Church Committee, Exhibit 6, p. 23.
4 *Presidential Talking Paper*, prepared by Tom Charles Huston and used by President Richard Nixon, Oval Office (June 5, 1970), Church Committee files (February 2, 1975). On the imperious J. Edgar Hoover, see Beverly Gage, *G-Man: J. Edgar Hoover and the Making of the American Century* (New York: Viking, 2022).
5 White, *Breach of Faith*, p. 133.
6 Tom Charles Huston, Memorandum to H. R. "Bob" Haldeman, the White House Chief of Staff (July 1970 – the precise day is unknown, but sometime during the first two weeks of the month), *Huston Plan Hearings*, Church Committee, Exhibit 2, p. 2. "Mail cover" refers to an examination of the external contexts of a letter, such as the address and the date of postage – a first step before an intelligence agency decides to open a suspect's letter and read its contents.
7 Huston, Memorandum to H.R. "Bob" Haldeman, p. 3.
8 Richard M. Nixon, answer to Church Committee interrogatory No. 17 (March 3, 1976).
9 For a more detailed account, see Loch K. Johnson, *America's Secret Power: The CIA in a Democratic Society* (New York: Oxford University Press, 1989), pp. 133–56.
10 Testimony of Tom Charles Huston, *Huston Plan Hearings*, Church Committee, p. 45.
11 Executive Order 12333, Sec. 3.5, as amended on July 31, 2008.
12 See Beverly Gage, *The Day Wall Street Exploded: A Story of America in Its First Age of Terror* (New York: Oxford University Press, 2009). This crime was never solved.

13 Jo Thomas, "Letter by McVeigh Told of Mind-Set," *New York Times* (May 9, 1977), p. A1.

14 For an account, see Stuart A. Wright, *Patriots, Politics, and the Oklahoma City Bombing* (New York: Cambridge University Press, 2007).

15 In 2007, researcher Stuart A. Wright, drawing on a 2003 Associated Press investigation, charged that the federal Bureau of Alcohol, Tobacco and Firearms (ATF) had an informant inside the McVeigh camp who provided advanced warning about the Oklahoma City attack, but was ignored (*Patriots, Politics, and the Oklahoma City Bombing*, p. 183).

16 Interview, MSNBC Network (September 11, 2023).

17 Mary Anne Weaver, "The Stranger," *The New Yorker* (November 13, 1995), pp. 59–72.

18 *Report on Terrorism in the United States*, Counterterrorism Center, CIA, Langley, VA (July 1995), provided to the Aspin–Brown Commission in unclassified form (August 1995).

19 See Jane Mayer, *The Dark Side* (New York: Doubleday, 2008); and Amy B. Zegart, *Spying Blind: The CIA, the FBI, and the Origins of 9/11* (Princeton, NJ: Princeton University Press, 2007).

20 Richard A. Clarke, *Against All Enemies: Inside America's War on Terror* (New York: Free Press, 2004), p. 237.

21 See *An Assessment of the Aldrich H. Ames Espionage Case and Its Implications for U.S. Intelligence*, Staff Report, Select Committee on Intelligence, U.S. Senate, S. Prt. 103–90, 103rd Cong., 2nd Sess. (Washington, DC: Government Printing Office, November 1, 1994); David Wise, *Nightmover: How Aldrich Ames Sold the CIA to the KGB for $4.6 Million* (New York: HarperCollins, 1993); and David Wise, *Spy: The Inside Story of How the FBI's Robert Hanssen Betrayed America* (New York: Random House, 2003).

22 Loch K. Johnson, *The Threat on the Horizon: An Inside Account of America's Search for Security after the Cold War* (New York: Oxford University Press, 2011).

23 See Paul J. Redmond, "The Challenges of Counterintelligence," in Loch K. Johnson, ed., *The Oxford Handbook of National Security Intelligence* (New York: Oxford University Press, 2010), pp. 537–54; quote at p. 541.

24 John Earl Haynes, Harvey Klehr, and Alexander Vassiliev, with translations by Philip Redko and Steven Shabad, *Spies: The Rise and Fall of the KGB in America* (New Haven, CT: Yale University Press, 2009). See also Timothy Gibbs, "Catching an Atom Spy: MI5 and the Investigation of Klaus Fuchs," in Johnson, ed., *Oxford Handbook of National Security Intelligence*, pp. 555–68.

25 See, for example, Cleveland C. Cram, "Of Moles and Molehunters: A Review of Counterintelligence Literature, 1977–92," Center for the Study of Intelligence, CIA, *Report No. CSI 93–002* (October 1993).

26 See David C. Martin, *Wilderness of Mirrors* (New York: Harper & Row, 1980); and John Ranelagh, *The Agency: The Rise and Decline of the CIA*, rev. edn (New York: Simon & Schuster, 1987).

27 Redmond, "The Challenges of Counterintelligence."
28 For profiles of Kampiles and many of the other traitors mentioned here, see the useful compilation by Norman Polmar and Thomas B. Allen, eds., *The Encyclopedia of Espionage* (New York: Gramercy Books, 1997).
29 See David Wise, *The Spy Who Got Away: The Inside Story of Edward Lee Howard* (New York: Random House, 1988).
30 See Seymour M. Hersh, "The Traitor," *The New Yorker* (January 18, 1999), pp. 26–33.
31 See David Johnston and Tim Weiner, "On the Trail of a C.I.A. Official, From Asia Travel to Bank Files," *New York Times* (November 21, 1996), p. A1; and Walter Pincus and Roberto Suro, "Rooting Out the 'Sour Apples' Inside the CIA," *Washington Post*, National Weekly Edition (November 25–December 1, 1996), p. 30.
32 Tim Weiner, "Former South Korean Pleads Guilty in Spying Case," *New York Times* (May 8, 1997), p. A16.
33 See Adam Goldman and Jill Cowan, "Two U.S. Navy Sailors Charged with Helping China," *New York Times* (August 3, 2023); and Adam Goldman, "Former US. Soldier Is Accused of Trying to Give Classified Secrets to China," *New York Times* (October 6, 2023). For more on the aggressiveness of contemporary Chinese spying against the United States, see Edward Wong, Julian E. Barnes, Muyi Xiao, and Chris Buckley, "Chinese Spy Agency Rising to Challenge the C.I.A.," *New York Times* (December 28, 2003). These journalists report that spending by the Agency against the Chinese target has doubled since William J. Burns became D/CIA in 2021, and that he has created a special Chinese Mission Center at Langley to focus on this threat from Beijing.
34 Frederick L. Wettering, "Counterintelligence: The Broken Triad," *International Journal of Intelligence and Counterintelligence* 13 (Fall 2000), pp. 265–99; quote at p. 276.
35 For examples, see Percy Cradock, *Know Your Enemy* (London: John Murray, 2002); Michael S. Goodman, *Spying on the Nuclear Bear: Anglo-American Intelligence and the Soviet Bomb* (Stanford, CA: Stanford University Press, 2007); and Athan Theoharis, *Chasing Spies* (Chicago, IL: Ivan R. Dee, 2002).
36 Scott Shane, "A Spy's Motivation: For Love of Another Country," *New York Times* (April 20, 2008), p. WK 3.
37 Stan A. Taylor and Daniel Snow, "Cold War Spies: Why They Spied and How They Got Caught," *Intelligence and National Security* 12 (April 1997), pp. 101–25.
38 Reported by Shane, "A Spy's Motivation" (note 36).
39 On this recent case, see Julian E. Barnes and Edward Wong, "Global Espionage Grows Between U.S. and China," *New York Times* (September 17, 2023), p. A1.

40 On Angleton, see Seymour M. Hersh, "The Angleton Story," *New York Times Magazine* (June 25, 1978), pp. 13ff.; Loch K. Johnson, "James Angleton and the Church Committee," *Journal of Cold War Studies* 15 (Fall 2013), pp. 128–47; Tom Mangold, *Cold Warrior: James Jesus Angleton, the CIA's Master Spy Hunter* (New York: Simon & Schuster, 1991); and Robin W. Winks, *Cloak & Gown: Scholars in the Secret War, 1939–1961* (New York: Morrow, 1987), pp. 322–438.

41 On Angleton's early suspicions about Philby, see Ranelagh, *The Agency*, p. 151.

42 See the argument in Redmond, "The Challenges of Counterintelligence," pp. 540, 547.

43 Hersh, "The Angleton Story."

44 The phrase comes from a line in T. S. Eliot's poem, "Gerontion" (1920). For a recent – and likely false – charge from a former CIA operations officer that former Agency Deputy Chief of Counterintelligence (1991–6), Paul J. Redmond, was a Soviet spy, see Robert Baer, *The Fourth Man* (New York: Hachette, 2022); and Redmond's persuasive self-defense, "The Ghost of Angleton," *International Journal of Intelligence and Counterintelligence* (online, February 6, 2023), pp. 301–7.

45 Henry Brandon, "The Spy Who Came and Then Told," *Washington Post*, National Weekly Edition (August 24, 1987), p. 36.

46 Robert Jervis, "Intelligence, Counterintelligence, Perception, and Deception," in Jennifer E. Sims and Burton Gerber, eds., *Vaults, Mirrors, and Masks: Rediscovering U.S. Counterintelligence* (Washington, DC: Georgetown University Press, 2009), pp. 69–79; quote at p. 75.

47 Redmond, "The Challenges of Counterintelligence," p. 539.

48 Commission on the Intelligence Capabilities of the United States Regarding Weapons of Mass Destruction (the Silberman–Robb or WMD Commission), *Report to the President of the United States* (Washington, DC: Government Printing Office, 2005), p. 490.

49 Redmond, remarks to the Aspin–Brown Commission. Canadian intelligence scholar Wesley K. Wark notes in a similar vein: "Treason perpetually beckons and those with access to secrets will, on occasion, succumb to the temptations of leading a double life, and of the banalities of greed and folly": "For Love of Money," *Ottawa Citizen* (February 7, 2009), p. A16.

50 J.H. Plumb, *The Italian Renaissance* (Boston: Houghton Mifflin, 1961), pp. 102–3.

51 See Edward Jay Epstein, "The Spy War," *New York Times Sunday Magazine*, sec. 6 (September 28, 1980), p. 108.

52 Communication to the author (April 15, 2010).

53 See Mark Mazzetti, "Officer Failed to Warn CIA Before Attack," *New York Times* (October 20, 2010), p. A1.

54 Quoted by Ken Dilanian, "U.S. Counter-Terrorism Agents Still Hamstrung by Data-Sharing Failures," *Los Angeles Times* (October 5, 2010), p. A1.

55 David E. Sanger and Steven Lee Myers, "China Sows Disinformation About Hawaii Fires Using New Techniques," *New York Times* (September 11, 2023). For evidence that Russia's use of cyberwarfare has had limited effects in Ukraine and elsewhere, see Lennart Maschmeyer, *Subversion* (New York: Oxford University Press, 2024).

56 *CBS Sunday Morning News* (September 17, 2023).

57 Magda Long, "An Essential Tool of American Foreign Policy: US Covert Action since 1947," *The International Spectator* 58/2 (2023), p. 162.

58 Redmond, remarks to the Aspin–Brown Commission.

59 On Clapper's views, see, for example, Mark Mazzetti and Scott Shane, "Spy Chief Calls Cyberattacks Top Threat to the U.S.," *New York Times* (March 13, 213), p. A1.

60 Avril D. Haines, Director of National Intelligence (DNI) Carnegie Endowment online lecture, April 24, 2023.

61 Yudhijit Bhattacharjee, "How the Downfall of One Intelligence Agent Revealed the Astonishing Depth of China's Espionage Against America," *New York Times Sunday Magazine* (March 12, 2023), p. 27.

62 See David Sanger, "U.S. Indicts 7 Tied to Iranian Unit in Cyberattacks," *New York Times* (March 25, 2016), p. A3. An important ethical issue is how far the democracies should go in using highly aggressive cyberattacks – electronic covert action – against rivals. Reportedly, U.S. intelligence agencies, operating in a joint effort with Israeli intelligence, inserted a Stuxnet virus into key Iranian computers as a means for sabotaging Tehran's nuclear weapons program. The operation is said to have wiped out about 20 percent of that nation's nuclear centrifuges. See Isabel Kershner, "Meir Dagan, Israeli Who Disrupted Iranian Nuclear Program, Dies at 81," *New York Times* (March 18, 2016), p. B15; and David E. Sanger, *Confront and Conceal: Obama's Secret Wars and Surprising Use of American Power* (New York: Crown, 2012).

63 James R. Clapper, remark, Jackson Institute for Global Affairs Discussion Forum, Yale University (Internet, October 20, 2020).

64 Paul R. Kolbe, "With Hacking, the United States Needs to Stop Playing the Victim," *New York Times* (December 23, 2020), p. A15.

65 Redmond, "The Challenges of Counterintelligence," p. 540. Mistakes in the sharing of intelligence among elements of a nation's security services is hardly limited to the United States. In the United Kingdom, for instance, its CI service (MI5) is said to have failed to share vital intelligence with local counterterrorism police who might have been able to halt the attack carried out in 2017 by a suicide bomber in Manchester, Salman Abedi. See Euan Ward, "U.K. Spy Agency Missed Chance to Stop Manchester Bombing," *New York Times* (March 3, 2023), p. A9. See also, US Government Accountability Office (GAO), *Domestic Terrorism: Further Actions*

Needed to Strengthen FBI and DHS Collaboration to Counter Threats (February 2023).

66 See the essays on CI in the following "handbooks": Johnson, ed., *Oxford Handbook of National Security Intelligence*; Loch K. Johnson, ed., *Strategic Intelligence, Vol. 4: Counterintelligence and Counterterrorism, Defending the National against Hostile Forces* (Westport, CT: Praeger, 2007); and Loch K. Johnson, ed., *Handbook of Intelligence Studies* (New York: Routledge, 2007). See also Raymond J. Batvinis, *The Origins of FBI Counterintelligence* (Lawrence: University Press of Kansas, 2007); and Theoharis, *Chasing Spies* (note 35).

67 Declassified CIA memorandum, Church Committee, p. 167.

68 Karen DeYoung and Walter Pincus, "Success Against al-Qaeda Cited," *Washington Post* (September 30, 2009), p. 1A.

69 George Tenet, public testimony, National Commission on Terrorist Attacks upon the United States (the 9/11 Commission), April 14, 2004, p. 5, cited in Zegart, *Spying Blind*, p. 113.

70 Jervis, "Intelligence, Counterintelligence, Perception, and Deception," p. 71.

71 Jervis, "Intelligence, Counterintelligence, Perception, and Deception," p. 77; see also Thaddeus Holt, *The Deceivers: Allied Military Deception in the Second World War* (New York: Scribner, 2004).

72 Duncan Campbell, "Afghan Prisoners Beaten to Death," *Guardian* (March 7, 2003), p. 1.

73 For arguments that harsh interrogation is inappropriate and yields poor results, see Loch K. Johnson, "Educing Information: Interrogation: Science and Art," *Studies in Intelligence* 51 (December 2007), pp. 43–6; William R. Johnson, "Tricks of the Trade: Counterintelligence Interrogation," *International Journal of Intelligence and Counterintelligence* 1 (1986), pp. 103–33; Mayer, *The Dark Side*; and Ali H. Soufan (an FBI interrogator), "What Torture Never Told Us," *New York Times* (September 6, 2009), p. WK 9, who refers to this approach as "ineffective, unreliable, unnecessary and destructive." As two astute observers have emphasized, the use of torture by the CIA blurred "the moral distinction between terrorists and the Americans who hunted them": Scott Shane and Mark Mazzetti, "Adopting Harsh Tactics, No Look at Past Use," *New York Times* (April 21, 2009), p. A16.

74 Quoted by Toby Harden, "CIA 'Pressure' on Al Qaeda Chief," *Washington Post* (March 6, 2003), p. A1.

75 Quoted in the *New York Times* (February 26, 1976), p. A1.

76 Raoul Berger, *Executive Privilege: A Constitutional Myth* (Cambridge, MA: Harvard University Press, 1974), pp. 7, 14.

77 403 U.S. 713, 91 S.Ct. 2140, 29 L. Ed. 2nd 822 (1971); emphasis added.

78 For example, in a remark to the author, Athens, George (July 4, 1983).

79 Author's interview with Senator Frank Church, Washington, DC (October 16, 1976); see also Church's "Which Secrets Should Be Kept Secret?"

Washington Post (March 14, 1977), p. A27. The Agee book, *Inside the Company: CIA Diary*, published by Penguin (Harmondsworth, UK) in 1975, made the author a pariah in the United States and many European democracies.

CHAPTER 6: SAFEGUARDS AGAINST THE ABUSE OF SECRET POWER

1 Author's interview with DCI James R. Schlesinger, Washington, DC (June 16, 1994).
2 *Myers* v. *United States*, 272 U.S. 52 293 (1926).
3 David M. Barrett, *The CIA and Congress: The Untold Story from Truman to Kennedy* (Lawrence: University Press of Kansas, 2005); for works that have found little meaningful accountability in these early days, see Harry Howe Ransom, *The Intelligence Establishment* (Cambridge, MA: Harvard University Press, 1970); and Jerrold L. Walden, "The CIA: A Study in the Arrogation of Administrative Power," *George Washington Law Review* 39 (January 1975), pp. 66–101. For more current accounts that continue to find Congress lacking in the department of intelligence oversight, see Kathleen Clark, "'A New Era of Openness?' Disclosing Intelligence to Congress under Obama," *Constitutional Commentary* 26 (2010), pp. 1–20; Jennifer Kibbe, "Congressional Oversight of Intelligence: Is the Solution Part of the Problem?" *Intelligence and National Security* 25 (February 2010), pp. 24–49; Anne Joseph O'Connell, "The Architecture of Smart Intelligence: Structuring and Overseeing Agencies in the post–9/11 World," *California Law Review* 94 (December 2006), pp. 1655–744; Amy B. Zegart, "The Domestic Politics of Irrational Intelligence Oversight," *Political Science Quarterly* 126 (Spring 2011), pp. 1–27; and Amy B. Zegart, with Julie Quinn, "Congressional Intelligence Oversight: The Electoral Disconnection," *Intelligence and National Security* 25 (December 2010), pp. 744–66.
4 See the reporting of Seymour Hersh in the *Times* throughout the autumn and winter months of 1974, especially on December 22.
5 Church Committee, Select Committee on Intelligence Activities, U.S. Senate, 94th Cong., 1st Sess. (September 25, 1975), as well as two special reports: *Alleged Assassination Plots Involving Foreign Leaders*, Interim Rept., S. Rept. No. 94–465 (Washington, DC: Government Printing Office, November 20, 1975); and *Covert Action in Chile, 1963–1973, Staff Report* (Washington, DC: Government Printing Office, December 18, 1975). "The Church Committee hearings remain the single most significant inquiry every undertaken by Congress into the conduct of the nation's intelligence agencies," writes Yale University historian Beverly Gage, who concludes that the inquiry "resulted in real reform": *G-Man* (New York: Knopf, 2022), p. 729. Political scientist Paul C. Light examined 100 top investigations conducted by federal lawmakers between 1945 and 2012, giving the Church Committee special praise as a model of congressional inquiry: see *Government by Investigation* (Washington, DC: Brookings Institution, 2014), p. 193. The leading works

about the committee are Loch K. Johnson, *A Season of Inquiry* (Lexington: University Press of Kentucky, 1985), republished as *A Season of Inquiry Revisited: The Church Committee Confronts America's Spy Agencies* (Lawrence: University Press of Kansas, 2015); James Risen, *The Last Honest Man* (New York: Little, Brown, 2023); Frederick A. O. Schwarz Jr., and Aziz Z. Huq, *Unchecked and Unbalanced: Presidential Power in a Time of Terror* (New York: New Press, 2007); and Frank J. Smist, Jr., *Congress Oversees the United States Intelligence Community, 1947–1989* (Knoxville, University of Tennessee Press, 1990). The Committee's chief counsel, Frederick "Fritz" A.O. Schwarz Jr., viewed the FBI as the nation's "greatest problem," for it undermined American democracy at home with its COINTELPRO activities against civil rights activists and anti-Vietnam War protestors; interview, *The Harvard Gazette* (March 3, 2023), pp. 1–5.

6 Author's interview, Minneapolis, Minnesota (February 17, 2000). See also Walter F. Mondale, *The Good Fight: A Life in Liberal Politics* (New York: Simon & Schuster, 2010), Ch. 7. In one instance, the Bureau infiltrated a perfectly benign women's group whose purpose was to "free women from their humdrum existence"; see Johnson, *A Season of Inquiry*, p. 128.

7 Henry Steele Commager, "Intelligence: The Constitution Betrayed," *New York Review of Books* (September 30, 1976), p. 32.

8 On the seven Boland Amendments, each more restrictive, see "Boland Amendments: A Review," *Congressional Quarterly Weekly Online* (May 23, 1987), p. 1043; and Henry K. Kissinger, "A Matter of Balance," *Los Angeles Times* (July 26, 1987), p. V1.

9 See Barrett, *The CIA and Congress*, p. 459.

10 Joel D. Aberbach, "What's Happened to the Watchful Eye?" *Congress & the Presidency* 29 (2002), pp. 20–3; quote at p. 20.

11 Stephen F. Knott, "The Great Republican Transformation on Oversight," *International Journal of Intelligence and Counterintelligence* 13 (2002), pp. 49–63; quote at p. 57.

12 Marvin C. Ott, "Partisanship and the Decline of Intelligence Oversight," *International Journal of Intelligence and Counterintelligence* 16 (2003), pp. 69–94; quote at p. 87.

13 See Charles Babington, "Senate Intelligence Panel Frayed by Partisan Infighting," *Washington Post* (March 12, 2006), p. A9.

14 L. Britt Snider, "Congressional Oversight of Intelligence after September 11," in Jennifer E. Sims and Burton Gerber, eds., *Transforming U.S. Intelligence* (Washington, DC: Georgetown University Press, 2005), p. 245. See, also, Snider's *The Agency and the Hill: CIA's Relationship with Congress, 1946–2004* (Washington, DC: Center for the Study of Intelligence, Central Intelligence Agency, 2008).

15 Bob Drogin, "Senator Says Spy Agencies are 'in Denial,' " *Los Angeles Times* (May 4, 2004), p. A1.

16 Kean Commission (led by former Governor Thomas H. Kean, R, New Jersey), *The 9/11 Commission: Final Report of the National Commission on Terrorist Attacks upon the United States* (New York: Norton, 2004).

17 See, respectively, Loch K. Johnson, *Secret Agencies: U.S. Intelligence in a Hostile World* (New Haven, CT: Yale University Press, 1996), p. 96; and Zegart, "The Domestic Politics of Irrational Intelligence Oversight."

18 Remarks, "Meet the Press," *NBC Television* (November 21, 2004).

19 Kean Commission, *The 9/11 Commission*, p. 420.

20 Gregory F. Treveton, *Intelligence in an Age of Terror* (New York: Cambridge University Press, 2009), p. 232.

21 Bill Gertz, *Breakdown* (Washington, DC: Regnery, 2002), p. 113.

22 On the Snowden affair, see Glenn Greenwald, *No Place to Hide: Edward Snowden, the NSA, and the U.S. Surveillance State* (New York: Metropolitan Books, 2014).

23 Quoted in Ken Dilanian, "NSA Weighed Ending Phone Program Before Leak," *Associated Press* (March 30, 2015).

24 Quoted in Darren Samuelsohn, "Hill Draws Criticism over NSA Oversight," *Politico* (March 2, 2014), p. 2.

25 Paul J. Quirk and William Bendix, "Secrecy and Negligence: How Congress Lost Control of Domestic Surveillance," *Issues in Governance Studies*, Brookings Institution, Washington, DC (March 2, 2015), pp. 9, 13.

26 The formal name of the panel is the President's Review Group on Intelligence and Communications Technologies, which urged that as a "central aspect of liberty" privacy must be protected; *Liberty and Security in a Changing World*, U.S. Government Printing Office, Washington, DC (December 12, 2013), p. 47.

27 Jack Goldsmith, "United States of Secrets (Part One): The Program," Transcript, *Nightline*, PBS Television (May 2015), p. 16.

28 See, respectively: Jennifer Steinhauer, "Senate Is Sharply Split Over Extension of NSA Phone Data Collection," *New York Times* (May 22, 2015), p. A15; and unsigned editorial, "Rand Paul's Timely Takedown on the Patriot Act," *New York Times* (May 22, 2015), p. A24.

29 Jonathan Weisman and Jennifer Steinhauer, "Patriot Act Faces Curbs Supported by Both Parties," *New York Times* (May 1, 2015), p. A1.

30 Jennifer Steinhauer, "Senate to Try Again Next Week after Bill on Phone Records Is Blocked," *New York Times* (May 24, 2015), p. A14.

31 Charlie Savage, "Surveillance Court Rules that NSA can Resume Bulk Data Collection," *New York Times* (July 1, 2015), p. A14.

32 Lawrence Wright, "The Al Qaeda Switchboard," Comment, *The New Yorker* (January 13, 2014), p. 3.

33 For a chronology of the torture program, see Wilson Andrews and Alicia Parlapiano, "A History of the CIA's Secret Interrogation Program," *New York Times* (December 9, 2014).

34 Jane Mayer, "Torture and the Truth," *The New Yorker* (December 22, 2014). A columnist remembered in 2023 that her newspaper had referred to the Torture Report when it was finally released as "a portrait of depravity": Maureen Dowd, "DiFi, Breaking into the Boys's Club," *New York Times* (October 1, 2023): SR3.

35 Steven Aftergood, "CIA Torture Report: Oversight, but No Remedies Yet," *Secrecy News*, 2014/83 (December 10, 2014), p. 2.

36 A high-ranking HPSCI member remembers urging the CIA, in a letter to the Agency's General Counsel (Scott Muller) in 2003, not to destroy the interrogation videotapes; see Jane Harman (D, California), "America's Spy Agencies Need an Upgrade," *Foreign Affairs* (March/April 2015), p. 103.

37 Senator Dianne Feinstein, "Dianne Feinstein: The CIA 'Cannot Shove the Laws Aside,'" *Nightline*.

38 Feinstein, "Dianne Feinstein."

39 Dianne Feinstein, remarks concerning the *Committee Study of the Central Intelligence Agency's Detention and Interrogation Program*, Senate Select Committee on Intelligence, U.S. Senate, 113th Cong., 2d Sess. (December 3, 2014; hereafter the *Senate Torture Report*), U.S. Senate floor (December 9, 2014).

40 Senator Chambliss retired from the Congress soon after the release of the torture report; he became a member of the CIA's Advisory Board.

41 *Senate Torture Report*, Findings and Conclusions Section, p. 3. For a series of thoughtful essays on the Report, see Mark Phythian, editor, "An INS Special Forum: The US Senate Select Committee Report on the CIA's Detention and Interrogation Program," *Intelligence and National Security* 31/1 (January 2016), pp. 8–27.

42 See Adam Goldman, "Military Prosecutor: Senate Report on CIA Interrogation Program is Accurate," *Washington Post* (February 10, 2016), p. A1.

43 See remark to Eric Bradner, "John Brennan Defends CIA," *CNN Politics* (December 12, 2014); and John Brennan, Letter to the Editor, *Washington Post* (October 14, 2023). My thanks to William E. Jackson for bringing this letter to my attention.

44 President Barack Obama, Statement, White House (December 9, 2014).

45 Feinstein, "Dianne Feinstein," p. 4.

46 Quoted by Connie Bruck, "The Inside War," *The New Yorker* (June 22, 2015), p. 45.

47 Quoted anonymously by Jeremy Herb in *The Hill* (March 6, 2014), p. 11.

48 Bruck, "The Inside War," p. 46.

49 Bruck, "The Inside War," p. 48.

50 See Mark Mazzetti and Matt Apuzzo, "CIA Officers Are Cleared in Senate Computer Search," *New York Times* (January 15, 2015), p. A8.

51 Remarks to the Senate (December 9, 2014), cited by James P. Pfiffner in Phythian, ed., "INS Special Forum," p. 23.

52 George J. Tenet, et al., "Ex-CIA Directors: Interrogations Saved Lives," *Wall Street Journal* (December 10, 2014).

53 David Ignatius, "The Torture Report's One Glaring Weakness," *Washington Post* (December 11, 2014). A senior CIA official has argued that when it came to keeping lawmakers informed about the interrogation program, their claim to have been misled is "farcical, not true. I can tell you, I had difficulty getting on the calendars of senators I wanted to brief. Their ardor for the truth is greater now than it was then, in some cases"; interview with Robert Grenier, former CIA/ CTC Director, 2004-2006, *News Hour*, PBS Television (December 9, 2014).

54 Michael Glennon, Fletcher School of Law and Diplomacy, remarks, Levin Center Conference on Intelligence Accountability, U.S. Senate (October 20, 2015).

55 See Amy Zegart, "INS Special Forum," in Phythian, ed., "An INS Special Forum," p. 25. The denials of normative bias in the report were expressed during the Levin Center Conference by the leading Democratic staffer.

56 Dianne Feinstein, "NSA's Watchfulness Protects America," *Wall Street Journal* (October 13, 2013). In a Senate hearing, Feinstein spoke in support of the NSA metadata collection, ruing "how little information" the United States had about Al Qaeda before the 9/11 attacks. "They will come after us," she said, "and I think we need to prevent an attack wherever we can"; Mattathias Schwartz, "Who Can Control NSA Surveillance?" *The New Yorker* (January 23, 2015).

57 Feinstein, "Dianne Feinstein," p. 6.

58 Statement, U.S. Senate floor (December 9, 2014), cited by Professor Pfiffner in "INS Special Forum," p. 23. McCain, a former GOP presidential nominee, said elsewhere that he "totally agree[d] with the report"; quoted by Matt Sledge and Michael McAuliff, "CIA Torture Report Approved by Senate Intelligence Committee," *Huffington Post* (October 13, 2012). Even D/CIA Brennan eventually ended up speaking out against the use of waterboarding in the future, declaring that "as long as I'm director of CIA, irrespective of what the president says, I'm not going to be the director of CIA that gives that order. They'll have to find another director"; John Brennan, public remarks, Brookings Institution, Washington, DC (July 13, 2016).

59 Harry H. Ransom, "Secret Intelligence Agencies and Congress," *Society* 123 (1975), pp. 33–6; quote at p. 38.

60 See, for example, Joel D. Aberbach, *Keeping a Watchful Eye: The Politics of Congressional Oversight* (Washington, DC: The Brookings Institution, 1990); Christopher J. Deering, "Alarms and Patrols: Legislative Oversight in Foreign and Defense Policy," in Colton C. Campbell, Nicol C. Rae, and John F. Stack, Jr., *Congress and the Politics of Foreign Policy* (Upper Saddle River, NJ: Prentice-Hall, 2003), pp. 112–38.

61 David Mayhew, *The Electoral Connection* (New Haven, CT: Yale University Press, 1974).

62 Matthew D. McCubbins and Thomas Schwartz, "Congressional Oversight Overlooked: Police Patrols and Fire Alarms," *American Journal of Political Science* 28 (1984), pp. 165–79.

63 Quoted by Philip Shenon, "As New 'Cop on the Beat,' Congressman Starts Patrol," *New York Times* (February 6, 2007), p. A18.

64 See Loch K. Johnson, John C. Kuzenski, and Erna Gellner, "The Study of Congressional Investigations: Research Strategies," *Congress & the Presidency* 19 (Autumn 1992), pp. 138–56.

65 See Johnson, *A Season of Inquiry Revisited*; and Schwarz and Huq, *Unchecked and Unbalanced*.

66 U.S. Congress, *Report of the Congressional Committees Investigating the Iran–Contra Affair*, U.S. Senate Select Committee on Secret Military Assistance to Iran and the Nicaraguan Opposition and U.S. House of Representatives Select Committee to Investigate Covert Arms Transactions with Iran, S. Rept. 100–216 and House Rept. 100–433, 100th Cong., 1st Sess. (November 1987), chaired by Daniel K. Inouye (D, Hawaii) and Representative Lee H. Hamilton (D, Indiana).

67 *Preparing for the 21st Century: An Appraisal of U.S. Intelligence*, Report of the Commission on the Roles and Capabilities of the United States Intelligence Community (the Aspin–Brown Commission) (Washington, DC: Government Printing Office, March 1, 1996).

68 Joint Inquiry into Intelligence Community Activities before and after the Terrorist Attacks of September 11, 2001, *Final Report*, U.S. Senate Select Committee on Intelligence and U.S. House Permanent Select Committee on Intelligence, led respectively by Senator Bob Graham (D, Florida) and Representative Porter J. Goss (R, Florida), Washington, DC: December 2002; and the Kean Commission, *The 9/11 Commission*.

69 *Intelligence Authorization Act for Fiscal Year 2005*, Report 108–558, Permanent Select Committee on Intelligence (the Goss Committee), U.S. House of Representatives, 108th Cong., 2nd Sess. (June 21, 2004), pp. 23–7.

70 *Report of the Commission on the Intelligence Capabilities of the United States Regarding Weapons of Mass Destruction*, led by Judge Laurence H. Silberman and former Senator Charles S. Robb (D, Virginia).

71 Report on the U.S. Intelligence Community's Prewar Intelligence Assessments on Iraq (the Roberts Report), Senate Select Committee on Intelligence (the Roberts Committee), U.S. Senate, 108th Cong., 2nd Sess. (July 7, 2003).

72 See Alfred Cumming, "Sensitive Covert Action Notifications: Oversight Options for Congress," *CRS Report for Congress*, Congressional Research Service (July 7, 2009), pp. 1–12.

73 Cited by intelligence scholar Harry Howe Ransom, "Congress, Legitimacy and the Intelligence Community," paper, Western Political Science Association, Annual Convention, San Francisco, California (April 20, 1976).

74 Quoted by Tom Braden, "What's Wrong with the CIA?" *Saturday Review* (April 5, 1975), p. 14.

75 While serving as D/CIA, Leon E. Panetta, said: "I do not want to just do a Gang of Four briefing – in other words, just inform the leaders of the party. My view is, and I said this at my confirmation hearings, I think it's very important to inform all the members of the Intelligence Committees about what's going on when we have to provide notification"; remarks during Q&A, Pacific Council on International Policy, California (May 18, 2009).

76 Mike Soraghan, "Reyes Backs Pelosi on Intel Briefings," *The Hill* (May 1, 2009), p. 1.

77 *Congressional Quarterly Almanac*, vol. XLVII, 102nd Cong., 1st Sess. (1991), p. 482.

78 See David M. Barrett, "Congressional Oversight of the CIA in the Early Cold War, 1947–1963," in Loch K. Johnson, ed., *Strategic Intelligence, Vol. 5: Safeguards against the Abuse of Secret Power* (Westport, CT: Praeger, 2007), pp. 1–18; Loch K. Johnson, *America's Secret Power: The CIA in a Democratic Society* (New York: Oxford University Press, 1989); and Ransom, The Intelligence Establishment.

79 On the frequency and seriousness with which intelligence officers are questioned by lawmakers in public hearings, see Loch K. Johnson, "Playing Ball with the CIA: Congress Supervises Strategic Intelligence," in Paul E. Peterson, ed., *The President, the Congress, and the Making of American Foreign Policy* (Norman: University of Oklahoma Press, 1994), pp. 49–73.

80 Daniel Patrick Moynihan, "Do We Still Need the CIA? The State Dept. Can Do the Job," *New York Times* (May 19, 1991), p. E17.

81 Quoted by Ann Davis, "GOP-Controlled Senate Expected to Give Less Scrutiny to War on Terror," *Miami Herald* (November 7, 2002), p. A1.

82 Interviewed by Cynthia Nolan, Washington, DC (October 15, 2003), "More Perfect Oversight: Intelligence Oversight and Reform," in Johnson, ed., *Strategic Intelligence*, Vol. 5; quote at pp. 126–7.

83 Author's conversation with William J. Casey, CIA, Langley, VA (June 11, 1984).

84 The letter was dated April 9, 1984; Letters to the Editor, *Washington Post* (April 11, 1984), p. A17.

85 Robert M. Gates, *From the Shadows* (New York: Simon & Schuster, 1996), p. 559.

CHAPTER 7: NATIONAL SECURITY INTELLIGENCE: HIDDEN SHIELD AND SWORD OF THE DEMOCRACIES

1 This point is well made by David Kahn, "The Rise of Intelligence," *Foreign Affairs* 85 (September/October 2006), pp. 125–34; and John Keegan, *Intelligence in War: Knowledge of the Enemy from Napoleon to Al-Qaeda* (New York: Random House, 2003).

2 On the virtues of soft power, see Joseph S. Nye, Jr., *Soft Power: The Means to Success in World Politics* (New York: Public Affairs, 2004); and on public diplomacy, Kristin M. Lord, *Voices of America: U.S. Public Diplomacy for the 21st Century* (Washington, DC: Brookings Institution, November 2008). On the strengthening of American foreign policy across the board, see Loch K. Johnson, *American Foreign Policy and the Challenges of World Leadership: Power, Principle, and the Constitution* (New York: Oxford University Press, 2015).

3 See Business Executives for National Security (BENS), *Domestic Security: Confronting a Changing Threat to Ensure Public Safety and Civil Liberties* (Washington, DC, February 2015, and February 2016 update).

4 This successful experiment in liaison relationships between an intelligence agency and a policy agency is discussed in Loch K. Johnson, "Analysis for a New Age," *Intelligence and National Security* 11 (October 1996), pp. 657–71.

5 Barton Gellman, "U.S. Spied on Iraqi Military via U.N.," *Washington Post* (March 2, 1999), p. A1; Loch K. Johnson, *Bombs, Bugs, Drugs, and Thugs: Intelligence and America's Quest for Security* (New York: New York University Press, 2000), pp. 170–1.

6 Matthew Aid, expert on the NSA, comment, "Panel on Security Intelligence, and the Internet," CASIS (Canadian Association of Security and Intelligence Studies) International Conference, Ottawa, Canada (2009, author's notes).

7 Loch K. Johnson, *The Third Option: Covert Action and American Foreign Policy* (New York: Oxford University Press, 2022; paperback, 2024).

8 For Clapper's reflections on these disputes, see James R. Clapper, *Facts and Fears: Hard Truths from a Life in Intelligence* (New York: Viking, 2018), pp. 362, 379–80. On President Trump's dealing with the IC, see Loch K. Johnson, "The National Security State Gone Awry: Returning to First Principles," in Karen J. Greenberg, ed., *Reimaging the National Security State* (New York: Cambridge University Press, 2020), pp. 37–70. See also Special Counsel Robert S. Mueller, III, *Report on the Investigation into Russian Interference in the 2016 Presidential* (the Mueller Report) (Washington, DC, 2019); and *Russian Active Measures Campaign and Interference in the 2016 U.S. Election, Senate Report 116-290*, Senate Select Committee on Intelligence (SSCI), U.S. Senate, 116th Cong., 2d Sess., Government Printing Office, Washington, DC (November 10, 2020).

9 Connie Bruck, "The Guantanamo Failure," *The New Yorker* (August 1, 2016), p. 34. When he served as D/CIA, Mike Pompeo enthusiastically supported

the President's no-holds-barred approach. "The CIA, to be successful," he argued, "must be aggressive, vicious, unforgiving, relentless"; speech, 2017, cited in Luke Mogelson, "The Afghan Way of Death," *The New Yorker* (October 28, 2019), p. 43.

10 Quoted in Adam Entous and Evan Osno, "Last Man Standing," *The New Yorker* (February 10, 2020), p. 43. See also "A Discussion with John O. Brennan," Center on National Security, Fordham University (January 30, 2020). Brennan served as D/CIA from 2013 to 2018; and Luca Trenta, *The President's Kill List: Assassination and US Foreign Policy since 1945* (Edinburgh: Edinburgh University Press, 2024).

11 Loch K. Johnson, "The Show Trial of the Century?" *New Lines Magazine* (December 14, 2022), pp. 1–7.

12 Loch K. Johnson, *The Threat on the Horizon* (New York: Oxford University Press, 2011), p. 93.

Appendix

Intelligence leadership in the United States, 1946–2024

Directors, National Intelligence (DNI)

2005–7	Amb. (ret.) John D. Negroponte
2007–9	Gen. (ret.) J. M. "Mike" McConnell
2009–10	Adm. (ret.) Dennis C. Blair
2010–17	Gen. (ret.) James R. Clapper, Jr.
2017–19	Dan Coates
2019–20	Joseph Maguire (Acting)
2020–1	John Ratcliffe
2021–	Avril D. Haines

Directors, Central Intelligence (DCI), an office terminated in 2004

1946	Adm. Sidney William Souers
1946–7	Lt. Gen. Hoyt Sanford Vandenberg
1947–50	Rear Adm. Roscoe H. Hillenkoetter
1950–3	Gen. Walter Bedell Smith
1953–61	Allen W. Dulles
1961–5	John A. McCone
1965–6	Vice Adm. William F. Raborn, Jr.
1966–73	Richard Helms
1973	James R. Schlesinger
1973–6	William E. Colby
1976–7	George H.W. Bush
1977–81	Adm. Stansfield Turner
1981–7	William J. Casey
1987–91	William H. Webster
1991–3	Robert M. Gates
1993–5	R. James Woolsey
1995–7	John M. Deutch
1997–2004	George J. Tenet
2004	Porter J. Goss [the last DCI]

Directors, Central Intelligence Agency (D/CIA)

2005–6	Porter J. Goss
2006–9	Gen. Michael Hayden
2009–11	Leon Panetta
2011–13	Gen. David Petraeus
2013–18	John Brennan
2018–21	Gina Haspel
2021–	William J. Burns

Chairs, Senate Select Committee on Intelligence (SSCI)

1976–7	Daniel K. Inouye, Democrat, Hawaii
1977–81	Birch Bayh, Democrat, Indiana
1981–5	Barry Goldwater, Republican, Arizona
1985–7	David Durenberger, Republican, Minnesota
1987–93	David L. Boren, Democrat, Oklahoma
1993–5	Dennis DeConcini, Democrat, Arizona
1995–7	Arlen Specter, Republican, Pennsylvania
1997–2001	Richard C. Shelby, Republican, Alabama
2001–3	Bob Graham, Democrat, Florida
2003–6	Pat Roberts, Republican, Kansas
2007–8	John D. Rockefeller IV, Democrat, West Virginia
2009–14	Dianne Feinstein, Democrat, California
2015–20	Richard M. Burr, Republican, North Carolina
2020–21	Marco Rubio, Republican, Florida
2021–	Mark Warner, Democrat, Virginia

Chairs, House Permanent Select Committee on Intelligence (HPSCI)

1977–85	Edward P. Boland, Democrat, Massachusetts
1985–7	Lee H. Hamilton, Democrat, Indiana
1987–9	Louis Stokes, Democrat, Ohio
1989–91	Anthony C. Beilenson, Democrat, California
1991–3	Dave McCurdy, Democrat, Oklahoma
1993–5	Dan Glickman, Democrat, Kansas
1995–7	Larry Combest, Republican, Texas
1997–2004	Porter J. Goss, Republican, Florida
2004–6	Peter Hoekstra, Republican, Michigan
2006–11	Silvestre Reyes, Democrat, Texas
2011–14	Mike Rogers, Republican, Michigan
2015–19	Devin Nunes, Republican, California
2019–23	Adam Schiff, Democrat, California
2023–	Michael R. Turner, Republican, Ohio

Suggested Readings

Aid, M.A. *The Secret Sentry: The Untold History of the National Security Agency.* New York: Bloomsbury, 2009.

Aldrich, R.J. *The Hidden Hand: Britain, America and Cold War Secret Intelligence, 1945–1964.* London: John Murray, 2001.

Aldrich, R.J., and Cormac, R. *The Back Door: Spies, Secret Intelligence and British Prime Ministers.* New York: HarperCollins, 2017.

Allen, M. *Blinking Red: Crisis and Compromise in American Intelligence after 9/11.* Washington, DC: Potomac Books, 2013.

Andrew, C. *For the President's Eyes Only.* New York: HarperCollins, 1996.

Andrew, C. *The Secret World: A History of Intelligence.* New York: Penguin, 2018.

Aspin–Brown Commission. *Preparing for the 21st Century: Appraisal of U.S. Intelligence, Report of the Commission on the Roles and Capabilities of the United States Intelligence Community.* Washington, DC: Government Printing Office, March 1, 1996.

Bar-Joseph, U., and McDermott, R. *Intelligence Successes and Failures: The Human Factor.* New York: Oxford University Press, 2019.

Barrett, D.M. *The CIA and Congress: The Untold Story from Truman to Kennedy.* Lawrence: University Press of Kansas, 2005.

Batvinis, R.J. *The Origins of FBI Counterintelligence.* Lawrence: University Press of Kansas, 2007.

Betts, R.K. "Analysis, War and Decision: Why Intelligence Failures Are Inevitable," *World Politics* 31 (1978), pp. 61–89.

Betts, R.K. *Enemies of Intelligence: Knowledge and Power in American National Security.* New York: Columbia University Press, 2007.

Born, H., Johnson, L.K., and Leigh, I., eds. *Who's Watching the Spies? Establishing Intelligence Service Accountability.* Washington, DC: Potomac Books, 2005.

Brantly, A.F. *The Decision to Attack Military and Intelligence Cyber Decision-Making.* Athens: University of Georgia Press, 2016.

Brantly, A.F., and Van Puyvelde, D. *Cybersecurity: An Introduction.* Cambridge: Polity, 2018.

Byrne, M. *Iran–Contra: Reagan's Scandal and the Unchecked Abuse of Presidential Power.* Lawrence: University Press of Kansas, 2014.

Caddell, J.W. Jr. "Corona over Cuba: The Missile Crisis and the Early Limitations of Satellite Intelligence," *Intelligence and National Security* 31/3 (2016), pp. 416–38.

Chesney, R., and Smeets, M., eds. *Deter, Disrupt, or Deceive: Assessing Cyber Conflict as an Intelligence Contest.* Washington, DC: Georgetown University Press, 2023.

Church Committee. *Alleged Assassination Plots Involving Foreign Leaders: An Interim Report.* S. Rept. No. 94-465. Washington, DC: U.S. Government Printing Office, November 20, 1975.

Church Committee. *Final Report. Select Committee to Study Governmental Operations with Respect to Intelligence Activities.* U.S. Senate, 94th Cong., 2nd. Sess., 1976.

Clapper, J.R., with T. Brown. *Facts and Fears: Hard Truths from a Life in Intelligence.* New York: Viking, 2018.

Clark, R.M. *The Technical Collection of Intelligence.* Washington, DC: CQ Press, 2011.

Clarke, R.A. *Against All Enemies: Inside America's War on Terror.* New York: Free Press, 2004.

Cohen, W.S., and Mitchell, G.J. *Men of Zeal.* New York: Penguin Press, 1988.

Colby, W.E., and Forbath, P. *Honorable Men: My Life in the CIA.* New York: Simon & Schuster, 1978.

Coll, S. *Ghost Wars.* New York: Penguin Press, 2004.

Coll, S. *Directorate S: The C.I.A.'s Secret Wars in Afghanistan and Pakistan.* New York: Penguin, 2018.

Corke, S.-J. *US Covert Operations and Cold War Strategy: Truman, Secret Warfare, and the CIA, 1945–1953.* New York: Routledge, 2008.

Cradock, P. *Know Your Enemy.* London: John Murray, 2002.

Crumpton, H.A. *The Art of Intelligence: Lessons from a Life in the CIA's Clandestine Service.* New York: Penguin, 2012.

Cunliffe, K.S. "Hard Target Espionage in the Information Era: New Challenges for the Second Oldest Profession," *Intelligence and National Security* 36/7 (July 2021), pp. 1018–39.

Daugherty, W.J. *Executive Secrets: Covert Action and the Presidency.* Lexington: University Press of Kentucky, 2004.

Dorn, A.W., and Webb, S. "Cyberpeacekeeping: New Ways to Prevent and Manage Cyberattacks," *International Journal of Cyber Warfare and Terrorism* 9/1 (2019).

Dylan, H., Gioe, D., and Goodman, M.S. *The CIA and the Pursuit of Security.* Edinburgh: Edinburgh University Press, 2020.

Elias, B. *Why Allies Rebel: Defiant Local Partners in Counterinsurgency Wars.* Cambridge: Cambridge University Press, 2020.

Farson, A.S., Stafford, D., and Wark, W., eds. *Security and Intelligence in a Changing World.* London: Frank Cass, 1991.

Ferris, J. *Behind the Enigma: The Authorised History of Britain's Cyber Security Agency.* New York: Bloomsbury, 2020.

Fisher, L. *The Constitution and 9/11: Recurring Threats to America's Freedoms.* Lawrence: University Press of Kansas, 2008.

Ford, H.P. *Estimative Intelligence: The Purposes and Problems of National Intelligence Estimating.* Lanham, MD: University Press of America, 1993.

Freedman, L. "The CIA and the Soviet Threat: The Politicization of Estimates, 1966–1977," *Intelligence and National Security* 12 (January 1997), pp. 122–42.

Gage, B. *G-Man: J. Edgar Hoover and the Making of the American Century.* New York: Viking, 2022.

Garthoff, D.F. *Directors of Central Intelligence as Leaders of the U.S. Intelligence Community, 1946–2005.* Washington, DC: Center for the Study of Intelligence, CIA, 2005.

Garthoff, R.L. *Soviet Leaders and Intelligence: Assessing the American Adversary during the Cold War.* Washington, DC: Georgetown University Press, 2015.

Gates, R.M. "The CIA and American Foreign Policy," *Foreign Affairs* 66 (Winter 1987–88), pp. 215–30.

Gates, R.M. *From the Shadows.* New York: Simon & Schuster, 1996.

Gentry, J.A. *Influence Operations of China, Russia, and the Soviet Union: A Comparison.* Occasional Paper 3/5 (May 2023).

Gill, P., and Phythian, M. *Intelligence in an Insecure World*, 2nd edn. Cambridge: Polity, 2012.

Gill, P., Marrin, S., and Phythian, M., eds. *Intelligence Theory.* London: Routledge, 2009.

Gioe, D.V., Goodman, M.S., and Frey, D.S. "Unforgiven: Russian Intelligence Vengeance as Political Theater and Strategic Messaging," *Intelligence and National Security* 34/4 (2019), pp. 561–75.

Glennon, M.J. *National Security and Double Government.* New York: Oxford University Press, 2015.

Goldman, J. *Ethical Espionage: Ethics and the Intelligence Cycle.* Boulder, CO: Lynne Rienner, 2024.

Goldsmith, J. *The Terror Presidency.* New York: Norton, 2007.

Goodman, M.S. *Spying on the Nuclear Bear: Anglo-American Intelligence and the Soviet Bomb.* Stanford, CA: Stanford University Press, 2007.

Graham, B., with Nussbaum, J. *Intelligence Matters: The CIA, the FBI, Saudi Arabia, and the Failure of America's War on Terror.* Lawrence: University Press of Kansas, 2008.

Greenberg, K.J. *Rogue Justice: The Making of the Security State.* New York: Crown, 2016.

Greenwald, G. *No Place to Hide: Edward Snowden, the NSA, and the U.S. Surveillance State.* New York: Henry Holt, 2014.

Hadley, D.P. *The Growing Clamor: The American Press, the Central Intelligence Agency, and the Cold War.* Lexington: University Press of Kentucky, 2019.

Hamilton–Inouye Committee. *Report of the Congressional Committees Investigating the Iran–Contra Affair.* U.S. Senate Select Committee on Secret

Military Assistance to Iran and the Nicaraguan Opposition, U.S. House of Representatives Select Committee to Investigate Covert Arms Transactions with Iran, S. Rept. 100–216 and H. Rept. 100–433, 100th Cong., 1st Sess. (November 1987).

Hannas, W.C., Mulvenon J., and Puglisi, A.B. *Chinese Industrial Espionage*. New York: Routledge, 2013.

Hastedt, G. *Espionage: A Reference Handbook*. New York: Bloomsbury, 2003.

Hayden, M.V. *Playing to the Edge: American Intelligence in the Age of Terror*. New York: Random House, 2016.

Haynes, J.E., and Klehr, H. *Verona: Decoding Soviet Espionage in America*. New Haven, CT: Yale University Press, 1999.

Haynes, J.E., Klehr, H., and Vassiliev, A. *Spies: The Rise and Fall of the KGB in America*. New Haven, CT: Yale University Press, 2010.

Helms, R.M., with Hood, W. *A Look Over My Shoulder: A Life in the Central Intelligence Agency*. New York: Random House, 2003.

Herman, M. *Intelligence Power in Peace and War*. Cambridge: Cambridge University Press, 1996.

Hitz, F. *The Great Game: The Myth and Reality of Espionage*. New York: Knopf, 2004.

Hughes, T.L. "The Power to Speak and the Power to Listen: Reflections in Bureaucratic Politics and a Recommendation on Information Flows," in T. Franck and W. Weisband, eds., *Secrecy and Foreign Policy*. New York: Oxford University Press, 1974, pp. 13–41.

Hughes, T.L. *The Fate of Facts in a World of Men: Foreign Policy and Intelligence-Making*, Headline Series, No. 233. Washington, DC: Foreign Policy Association, 1976.

Hulnick, A.S. *Fixing the Spy Machine: Preparing American Intelligence for the Twenty-First Century*. Westport, CT: Praeger, 1999.

Immerman, R.H. *The CIA in Guatemala: The Foreign Policy of Intervention*. Austin: University of Texas Press, 1982.

Inderfurth, K.F., and Johnson, L.K., eds. *Fateful Decisions: Inside the National Security Council*. New York: Oxford University Press, 2004.

Jackson, P., and Scott, L. *Understanding Intelligence in the Twenty-First Century*. New York: Routledge, 2004.

Jeffreys-Jones, R. *The CIA and American Democracy*. New Haven, CT: Yale University Press, 1989.

Jeffreys-Jones, R. *In Spies We Trust: The Story of Western Intelligence*. New York: Oxford University Press, 2013.

Jeffreys-Jones, R. *A Question of Standing: The History of the CIA*. New York: Oxford University Press, 2022.

Jervis, R. *Why Intelligence Fails: Lessons from the Iranian Revolution and the Iraq War*. Ithaca, NY: Cornell University Press, 2010.

Johnson, L.K. *A Season of Inquiry: The Senate Intelligence Investigation*. Lexington: University Press of Kentucky, 1985.

Johnson, L.K. *America's Secret Power: The CIA in a Democratic Society.* New York: Oxford University Press, 1989.

Johnson, L.K., ed. *Handbook of Intelligence Studies.* New York: Routledge, 2007.

Johnson, L.K., ed. *Strategic Intelligence,* 5 vols. Westport, CT: Praeger, 2007.

Johnson, L.K., ed. *The Oxford Handbook of National Security Intelligence.* New York: Oxford University Press, 2010.

Johnson, L.K., ed. *Intelligence: Critical Concepts in Military, Strategic & Security Studies,* vols. I–IV. New York: Routledge, 2011.

Johnson, L.K. *The Threat on the Horizon: An Inside Account of America's Search for Security after the Cold War.* New York: Oxford University Press, 2011.

Johnson, L.K., ed. *Essentials of Strategic Intelligence.* Santa Barbara, CA: ABC-CLIO/Praeger, 2015.

Johnson, L.K. *Spy Watching: Intelligence Accountability in the United States.* New York: Oxford University Press, 2018.

Johnson, L.K. *The Third Option: Covert Action and American Foreign Policy.* New York: Oxford University Press, 2022.

Johnson, L.K., and Wirtz, J.J., eds. *Intelligence: The Secret World of Spies,* 6th edn. New York: Oxford University Press, 2023.

Johnston, J.H. *Murder, Inc.: The CIA Under John Kennedy.* Lincoln: University of Nebraska Press, 2019.

Jones, D.M., and Smith, M.L.R., eds. *Handbook of Terrorism and Counter Terrorism Post 9/11.* Cheltenham, UK: Elgar, 2019.

Jones, S.G. *A Covert Action: Reagan, the CIA, and the Cold War Struggle in Poland.* New York: Norton, 2018.

Kaag, J., and Kreps, S. *Drone Warfare.* Cambridge: Polity, 2014.

Kahn, D. *The Codebreakers: The Story of Secret Writing.* New York: Macmillan, 1967.

Kibbe, J.D. "The Rise of the Shadow Warriors," *Foreign Affairs* 83 (2004), pp. 102–15.

Kibbe, J.D. "Congressional Oversight of Intelligence: Is the Solution Part of the Problem?" *Intelligence and National Security* 25 (February 2010), pp. 24–49.

Kinzer, S. *Overthrow: America's Century of Regime Change from Hawaii to Iraq.* New York: Times Books, 2013.

Kinzer, S. *Poisoner in Chief: Sidney Gottlieb and the CIA Search for Mind Control.* New York: Henry Holt, 2019.

Krieger, W. *German Intelligence History.* New York: Routledge, 2004.

Lowenthal, M.M. *U.S. Intelligence: Evolution and Anatomy,* 2nd edn. Westport, CT: Praeger, 2015.

Lowenthal, M.M. *Intelligence: From Secrets to Policy,* 8th edn. Washington, DC: CQ Press, 2020.

Lowenthal, M.M., and Clark, R.M., eds. *The 5 Disciplines of Intelligence Collection.* Los Angeles: Sage/CQ, 2016.

Lubin, A. *The International Law of Intelligence: The World of Spycraft and the Law of Nations*. New York: Oxford University Press, 2024.

MacEachin, D.J. *CIA Assessments of the Soviet Union: The Record vs. the Charges*. Langley, VA: Center for the Study of Intelligence, CIA, 1996.

Macrakis, K. *Prisoners, Lovers, & Spies: The Story of Invisible Ink from Herodotus to al-Qaeda*. New Haven, CT: Yale University Press, 2014.

Mangold, T. *Cold Warrior: James Jesus Angleton, the CIA's Master Spy Hunter*. New York: Simon & Schuster, 1991.

Manosevitz, J. U. "The Intelligence Politics of Early Congressional Oversight of the CIA," *Intelligence and National Security* 38 (August 2023), pp. 706–25.

Marrin, S. "Evaluating the Quality of Intelligence Analysis: By What (Mis) Measure," *Intelligence and National Security* 27 (December 2012), pp. 896–912.

Martin, D. *Wilderness of Mirrors*. New York: Harper & Row, 1980.

Maschmeyer, L. *Subversion: From Covert Operations to Cyber Conflict*. New York: Oxford University Press, 2024.

Masterman, J.C. *The Double-Cross System in the War of 1939 to 1945*. New Haven, CT: Yale University Press, 1972.

Mazzetti, M. *The Way of the Knife: The CIA, a Secret Army, and a War at the Ends of the Earth*. New York: Penguin, 2013.

Miller, R.A., ed. *US National Security, Intelligence and Democracy: From the Church Committee to the War on Terror*. New York: Routledge, 2008.

Millis, J.L. "Our Spying Success Is No Secret," Letter to the Editor, *New York Times* (October 12, 1994).

Mondale, W.F., Stein, R.A., and Fisher, C. "No Longer a Neutral Magistrate: The Foreign Intelligence Surveillance Court in the Wake of the War on Terror," *Minnesota Law Review* 100/6 (June 2016), pp. 2251–312.

Moran, C. *Company Confessions: Revealing CIA Secrets*. London: Biteback, 2015.

Nolte, W. "Keeping Pace with the Revolution in Military Affairs," *Studies in Intelligence* 48 (2004), pp. 1–10.

Nye, J.S., Jr. "Peering into the Future," *Foreign Affairs* 77 (July/August 1994), pp. 82–93.

Omand, D. *How Spies Think: 10 Lessons in Intelligence*. New York: Viking, 2020.

Omand, D., and Phythian, M. *Principled Spying: The Ethics of Secret Intelligence*. Washington, DC: Georgetown University Press, 2018.

Pallitto, R.M., and Weaver, W.G. *Presidential Secrecy and the Law*. Baltimore, MD: Johns Hopkins University Press, 2007.

Phythian, M., ed. *Understanding the Intelligence Cycle*. New York: Routledge, 2013.

Phythian, M., ed. "An *INS* Special Forum: The US Senate Select Committee Report on the CIA's Detention and Interrogation Program," *Intelligence and National Security* 31/1 (January 2016), pp. 8–27.

Phythian, M., and Gill, P. *Intelligence in an Insecure World*, 2nd edn. London: Routledge, 2012.

Pillar, P.R. *Intelligence and U.S. Foreign Policy: Iraq, 9/11, and Misguided Reform.* New York: Columbia University Press, 2011.

Posner, R.A. *Not a Suicide Pact: The Constitution in a Time of National Emergency.* New York: Oxford University Press, 2009.

Powers, T. *The Man Who Kept the Secrets: Richard Helms and the CIA.* New York: Knopf, 1979.

Poznansky, M. *In the Shadow of International Law: Covert Action in the Postwar World.* New York: Oxford University Press, 2020.

Prados, J. *Safe for Democracy: The Secret Wars of the CIA.* Chicago, IL: Ivan R. Dee, 2007.

Ranelagh, J. *The Agency: The Rise and Decline of the CIA*, rev. edn. New York: Simon & Schuster, 1987.

Ransom, H.H. *The Intelligence Establishment.* Cambridge, MA: Harvard University Press, 1970.

Ransom, H.H. "Don't Make the C.I.A. a K.G.B," *New York Times* (December 24, 1981), p. A23.

Reisman, W.M., and Baker, J.E. *Regulating Covert Action.* New Haven: CT: Yale University Press, 1992.

Richelson, J. *America's Eyes in Space: The U.S. Keyhole Spy Satellite Program.* New York: Harper & Row, 1990.

Richelson, J. *The Wizards of Langley: Inside the CIA's Directorate of Science and Technology.* Boulder, CO: Westview Press, 2001.

Richelson, J. *The U.S. Intelligence Community*, 5th edn. Boulder, CO: Westview Press, 2008.

Risen, J. *State of War: The Secret History of the CIA and the Bush Administration.* New York: Free Press, 2006.

Risen, J. *The Last Honest Man: The CIA, the FBI, the Mafia, and the Kennedys – One Senator's Fight to Save Democracy.* New York: Little, Brown, 2023.

Robarge, D. *The Solider-Statesman in the Secret World: George C. Marshall and Intelligence in War and Peace.* Langley, VA: Center for the Study of Intelligence, CIA, 2023.

Rohde, D. *In Deep: The FBI, the CIA, and the Truth about America's "Deep State."* New York: Norton, 2020.

Roosevelt, K. *Countercoup: The Struggle for the Control of Iran.* New York: McGraw-Hill, 1981.

Rusk, D. *As I Saw It*, as told to R. Rusk and edited by D. Papps, New York: W.W. Norton, 1990.

Russell, R.L. *Sharpening Strategic Intelligence.* New York: Cambridge University Press, 2007.

Schwarz, F.A.O., Jr. "The Church Committee and a New Era of Intelligence Oversight," *Intelligence and National Security* 22 (April 2007), pp. 270–97.

Schwarz, F.A.O., Jr. "Intelligence Oversight: The Church Committee," in L.K. Johnson, ed., *Strategic Intelligence, Vol. 5: Intelligence and Accountability,*

Safeguards against the Abuse of Secret Power. Westport, CT: Praeger, 2007, pp. 19–46.

Schwarz, F.A.O., Jr. *Democracy in the Dark: The Seduction of Government Secrecy*. New York: Free Press, 2015.

Schwarz, F.A.O., Jr., and Huq, A.Z. *Unchecked and Unbalanced: Presidential Power in a Time of Terror*. New York: The New Press, 2007.

Scott, L., and Jackson, P. "The Study of Intelligence in Theory and Practice," *Intelligence and National Security* 19 (Summer 2004), pp. 139–69.

Shane, S. *Objective Troy: A Terrorist, a President, and the Rise of the Drone*. New York: Duggan Books, 2015.

Sharp, D.H. *The CIA's Greatest Covert Operation: Inside the Daring Mission to Recover a Nuclear-Armed Soviet Sub*. Lawrence: University Press of Kansas, 2012.

Shorrock, T. *Spies for Hire: The Secret World of Intelligence Outsourcing*. New York: Simon & Schuster, 2008.

Sims, J.E., and Gerbers, B., eds. *Vaults, Mirrors, and Masks: Rediscovering U.S. Counterintelligence*. Washington, DC: Georgetown University Press, 2008.

Sirrs, O.L. *The Egyptian Intelligence Service: A History of the Mukhabarat, 1910–2009*. New York: Routledge, 2010.

Snider, L.B. *The Agency and the Hill: CIA's Relationship with Congress, 1946–2004*. Washington, DC: Central Intelligence Agency, 2008.

Stuart, D.T. *Creating the National Security State: A History of the Law that Transformed America*. Princeton, NJ: Princeton University Press, 2008.

Tenet, G., with Harlow, B., Jr. *At the Center of the Storm: My Years at the CIA*. New York: HarperCollins, 2007.

Theoharis, A. *Chasing Spies*. Chicago: Ivan R. Dee, 2002.

Trenta, L. *The President's Kill List: Assassination and US Foreign Policy since 1945*. Edinburgh: Edinburgh University Press, 2024.

Treverton, G.F. *Covert Action: The Limits of Intervention in the Postwar World*. New York: Basic Books, 1987.

Treverton, G.F. "Estimating beyond the Cold War," *Defense Intelligence Journal* 3 (Fall 1994), pp. 5–20.

Treverton, G.F. *Intelligence in an Age of Terror*. New York: Cambridge University Press, 2009.

Tromblay, D. *Securing the Private Sector: Protecting U.S. Industry in Pursuit of National Security*. Boulder, CO: Lynne Rienner, 2021.

Turner, M.A. *Why Secret Intelligence Fails*. Dulles, VA: Potomac Books, 2005.

Turner, S. *Secrecy and Democracy: The CIA in Transition*. Boston, MA: Houghton Mifflin, 1985.

Turner, S. *Burn before Reading: Presidents, CIA Directors, and Secret Intelligence*. New York: Hyperion, 2005.

Van Puyvelde, D. *Outsourcing U.S. Intelligence: Contractors and Government Accountability*. Edinburgh: Edinburgh University Press, 2019.

Vogel, K.M., Reid, G., Kampe, C., and Jones, P. "The Impact of AI on Intelligence Analysis: Tackling Issues of Collaboration, Algorithmic Transparency, Accountability, and Management," *Intelligence and National Security* 36/6 (2021), pp. 827–48.

Wallace, R., and Smith, H.K., with Schlesinger, H.R. *Spycraft: The Secret History of the CIA's Spytechs from Communism to Al-Qaeda*. New York: Dutton, 2008.

Walsh, P.F., Ramsay, J. and Bernot, A. "Health Security Intelligence Capabilities Post-COVID-19: Resisting the Passive 'New Normal' Within the Five Eyes," *Intelligence and National Security* 38/7 (August 2023), pp. 1095–111.

Walton, C. *The Epic Intelligence War Between East and West*. New York: Simon & Schuster, 2023.

Warner, M. *The Rise and Fall of Intelligence: An International Security History*. Washington, DC: Georgetown University Press, 2014.

Weiner, T. *Legacy of Ashes: The History of the CIA*. New York: Doubleday, 2007.

Weiner, T., Johnston, D., and Lewis, N.A. *Betrayal: The Story of Aldrich Ames, An American Spy*. New York: Random House, 1995.

Weissberg, J. *An Ordinary Spy*. New York: Bloomsbury, 2008.

Weissman, S.R. "Covert Action: Congressional Inaction," *Foreign Affairs* (December 9, 2020).

Westerfield, H.B., ed. *Inside CIA's Private World: Declassified Articles from the Agency's Internal Journal, 1955–1992*. New Haven, CT: Yale University Press, 1995.

Whipple, C. *The Spymasters: How the CIA Directors Shape History and the Future*. New York: Simon & Schuster, 2020.

Wilford, H. *The Mighty Wurlitzer: How the CIA Played America*. Cambridge, MA: Harvard University Press, 2008.

Winks, R.W. *Cloak & Gown: Scholars in the Secret War, 1939–1961*. New York: William Morrow, 1987.

Wirtz, J.J. *The Tet Offensive: Intelligence Failure in War*. Ithaca, NY: Cornell University Press, 1991.

Wise, D. *Spy: The Inside Story of How the FBI's Robert Hanssen Betrayed America*. New York: Random House, 2002.

Wise, D., and Ross, T. *The Invisible Government*. New York: Random House, 1964.

Wohlstetter, R. *Pearl Harbor: Warning and Decision*. Stanford, CA: Stanford University Press, 1962.

Wyden, P. *Bay of Pigs: The Untold Story*. New York: Simon & Schuster, 1979.

Zegart, A.B. "Cloaks, Daggers, and Ivory Towers: Why Academics Don't Study U.S. Intelligence," in L.K Johnson, ed., *Strategic Intelligence, Vol. 1: Understanding the Hidden Side of Government*. Westport, CT: Praeger, 2007, pp. 21–34.

Zegart, A.B. *Spying Blind: The CIA, the FBI, and the Origins of 9/11*. Princeton, NJ: Princeton University Press, 2007.

PROMINENT INTELLIGENCE STUDIES JOURNALS

Cryptologia
Intelligence and National Security
International Journal of Intelligence and Counterintelligence
Journal for Intelligence, Propaganda and Security Studies
Journal of Intelligence History
Studies in Intelligence

Index

9/11, 1–7, 9, 71, 74, 100, 148–50, 193, 209
  aftermath, 103, 110, 119, 126, 138–9, 165,
    173, 192, 196, 198–9
9/11 Commission, *see* Kean Commission

A-12 spy plane, 60
Aberbach, Joel D., 192
Abu Zubaydah, *see* Zubaydah, Abu
Academi, 33
accountability, *see* intelligence oversight
  (accountability)
active measures, 111, 233
Acton, Lord, 11, 20, 241nn3, 4
aerial terrorism, 4, 12, 48, 87, 93, 148
Afghanistan
  and Al Qaeda, 2, 4–6, 43, 48, 53, 61, 71, 74,
    89, 101, 103, 116, 119, 122, 125–7, 137,
    139–41, 150, 165, 173, 191, 193, 198
  covert action in, 107, 119, 125, 137, 139,
    173
  mujahideen, 119, 137
  Northern Alliance, 137, 139
  Soviet invasion of, 129–30
  Taliban regime, 2, 5, 9, 66, 103, 107, 119, 122,
    133, 137, 139
  U.S. retreat from, 9, 81, 88
Agee, Philip, 177
agent provocateur, 172
agents, *see* Central Intelligence Agency, assets
agents of influence, 116
agents-in-place, 171
Aidid, Mohamed Ali Farrah, 127
Air Force intelligence unit, 25
al-Awlaki, Anwar, 125–6
al-Balawi, Humam Khali Abu-Mulal, 165
Alfred P. Murrah Federal Building (Oklahoma
  City), 46, 146–7
Al Qaeda
  9/11 attacks, 1–6, 22, 26, 36, 61, 65, 71, 77, 93,
    100, 131, 140, 197
  in Afghanistan, 2
  assassination plots against, 6, 125
Allende, Salvador, 113–14, 117–18, 129, 186
Alwan, Rafid Ahmed ("Curveball"), 51, 63, 70, 88,
  100–3
ambition instinct, 12
American Pilots Association, 4, 149
Ames, Aldrich "Rick" Hazen, 21, 150–3, 157–9,
  162, 164–5, 167, 207

analysis, 18, 21, 73
  ideal attributes, 92–5
Angleton, James, 160–2, 171
ante facto reporting, 216
antiwar movement, 31–2, 142–3
Appropriations Committees, 30, 34, 179, 181,
  210, 213, 228
Arab–Israeli War, 85
Arbenz, Jacobo, 114, 118
Army intelligence unit, 25
Artificial Intelligence (AI), 65, 115
Aspin, Les, 44, 181–2
Aspin–Brown Commission, 44, 49–50, 78, 97,
  100, 150, 152, 163, 230
assassination plots, 55, 66, 100, 103, 129, 135,
  138–9, 179
Atta, Mohamed, 1
Australia, 223
Auth (*Philadelphia Inquirer*), 184

Backfire bomber, 44
ballistic missiles, 68, 157
  see also weapons of mass destruction (WMDs)
Barrett, David M., 185
Barrett, Richard, 61
Barry, James A., 256n43
Bay of Pigs operation, 66, 68, 96, 107, 129–30,
  139, 185, 230
Bennett, Donald, 143
Berger, Raoul, 176
Betts, Richard K., 73, 88, 97
Biden, Joseph R., 10, 38, 46, 57, 95, 101, 125, 131,
  155, 166, 231, 236–7
Biden Administration, 50, 52, 117, 124, 155, 160,
  230, 232, 235
Bin Laden, Osama, 5–6, 125–7, 137, 139
biological weapons, 5, 45, 59, 63, 88, 99, 100,
  112, 136, 148
  see also weapons of mass destruction (WMDs)
Bissell, Richard, 96–7
Black, Cofer, 173–4, 242n15
black propaganda, 111
black sites (secret prisons), 173, 198
Blackwater, 33
Blair, Dennis C., 37–8, 170
blow-back ("replay"), 112, 134
Boland, Edward P., 110, 179–84, 210, 214
Boland Amendments, 110, 130, 188, 190
bomber gap, 56

Booz Allen Hamilton corporation, 194
Branch Davidian sect, 146
Brandeis, Louis, 184–5
Brazil, 53
Brennan, John O., 97, 125, 127, 200–2, 232–3, 235
British intelligence, *see* MI6; United Kingdom (UK)
Brookings Institution, 195
Brown, Harold, 209
Brzezinski, Zbigniew, 129
Buckley, David, 202–3
Bundy, McGeorge, 117, 137–8
Bunga (parasite), 117, 135
Bureau of Intelligence and Research (INR), 26, 84
Burns, William J., 10, 58, 95, 236
Burr, Richard, 127
Bush, George H. W., 96, 122–3, 130
Bush, George W., 56, 65, 77, 89, 99, 123, 131, 172, 211, 225
Bush Administration (1st), 4
Bush Administration (2nd), 28, 30, 75, 131, 149, 150, 193–4, 196, 206, 210–11, 227

cable and telegram intercepts, 4, 24, 52, 56, 61, 71, 78, 127, 164, 175, 187, 214
Cali drug cartel, 100
Cambodia, 88, 119, 130
Cambridge Spy Ring, 161
Canada, 223
Carlos the Jackal, 100
Carter, Jimmy, 52–3, 129, 179, 180, 181
Carter Administration, 28, 58, 60, 77, 79, 107, 110, 140
case officers, *see* operations officers
Casey, William J., 95, 98, 174, 190, 214, 216
Castro, Fidel, 66, 96–7, 113, 117, 121, 127, 138
Castro, Raoul, 138
Center for Open-Source Intelligence, 58
Central Intelligence Agency (CIA)
    appointment of chiefs of station, 37
    assassination plots, 66, 105, 120–7, 144, 138, 189. 211, 235
    assets, 30–1, 37, 49–51, 61, 54–8, 73, 106, 111, 114, 132, 157, 171, 209, 219, 237
        agents of influence, 116
        betrayal of, 150–4
        in Cuba, 62–70
        media assets, 111
        recruiting of, 223
    attack on employees at Langley, 148
    co-location of operations officers and analysts, 96, 225
    counterintelligence, 142, 146
    Counterproliferation Center, 97
    Counterterrorism Center, 22, 48, 148, 163
    cover, 61–2
    Covert Action Staff, 108, 111, 121, 128
    Cuban Missile Crisis, 65–9
    definition of intelligence, 18
    Directorate of Analysis, 31, 96
    Directorate of Operations, 28
    Directorate of Science and Technology, 28, 31
    Directorate of Support, 31

    domestic spying, 31–2, 129, 144, 185–6, 207
    economic covert action, 116–18
    establishment of, 27–8
    Huston Plan, 144–5
    internal structure, 28–31
    interrogation methods, 126, 171–4, 198–203, 239
    journalistic cover, 62
    lawyers in, 20
    numbers of operations officers, 31, 50, 65
    Office of Security, 171
    Operation CHAOS, 16, 32, 187, 206–7, 213
    organization of, 29
    paramilitary activities, 15, 118–28
    penetrated by Russian intelligence, 15, 150–3
    Phoenix Program, 15, 122, 150–3
    photography of, 17
    political covert action, 115–16
    position in the Intelligence Community, 27–8
    Project Jennifer, 59–60
    Project NIMBUS, 65–6
    propaganda, 111–15
    relations with the FBI, 4, 36, 100, 149
    Reserve for Contingency Fund, 189
    Senate Torture Report, 198–204
    as set of "baronies," 28
    and Silicon Valley, 167
    Special Activities Division, 108
    Special Operations Group, 109, 139
    stations, 28–9
    treason within, 150–2, 157–8
    use of torture, 198–204
    see also Cold War; covert action; Operation CHAOS
Chambliss, Saxby, 199, 201–2, 207
CHAOS Operation, *see* Operation CHAOS
Charles, Prince of Wales (now King Charles III), 103
"chatter," 24, 94
"cheerleader" intelligence overseers, 212–14, 228
cherry-picking, 97
Chief of Station (COS), 30–1, 37, 126, 192
Chile, 109, 112, 122, 129, 140, 186
Chin, Larry Wu-tai, 116
China,
    Belgrade embassy bombing by US, 91–2
    Covid-19 origins, 22–5, 50
    cyberattacks, 53
    electronic spying by, 165, 238
    humint espionage, 15, 22, 146, 158
    missile sales to Pakistan (covert), 78
    nuclear weapons, 238
    shipments of illegal narcotics, 52, 222
    sigint station in Cuba, 56
    skewed analysis of, 112
    spying by aerial balloons, 166–7
    threat posed by, 45, 74
    "wet markets," 6–7, 88
Christian Democratic Party (Italy), 116
Chung, Dongfan, 158
Church, Frank, 16, 60, 88, 109, 186

Church Committee, 16, 113–14, 118, 121–2, 126, 128–9, 140, 144, 168, 186, 188–95, 204–5, 207, 213, 237
Churchill, Winston, 93, 108
civil liberties, 12, 144, 153, 175, 185, 197
 see also domestic spying; civil rights movement, 187
Clapper, James R., 32, 38, 167–8, 220, 232, 238
Clark, Kathleen, 150
Clarke, Richard A., 107, 140
Clausewitz, Karl von, 9
Clifford, Clark, 107, 140
Cline, Ray, 112, 136–7
Clinton, Bill, 40, 99, 192, 214, 230
Clinton, Hillary, 232, 234
Clinton Administration, 28, 44, 47, 75, 77, 81, 125, 131, 192
Coast Guard Intelligence, 26
codebreaking, 24, 71
Colby, William E., 53, 56, 59, 65, 70, 76, 108–9, 122, 138, 162, 228
Cold War
 aftermath, 43, 58, 61, 69
 CIA preeminence, 27–8
 covert action expansion, 108, 128, 131
 early lax intelligence oversight, 80
 ideological dimensions, 160
 McCarthyism, 19
 NIE prediction of Sputnik, 86
 objections to strong CIA, 36
 Second Cold War (potential), 7
 stresses on IC, 158
 US focus on USSR, 55, 108, 136, 150
 US spying successes, 10, 100–1
 see also communism; Russia/Soviet Union
collection
 analysis phase, 43
 collection phase, 43
 dissemination phase, 43, 97–9
 intelligence cycle, 43
 intelligence disciplines, 24
 intelligence reports, 9, 20, 58, 73–4, 91–6, 97–8
 planning and direction phase, 43
 processing phase, 43
 weaknesses in, 99–101
combatant commanders (COCOMs), 51
Comey, John B., 232
Commager, Henry Steele, 187
communications intelligence (comint), 56
communism, 108–9, 113, 120, 138, 161
 see also Cold War; propaganda
Congo, 25, 105–6
Conrad, Clyde, 151
Constitution, 11, 16, 46, 130, 135, 140, 173–4, 176, 184–9, 193, 202, 219, 227–8, 231, 235, 239
contras, Nicaraguan, 110
Convention Against Torture, 198
Coons, Chris, 197
counterespionage (CE), 169–71
counterintelligence (CI)
 counterespionage activities, 171–4

cybersecurity, 26–7, 103, 167
 definition, 146
 difficulty of catching spies, 162
 domestic use of, 144–5, 162–4, 168, 170–3, 182–4, 185, 213–14
 failures in, 146–53
 as key intelligence mission, 15
 motivations for treason, 159–60
counterproliferation, 38, 97
Counterproliferation Center, 97
counterterrorism, 22, 26, 55, 61, 72, 97, 100, 120, 150, 163–5, 170, 193, 196
Counterterrorism Center (CTC), 22, 48, 148, 179
covert action (CA) covert action,
 assassination plots, 194–206, 120–8
 definition of, 107
 as "dirty tricks," 15, 129
 and dollar subversion, 120
 economic activities, 116–18
 environmental activities, 135–6
 euphemisms for, 107
 evaluation of, 136–8
 funding for, 128–31, 189
 guidelines for, 139–41
 HPSCI and SSCI briefings on, 179–83, 203–4, 210–12
 implementation of, 109–11
 ladder of escalation, 131–6
 legal context, 107
 levels of use, 131–6
 methods of, 111
 oversight of, 203–7
 paramilitary activities, 118–28
 political activities, 113–16
 and presidential approval, 181–2
 propaganda, 111–15
 rationale, 107–9
Covert Action Staff (CAS), 108, 111, 121, 128
covert mail cover, 145
Covid-19 pandemic, 7, 50, 56, 88, 114, 167
Coyle, Philip E., 44–5
Cuba, 56–8, 63–9, 96, 98, 114, 116–17, 121–2
Cuban Missile Crisis, 65–9, 82, 87
current intelligence, 76–7
Curveball, *see* Alwan, Rafid Ahmed ("Curveball")
cyberespionage, 27, 166–8, 238–9
cyberhackers, 165, 168
cybersecurity, 26–7, 103, 167–8
cyberwarfare, 15, 27, 167–8
Cyprus, 86–8
Czechoslovakia, 88

D-Day landings, 171
Daesh, *see* ISIS
Damrosch, Lori Fisler, 134
"dangles," 64, 172
data integration, 72
Daugherty, William J., 128, 138
deception operations, 15, 70, 84, 115, 133, 169, 171–2, 219
"Deep State," 237, 237
defectors, 51, 63, 170–2

Defense Intelligence Agency (DIA), 25
democracy, and secrecy, 174–8
Department of Defense (DoD), 24, 35, 84, 124
Department of Energy, 26
Department of Homeland Security (DHS), 26
Department of Justice, 23
Department of State, 26, 36, 67, 112, 178, 234
Department of Transportation, 149
Department of Treasury, 26
Deputy Director for Operations (DDO), 28, 37,
    139
Deputy Directors of National Intelligence
    (DDNIs), 22
Deutch, John, 32, 49, 97, 131, 139, 153
Dicks, Norm, 214
Diem, Ngo Dinh, 122
diplomacy, 51, 107, 120, 123, 218–19
Director of Central Intelligence (DCI), 22, 27–8,
    32–3, 36–7, 42, 49, 80, 182
Director of the CIA (D/CIA), 22–3, 32, 37–8, 75,
    82, 98, 124, 126, 189, 225, 232–3
Director of National Intelligence (DNI), 22, 27, 36,
    98, 124, 219, 225, 232–3
Directorate of Administration (DA), 31
    see also Directorate of Support (DS)
Directorate of Analysis (DA), 31, 96
Directorate of Intelligence (DI) 76
    see also Directorate of Analysis (DA)
Directorate of Operations (DO), 28–31
    see also National Clandestine Service (NCS)
Directorate of Science and Technology (DS&T),
    31–2
Directorate of Support (DS), 31–2
disinformation, 10, 15, 20, 45, 95, 112, 133, 162,
    166, 171, 236
dissemination, see intelligence dissemination
domestic spying, 142–6, 185–6, 207
    see also Huston Plan; Operation CHAOS
domestic violent extremists (DVEs), 7
dominant battlefield awareness (DBA), 51
Dominican Republic, 118, 122
double agents, 20, 65, 103, 170
drones, 24
    see also Unmanned Aerial Vehicles (UAVs)
Drug Enforcement Administration (DEA), 23, 26
Drugs-related operations, 43, 50–2, 100, 167,
    219
Dulles, Allen, 34, 94, 105–6, 214, 211
Dulles, John Foster, 114
Dunlap, Jack E., 157
Durban, Richard, 89
Duvalier, François "Papa Doc," 122

economic covert action, 15, 66, 103, 116–18, 136,
    146, 166, 168
Egypt, 86, 115, 137
Ehrlichman, John, 142–3
Eisenhower, Dwight D., 109, 224
Eisenhower Administration, 24, 32, 34, 105–6,
    114, 128
El Salvador, 65, 130
electronic intelligence (elint), 56

"Elimination by Illumination" (proposed CIA
    operation), 114
Ellsberg, Daniel, 176–7
embassies, 58, 64, 165
"Enterprise, The," 110, 182, 190, 203
environmental intelligence, 48–9, 92
    collection, 238
    covert action, 135, 140
    degradation, 47, 93
    MEDEA, 50
    NIE on (2021), 83–4
Environmental Intelligence Center, 32
Environmental Protection Agency, 49, 222
Ervin, Sam, 174
Ervin Committee, 174
executive privilege, 174–6, 204
ex post facto reporting, 211
extraordinary renditions, 126, 172–4, 218

false defector, 63, 172
Federal Aviation Administration, 1
Federal Bureau of Investigation (FBI)
    and 9/11, 149, 197, 222
    counterintelligence, 23, 27, 61, 100, 142, 145,
        152, 155, 157, 171, 195, 232–8
    domestic spying, 143–6
    establishment of, 34–5
    Huston Plan, 143–6
    and the Oklahoma City bombing, 146
    Operation COINTELPRO, 187, 193, 211, 216,
        239, 265n5
    penetrated by Russian intelligence, 150–3
    position in the Intelligence Community, 26
    relations with the CIA, 150, 152, 171
    special agents, 61
    treason within, 147, 150
    and the Waco siege, 146
    "weaponized" (politically), 46, 155–6, 210,
        230–1
Federalist Papers, 228
Federation of American Scientists Project on
    Government Secrecy, 26
Feinstein, Dianne, 127, 198–9, 202, 204
Filkins, Dexter, 139
"finding" (presidential), 180–3, 186–9, 191,
    210–11
    "generic" ("worldwide"), 189
"firefighting" (oversight), 205–7, 228
First Amendment (US Constitution), 16, 177–8
Fisher, Roger, 140
"Five Eyes," 101–2, 223
Ford, Gerald R., 75, 122
Ford Administration, 75, 175, 186
foreign instrumentation signals intelligence
    (fisint), 56
foreign intelligence liaison, 101, 165
Foreign Intelligence Surveillance Act, 126, 189,
    192, 194–8, 208
Foreign Intelligence Surveillance Court (FIS
    Court), 190, 194, 196–7, 207, 228
France, 159
Freedom Caucus, 237

Fuchs, Klaus, 156–7, 160
funding, *see* intelligence funding
fusion centers, intelligence, 38, 72, 165, 221

Gang of Eight, 210–11
Gang of Four, 210, 270n75
"Gang of None," 211
Gates, Robert M., 49, 65, 87, 125, 192, 211, 216, 228
Gayler, Noel, 71, 143
Geneva Conventions, 198
geospatial intelligence (geoint), 24–5, 41, 49, 59, 60–1, 64, 71, 78, 172, 224
Germany, 54, 63, 102–3, 108, 118, 159, 204, 218, 223
Giancana, Sam, 121
Gill, Peter, 21
Gingrich, Newt, 191
Glennon, Michael, 203
globalization, 222
Goldsmith, Jack, 196
Goldwater, Barry, 60, 213, 216
Gore, Al, 47–9, 52
Goss, Porter, 103, 209
Graham, Bob, 89–90, 198
Graham–Goss Committee, 209
Grass, Günter, 109
Greece, 115, 118, 172
Greene, Graham, 106
Greenglass, David, 156
GRU, 108, 156
Guantánamo Bay, 109, 114, 118, 128, 135, 137
Guardian (UK newspaper), 153, 194
"guardian" intelligence overseers, 214–15, 216–17, 219, 220, 228, 230, 236
Guatemala, 109, 114, 118, 128, 137
Gulf Wars, 32, 40, 115, 122–3, 218–19
Guterres, António, 128

Hagel, Chuck, 90
Haines, Avril D. (DNI), 167, 221, 236
Haiti, 118, 122, 131
Hamilton, Lee H., 183, 214–15
Hanssen, Robert, 150, 152–3
Hayden, Michael V., 198–200, 203–4
Haynes, John Earl, 156
Health Alteration Committee (CIA), 121
Hellfire missiles, 123, 126, 135
Helms, Richard, 76, 94, 98, 118, 139, 143, 233
Henze, Paul, 60
Herbig, Katherine L., 160
Herron, Mick, 54
Hiss, Alger, 156
Hitler, Adolf, 9, 94, 108, 171, 234
Hmung tribesmen, 118–19
Hoekstra, Peter, 211
Homeland Security, Department of, *see* Department of Homeland Security (DHS)
Homeland Security Committee, 17
"honeytraps," 159
Hoover, J. Edgar, 34–5, 143–4, 169, 187, 219, 239

Hoover Commission, 136
Hostage-rescue operations, 132, 134
House Permanent Select Committee on Intelligence (HPSCI), 33, 124, 126–7, 140, 179–84, 188–94, 196, 198, 203, 207, 209–17, 227–9, 232, 235–6
Howard, Edward Lee, 157, 178
Hughes, Howard, 59–60
Hughes–Ryan Act, 110, 127, 130, 180, 188–90, 211–12, 226
Hulnick, Arthur S., 88–9
human intelligence (humint), 5, 37, 42, 49–50, 57, 60–5, 67, 69–70, 77–8, 88, 116, 209, 224, 229, 232, 237
human nature, 12
Hungary, 47, 88, 118
Hurricane Katrina, 149
Hussein, Saddam, 40, 51, 89, 99–100, 115, 122, 127
Huston, Tom Charles, 142–6, 239
Huston Plan, 142–6, 172, 178, 216

Ignatius, David, 203
imagery intelligence (imint), *see* geospatial intelligence (geoint)
India, 31, 47, 57, 83
India–Pakistan War, 86
indications and warnings (I & W), 17
Indonesia, 118, 122
information technology (IT), 224
Inouye, Daniel K., 179
Inouye–Hamilton Committee, 179, 207
Inspector General Act (IG Act), 191, 207
inspectors general (IGs), 20
insurrectionists (US, 2021), 46, 146, 234
Intelligence Community, 22–7
Intelligence Community Whistleblower Protection Act (1998), 152
intelligence cycle, 12, 42–3
  see also collection
intelligence dissemination, 42, 43, 95, 97–9, 225–6
intelligence funding, 25–6
Intelligence Identities Act, 208
intelligence oversight (accountability), 183, 204–8, 239
Intelligence Oversight Acts, 127, 211, 226, 230
Intelligence Oversight Board (IOB), 32, 154
intelligence to please, 98
intelligence, politicization of, 85, 94, 98, 226, 229, 233
Intelligence Reform and Terrorism Prevention Act (IRTPA), 36, 208
intelligence reports
  current and research intelligence, 75–6, 78
  critical review of, 74, 77, 99, 249n24, 252n67
  National Intelligence Estimates (NIEs), 78
  President's Daily Brief (PDB), 75–8
intelligence–risk relationship, 54, 139
intelligence task forces, 32
International Telephone and Telegraph Corporation (ITT), 113

interrogation methods, 126, 149, 239
  see also torture
Inter-Services Intelligence (ISI) (Pakistan), 103
Iran, 18, 27, 47, 48, 117–18, 128, 137, 167, 222, 235, 237
Iran–*contra* affair, 14, 110, 119, 130–1, 135, 139–40, 174, 182, 203, 207, 212, 215, 227
Iranian revolution, 44
Iraq, 6, 9, 32, 40, 51, 63, 88–90, 122, 209
Iraqi Task Force, 32
iron pentagon, 33–4
iron triangle, 34
ISIS, 6, 53, 60–1, 71, 101, 119, 122, 127–9, 131, 138, 157, 162, 164
Israel, 5, 18, 53, 86
Italy, 116, 218

Jervis, Robert, 163, 171
jihadist, 5
Johnson, Lyndon B., 84–5, 140
Johnson, Mike, 238
jointness, 93–4
Jordan, Jim, 237
judiciary branch, 190
Judiciary Committees, 210, 228

Kahn, Herman, 131
Kampiles, William, 157
Kansi, Mir Aimal, 148
Kant, Immanuel, 136
Kean, Thomas, 75
Kean Commission, 65, 94, 209
Keating, Kenneth, 67
Kennan, George F., 93
Kennedy, John F., 68, 96, 129, 171, 230
Kennedy Administration, 65, 66, 67, 106, 114, 116, 121, 128
Kent, Sherman, 85, 98
Key Judgments (KJs), 82, 90, 95
KGB, 20, 58, 108, 122, 143, 144, 152, 156, 157, 162
"King George's cavalry," 115
King, Martin Luther, Jr., 187
Klehr, Harvey, 156
Kleindienst, Richard, 174
Khrushchev, Nikita, 67–8, 162
Kim (Kipling), 57
Kim, Robert C., 158
Kipling, Rudyard, 57
Kissinger, Henry, 75–6, 107, 118, 178
Knott, Stephen F., 192
Kolbe, Paul R. 169
Korea (North), 8, 18, 44–5, 47, 60, 69, 100, 115, 146, 167, 178, 220, 222, 234, 238
Korea (South), 158, 160
Korean War, 158, 160
Ku Klux Klan, 187
Kuwait, 40–2, 123

ladder of escalation (covert action), 131–6, 140
Lake, Anthony, 192
Land, Edward, 32

Langan-Riekhof, Maria, 103
Langley, VA, 23, 27–8, 31–2, 69, 79, 96, 106, 123, 128, 147, 162, 167, 180, 202, 212, 230
  see also Central Intelligence Agency (CIA)
Laos, 118–19, 135
Laurent, Sébastien, 16
leaks, 153–6, 211
"lemon-sucker" intelligence overseers, 212–14, 216
Leno, Jay, 91
Levin, Carl, 89
Lewis, Anthony, 137
Liberty Crossing, VA, 37, 96
Library of Congress, 58
Libya, 6, 101, 122, 131, 158, 235
Liddy, G. Gordon, 137
"lone wolf" attacks, 88, 147
Long, Magda, 167
Lowenthal, Mark M., 44, 91
Lumumba, Patrice, 105–6
Luna, Anna Paulina, 236

Madison, James, 11, 20, 147, 178, 193
Mafia, 121
MAGA movement, 46, 231
mail coverage, 145
Mak, Chi, 158
Manhattan Project, 156
Marines intelligence unit, 25
Marshall, George Catlett, 93, 241n10
Marshall Plan, 108
Martins, Mark, 197
Matthews, Jennifer, 163
Maugham, Somerset, 17
Mayer, Jane, 198
Mazzoli, Roman, 180–3
McCain, John, 67–8, 82, 98, 170
McCarthy, Joseph, 19
McCone, John A., 36–7, 71
McConnell, Mike, 36–7, 71
McCubbins, Matthew D., 205
McFarlane, Robert C., 190, 203
McNamara, Robert S., 69
McNutt, Russell, 156
McVeigh, Timothy, 46, 147
measurement and signatures intelligence (masint), 59
media, role in intelligence oversight, 206
media assets, 111–15
metadata collection program, 153–4, 194–8
MI6, 12, 21, 33, 37, 54, 57, 64, 99, 102–3, 115, 161
militia violent extremists (MVEs), 7
Military Intelligence Program (MIP), 25–6
Milley, General Mark, 234
Millis, John, 65
Milton, John 11
Mitchell, John, 118, 144
Mobutu, Joseph, 106
mock executions, 200
Mohammed, Khalid Sheikh ("KSM"), 173, 200
Mondale, Walter, 187
Moore, Richard, 8, 102

Morell, Michael, 232
Morgan Bank (Wall Street), 147
Mosman, Michael W., 197
Moss, John E., 175
Mossadeq, Mohammed, 118
Moussaoui, Zacarias, 149
Moynihan, Daniel Patrick, 100, 214
Mueller, Robert S. III, 232
mujahideen, 119, 137–8
mysteries, 7–8

National Center for Medical Intelligence (NCMI), 25, 50–1
National Clandestine Service (NCS), 28, 30 37
  see also Directorate of Operations (DO)
National Command Authority (NCA), 22
National Counterproliferation Center, 97
National Counterterrorism Center (NCTC), 22, 163
National Geospatial-Intelligence Agency (NGA), 24
National Intelligence Board (NIB), 82
National Intelligence Council (NIC), 21, 23, 29, 78–81, 84
National Intelligence Estimates (NIEs)
  accuracy and inaccuracy of, 85–6
  incorporation of dissenting views, 82–4
  and internal liaison, 84–5
  Iraq NIE controversy, 89–90
  Key Judgments section, 82, 90, 95, 229
  preparation process, 79–82
  range of topics, 79
  special NIEs, 85–6
  timing and frequency, 85
National Intelligence Managers (NIMs), 38, 81
National Intelligence Officers (NIOs), 81
National Intelligence Priorities Framework (NIPF), 53
National Intelligence Program (NIP), 25
National Photographic Interpretation Center (NPIC), 42, 67
National Reconnaissance Office (NRO), 24–5
National Security Act, 27, 36, 107
National Security Agency (NSA)
  and 9/11, 71
  appointment of chiefs of station, 37
  funding, 25–6
  Huston Plan, 143
  intelligence processing, 71
  metadata collection program, 153–4
  Operation MINARET, 187, 211, 239
  Operation PRISM, 194
  Operation SHAMROCK, 175, 187, 195, 211, 239
  position in the Intelligence Community, 24
  Snowden leaks, 153–5
  warrantless wiretaps, 193, 206, 209, 211
  treason within, 157
National Security Council (NSC), 22–3, 107, 185, 233
national security intelligence (NSI)
  and accountability, 11
  definitions of, 21

as first line of defense, 219
holistic view of, 19–22
as organization, 19
as a process, 18, 43
as a "river" of information, 14
as secret information, 17–18
as set of missions, 18, 223–7
"signals" v. "noise," 224
National Student Association, 185
Navy intelligence unit, 25
Negroponte, John D., 36
New Zealand, 53, 233
New York Times, 14, 16, 38, 176, 185, 194, 197, 198, 205, 211
New York Times v. United States (Pentagon Papers case), 176
Nicaragua, 19, 109, 110, 118, 119–20, 130, 188, 190, 206, 216
  see also Iran–*contra* affair
Nicolson, Harold J., 157–8
NIMBUS, Project, 66
Nixon, Richard, 75–6, 94, 142–4, 174–5, 230
Nixon Administration, 107, 119, 129, 142, 176, 239
"nondiscernible microbioinoculator," 121, 186
non-official cover officers (NOCs), 61–2, 96, 224
North Atlantic Treaty Organization (NATO), 7–8, 45, 52, 79, 91, 108, 218–19, 223
Northern Alliance, 137–9
Norway, 53
Nosenko, Yuri, 171
Nuclear Emergency Support Team (NEST), 10
Nunes, Devin, 235
"nut-cut" (MI6 slang), 33
Nye, Joseph S., 55

Obama, Barack, 30, 38, 139, 196, 201, 220, 234–6
Obama Administration, 50, 75, 123–31, 155, 199, 203–4
Office of the Director of National Intelligence (ODNI), 22, 27, 32, 36–8, 79, 96, 208, 230, 232
Office of Intelligence and Analysis
  Department of Homeland Security, 26
  Department of Treasury, 26
Office of Intelligence and Counterintelligence, 26
Office of National Security Intelligence, 26
Office of Security (CIA), 171
official cover officers (OCs), 62
Ogonowski, Captain John, 1
Oklahoma City bombing, 46, 146–7
O'Neill, Thomas "Tip," 179
open source intelligence (osint), 58
Operation CHAOS, 16, 32, 187, 193, 206–7, 211, 213, 216, 239
Operation COINTELPRO, 187, 193, 211, 216, 239, 265n5
Operation MINARET, 187, 211, 239
Operation PRISM, 194
Operation SHAMROCK, 175, 187, 195, 211, 239
Operation SQUARE DANCE (proposed), 117
operations officers, 31, 50, 62, 65, 70, 116

oral briefings, 18–19, 21, 59, 73, 77, 234
Organization of Petroleum Exporting Countries (OPEC), 87
Orlando shootings, 6, 88
Ortega, Daniel, 130
"ostrich" intelligence overseers, 212–13, 216, 228
Oswald, Lee Harvey, 171
outsourcing, 33
oversight, intelligence, see intelligence oversight (accountability); Intelligence Oversight Acts; Intelligence Oversight Board
Owens, William A., 55

Pakistan, 5, 7, 61, 63, 78, 86, 101, 103, 115, 122, 125, 131, 133, 137, 148, 173
pandemics, threat of global, 11, 25, 45, 50, 219, 238
    see also Covid-19 pandemic
Panetta, Leon E., 37–8, 97, 270n75
Panetta Review (CIA torture), 201
paramilitary activities, 15, 33, 60, 66–8, 103, 109, 118–28, 139, 232
Pathet Lao, 119
Patriot Act, 125, 196–7, 208
Paul, Rand, 197
Pearl Harbor, 4, 9–10, 13, 56, 147
Pence, Mike, 155, 236
penetration, 15, 20, 145, 159, 162, 169–70
Penkovsky, Oleg, 57–8, 64, 171
Pentagon, see Department of Defense (DoD)
Pentagon Papers, 176–7
Perry, William J., 40–2
Persian Gulf Wars, see Gulf Wars
Peru, 100
Philby, Kim, 21, 102, 161–2, 227
Philippines, 115
photographic interpretation, 42, 67
Phoenix Program, 122
physical security, 22, 163–5
Phythian, Mark, 21
Pike Committee, 186, 188, 207
Pipes, Richard E., 81
plausible deniability doctrine, 109–10
Poindexter, John M., 190
Poland, 19, 118–19, 130–1, 138
police (Capitol Hill), 231
"police patrolling," 180–2, 205–7, 227–8, 230
Policy Planning Staff (State Department), 93
political covert action, 115–16
Pollard, Jonathan Jay, 157
polygraph tests, 151, 158, 164
Portugal, 65
Powell, Colin, 97–8
Predator drones, 60, 123, 126, 135
President, the
    covert action findings, 180–1
    decision-making, 18, 35, 52, 95, 98, 124, 216
    executive privilege, 174–6
    oral briefings to, 59
    oversight of IC, 185–91, 210, 228, 239
    PDBs, 75–8
    PFIAB/PIAB, 32

plausible denial, 109–11
    position of, 20, 22–3
    possession of classified documents, 155–6
    sigint controversies, 195–6
President's Daily Brief (PDB), 51, 75–8, 96, 225, 234
President's Intelligence Advisory Board (PIAB), 32
President's Review Group (Obama), 196
prior restraint, 176–8
private contractors, 100
    see also outsourcing
processing of intelligence, see collection, processing phase
Project Jennifer, 59
Project NIMBUS, 66
propaganda, 15, 52, 103, 111–15, 118, 132–40
provocation operations, 192
Putin, Vladimir V., 7–8, 10, 74, 112, 114, 169, 223, 232–3
"puzzles," 7–8

Qaddafi, Muammar, 122, 131

racially or ethnically motivated violent extremists (RMVEs), 7
Radio Free Europe (RFE), 112
Radio Liberty (RL), 112
Ranelagh, John, 128
Ransom, Harry H., 204
Ratcliffe, John, 232
Reagan, Nancy, 14
Reagan, Ronald, 19, 21, 95, 182, 190–1, 198
Reagan Administration, 75, 87, 110, 118–20, 122, 128–31, 137–9, 174, 206, 212
Reagan Doctrine, 19, 130
Reaper drones, 60, 123, 124, 135, 235
reconnaissance aircraft, 8, 18, 24, 52, 55, 57, 60, 61, 64–9, 109
Redmond, Paul J., 167, 169, 261n44
Reed, Harry, 202
Regan, Brian P., 158
renditions, see extraordinary renditions
research intelligence, 78, 91–2
Reserve for Contingency Fund, 189
Ribbentrop, Joachim von, 94
Rice, Condoleezza, 89, 150
risk–intelligence relationship, 53–4
Roberts, Pat, 192
Rockefeller IV, John D. "Jay," 2–3, 192
Rockefeller, Nelson, 186
Rockefeller Commission, 121
Roosevelt, Franklin D., 9, 35, 158
Rosenberg, Ethel, 156
Rosenberg, Julius, 156
Rosselli, John, 121
Rusk, Dean, 43, 65, 67, 69, 74 177, 211–12, 241n9, 249n24
Russia/Soviet Union
    Backfire bomber, 44
    collection of intelligence about, 57, 68
    covert action against, 19, 68–9, 112, 116
    Cuban Missile Crisis, 57, 67–9
    cyberattacks, 16, 167–8

espionage against the West, 8, 10–11, 56, 103, 112, 146, 150–3, 157–9, 164, 168, 185
friendly ties with the US, 14, 129
invasion of Afghanistan, 119
propaganda activities, 112, 166, 232–3
shoots down US reconnaissance aircraft, 109, 185
suspected involvement in US antiwar movement, 142
ties with Donald J. Trump, 52, 232, 235–6
use of assassination, 121, 172
use of NOCs, 63
see also Cold War
Russian/Soviet intelligence, *see* GRU; KGB; Russia/ Soviet Union; SVR
Rwanda, 44

San Bernardino shootings, 6, 88
Sandinistas, 110, 130
Saudi Arabia, 115, 137
Schiff, Adam, 216–17, 235–6
Schlesinger, James R., 76, 184
Schneider, René, 122
Schwartz, Thomas, 205
Second Gulf War, *see* Gulf Wars
Secretary of Defense (SecDef), 23, 36, 40–1, 44, 49, 69, 97–8, 111, 140
secrets, 7–8, 15, 20, 56, 152, 158, 174–8
  see also President's Daily Brief
security breaches, *see* leaks
"self-licking ice cream cones," 85, 92
Senate Select Committee on Intelligence (SSCI), 33, 89–90, 124, 126–7, 140, 167, 173, 179, 183, 188–95, 198–217
Senate Torture Report, 198–204
sensitive compartmented information facilities (SCIFs), 30
September 17th group, 172
Shakespeare, William, 93
SHAMROCK, *see* Operation SHAMROCK
Shane, Scott, 159–60
Shining Path, 100
Shultz, George P., 252n67
signals intelligence (sigint), 24–5, 34–5, 37, 56–7, 60–1, 69, 71, 78, 153, 157, 194, 198, 204, 209, 224
Silberman–Robb Commission, 65, 209
sleep deprivation, *see* torture
"slow-rolling," 176
Smith, Walter Bedell (DCI), 35
Snider, L. Britt, 192–3
Snow, Daniel, 159
Snowden, Edward J., 153–5, 178, 194–6
Snowe, Olympia, 204
Somalia, 5, 101, 103
South Korea, 158
Soviet Union, *see* Russia/Soviet Union
Space Force Agency, 23, 25
Spann, Johnny Michael, 139
Special Activities Division (SA Division), *see* Covert Action Staff (CAS)
Special Forces, 110, 139, 232

Special National Intelligence Estimates (SNIEs), 85–6, 96–7
Special Operations Group (SOG), 109, 139
Sputnik, 86
SQUARE DANCE, *see* Operation SQUARE DANCE
SR-71 spy plane, 60
Stalin, Joseph, 9, 160, 162
Stennis, John, 184–5
Stewart, Justice Potter, 177
Stone, Geoffrey, 196
Stone, I. F., 156
"stonewalling," 176
"stovepipes," 169
student antiwar protests, 116–21
Suez crisis, 85
Sukarno, president of Indonesia, 122
Sullivan, William C., 143
support to diplomatic operations (SDO), 51
support to military operations (SMO), 42, 51, 129
Supreme Court, 175–6, 184, 190
surreptitious surveillance, 8–9, 25, 41–2, 52, 61, 157
surveillance satellites, 8, 18, 24–5, 32, 40–2, 48, 52, 55–9, 60–1, 238
survival instinct, 12
SVR, 121, 146, 152–3, 173, 232
Swalwell, Eric, 216–17
Syria, 6, 47, 50, 86, 101, 127, 140, 164, 257n55

tactical intelligence and related activities (TIARA), 25
Taliban, 2, 5, 8, 61–3, 88, 103, 107, 116, 119, 122, 129, 133, 137–9, 208
tasking, 238–9
Taylor, Stan, 159
Team A, Team B, 81, 225
technical intelligence (techint), 57, 60–5, 70, 77, 224, 232, 237
telemetry (telint), 56
telephone intercepts, 4, 24, 52, 56, 61, 70–1, 78, 94, 127, 144, 164, 194, 196–7, 214
Tenet, George J., 53, 75, 77, 89, 99, 171, 225
Terms of Reference (TOR), 79
terrorist organizations
  attacks against US, 147–50, 185, 189, 193–201, 209
  defenses against, 163–74, 207, 222–3
  domestic, 6–7, 46–7, 88, 146
  expansion, 43, 119–20, 137
  successes against, 100–1, 137
  targeting by, 93, 131
  use of drones against, 123–8
  see also 9/11; Al Qaeda; ISIS
Thailand, 118
threat assessment, 45–52
torture, 103, 132, 135, 173, 197, 200, 204, 206–10
tradecraft, 22, 56, 201, 224, 238
  counterintelligence, 61–3, 145, 153–4, 163, 170–2
  "dead drops," 58
  "traffic analysis," 94
Trafficante, Santo, 121

translation (foreign language), 71, 95, 224, 229
treason
    examples of, 18, 64, 150–9, 156–7
    motivations for, 159–60
Treasury, Department of, *see* Department of
    Treasury
Trotsky, Leon, 120
Trujillo, Rafael, 122
Truman, Harry S., 11, 35
Truman Administration, 175
Trump, Donald J., 155, 217, 231–8
Trump Administration, 50, 52, 117, 124, 155, 160
    230, 232, 235
Turkey, 88, 118
Turner, Stansfield, 28, 58, 122, 138, 179–83

U-2 reconnaissance aircraft, 56–7, 60, 64–9, 109,
    185
Udall, Mark, 195
Ukraine, Eastern, invasion by Russia (2014), 45
Ukraine, invasion by Russia (2022–), 6
    ad hoc targeting, 44
    CIA assistance, 10, 112, 114, 131, 236
    CIA Mission Center, 28
    harmful leaks, 154
    IC support to, 238
    and "iron pentagon," 34
    NATO, 79, 218
    Russian imperialism, 103, 227
    tasking debates, 52
    trade sanctions, 46
United Arab Emirates (UAE), 125
United Fruit Company, 114, 137
United Kingdom (UK), 10, 15, 17, 37, 53, 101, 137,
    153, 223
United Nations, 223
United States Cyber Command (USCYBERCOM),
    24, 27, 168–9
United States Information Agency (USIA), 111
United States v. Nixon, 175
Unmanned Aerial Vehicles (UAVs), 24, 60, 100,
    123–9, 135
USA Freedom Act, 196–7, 208
US Cyber Command (USCYBERCOM), 24
USS *Cole*, 165
USS *George Washington*, 40
USS *Pueblo*, 178

Vance, Cyrus, 140
Vassiliev, Alexander, 156
Venezuela, 118
Venice Council of Ten, 163–4
Viet Cong, 119, 122
Vietnam War, 86–8, 128, 176, 187, 230
Vietnam War protestors, 31, 142–6, 263n5

Waco siege, 146
"walk-ins," 64
Walker family, 157, 178
Warks, Wesley, 261n49
Warner, Mark, 191, 236
Warner, Michael, 36
warrantless wiretaps, 193–4, 206, 209, 211
Warsaw Pact, 162
Washington Post, 14, 33, 194, 198, 216, 234
waterboarding, 200, 203, 235, 268n58
Watergate, 137, 174
"watch lists," 71
Waxman, Henry A., 205
weapons manufacturers, 34
weapons of mass destruction (WMDs)
    counterproliferation, 38
    Counterproliferation Center (CIA), 97
    covert acquisition, 55
    Cuban missile crisis, 68–9
    dangers, 45, 53, 103, 120
    Iraq (wrongly identified), 9, 51, 63, 74, 88–90,
        99–100
    North Korea, 100
    Soviet/Russian capabilities, 81, 238
    "watch lists," 71–2
    see also ballistic missiles; biological weapons
"weather weapon," 166
Webster, William H., 32, 139, 226
Weisband, William, 156–7
"wet affairs," 120
whistleblowers, 153–4, 157, 208, 227
    see also Intelligence Community Whistleblower
        Protection Act (1998); Snowden, Edward J.
White, Theodore H., 142, 144
WikiLeaks, 154
wiretaps, *see* cable and telegram intercepts;
    metadata collection program; telephone
    intercepts; warrantless wiretaps
"witting circle," 210
Wodehouse, P.G., 13
Woolsey, R. James, 28, 43, 69, 95, 99, 160
World Trade Center (Twin Towers), 2
Wyden, Ron, 195

Xe Services, 33

"Year of Intelligence" (1975), 185, 189, 214
"Year of the Spy" (1985), 158
Yemen, 5, 101, 125–6, 165, 189, 235
Young Americans for Freedom (YAF), 142
Yugoslavia, 87, 133
Yurchenko, Vitaliy Sergeyevich, 172

Zegart, Amy B., 36, 193
Zubaydah, Abu, 200